STUDY GUIDE and PRACTICE TESTS

to accompany

Wade * Tavris

PSYCHOLOGY
Fourth Edition

Tina E. Stern

DeKalb College

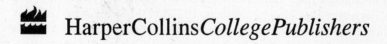 HarperCollins*CollegePublishers*

Study Guide and Practice Tests to accompany Wade/Tavris, PSYCHOLOGY, Fourth Edition

Copyright © 1996 HarperCollins*Publishers*

HarperCollins® and 🏭® are registered trademarks of HarperCollins Publishers Inc.

ISBN: 0-673-99651-4

96 97 98 99 00 9 8 7 6 5 4 3 2 1

CONTENTS

TIRED??

* of reading a chapter and not remembering any of the contents five minutes later?

* of fighting against drooping eyelids and losing?

* of thinking you've studied enough only to find that you can't remember anything that's on the test?

* of studying definitions and terms only to find that the test questions don't ask for definitions and terms; instead, they ask for examples that you never saw in the text?

* of test scores that don't reflect what you know?

I'd like to be able to say, "Guaranteed, 100%!!! Follow these simples guidelines and you, too, can get a 4.0! Simple! Easy! Money-back guarantee! Teachers and parents will love you, and it will change your life!!" Of course, I cannot make those claims, but I can say the following: "**YOU CAN** change the above behaviors **IF** you read **AND** attempt to use the techniques that are described in this section of the Study Guide." Changing your study habits is like going on a diet. First, you must know the details of the diet: How does it propose to help you eat healthier? **BUT** knowing how the diet works and what you are supposed to eat will **NOT** cause you to develop healthier eating habits. You must implement the diet. In other words, to receive the benefits, you must **DO IT!** It is not enough to know what you are supposed to do...you must actually do it! It is the same thing with changing your study habits. It is not enough to know the changes you need to make...you must **MAKE THE CHANGES!**

STEP 1: DIAGNOSING THE PROBLEM

Some students have developed study skills that work well for them, and they do not wish to change their habits. Some students have many study skills with which they are generally satisfied, but they have one or two areas that need improvement. Other students have difficulty with a number of their study skills. Below is a list of some study skills. Review this list and try to identify whether you are satisfied or dissatisfied with each of these abilities. The preface to this Study Guide focuses on study skills and how to use this manual. As you read the preface, focus on the areas in which you need improvement. If this chapter does not cover that particular area, identify and **USE** the resources that are available on your campus to get assistance. **DON'T** ignore study problems. It is unlikely that they will just disappear on their own or improve simply by your trying to do more of what you are already doing!

Check all of the following areas that are problems for you:

Reading the text
    Comprehending the material   _____
    Concentrating while reading   _____
    Identifying what is important   _____
    Recalling what you have read   _____
    Being distracted easily   _____

Time Management
    Not planning your time   _____
    Not having enough time to study   _____
    Not using the time you have allotted to study   _____
    Underestimating the time you need to study   _____
    Difficulty saying no to other plans   _____
    Not sticking to your study schedule   _____

Getting the Most out of Class
    Trouble paying attention in class   _____
    Not going to classes   _____
    Not understanding what is important   _____

Taking Notes
    Your notes aren't helpful   _____
    Your notes are disorganized   _____

Taking Tests
    Trouble recalling information   _____
    Test anxiety   _____
    Trouble on multiple choice questions   _____
    Trouble on fill-in-the-blank questions   _____
    Trouble on essay questions   _____
    Trouble predicting what will be on the test   _____
    Trouble going from definitions to examples   _____

Identifying your problem areas should help you to focus on the skills that you most need to improve. Think about your problem areas as you read the preface and apply the information to your particular situation.

ON BEING A LEARNER or DON'T STOP BEFORE YOU BEGIN!

What was the last new skill you tried to learn? Were you learning to play basketball, softball, tennis, the guitar? Or were you learning a new language? Whatever you were learning to do, it is very likely that you were not very good at it at first. In fact, you were probably **BAD** at it! That is how it is supposed to be! Your ability to do something well depends on gaining experience with that activity: the more you do it, the better you become at the task. This means that it is necessary to go beyond the beginning period of learning when the new skill is difficult and awkward and you are not very good at it. This can be frustrating for students who often think they already should know how to study, and if they have to learn new study skills, they should be learned quickly and easily. During the early stages of learning a new skill, a person may be tempted to say, "This isn't working," or "This will never work" or "These techniques feel so artificial." **RESIST** those thoughts. Learning these skills may be difficult at first, but no more difficult than continuing to use skills that you already know **DO NOT WORK!!** If you want to change any long-standing behavior, you will have to tolerate the early phases of learning when the new behaviors won't yet feel like "your own." In college, graduate school and employment, you will find that persistence pays. So, **RESIST** returning to your old habits and **PERSIST** with learning the new habits. Don't stop before you begin...give it some time.

MASTERING YOUR MEMORY (OR AT LEAST GETTING THE UPPER HAND!)

A great deal of the information contained in most study skills manuals and courses is based on what is known about how human memory works. Experimental psychologists study memory and how it works; therefore, it is appropriate in this course for you to understand the findings of scientific research on memory and how they apply to **YOU**. Ignore these findings at your peril! This section will present a few general findings about memory that are particularly relevant to your studying. This information comes directly from Chapter 9, which will discuss memory in more detail. Information about memory has applicability not only to your psychology class, but to all your classes.

KEEPING INFORMATION IN SHORT-TERM MEMORY
The three-box model of memory suggests there are three types of memory: sensory memory, short-term memory (STM) and long-term memory (LTM). Sensory memory is a very brief type of memory that lasts less than a second. Sensory memory is important because if information does not get noticed in sensory memory, it cannot be transferred into either short-term or long-term memory. The limits of short-term memory are known. Short-term memory can hold seven (plus or minus two) pieces of information for about 30 seconds or less. A person can extend the amount of time information is held in STM by repeating it over and over (this is called maintenance rehearsal); however, once you stop repeating the information, it is quickly lost. Think of times that you have called information to get the number of the nearest pizza place. You repeat the number over and over and hope your roommate does not come along and ask to borrow your comb, because if your repetition is interrupted, you will forget the number. Many professors believe that most students study in ways that get information into short-term memory, but not in ways that get it into long-term memory.

GETTING INFORMATION INTO LONG-TERM MEMORY

Long-term memory can hold an infinite amount of information for an unlimited amount of time. **THAT'S** where you want to store all the information you are studying!! The important question becomes how to transfer information from short-term memory into long-term memory. The transfer of memory from STM into LTM relies upon the use of elaborative rehearsal. Elaborative rehearsal involves more than the simple repetition of information required by short-term memory; it requires that you make the information meaningful. Making information meaningful requires more than saying "This has deep meaning to me." Meaningfulness can be accomplished by interacting with the material in any **ACTIVE** way. Some examples of ways to make information meaningful include putting it into a story, putting it into a rhyme (i.e. "30 days has September"), forming visual images of the information, forming associations with people or things already familiar to you or associating information to other pieces of information, organizing it into categories, putting it into your own words, explaining it to someone else--almost anything that you do with the information that is **ACTIVE**. Being **ACTIVE** with the information and aiming for **UNDERSTANDING** and not simple repetition of the material are the keys. Almost anything you do with the material that is active will help move it into long-term memory. Passively reading the material will not help the information transfer into long-term memory, and this is the technique most students use.

CRITICAL THINKING AND LONG-TERM MEMORY

Critical thinking is emphasized throughout this textbook. Every chapter includes information on how to approach that topic critically. Critical thinking requires organizing, analyzing and evaluating information. This may sound suspiciously like elaborative rehearsal. Critical thinking is important for many reasons. In the context of study skills, critical thinking is important because it involves the same processes that promote the transfer of information into long-term memory.

GETTING MORE INFORMATION INTO SHORT-TERM AND LONG-TERM MEMORY

One last piece of information about memory has to do with expanding the amount of information contained in short-term memory. To get information into LTM, it must pass through STM, and we know that STM holds only about seven (plus or minus two) units of information. That does not seem like a practical system, since most text book chapters seem to contain hundreds of pieces of new information in each chapter! Short-term memory holds **units** or chunks of information, and your chance to increase the amount of information being held in STM is to include more information in each chunk. For example, you can change 26 separate pieces of information (which far exceeds the capacity of STM) into one piece of information (well within the capacity of STM) by chunking! Whenever you use the word "alphabet" to refer to 26 separate letters, you are chunking. If you organize the information you are studying into categories, or chunks, you will improve your chances of getting more information into LTM in two ways: 1) you will increase the information contained in the units getting into STM, and 2) you will be making the information meaningful by the act of organizing in into the chunks! You can't lose! Making outlines is a good way to chunk information. Outlines naturally organize information into categories (chunks) and subcategories. This study guide presents the information in ways that help you to organize information into chunks, which also helps make the information meaningful.

STUDYING WITH THE SQ3R OR STAYING AWAKE, STAYING ACTIVE AND OPENING THE DOOR TO LONG-TERM MEMORY

The SQ3R method was developed by Francis Robinson, a psychology professor at Ohio State University. It is a method of reading assignments that implements many techniques that promote the transfer of information into long-term memory. The letters "SQ3R" stand for survey, question, read, receive, review.

SURVEY
Before you read a chapter or reading assignment, it is important to survey what is in the chapter and how the information is organized. You can do this by simply looking over the headings or the chapter outlines at the beginning of each chapter. This Study Guide also provides more detailed preview outlines for this purpose. It is important that you survey the information before you read, because surveying turns what otherwise would seem like hundreds of independent facts (which far exceeds the capacity of STM) into a much smaller number (probably five to nine--text book authors know how memory works) of main topics identified in separate headings. Once you have seen the main headings, you have an organizational structure to begin your reading. This helps you organize the information when you begin reading (remember that organizing is one way to make information meaningful, which transfers it into LTM). Surveying a chapter in the text is like going on a trip. Before you arrive at a city you do not know, it is very helpful to look at a map. You quickly can see the location of the airport, your hotel, downtown, the river and the three important sites you want to see. This orients you to your journey. If you do not look at a map before your arrival, you are wandering around without knowing where you are going. You do not want to wander around a 40-page chapter that contains a great deal of information without knowing where you are going.

QUESTION
Assume you are taking a college entrance exam that contains a comprehension section. There are several paragraphs for you to read, and then you are to answer five questions about the reading. Would you read the questions before you read the paragraphs, or would you read the paragraphs and then begin to try to answer the questions? Most of you would read the questions first, so that as you read the paragraphs, you could keep the questions in mind and look for the answers while you read. The reasons for formulating questions before you read your text are: 1) to help you read with a purpose, and 2) to help you be more active while you read.

After you have surveyed the chapter, formulate questions by converting the headings, key terms and definitions into questions. For example, "Psychology's Relatives" is a subheading in Chapter 1. "What are some of psychology's relatives?" would be an example of changing that subheading into a question. This Study Guide has listed the relevant learning objectives for each section below the preview outline for that section of text. In addition, there are several extra lines for you to formulate additional questions. The intention is that you will write the answers to all these questions while you read the chapter. This helps you read with a purpose: your purpose is to answer the questions. This also helps you to be active while you read. You are being active by looking for the answers to the questions **AND** by writing down the answers as you find them.

READ
You are now ready to read. You have surveyed the chapter in order to know where you are going and how the chapter is organized. You have formulated your questions in order to know what you are looking for as you read. As you read, you will be organizing the information and answering the questions. These are both ways to increase the transfer of information into long-term memory. As you begin your reading, look at your first question. Open your textbook to the part of the chapter that applies to the question and read to answer that question.

RECITE
After you have surveyed the reading assignment to get the general idea of its content, have turned the first heading into a question, and have read that section to answer the question, you are now ready to recite. Reciting helps make information meaningful (did you ever notice that when you speak in class, you tend to remember the information you spoke or asked about?). Also, it is another way that you can be active (which also makes the information meaningful). Reciting requires that you put the information into your own words, and it is an excellent way to identify what you don't yet understand. There are a number of ways to recite.

Using the questions that you have formulated, recite aloud the answers to the questions (without looking at the answers). You can give definitions or examples of key terms, terms that are listed in bold, or terms that are underlined as a vehicle for reciting information. You can recite responses to learning objectives. You can use the flash cards in this Study Guide to explain key concepts and terms, and then check your responses against the answers on the flash cared. Explaining information to other people, either classmates or patient friends who are willing to help, is also a good way to recite the information. Explaining the information to others also allows you to identify areas that you do not understand well. Remember, your recitation of information should be in your own words and should attempt to give examples of the concepts you are describing. If you simply try to memorize definitions given in the text and recite these definitions, you are simply camouflaging maintenance rehearsal. Remember, getting information into long-term memory involves meaning--so make sure you understand the material and can make it "your own" to get it into long-term memory.

REVIEW

The final step in the SQ3R approach is to review the material again. Frequent reviews, even brief reviews, are among the important keys to learning. After at least one hour, review the material once more. This can be done by going over the main points of the chapter (with your book closed), going over the answers to the questions you have written (without looking at them), reviewing key terms and concepts. Limit your reviews to about five minutes. Reviews can be used in other ways too. Begin each study session with a five-minute review. Before each class, review notes from the previous class for five minutes. At the end of every class, review your notes for five minutes.

SUMMARY

The SQ3R method incorporates the information that psychologists know about how people learn and remember. The key points to remember include: **BE ACTIVE, MAKE INFORMATION MEANINGFUL, INTERACT WITH THE INFORMATION, AIM FOR UNDERSTANDING NOT JUST REPETITION, THINK CRITICALLY.** All this can be achieved by writing, talking, thinking, making outlines, forming associations, developing questions and examples and putting definitions in your own words. The SQ3R method suggests that you can achieve these goals by:

1. Survey the information: Use headings and chapter summaries to orient yourself to the information you plan to read. Give the information an organizational structure.
2. Question: Turn the headings, terms, concepts into questions.
3. Read: Read each section to answer the specific questions that you asked. Write your answers on a separate sheet of paper.
4. Recite: Close your book and rehearse the information contained in the section by answering the relevant questions or giving examples of key terms or concepts.
5. Review: After at least an hour-long break, close your book, turn over your notes and list the main points of the chapter and the answers to your questions.

REMEMBER, this may feel awkward or cumbersome at first, **BUT** the more you use this method, the easier it will become.

WHEN AND WHERE TO STUDY

In many courses, several weeks can pass between tests. You might wonder whether it is better to study intensely the night before the test or to spread out your studying time. Memory research clearly suggests that "cramming" just doesn't work. You may know this from personal experience. Rather than studying for hours and hours just before the test, it is much more effective to study as you go along in the course.

In terms of when to study, the best time to study is immediately after class. **BEFORE** going to class, you should preview the material to be covered, form general questions and read the text.

Study the subject that was covered as soon after the lecture as possible. You will find it easier to master the material and will have an opportunity to test your understanding of the lecture if you study right away. The procedure of continuously studying fairly small chunks will also help you to avoid the nightmare of the infrequent studier--the sudden realization that you don't understand any of what you have been covering for the last few weeks. If you study for a short period after each lecture, you will not have to worry about this. You will also find that tomorrow's lecture will be easier to understand if you study today's material and master the essential points covered by your teacher. Most professors structure lectures so that each one builds on earlier lectures and readings. Studying as you go along will guarantee that you are well prepared to get the most out of each new lecture. It is also a good idea to set a specific time to study. Even if it is for a short time, you should study at a regular time every day.

In terms of where to study, many students indicate that they have difficulty concentrating. Upon further examination, it seems that many students study with their T.V. or CD player on at the same time and place their roommates are having a snack or are on the phone. Some general guidelines about where to study include:
1.   Limit the places that you study to one or two special locations. These could be the library, a desk or a designated study area. They are special in the sense that they should be places where the only thing you do there is study. That means you should not study in places where you regularly do something else (such as the dining room table or bed).
2.   Make these places free from distractions. Distractions like the T.V., telephone or friends can cause studying to be abandoned.
3.   Set a specific time to begin studying and then study in that same place every day. In that way, that place will become a cue to study.

OTHER SKILLS THAT INFLUENCE STUDYING

Many skills influence study habits. The diagnostic check list at the beginning of this section identifies some of the skills that students must possess to study effectively. Skills that affect studying include the following: time management, note-taking, test-preparation, test-taking, stress-management, using the library, dealing with professors and classroom participation. All of these abilities are important. In fact, they are so important that entire books have been devoted to helping students develop these skills. Many colleges and universities offer various types of academic assistance, from courses on study skills to individual counseling on study skills. One of the survival skills necessary for college students is to be aware of the services offered by your institution and to make use of them as needed. If you have identified problem areas that influence your performance, you have several choices: find a book on study skills in your library, look for courses at your school that deal with study skills or identify other campus resources that are available to assist you in developing these abilities.

THE BEST WAY TO USE THIS STUDY GUIDE

This Study Guide is structured to incorporate the research information on learning and memory. Each chapter is set up so that students can easily utilize the SQ3R method. The structure of the Study Guide is designed so students can be actively involved in their learning.

LEARNING OBJECTIVES
Learning Objectives begin each chapter. Knowing the main objectives for each chapter can help students to know what to look for as they read the chapter and to discern the most important aspects of each chapter. Students should read the Learning Objectives **BEFORE** they begin reading the chapter.

CONCEPT MAPS AND CHAPTER SUMMARIES
Following the Learning Objectives, each chapter begins with a concept map and chapter summary. Broad concepts are identified and the concept map displays relationships that exist among the concepts. This allows students to identify the main chunks, or ideas, in the chapter along with the subdivisions that come underneath each main concept. This provides a general overview to the chapter. The chapter summary uses a narrative format to tell the student what the chapter will cover. Both the concept map and the chapter summaries give the student the overall survey (the "S" in SQ3R) to the entire chapter.

SECTION-BY-SECTION PREVIEW OUTLINES
The entire chapter is then broken down by section. Each section of the chapter is presented in a general outline format, which students are intended to examine **BEFORE** they read the chapter. Once again, a section of text can be previewed or surveyed before the student reads. The outline format is used to help students organize the section of the chapter into main topic areas. It is suggested that students use the SQ3R method for each section of the text before going on to the next section. The preview outlines have some blank spaces in them. Some key terms and concepts have been left blank so that students may look for the terms during their reading. While students read the text, they should find the terms that fit the blanks in the outline.

SECTION-BY-SECTION LEARNING OBJECTIVES AND STUDENT-GENERATED QUESTIONS
The Learning Objectives that relate to each section of the text are listed below the preview outline for each section so that students can look for the answers as they read. Students should also formulate additional questions by using headings, key terms and concepts. For example, empirical evidence is a highlighted term in Chapter 1. "How is empirical evidence different from other types of evidence?" is an example of using a term as the basis of a question. Students should examine all these questions before reading the text and answer them while reading that particular section of text. This represents the "Q" or question aspect of the SQ3R.

CROSSWORD PUZZLES
Each chapter has a crossword puzzle that utilizes key terms, figures or concepts from the chapter. This is another way students can attempt to make the information meaningful, interact with it actively and improve the transfer of information into long-term memory.

FLASH CARDS
Each chapter has tables with key terms. The reverse sides of the tables gives the definitions of the terms. The tables are designed so they can be cut out and used as flash cards. Students can use the flash cards to review the information and to test themselves. This feature helps students use the key terms as questions (the "Q" part of the SQ3R) and to recite (one of the "R"s in SQ3R) the material to themselves or to a study partner.

TABLES
Some chapters have tables that help students organize, categorize and form associations to the information in the chapters. The completed table will be great study aid, but the act of completing the table is just as important: it is another way of making the information meaningful.

PRACTICE TESTS
Each chapter has three practice tests. Practice tests one and two are multiple choice tests. All three practice tests try to tap into different types of thinking skills. The first practice test in each chapter requires that students know definitions, terms, concepts and figures. The second practice test in each chapter requires students to identify, analyze, interpret, compare, contrast and synthesize information. The third practice test in each chapter requires that students apply, analyze and synthesize the information in essay or short-answer responses. The fill-in-the-blanks provided in the preview outlines and the different types of practice tests offer students the opportunity to practice and review the information in different formats and at different levels of analysis.

CONCLUSION

This Study Guide has been developed utilizing psychological research findings in the areas of learning and memory. As a beginning psychology student, you have the opportunity to apply the findings of psychological research to your lives by using this Study Guide. In essence, that is the goal of this course: for you to learn the information, think about it critically and make use of it in your life.

CHAPTER 1

What Is Psychology?

LEARNING OBJECTIVES

After studying this chapter, you should be able to do the following:

1.   Define psychology.

2.   Distinguish psychology from pseudoscience and "psychobabble."

3.   Summarize the relationship between the discipline of psychology and common sense.

4.   Distinguish between psychology and related sciences and social sciences.

5.   Summarize the early history and development of psychology.

6.   Describe the aims of structuralism and functionalism.

7.   Compare and contrast the major principles of the learning, psychodynamic, cognitive, biological and sociocultural perspectives in psychology.

8.   Discuss humanistic psychology and feminist psychology.

9.   Distinguish between applied and basic research in psychology.

10.   Discuss and give examples of the concerns of various specialties in psychology.

11.   Distinguish between a psychotherapist, a psychoanalyst, a psychiatrist, a clinical psychologist and other practicing mental health professionals.

12.   List and discuss the essential elements of critical thinking.

CONCEPT MAP OF CHAPTER

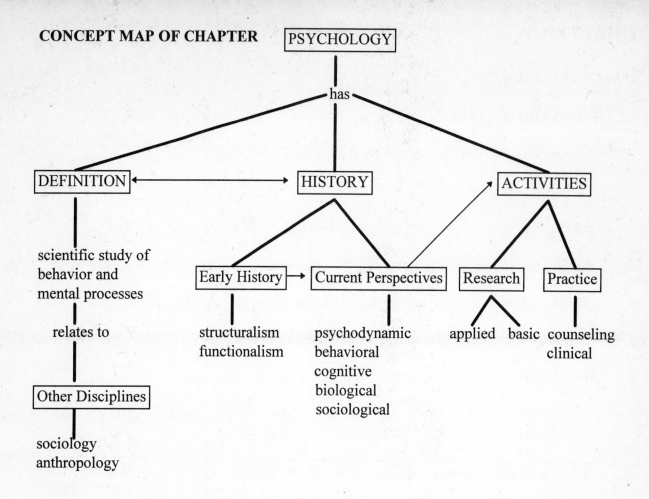

BRIEF CHAPTER SUMMARY

Chapter 1 defines psychology and follows the historical and disciplinary roots of the field to its current perspectives, specialty areas and activities. Five current perspectives and two important movements are identified. The current perspectives include the learning perspective, psychodynamic perspective, biological perspective, cognitive perspective and sociocultural perspective. Each of these reflects a different emphasis and approach to understanding human behavior. A review of the specialty areas within the field helps students appreciate that psychology includes many diverse topics. The practice of psychology, which helps people with mental health problems, is discussed along with a description of practitioners both within the field of psychology and outside of it. Critical thinking guidelines are described and students are encouraged to understand and apply these as they read the text. The complexity of human behavior requires that psychology students resist simplistic thinking and the search for simple answers.

PREVIEW OUTLINE AND REVIEW QUESTIONS

Before you read the chapter, review the preview outline and the Learning Objectives for each section of the text. Develop additional questions of your own based on key concepts and terms and write them in the designated spaces. Answer all questions as you read the text.

SECTION 1 - A MATTER OF DEFINITION (PP. 3-7)

I.   **A MATTER OF DEFINITION**
  A.   **Formal definition** - scientific study of _____ and _____ _____ and how they are affected by an organism's physical state, mental state and the external environment
  B.   **Psychology and common sense**
    1.   Psychology is based on _____ evidence; common sense is not
    2.   Research in psychology may confirm or disconfirm common sense
  C.   **Psychology's relatives**
    1.   In the social sciences
      a.   Sociology
      b.   _____
    2.   In other fields
      a.   Biology
      b.   _____
      c.   Neuroscience
      d.   Management science

Answer these Learning Objectives while you read Section 1.

1.   Define psychology.

2.   Distinguish psychology from pseudoscience and "psychobabble."

3.   Summarize the relationship between the discipline of psychology and common sense.

4.   Distinguish between psychology and related sciences and social sciences.

Write the questions that you have formulated below and answer them while you read.

A.   _____

B.   _____

SECTION 2 - PSYCHOLOGY'S PAST: FROM THE ARMCHAIR TO THE LABORATORY (PP. 7-11)

II. **PSYCHOLOGY'S PAST: FROM THE ARMCHAIR TO THE LABORATORY**
    A.   **Early history**
        1.   Originated within philosophy
        2.   Forerunners of psychology
            a.   Hippocrates
            b.   Aristotle
            c.   _____
        3.   Not yet a separate field of study
        4.   Did not use the scientific method - prescientific
    B.   **The birth of modern psychology**
        1.   Wilhelm _____ is considered the "father of psychology"
        2.   Wundt used introspection and established the first psychology laboratory
    C.   **Two early psychologies**
        1.   E.B. _____ and structuralism
            a.   Popularized Wundt's ideas in the United States
            b.   Used structuralism to analyze sensations, images and feelings into their most basic elements
            c.   Relied on Wundt's method of _____
        2.   William James and functionalism
            a.   Critical of structuralism and introspection
            b.   Interested in how and why behavior occurs
            c.   Emphasized causes and consequences of behavior

Answer these Learning Objectives while you read Section 2.

5.   Summarize the early history and development of psychology.

6.   Describe the aims of structuralism and functionalism.

Write the questions that you have formulated below and answer them while you read.

A. _____

B. _____

III. **PSYCHOLOGY'S PRESENT: BEHAVIOR, BODY, MIND, AND CULTURE**
   A. **The learning perspective**
       1. Introduced by John Watson
       2. Maintains that psychology should only study directly _____ and measurable events, not private experiences like mental events
       3. Emphasizes learning and the influence of the environment
       4. Pavlov's experiments explained automatic or _____ behavior
       5. _____ extended behaviorism to explain the learning of voluntary behaviors
       6. Social learning theory an outgrowth of behaviorism
           a. Expands behaviorism beyond the study of behavior to include learning by observation, insight, imitation
           b. Combines classic behaviorism with research on thinking
           c. _____ is a key figure
   B. **The psychodynamic perspective**
       1. Based on the work of _____ in the early 1900s
       2. Maintains that psychological distress due to childhood conflicts
       3. Introduced idea of the unconscious
       4. Emphasizes biological instincts like aggression
       5. Launched theories based on Freudian approach called _____
           a. Emphasize inner forces and conflicts
           b. Emphasize instinctual energy
   C. **The biological perspective**
       1. Associates all actions, feelings and thoughts with bodily events
       2. Examines how bodily events interact with the environment to produce perceptions, memories and behavior
       3. Related to _____ psychology, which examines how evolutionary past may help explain some present behaviors and psychological traits
   D. **The cognitive perspective**
       1. Popularized in the 1950's and 1960's
       2. Returns to the study of _____ _____
       3. Studies perception, memory, language, problem solving using new research methods
       4. Shows how explanations and perceptions affect behavior and feelings
       5. Serves as one of the strongest forces in psychology today
   E. **The sociocultural perspective**
       6. Examines how the cultural values and political systems affect experience
       7. Looks at the influence of the historical and social context on behavior

F.   Two influential movements in psychology
    1.   Humanistic psychology or the "third force"
         a.   Rejects psychoanalytic perspective as too pessimistic and behaviorism as too mechanistic
         b.   Rejects determinism by the unconscious (psychoanalysis) or by the environment (behaviorism); believes in free will
         c.   Goals of humanism
             (1)   _____
             (2)   To help people reach their full potential
         d.   Has influenced psychotherapy not scientific psychology
    2.   Feminist psychology
         a.   Examines how social, economic and political inequities affect gender relations and behavior of the sexes
         b.   Identifies biases in research methods of psychology
         c.   Motivated the study of new topics such as _____, menstruation

G.   Eclecticism
    1.   Incorporates features of diverse theories and approaches
    2.   Employs broad guidelines
         a.   Relies on _____ evidence
         b.   Rejects supernatural explanations

Answer these Learning Objectives while you read Section 3.

7.   Describe the major principles of the following perspectives:
learning

psychodynamic

cognitive

biological

sociocultural

8.   Discuss humanistic psychology and feminist psychology.

Write the questions that you have formulated below and answer them while you read.

A.   _____

B.   _____

IV. **WHAT PSYCHOLOGISTS DO**
   A. **Overview of professional activities**
      1. Teach and conduct research in colleges and universities
      2. Provide health or mental health services (psychological practice)
      3. Conduct research or apply its findings in nonacademic settings
      4. Combination of the above
   B. **Psychological research**
      1. _____ research - knowledge for its own sake
      2. Applied research - concerned with the practical uses of knowledge
      3. Some major nonclinical specialties in psychology
         a. Experimental psychologists - conduct laboratory studies of learning, motivation, emotion, sensation and perception, physiology, human performance and cognition
         b. _____ psychologists - study principles that explain learning and look for ways to improve learning in educational systems
         c. Developmental psychologists - study how people change and grow over time physically, mentally and socially
         d. Industrial/organizational psychologists - study behavior in the workplace
         e. _____ psychologists - design and evaluate tests of mental abilities, aptitudes, interests and personality
         f. Social psychologists - study how groups, institutions and the social context influence individuals and vice versa
   C. **The practice of psychology**
      1. Those who try to understand and improve physical and mental health
      2. Settings in which those who practice psychology work
         a. Mental or general hospital
         b. _____
         c. Schools
         d. Counseling centers
         a. Private practice
      3. Types of psychologist practitioners
         a. _____ psychologists deal with problems of everyday life
         b. School psychologists try to enhance students' performance and emotional development
         c. Clinical psychologists diagnose, treat and study mental or emotional problems
      4. Degrees for practice may include Ph.D., Ed.D. (doctorate in education), and Psy.D. (doctorate in psychology)

5. Types of non-psychologist practitioners
    a.   _____ - anyone who practices psychotherapy; unrelated to formal education and rarely requires licensing
    b.   Psychoanalyst - someone with specialized training at a recognized psychoanalytic institute
    c.   Psychiatrist - a medical doctor (M.D.) with a residency in psychiatry
        (1)   May treat the more severely disturbed
        (2)   More medically oriented
        (3)   Can write prescriptions
        (4)   May not have thorough training in theories and methods of psychology
    d.   Counselors, social workers and other mental health professionals - treat general problems in adjustment, licensing requirements vary

D.   **Psychology in the community**
1. Psychologists work in other areas within the community
2. Psychogists work with diverse groups of people and in a variety of types of settings

Answer these Learning Objectives while you read Section 4.

9. Distinguish between applied and basic research in psychology.

10. Discuss and give examples of the concerns of various specialties in psychology.

11. Distinguish between a psychotherapist, a psychoanalyst, a psychiatrist, a clinical psychologist and other practicing mental health professionals.

Write the questions that you have formulated below and answer them while you read.

A.   _____

B.   _____

SECTION 5 - THINKING CRITICALLY AND CREATIVELY ABOUT PSYCHOLOGY, AND WHAT PSYCHOLOGY CAN DO FOR YOU AND WHAT IT CAN'T (PP. 28-36)

V.   **THINKING CRITICALLY AND CREATIVELY ABOUT PSYCHOLOGY**
  A.   **Eight guidelines for critical thinking**
    1.   Ask questions; be willing to wonder
    2.   Define the problem
    3.   Examine the evidence
    4.   Analyze the assumptions and biases
    5.   Avoid _____ reasoning: "If I feel this way, it must be true"
    6.   Don't oversimplify
    2.   Consider other interpretations
    3.   Tolerate uncertainty
VI.   **WHAT PSYCHOLOGY CAN DO FOR YOU AND WHAT IT CAN'T**
  A.   **What psychology can do for you**
    1.   Make you a more informed person
    2.   Satisfy your curiosity about human nature
    3.   Help you increase control over your life
    4.   Help you on the job
    5.   Give you insights into political and social issues
  B.   **What psychology can't do for you**
    1.   Tell you the meaning of life
    2.   Relieve you of responsibility for your actions
    3.   Provide simple answers to complex questions

Answer this Learning Objective while you read Section 5.

12.   List and discuss the essential elements of critical thinking.

Write the questions that you have formulated below and answer them while you read.

A.   _____

B.   _____

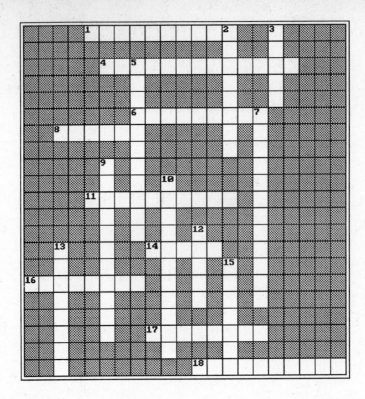

ACROSS

1. perspective of psychology that states that actions, feelings and thoughts are associated with bodily events
4. early approach that asks how and why
6. psychological perspective that studies perception, memory, problem solving and language
8. type of psychologist who works with students to enhance performance
11. the scientific study of behavior and mental processes
14. developed psychoanalysis
16. movement in psychology that studies motherhood and menopause
17. psychologists whose goal is to improve mental health engage in the _____ of psychology
18. type of psychology that studies behavior in the workplace

DOWN

2. the perspective of psychology that states that psychology should study observable events and not mental processes
3. research that explores knowledge for its own sake
5. experimental, educational, developmental, industrial and social psychology are _____ specialty areas in psychology
7. type of psychologist who studies learning, motivation, emotion and sensation
9. psychology, sociology, anthropology and biology are _____
10. Hippocrates, Aristotle and Descartes were psychology's _____
12. the "father" of psychology
13. movement in psychology that emphasizes human potential
15. type of research that is concerned with practical uses of knowledge

FLASH CARDS

Cut the following chart along the borders and test yourself with the resulting flash cards.

1.1 PSYCHOLOGY	1.8 SOCIOLOGY	1.15 ANTHROPOLOGY
1.2 WILHELM WUNDT	1.9 EMPIRICAL	1.16 CROSS-CULTURAL PSYCHOLOGY
1.3 TRAINED INTROSPECTION	1.10 STRUCTURALISM	1.17 FUNCTIONALISM
1.4 WILLIAM JAMES	1.11 CHARLES DARWIN	1.18 JOHN B. WATSON
1.5 BEHAVIORISM	1.12 IVAN PAVLOV	1.19 B.F. SKINNER
1.6 SOCIAL LEARNING OR COGNITIVE SOCIAL LEARNING	1.13 SIGMUND FREUD	1.20 PSYCHOANALYSIS
1.7 PSYCHODYNAMIC THEORIES	1.14 INTRAPSYCHIC	1.21 GESTALT PSYCHOLOGY

1.15 The study of the physical and cultural origins and development of the human species.	**1.8** The scientific study of groups and institutions within society, such as the family and religious institutions.	**1.1** The scientific study of behavior and mental processes and how they're affected by an organism's mental & physical state and external environment.
1.16 An area in psychology that investigates differences and similarities among cultures.	**1.9** Relying on or derived from observation, experimentation or measurement.	**1.2** The "father of psychology," established the first psychological laboratory and utilized trained introspection.
1.17 An early approach to psychology that stressed the function or purpose of behavior and consciousness.	**1.10** An early approach to psychology that stressed analysis of immediate experience into basic elements.	**1.3** A form of self-observation in which individuals examine and report the contents of their own consciousness.
1.18 Introduced the ideas of behaviorism and suggested that to be objective, psychology should not study the mind.	**1.11** A British naturalist who developed evolutionary theories that inspired the early psychological approach of functionalism.	**1.4** An American philosopher, physician and psychologist who was a proponent of functionalism.
1.19 Extended behaviorism to voluntary acts and showed that the consequences of an act affect its recurrence.	**1.12** Russian psychologist who showed that involuntary behaviors are learned responses to the environment.	**1.5** An approach emphasizing the study of observable behavior and the role of the environment as a determinant of behavior.
1.20 Personality theory and method of psychotherapy, originally formulated by Freud.	**1.13** A neurologist who developed the theory of personality and method of treating problems called psychoanalysis.	**1.6** Theory that behavior is learned through observation and imitation of others, consequences and cognitive processes.
1.21 Movement that studied how people interpret sensory information as patterns and whole objects.	**1.14** Within the mind or self.	**1.7** Approaches that emphasize unconscious dynamics within the individual, such as inner forces and conflicts.

1.22 BIOLOGICAL PERSPECTIVE	**1.29 EVOLUTIONARY PERSPECTIVE**	**1.36 COGNITIVE PERSPECTIVE**
1.23 SOCIOCULTURAL PERSPECTIVE	**1.30 CULTURE**	**1.37 HUMANISTIC PERSPECTIVE**
1.24 FEMINIST PSYCHOLOGY	**1.31 BASIC PSYCHOLOGY**	**1.38 APPLIED PSYCHOLOGY**
1.25 EXPERIMENTAL PSYCHOLOGIST	**1.32 DEVELOPMENTAL PSYCHOLOGIST**	**1.39 INDUSTRIAL OR ORGANIZATIONAL PSYCHOLOGIST**
1.26 PSYCHOMETRIC PSYCHOLOGIST	**1.33 SOCIAL PSYCHOLOGIST**	**1.40 COUNSELING PSYCHOLOGIST**
1.27 EDUCATIONAL PSYCHOLOGIST	**1.34 SCHOOL PSYCHOLOGIST**	**1.41 CLINICAL PSYCHOLOGIST**
1.28 PSYCHIATRY	**1.35 PSYCHOTHERAPIST**	**1.42 CRITICAL THINKING**

1.36 Approach that emphasizes mental processes in perception, memory, language, problem solving and other areas of behavior.	1.29 Researchers who study how our species' evolutionary past may help explain some of our present behaviors and psychological traits.	1.22 An approach to behavior that emphasizes bodily events and changes associated with actions, feelings and thoughts.
1.37 Approach emphasizing personal growth and human potential more than scientific understanding, prediction and control of behavior.	1.30 Shared rules that govern the behavior of members of a society; a set of values, beliefs and attitudes shared by most members of that community.	1.23 Approach that emphasizes social and cultural influences on behavior.
1.38 Study of psychological issues that have direct practical significance and the application of psychological findings.	1.31 Study of psychological issues in order to seek knowledge for its own sake rather than for its practical application.	1.24 Approach that analyzes the influence of social inequities on gender relations and the behavior of the two sexes.
1.39 Psychologist who studies behavior in the work place.	1.32 Psychologist who studies how people change and grow over time, physically, mentally and socially.	1.25 Psychologist who conducts laboratory studies of learning, motivation, emotion, sensation and perception, physiology and cognition.
1.40 Psychologist who helps people deal with problems of everyday life, such as test anxiety, family and marital problems.	1.33 Psychologist who studies how groups, institutions and the social context influence individuals and vice versa.	1.26 Psychologist who designs and evaluates tests of mental abilities, aptitudes, interests and personality.
1.41 Psychologist who diagnoses, treats and studies mental or emotional problems and disabilities.	1.34 Psychologist who works with parents, teachers and students to enhance students' performance and emotional development.	1.27 Psychologist who studies psychological principles that explain learning and search for ways to improve learning in educational systems.
1.42 The ability and willingness to assess claims and make objective judgments on the basis of well-supported reasons.	1.35 Anyone who does any kind of psychotherapy and may not have any training at all.	1.28 The medical specialty concerned with mental disorders, maladjustment and abnormal behavior.

PERSPECTIVES TABLE

Complete this table, then identify similarities and differences between perspectives.

PERSPECTIVES	KEY FIGURES	KEY CONCEPTS AND TERMS	MAJOR INFLUENCES ON BEHAVIOR
LEARNING PERSPECTIVE			
PSYCHODYNAMIC PERSPECTIVE			
BIOLOGICAL PERSPECTIVE			
COGNITIVE PERSPECTIVE			
SOCIOCULTURAL PERSPECTIVE			
HUMANISTIC PERSPECTIVE			
FEMINIST PERSPECTIVE			

PRACTICE TEST 1

1. Psychology is defined as
    A. the scientific study of behavior and how it is affected by an organism's physical state, mental state and the external environment.
    B. the scientific study of behavior and mental processes and how they are affected by an organism's physical state, mental state and the external environment.
    C. the scientific study of mental processes and how they are affected by an organism's physical state, mental state and the external environment.
    D. the scientific study of groups and institutions in society.

2. The main difference between psychological knowledge and knowledge gained through common sense is that
    A. psychological knowledge is contained in text books, common sense is not.
    B. psychological knowledge is based on research evidence, common sense is not.
    C. findings based on psychological knowledge are often the opposite of findings based on common sense. ·
    D. common sense is usually very obvious and psychological knowledge is rarely the expected result.

3. The study of the physical and cultural origins and development of the human species is the definition of
    A. anthropology.   B. biology.
    C. sociology.   D. psychology.

4. Hippocrates and Aristotle
    A. were early psychologists.
    B. did not use the scientific method and therefore their ideas were rarely correct.
    C. had nothing to do with psychology.
    D. were the forerunners of psychology.

5. _____ established the first psychology lab in 1879 and is considered the "father of psychology."
    A. E.B. Titchener   B. William James
    C. B.F. Skinner   D. Wilhelm Wundt

6. An early school of psychology, popularized by E.B. Titchener, attempted to analyze sensations, images and feelings into their most basic elements. This school was called
   A. structuralism.   B. introspection.
   C. functionalism.   D. behaviorism.

7. A second early school of psychology asked how and why an organism's behavior helps it to adapt to its environment. It was called
   A. structuralism.   B. introspection.
   C. functionalism.   D. behaviorism.

8. "To be objective, psychology should concentrate on directly observable and measurable events and eliminate from study private subjective experiences like thoughts, emotions or feelings." This statement reflects the position of the
   _____ perspective.
   A. behavioral   B. psychodynamic
   C. cognitive   D. biological

9. What do John Watson, Ivan Pavlov and B.F. Skinner have in common?
   A. They were students of Freud and further developed psychodynamic theory.
   B. They were the forerunners of psychology.
   C. They all made significant contributions to the behavioral perspective.
   D. They all used the technique of trained introspection in their research.

10. _____, and outgrowth of behaviorism, says that new behaviors can be acquired through observing and imitating others.
    A. Social learning theory   B. Psychodynamic theory
    C. Humanism   D. Gestalt psychology

11. "Psychological distress is a result of inner forces, specifically unresolved unconscious conflicts from early childhood." This statement reflects the position of the
    _____ perspective.
    A. behavioral   B. psychodynamic
    C. cognitive   D. biological

12. Proponents of the _____ perspective believe that to understand the mind one must study the nervous system, because all actions, feelings and thoughts are associated with bodily events.
    A. behavioral   B. psychodynamic
    C. cognitive   D. biological

17

13. The study of mental processes in perception, memory, language and problem solving are some of the topics studied by
    A. the sociocultural perspective.
    B. humanism.
    C. social learning theory.
    D. cognitive psychology.

14. "The answer to violence and cruelty doesn't reside in instincts, brain circuits or personal dispositions, but in political systems and cultural values." This statement is consistent with the thinking of _____ psychologists.
    A. sociocultural
    B. humanistic
    C. cognitive
    D. psychodynamic

15. Developed in reaction to Freudian pessimism and behavioristic "mindlessness," _____ emerged as a "third force" in psychology.
    A. feminist psychology
    B. social learning theory
    C. sociocultural psychology
    D. humanistic psychology

16. Which of the following might be one of the goals of feminist psychology?
    A. Encourage research on menstruation and motherhood.
    B. Analyze how social, economic and political inequities affect gender relations and behavior of the sexes.
    C. Make sure that both male and female subjects are used in research design.
    D. All of the above.

17. Which of the following best describes the difference between applied and basic research?
    A. Basic research examines the basic elements of sensations, images and feelings, whereas applied research studies how these processes help a person adapt to the environment.
    B. Basic psychological research seeks knowledge for its own sake, whereas applied psychological research is concerned with the practical uses of knowledge.
    C. Applied research seeks knowledge for its own sake, whereas basic research is concerned with the practical uses of knowledge.
    D. Basic research is based on the psychoanalytic perspective, whereas applied research is based on the humanistic approach.

18. Psychologists who conduct laboratory studies of learning, motivation, emotion, sensation and perception, physiology, human performance and cognition are called _____ psychologists.
    A. experimental
    B. educational
    C. developmental
    D. social

18

19. A psychometric psychologist
    A. studies how groups, institutions and the social context influence individuals.
    B. studies how people change and grow over time physically, mentally and socially.
    C. designs and evaluates tests of mental abilities, aptitudes, interests and personality.
    D. studies behavior in the workplace.

20. Psychologists who help people deal with problems of everyday life, such as test anxiety, family or marital problems, or low job motivation, are called _____ psychologists.
    A. psychometric   B. clinical
    C. counseling   D. school

21. Which of the following is a nonclinical specialty?
    A. counseling psychologist
    B. school psychologist
    C. clinical psychologist
    D. educational psychologist

22. Which type of psychologist would be most likely to work with highly disturbed people?
    A. clinical   B. experimental
    C. counseling   D. school

23. Which of the following has a medical degree and can prescribe medication?
    A. clinical psychologist   B. psychotherapist
    C. psychoanalyst   D. psychiatrist

24. A psychotherapist
    A. has specialized training at a psychoanalytic institute.
    B. is not required to have any training at all in most states.
    C. has a medical degree.
    D. is a psychologist.

25. Which of the following is one of the essential elements of critical thinking?
    A. Ask questions; be willing to wonder.
    B. Examine the evidence.
    C. Avoid emotional reasoning: "If I feel this way, it must be true."
    D. All of the above are essential elements of critical thinking.

PRACTICE TEST 2

1. Of the following studies, the one that meets the definition of psychology is
   A. a study of someone who engages in self-injurious behavior.
   B. a study examining the components of emotion.
   C. a study of the effects of peer pressure on adolescents.
   D. all of the above.

2. Your friend is fond of telling you all the latest psychological tips she hears on T.V., in magazines or in the latest self-help book. What would you tell her to help her determine what information is scientific and what is "psychobabble."
   A. If she hears something on the news, it is likely to be true.
   B. Information she reads in the newspaper or magazines is likely to be correct.
   C. Information from experts is usually accurate.
   D. Information must be supported by documented research evidence in order to be considered scientific.

3. Common sense knowledge and psychological knowledge
   A. are never the same.
   B. may be the same, but may be quite different.
   C. are almost always the same.
   D. cannot be compared, since common sense cannot be proven.

4. You are working on a research paper that examines homosexual practices in Russia, Tasmania, Burma and Peru for your _____ class.
   A. sociology   B. anthropology
   C. psychology   D. biology

5. What is the relationship between Hippocrates, Aristotle, Descartes and psychological science?
   A. The thinking and ideas of Hippocrates, Aristotle and Descartes influenced the thinking of psychological science.
   B. They introduced the scientific method to psychology.
   C. They were the first to establish psychology as a separate science.
   D. Hippocrates, Aristotle and Descartes had little impact on psychology because they were so often wrong in their findings.

6. Wilhelm Wundt is often considered the "father of psychology" because
   A. he established the first psychology laboratory.
   B. he was the first to announce that he intended to make psychology a science.
   C. he attempted to use scientific methods to study psychological phenomena.
   D. all of the above.

7. The year is 1900 and you are a participant in a research project. You are told to respond to a series of words, like triangle, by telling the researchers about the basic elements of your mental experience. This approach is known as
   A. functionalism.   B. behaviorism.
   C. trained introspection.   D. structuralism.

8. The _____ school is critical of the goals of the previous experiment because of the belief that the brain and the mind are constantly changing. This school is more interested in why you are participating in the study in the first place.
   A. functionalism   B. behaviorism
   C. trained introspection   D. structuralism

9. Titchener is to James as
   A. trained introspection is to Wundt.
   B. functionalism is to structuralism.
   C. trained introspection is to functionalism.
   D. structuralism is to functionalism.

10. You have recently started psychotherapy with a psychologist who believes in the learning perspective. Which of the following statements would she make?
   A. "To best address your problem, we must identify the behaviors that are causing problems, the environmental conditions that maintain the behaviors and then we must modify those behaviors."
   B. "To help you we must identify your unconscious inner conflicts, memories and emotional traumas from your early childhood."
   C. "Your actions are self-regulated. We must discover how they are shaped by your thoughts, values, self-reflections and intentions."
   D. "We must examine your problem in the context of the broader culture and how cultural expectations and beliefs are affecting your behavior."

11. Pavlov is to Skinner as
   A. behaviorism is to humanism.
   B. voluntary is to involuntary.
   C. involuntary is to voluntary.
   D. objectivity is to subjectivity.

21

12. Social learning theory
    A.   is unrelated to behaviorism.
    B.   expands the principles of behaviorism to include the study of the unconscious.
    C.   extends behaviorism to explain the learning of voluntary behaviors.
    D.   combines classic behaviorism with research on thinking.

13. You have started psychotherapy with a psychologist who believes in the psychodynamic perspective. Which statement is he most likely to make?
    A.   "To best address your problem, we must identify the behaviors that are causing problems and then we must modify those behaviors."
    B.   "We must examine your unconscious conflicts from your early childhood."
    C.   "Your actions are self-regulated. We must discover how they are shaped by your thoughts, values, self-reflections and intentions."
    D.   "We must examine your problem in the context of the broader culture and how cultural expectations, pressures and beliefs are affecting your behavior."

14. Dr. Pine is conducting a research project in which she is looking for genetic and biochemical causes of depression. Which perspective is she most likely to follow?
    A.   biological   B.   humanistic
    C.   behavioral   D.   cognitive

15. "It is not what happened at the party that is upsetting you. It is your perception of what happened and your explanation of those events that are causing problems." This statement best reflects which of the following perspectives?
    A.   biological   B.   humanistic
    C.   sociocultural   D.   cognitive

16. "To understand the causes of the high rates of anorexia nervosa among older adolescent women, we must consider the influence of society's norms for female beauty and thinness." This statement reflects which of the following perspectives?
    A.   humanistic   B.   psychodynamic
    C.   sociocultural   D.   cognitive

17. A _____ psychologist would say, "The goal of psychotherapy is to help people express themselves creatively and utilize their free will to reach their full potential."
    A.   humanistic   B.   cognitive
    C.   feminist   D.   sociocultural

18. A _____ psychologist examines research for bias in subject selection.
    A.   humanist   B.   cognitive
    C.   feminist   D.   sociocultural

19. Dr. Borynko is designing a research study to answer each of the following research questions. Which study would be considered basic research?
    A. Can rats learn to press a bar for a reward?
    B. Can emotionally disturbed children learn to control aggression for a reward?
    C. Can training in moral development be used to prevent teenage violence?
    D. Can behavioral approaches be used to reduce alcohol abuse?

20. Dr. Cassales is designing a program to increase student performance in math. Other psychologists will implement his program in the schools. He is a(n) _____
    A. experimental psychologist.   B. developmental psychologist.
    C. educational psychologist.   D. school psychologist.

21. Dr. Abee is helping teachers, students and parents know how to use the Gonzales Program at his school. He is a/n _____ psychologist.
    A. experimental   B. developmental
    C. educational   D. school

22. An activity that reflects the work of a social psychologist would be
    A. a study on infant attachment behavior.
    B. a study on the arousal in the experience of emotions.
    C. the development of a new test to measure personality.
    D. a study on gender differences in conformity.

23. Clinical and counseling psychologists, psychiatrists and psychoanalysts
    A. conduct psychotherapy and prescribe medication.
    B. conduct research and teach.
    C. are educated at the doctoral level.
    D. work in psychiatric hospitals.

24. Dr. Iriko believes that Jon's depression is biochemical and writes him a prescription for antidepressant drugs. She is most likely a
    A. counseling psychologist.   B. psychotherapist.
    C. psychiatrist.   D. social worker.

25. Which of the following are examples of critical thinking?
    A. After Yolanda was refused from veterinary school, she took a job at a zoo.
    B. To be open-minded, Hank discusses whether the Holocaust happened.
    C. Robert was taught that spanking is the best way to discipline children and he plans to parent in the same way.
    D. Shaquille has decided not to major in psychology because there are so many contradictory research findings and there are too few clear-cut answers.

PRACTICE TEST 3

1. Several activities are described below. For each activity, indicate whether it is an example of applied or basic psychology, the area of specialization most likely to be involved and whether that area of specialization is a clinical or non-clinical area. Explain the reasons for your answers.

    A. Psychologist David Wechsler designed an intelligence test expressly for use with adults.

    B. Researchers Hubel and Wiesel (1962, 1968) received a Nobel Prize for their work in the area of vision. They found that special cells in the brain are designed to visually code complex features of an object. Their research involved recording impulses from individual cells in the brains of cats and monkeys.

    C. Swiss biologist Jean Piaget observed that children understand concepts and reason differently at different stages. Based on his observations, he developed a theory of cognitive development.

    D. Several researchers have studied work motivation. They have been interested in the conditions that influence productivity and satisfaction in organizations.

    E. In 1963, Stanley Milgram conducted a classic study on obedience to authority. In subsequent variations of the original study, Milgram and his colleagues were interested in the conditions under which people might disobey.

    F. Strupp conducted research in 1982 to examine the characteristics of effective psychotherapy. He found that the relationship between the therapist and client greatly affects the success of the therapy.

    G. A national study of 3,000 children in fourth through tenth grades found that over this period of time girls' self-esteem plummeted (American Association of University Women, 1991). As a result of recommendations based on the findings of this and other research, changes in school systems have been suggested.

    H. Several psychologists have studied the process of career development and use career development theories to assist college students in selecting their careers.

2.   Harold is 17 years old and has been abusing alcohol and marijuana for the past year. He has been missing school and his academic performance is declining. Harold was formerly a "B" student and was involved in sports. He is now getting D's and F's and has dropped out of most extracurricular activities.   Answer the following questions: What influences would each of the five perspectives (learning, psychodynamic, biological, cognitive and sociocultural) and two movements in psychology (humanist and feminist) identify as central to the development of Harold's drug problem?

3.   A newly discovered tribe that has had no previous contact with the outside world is being studied by scientists from a variety of disciplines. Identify the social scientist most likely to propose each study and explain how you reached that conclusion.

   A.   Prepare a descriptive study of family life detailing roles, norms and important social determinants.
   B.   Conduct a comparative study of significant social practices in this tribe with those found in the nearest neighboring tribes.
   C.   Examine the presence of mental illness in the tribe, including the rates, the types of disorders and how people with mental illnesses are treated.

4.   Juanita is suffering from depression and she is interested in seeking professional help for her problem. Briefly describe the general types of treatment that would most likely be utilized by a psychologist, a psychiatrist, a psychoanalyst and a psychotherapist. Indicate the types of training they are likely to have had.

CHAPTER 2

How Psychologists Know What They Know

LEARNING OBJECTIVES

After studying this chapter, you should be able to do the following:

1. List the reasons for studying the research methods of psychology.

2. List and discuss the characteristics of scientific psychological research.

3. List and discuss the characteristics of descriptive research methods.

4. Describe and give examples of case studies, naturalistic observation, laboratory observation, psychological tests, and surveys and discuss the advantages and disadvantages of each.

5. List and discuss the characteristics of correlational studies and identify examples of positive and negative correlations.

6. Distinguish between independent and dependent variables and identify examples of each.

7. Distinguish between experimental and control groups.

8. Describe single-blind studies, experimenter effects and double-blind studies.

9. List and describe the types of descriptive statistics.

10. Describe how inferential statistics are used and explain statistical significance.

11. Compare and contrast cross-sectional and longitudinal studies.

12. Describe the technique of meta-analysis.

13. Discuss ethical problems that confront researchers, including the use of animals and the use of deception.

14. Describe postmodernism and the theory of social constructionism.

CHAPTER CONCEPT MAP

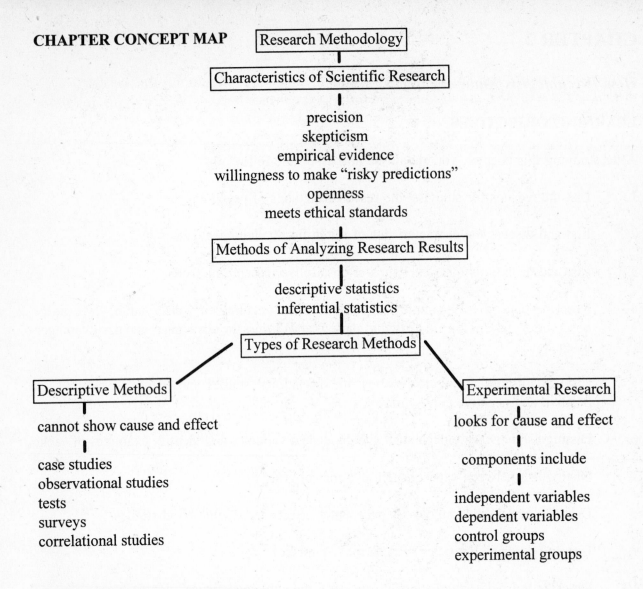

Research Methodology

Characteristics of Scientific Research

precision
skepticism
empirical evidence
willingness to make "risky predictions"
openness
meets ethical standards

Methods of Analyzing Research Results

descriptive statistics
inferential statistics

Types of Research Methods

Descriptive Methods

cannot show cause and effect

case studies
observational studies
tests
surveys
correlational studies

Experimental Research

looks for cause and effect

components include

independent variables
dependent variables
control groups
experimental groups

BRIEF CHAPTER SUMMARY

Chapter 2 discusses the importance of understanding scientific methodology to making a critical evaluation of research findings. Three major types of research studies are examined: descriptive studies, correlational studies and experimental studies. Descriptive studies include case studies, observational studies, studies based on psychological tests and studies based on surveys. Correlational studies are a special category of descriptive studies; they analyze the relationship between two variables. Experimental research is the only type that can examine cause and effect because it is conducted in a highly controlled fashion.

PREVIEW OUTLINE AND REVIEW QUESTIONS

Before you read the chapter, review the preview outline and the Learning Objectives for each section of the text. Develop additional questions of your own based on key concepts and terms and write them in the designated spaces. Answer all questions as you read the text.

SECTION 1 - SCIENCE VERSUS PSEUDOSCIENCE (PP. 41-47)

I. **SCIENCE VERSUS PSEUDOSCIENCE**
   A. **Why study methodology?**
      1. Helps identify fallacies in thinking such as _____ bias
      2. Promotes critical evaluation of psychological findings
   B. **What makes research scientific?**
      1. Precision
         a. Begin research with a precise hypothesis
         b. Base it on previous findings, observations or theory
            (1) Characteristics of a _____
               (a) Organized system of assumptions and principles that purports to explain certain phenomena
               (b) Accepted by a large part of scientific community
            (2) Terms must be defined in ways that can be observed and measured - called _____ definitions
      2. Skepticism
         a. Must accept conclusions with caution
         b. Balance caution with openness to new ideas and evidence
      3. Reliance on _____ evidence rather than on personal accounts
      4. Willingness to make "risky predictions" and the principle of falsifiability
      5. Openness - researchers must discuss ideas, testing procedures and results so their findings can be replicated to reduce fraud and error

Answer these Learning Objectives while you read Section 1.

1. List the reasons for studying the research methods of psychology.

2. List and discuss the characteristics of scientific psychological research.

Write the questions that you have formulated below and answer them while you read.

A. _____

B. _____

II.   **FERRETING OUT THE FACTS: DESCRIPTIVE STUDIES**

    A.   **General characteristics of descriptive methods**
        1.   Allow researcher to describe and predict behavior
        2.   Do not allow researcher to explain behavior

    B.   **Case Studies**
        1.   General characteristics
            a.   Detailed descriptions of particular individuals
            b.   Based on careful observation or psychological tests
        2.   Advantages
            a.   Produce detailed pictures of individuals
            b.   Can illustrate psychological principles well
            c.   Help avoid practical or _____ difficulties
        3.   Disadvantages
            a.   Rely on memories, which can be inaccurate
            b.   Difficult to interpret
            c.   Cannot use to _____ about human behavior
            d.   They are not tests of hypotheses

    C.   **Observational Studies**
        1.   General characteristics
            a.   Researchers observe behavior without interfering
            b.   Involve many subjects
            c.   Involve counting, rating or measuring specific behaviors
                (1)   _____ measuring reduces errors and biases
                (2)   Cross-checking by more than one rater occurs
            d.   Cannot explain behavior
        2.   Types of observational studies
            a.   _____ observation
                (1)   Describes behavior in the natural environment
                (2)   Can be used to describe animals or humans
            b.   Laboratory observation
                (1)   Subjects observed in the laboratory
                (2)   Observation might cause subjects to alter behavior

D.   Tests
    1.   Used for psychological assessment - procedures to measure personality traits, emotional states, aptitudes, interests, abilities and values
    2.   Types of tests
        a.   _____ tests - measure beliefs, behavior
        b.   Projective tests - designed to tap unconscious
    3.   Characteristics of a good test
        a.   Standardization - use of uniform procedures
        b.   Norms - established standards of performance
        c.   _____ - getting the same results over time
            (1)   Ways to measure reliability
                (a)   Test-retest reliability - giving the test twice to the same people
                (b)   Alternate forms reliability - giving different versions of the same test
        d.   Validity - test measures what it set out to
            (1)   _____ validity - test questions represent the trait
            (2)   Criterion validity - other measures of the trait can be predicted

E.   _____
    1.   Gather information by asking people directly
    2.   Potential problems with surveys
        a.   Representative sample - subjects should, but do not always, represent the larger population being described
        b.   Volunteer bias - volunteers differ from non-volunteers
        c.   Subjects may lie, forget or remember incorrectly
        d.   Potential biases or ambiguities in wording of questions

Answer these Learning Objectives while you read Section 2.

3.   List and discuss the characteristics of descriptive research methods.

4.   Describe and give examples of case studies, naturalistic observation, laboratory observation, tests and surveys. Discuss the advantages and disadvantages of each.

Write the questions that you have formulated below and answer them while you read.

A.   _____

B.   _____

SECTION 3 - LOOKING FOR RELATIONSHIPS: CORRELATIONAL STUDIES
(PP. 57-59)

III. **LOOKING FOR RELATIONSHIPS: CORRELATIONAL STUDIES**
- A. **Purpose and definitions**
  1. Purpose - to determine whether two or more phenomena are related, and if so, how strongly
  2. Definition - Numerical measure of the strength of the relationship
  3. _____ - anything that can be measured, rated or scored
- B. **Characteristics of correlations**
  1. Direction of a relationship between variables
     - a. Positive correlation - high values of one variable are associated with high values of the other; low values of one variable are associated with low values of the other
     - b. _____ correlation - high values of one variable are associated with low values of the other
     - c. Uncorrelated - no relationship between two variables
  2. Strength of relationship between the two variables expressed as correlation
     - a. Correlation _____ - statistic used to express a correlation
     - b. Possible range of correlation coefficient is -1 to +1
       - (1) -1 indicates a strong negative relationship
       - (2) +1 indicates a strong positive relationship
       - (3) _____ indicates no relationship
       - (4) The closer to either +1 or - 1, the stronger the relationship
       - (5) The closer to 0, the weaker the relationship
- C. **Benefits and limitations of correlations**
  1. Benefit - allows one to predict from one variable to another
  2. Limitation - cannot show causation

Answer these Learning Objectives while you read Section 3.

5. List and discuss the characteristics of correlational studies and identify examples of positive and negative correlations.

6. Distinguish between independent and dependent variables and identify examples of each.

Write the questions that you have formulated below and answer them while you read.

A. _____

B. _____

IV.   **HUNTING FOR CAUSES: THE EXPERIMENT**
   A.   **Purpose of experimentation** - to look for _____ of behavior
   B.   **Experimental variables** - the characteristics the researcher is studying
          1.   Independent variable - the one manipulated by the experimenter
          2.   _____ variable - the one the researcher tries to predict
   C.   **Experimental and control conditions**
          1.   Experimental condition - the condition or group in which subjects receive some amount of the independent variable
          2.   Control condition - the condition or group in which subjects do not receive any amount of the independent variable
                 a.   Subjects are treated the same in all other respects and are similar to experimental condition subjects
                 b.   Random assignment balances individual differences among subjects between the two groups
                 c.   A fake treatment or _____ controls for the expectations of control condition subjects
   D.   **Experimenter effects**
          1.   To control the effects of the expectations of subjects and experimenters
                 a.   Single-blind studies - subjects don't know whether they are in the experimental or control group
                 b.   _____ studies - neither experimenter nor subjects know which subjects are in which group
   E.   **Limitations of experimental research**
          1.   The setting is artificial and subjects' behavior may differ from real life
          2.   Subjects' behavior may be a reaction to the experimenter

Answer these Learning Objectives while you read Section 4.

6.   Distinguish between independent and dependent variables and identify examples of each.

7.   Distinguish between experimental and control groups.

8.   Describe single-blind studies, experimenter effects and double-blind studies.

Write the questions that you have formulated below and answer them while you read.

A.   _____

B.   _____

SECTION 5 - EVALUATING THE FINDINGS: WHY PSYCHOLOGISTS USE STATISTICS (PP. 64-70)

V.   **EVALUATING THE FINDINGS: WHY PSYCHOLOGISTS USE STATISTICS**
    A.   **General goals** - describe, assess and explain findings
    B.   **Descriptive statistics: Finding out what's so**
        1.   Steps in using descriptive statistics
            a.   Summarize individual data into _____ data
            b.   Compare group scores between two or more groups
            c.   Assess statistical significance of difference between group scores
        2.   Types of descriptive statistics
            a.   Arithmetic _____ - add scores, divide by number of scores
            b.   _____ - difference between highest and lowest scores
            c.   Variance - the spread of scores around the mean
    C.   **Inferential statistics: Asking "So What?"**
        1.   Determines the likelihood that the result of the study occurred by chance
        2.   Statistical _____ - the result is expected to occur by chance fewer than 5 times in 100; it does not necessarily indicate real-world importance
    D.   **From the Laboratory to the Real World: Interpreting the findings**
        1.   Choose among competing explanations for the one that best accounts for the greatest number of findings and makes most accurate predictions
        2.   Test a hypothesis in different ways several times
            a.   Cross-sectional studies - compare groups at one time
            b.   Longitudinal studies - study subjects across the life span
            c.   Meta-analysis - technique that combines data from many studies

Answer these Learning Objectives while you read Section 5.

9.   List and describe the types of descriptive statistics.

10.   Describe how inferential statistics are used and explain statistical significance.

11.   Compare and contrast cross-sectional and longitudinal studies.

12.   Describe the technique of meta-analysis.

Write the questions that you have formulated below and answer them while you read.

A.   _____

B.   _____

VI.   **KEEPING THE ENTERPRISE ETHICAL**
    A.   **American Psychological Association's ethical** _____
        1.   Dignity and welfare of subjects must be respected
        2.   Human subjects must voluntarily consent to participate
        3.   Subjects must know enough to make intelligent decision or informed _____
        4.   Subjects must be free to withdraw from a study at any time
        5.   Methods must follow governmental or institutional regulations
    B.   **Two controversial ethical issues**
        1.   Use of deception
            a.   Misleading subjects so the results are not affected
            b.   New guidelines govern use of deception
        2.   Use of animals
            a.   Many purposes for conducting research using animals
            b.   Opposition has resulted in improved treatment and regulations
    C.   **The meanings of knowledge** - questioning the many aspects of research
        1.   Assumptions on which research is based are being challenged
            a.   Do facts and theories reflect a reality that exists "out there"?
            b.   Can one study reality in a way that is objective, value-free and detached?
        2.   Postmodernism argues that detached objectivity is a myth
            a.   Observers' values, judgments affect how events are studied
            b.   Researchers are part of a culture that affects their research
            c.   Social _____ - believes knowledge is not discovered but created

Answer these Learning Objectives while you read Section 6.

13.   Discuss ethical problems that confront researchers, including the use of animals and the use of deception.

14.   Describe postmodernism and the theory of social constructionism.

Write the questions that you have formulated below and answer them while you read.

A.   _____

B.   _____

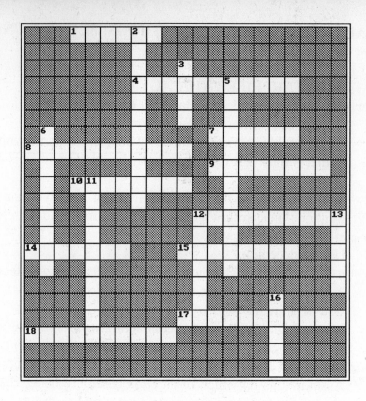

ACROSS

1. organized system of assumptions & principles that tries to explain a set of phenomena
4. the variable manipulated by the experimenter
7. type of descriptive research that gathers information by asking people directly
8. general term for scientific approach to research
9. whether a test measures what it sets out to
10. type of correlation in which high values of one variable are associated with low values of another
12. theory that argues that detached objectivity in science is a myth
14. the condition or group in an experiment in which subjects do not receive any amount of the independent variable
15. spread of scores around the mean
17. measure of how strongly two variables are related to one another
18. one of the characteristics that makes research scientific

DOWN

2. getting the same test results over time
3. average
5. type of observational study that describes behavior in the natural environment
6. a controversial ethical issue
11. the only type of research able to look for causes of behavior
12. fake treatment
13. established standards of performance in testing
16. difference between the highest and lowest scores in a group of scores

FLASH CARDS

Cut the following chart along the borders and test yourself with the resulting flash cards.

2.1 CONFIRMATION BIAS	2.9 OBSERVATIONAL STUDIES	2.17 ALTERNATE FORMS RELIABILITY
2.2 HYPOTHESIS	2.10 NATURALISTIC OBSERVATION	2.18 VALIDITY
2.3 THEORY	2.11 LABORATORY OBSERVATION	2.19 CONTENT VALIDITY
2.4 OPERATIONAL DEFINITION	2.12 PSYCHOLOGICAL TESTS	2.20 CRITERION VALIDITY
2.5 PRINCIPLE OF FALSIFIABILITY	2.13 STANDARDIZATION	2.21 SURVEYS
2.6 REPLICATE	2.14 NORMS	2.22 SAMPLE
2.7 DESCRIPTIVE METHODS	2.15 RELIABILITY	2.23 VOLUNTEER BIAS
2.8 CASE STUDY	2.16 TEST-RETEST RELIABILITY	2.24 CORRELATIONAL STUDY

2.17 A type of reliability in which different versions of a test are given to the same group on separate occasions.	2.9 A study in which the researcher systematically observes behavior without interfering with the behavior.	2.1 The tendency to look for evidence that supports our ideas and ignores evidence that does not.
2.18 The ability of a test to measure what it was designed to measure.	2.10 A study that describes behavior as it occurs in the natural environment.	2.2 A statement that attempts to predict or account for a set of phenomena.
2.19 Validity in which a test measures a broad sampling of beliefs and behaviors of the trait being measured.	2.11 A study in which researchers make observations of behavior in the laboratory rather than in the real world.	2.3 Organized system of assumptions and principles that purports to explain a specified set of phenomena.
2.20 A type of validity in which the test results predict other, independent measures of the trait in question.	2.12 Procedures to measure and evaluate personality traits, emotional states, aptitudes, interests, abilities and values.	2.4 A precise definition of a term in a hypothesis that specifies the operations for observing and measuring it.
2.21 Questionnaires and interviews that ask people directly about their experiences, attitudes or opinions.	2.13 In test construction, the development of uniform procedures for giving and scoring a test.	2.5 A scientific theory must make predictions that are specific enough that they may be disconfirmed.
2.22 Subjects selected from a population for study in order to estimate characteristics of the population.	2.14 In test construction, established standards of performance.	2.6 Scientists must tell others about their research procedures and results so others can repeat and verify their findings.
2.23 A shortcoming of findings derived from a sample of volunteers instead of a representative sample.	2.15 In test construction, the consistency, from one time and place to another, of scores derived from a test.	2.7 Methods that yield descriptions of behavior but not necessarily causal explanations.
2.24 A descriptive study that looks for a consistent relationship between two phenomena.	2.16 Reliability that is measured by giving a test twice to the same group of people, then comparing the sets of scores.	2.8 A detailed description of a particular individual under study or treatment.

2.25 VARIABLE	2.33 EXPERIMENTAL CONDITION/ GROUP	2.41 RANGE
2.26 POSITIVE CORRELATION	2.34 RANDOM ASSIGNMENT	2.42 VARIANCE
2.27 NEGATIVE CORRELATION	2.35 PLACEBO	2.43 INFERENTIAL STATISTICS
2.28 COEFFICIENT OF CORRELATION	2.36 SINGLE-BLIND STUDY	2.44 STATISTICALLY SIGNIFICANT
2.29 EXPERIMENT	2.37 EXPERIMENTER EFFECTS	2.45 CROSS-SECTIONAL STUDY
2.30 INDEPENDENT VARIABLE	2.38 DOUBLE-BLIND STUDY	2.46 LONGITUDINAL STUDY
2.31 DEPENDENT VARIABLE	2.39 DESCRIPTIVE STATISTICS	2.47 META-ANALYSIS
2.32 CONTROL CONDITION/GROUP	2.40 ARITHMETIC MEAN	2.48 SOCIAL CONSTRUCTIONISM

2.41 A measure of the spread of scores, calculated by subtracting the lowest score from the highest score.	2.33 In an experiment, the condition or group that is exposed to some amount of the independent variable.	2.25 Characteristics of behavior or experience that can be measured or described by a numeric scale.
2.42 A measure of the dispersion of scores around the mean.	2.34 A way to assign people to groups in which each person has the same probability of being assigned to a given group.	2.26 An association between increases in one variable and increases in another.
2.43 Statistical tests that allow researchers to assess the likelihood that their results occurred merely by chance.	2.35 An inactive substance or fake treatment used as a control in an experiment.	2.27 An association between increases in one variable and decreases in another.
2.44 A term used to refer to a result that would be expected by chance 5 or fewer times in 100 repetitions of the study.	2.36 An experiment in which subjects do not know whether they are in an experimental or control group.	2.28 A measure of correlation that ranges in value from -1.00 to +1.00
2.45 A study in which groups of subjects of different ages are compared at a given time.	2.37 Unintended changes in subjects' behavior due to cues inadvertently given by the experimenter.	2.29 A test of a hypothesis in which the researcher manipulates one variable to discover its effect on another.
2.46 A study in which subjects are followed and periodically reassessed over a period of time.	2.38 A study in which neither the subjects nor the researchers know whether subjects are in an experimental or control group.	2.30 A variable that an experimenter manipulates.
2.47 A statistical procedure for combining and analyzing data from many studies.	2.39 Statistics that organize and summarize research data.	2.31 A variable that an experimenter predicts will be affected by manipulations of the independent variable.
2.48 The view that there are no universal truths about human nature, because reality is constructed.	2.40 An average that is calculated by adding up a set of quantities and dividing the sum by the total number in the set.	2.32 In an experiment, a comparison condition in which subjects are not exposed to the independent variable.

PRACTICE TEST 1

1.   Introductory psychology students study research methodology to
     A.   find proof for our existing beliefs so we can argue against those who disagree.
     B.   be able to critically evaluate psychological findings.
     C.   be able to manipulate statistics to our advantage.
     D.   be able to use our own experiences as scientific proofs.

2.   Which of the following is <u>NOT</u> a characteristic of scientific research?
     A.   reliance on common sense   B.   precision
     C.   skepticism   D.   openness

3.   An organized system of assumptions and principles that purports to explain a specified set of phenomena is called a(n)
     A.   hypothesis.   B.   operational definition.
     C.   theory.   D.   risky prediction.

4.   Which of the following is an example of a hypothesis?
     A.   Alcohol decreases reaction time.
     B.   Studying improves grades.
     C.   Employees perform better in a supportive climate.
     D.   All of the above are examples of hypotheses.

5.   Defining terms in ways that can be observed and measured employs
     A.   operational definitions.   B.   theories.
     C.   common sense.   D.   skepticism.

6.   Descriptive research methods
     A.   explain behavior by identifying the causes of the behavior.
     B.   allow the researcher to describe and predict behavior.
     C.   include the experimental study.
     D.   all of the above

7.   Freud based his theory on studying a small number of particular individuals in great detail. This type of research method is called a(n)
     A.   survey.   B.   experiment.
     C.   naturalistic observation.   D.   case study.

8. One disadvantage of the research method used by Freud is that
    A. it relies on memories, which can be inaccurate.
    B. it is difficult to interpret.
    C. it cannot be used to generalize about human behavior.
    D. all of the above are disadvantages

9. Naturalistic observations involve
    A. giving subjects a series of psychological tests.
    B. assigning research participants to experimental and control groups.
    C. observing subjects in the natural environment.
    D. asking people a series of questions.

10. In the area of test construction, standardization refers to
    A. the use of uniform procedures in the administration and scoring of a test.
    B. the establishment of standards of performance.
    C. getting the same results over time.
    D. the condition that a test measures what it set out to.

11. _____ validity indicates that the test questions represent the trait being measured.
    A. test-retest   B. content
    C. criterion   D. alternate forms

12. A problem with surveys is that
    A. they can by weakened by volunteer bias.
    B. respondents may lie, forget or remember incorrectly.
    C. there may be biases or ambiguities in the wording of questions.
    D. all of the above may be problems with surveys

13. Correlations
    A. determine the causes of behavior.
    B. determine whether two or more phenomena are related, and if so, how strongly.
    C. can be expressed on a numeric scale from 1 to 10.
    D. require research participants to be observed in a laboratory.

14. The more Rupert studies, the more his test scores improve. This is an example of
    A. a naturalistic observation.   B. a positive correlation.
    C. a negative correlation.   D. proof of causation.

15. Dr. Smith is studying the relationship between hair color and shoe size. He is likely to find
    A.   a negative correlation.   B.   a positive correlation.
    C.   zero correlation.   D.   it is impossible to say

16. Experimentation is
    A.   a type of observational study.
    B.   the only research method that looks for the causes of behavior.
    C.   one of the descriptive research methods.
    D.   more limited in its conclusions than the other types of methodologies.

17. The independent variable is the one that
    A.   is manipulated by the researcher.
    B.   the researcher tries to predict.
    C.   is defined in a way that can be observed and measured.
    D.   cannot be controlled.

18. Dr. Knowles is conducting research on the effects of alcohol on reaction time. She assigns students to two groups. One group receives three ounces of alcohol and the other group receives an alcohol-free beverage that looks, smells and tastes like alcohol. Following ingestion of the beverage, the reaction time of subjects in both groups is tested. Which of the variables is the dependent variable?
    A.   alcohol   B.   control group
    C.   alcohol-free beverage   D.   reaction time

19. In the above study, the group of research participants who receive the alcohol-free beverage is called
    A.   the independent variable.   B.   the control group.
    C.   the experimental group.   D.   the random group.

20. In the study described in question 18, neither Dr. Knowles nor the research participants knew whether they were in the experimental or control group. This type of study is called a
    A.   single-blind study.   B.   longitudinal study.
    C.   double-blind study.   D.   case study.

21. The arithmetic mean, range and variance are all
    A.   types of descriptive statistics.   B.   inferential statistics.
    C.   examples of meta-analyses.   D.   statistically significant.

22. Inferential statistics
    A.   summarize individual data into group data.
    B.   combine data from many studies.
    C.   study abilities across the life span.
    D.   tell the researcher the likelihood that the result of the study occurred by chance.

23. Cross-sectional studies differ from longitudinal studies in that
    A.   cross-sectional studies compare different groups at one time, whereas longitudinal studies examine abilities across the life span.
    B.   cross-sectional studies examine groups in the laboratory, whereas longitudinal studies examine behavior in the natural environment.
    C.   cross-sectional studies examine abilities across the life span, whereas longitudinal studies compare different groups at one time.
    D.   cross-sectional studies cannot establish cause and effect, whereas longitudinal studies can.

24. Meta-analyses are helpful in the interpretation of research findings because they
    A.   determine which studies are accurate and which are not.
    B.   combine data from many studies.
    C.   establish whether the findings have any real-world importance.
    D.   establish the statistical significance of studies.

25. Postmodernism argues that
    A.   detached objectivity is a myth.
    B.   observers' values and judgments affect how events are studied.
    C.   researchers are part of a culture that affects their research.
    D.   all of the above are suggested by postmodernism

PRACTICE TEST 2

1. Which of the following is an example of confirmation bias?
    A. An article presents research evidence that supports its point of view and does not even mention the existence of well-known research that refutes it.
    B. Subjects in a study do not represent the larger population being described.
    C. A study uses only volunteer subjects who differ from non-volunteers.
    D. An experimenter's expectations subtly influence the outcome of a study.

2. Frank's neighbor was abused as a child and he is now abusive with his own children. Based on this, Frank now believes that adults who were abused become child abusers themselves.   Which characteristic of scientific research does this violate?
    A. precision   B. skepticism
    C. reliance on empirical evidence   D. openness

3. Scores on a depression test, changes in time spent sleeping and food intake might be
    A. hypotheses.   B. theories of depression.
    C. operational definitions of depression D. empirical evidence.

4. Which of the following is an example of a theory?
    A. The id, ego and superego interact to shape our personalities.
    B. Child abuse is correlated with alcoholism.
    C. Children of alcoholics will become alcoholic.
    D. People who exercise will have lower rates of depression.

5. To find out whether males or females talk more, Danielle goes to a cafe and systematically records the talking time of eight male-female pairs. This is an example of a(n)
    A. experiment.   B. case study.
    C. naturalistic observation.   D. survey.

6. To conduct research on attitudes toward abortion, Dr. Kim distributes surveys to people leaving church after a service. The problem with this survey is that
    A. people are likely to lie or forget.
    B. the questions are unclear.
    C. the sample is nonrepresentative.
    D. the procedures are not uniform.

7. Validity is to reliability as
    A. consistency is to accuracy.   B. accuracy is to consistency.
    C. criterion is to content.   D. objective is to projective.

8. You take an intelligence test on Monday and receive a high score. You repeat it on Tuesday and receive a low score. This test lacks
    A. content validity.   B. criterion validity.
    C. test-retest reliability.   D. alternate forms reliability.

9. Which of the following is an example of a positive correlation?
    A. The less students study, the worse their grades will be.
    B. The more people exercise, the fewer health problems they will have.
    C. The more alcohol people consume, the slower their reaction time will be.
    D. Hair color is unrelated to shoe size.

10. In general, older employees have fewer short-term absences. This is an example of
    A. a positive correlation.   B. a case study.
    C. a negative correlation.   D. zero correlation.

11. Based on a correlational study showing that those who exercise regularly experience lower rates of depression, which of the following conclusions can be reached?
    A. Exercise causes a reduction in depression.
    B. People who are depressed stop exercising.
    C. There is a relationship between exercise and depression.
    D. Self-esteem influences both exercise and depression levels.

12. Dr. Redbird is studying the effect of a new teaching method on learning psychology. Subjects come to her laboratory and she randomly assigns them to one of two groups. Though the subjects do not know this, one group gets instruction in the new teaching method while the other group receives instruction in the traditional method. The independent variable in this study is
    A. the new teaching method.   B. psychology grades.
    C. the control group.   D. Dr. Redmountain.

13. In the study in question 12, the group that receives the new teaching method is
    A. the control group.   B. the independent variable.
    C. the experimental group.   D. none of the above.

46

14. In question 12, the subjects did not know whether they were in the experimental or control group, but Dr. Redbird did know. This is a _____ study.
   A. descriptive
   B. single-blind
   C. double-blind
   D. laboratory observation

15. The way that Dr. Redbird tried to make subjects equal in the experimental and control group on <u>all</u> characteristics except the independent variable was to
   A. randomly assign them to groups.
   B. use single-blind techniques.
   C. select each subject individually.
   D. use only volunteers.

16. The purpose of single and double-blind studies is to
   A. control for the effects of volunteer subjects.
   B. equate subjects in the experimental and control groups.
   C. utilize a placebo.
   D. control for the expectations of subjects in a single-blind study and the expectations of both subjects and experimenter in a double-blind study.

17. The scores of the subjects in the experimental group in Dr. Redbird's study were: 93, 85, 75, 82, 77, 84, 92, 52. The mean is
   A. 93.
   B. 52.
   C. 80.
   D. 75.

18. What is the range of scores in the set of scores in question 17?
   A. 80
   B. 41
   C. 52
   D. 93

19. Subjects in the control group received a mean score of 77. Before Dr. Redbird can say whether the new technique was superior in this study, she must
   A. calculate the statistical significance of the results to evaluate the probability that this result could have happened by chance.
   B. conduct a meta-analysis.
   C. calculate the statistical significance to determine the real-world importance.
   D. conduct a longitudinal study to see if the improved learning lasts.

20. To calculate the statistical significance, _____ must be used.
   A. descriptive statistics
   B. meta-analysis
   C. inferential statistics
   D. cross-sectional analysis

21. Assessing a group's IQ scores across the life span requires using
   A. cross-sectional research.
   B. a case study approach.
   C. longitudinal research.
   D. a naturalistic study.

22. Meta-analysis would be used to
    A. establish a relationship between two variables.
    B. examine the causes of behavior.
    C. combine data from many studies.
    D. examine abilities across the life span.

23. A situation that violates the ethical code of the American Psychological Association governing research using human subjects is
    A. providing subjects with an informed consent form that informs them of potential risks of participation in a study.
    B. allowing subjects to withdraw from the study at any time.
    C. requiring subjects to participate in a study for class credit.
    D. following institutional regulations governing research.

24. Psychologists use animals in research
    A. because sometimes practical or ethical considerations prevent the use of human beings as subjects.
    B. to study principles that apply to both animals and people, such as certain biological systems.
    C. to compare different species.
    D. all of the above are reasons that animals are used in research

25. Physiologist Jared Diamond says, "There are many different, equally valid procedures for defining races, and those different procedures yield very different classifications." This statement represents the position of
    A. social constructionism.   B. the ethics code.
    C. empirical science.   D. those who use deception.

PRACTICE TEST 3

1. Determine which research method is best for each situation below and explain why.

    A.   Determine the favorite foods of adolescents.

    B.   Determine whether a person is introverted or extroverted.

    C.   Determine whether or not frustration causes aggression.

    D.   Determine whether level of education is associated with criminal behavior.

    E.   Determine conversational patterns of men and women.

    F.   Determine why a violinist gave up a flourishing career in business to play in the local symphony.

    G.   Determine the parenting patterns used on a child who is having behavior problems and whose parents cannot control him.

2. In the following experiments identify: 1) a possible hypothesis, 2) the independent and dependent variables, 3) their operational definitions, and 4) experimental and control conditions.

    A.   A study was conducted on the effects of caffeine on studying. Experimental subjects were given 32 ounces of caffeine. Subjects in the control group were given a decaffeinated beverage that looked and tasted like the beverage consumed by the experimental group. After consuming the drinks, all subjects were provided with a chapter of a text to read and then were tested.

    B.   A study was conducted on the effects of types of music on aggressive behavior. There were three experimental groups: one listened to classical music, the second listened to jazz, and the third listened to heavy metal music. Subjects in the control condition were exposed to a white noise machine for the same period of time. Following exposure to the 45 minute music session, all subjects were put in a situation in which they were able to engage in aggressive behavior (punch a punching bag).

    C.   A study was conducted on the effects of exercise on relaxation. There were two experimental groups of subjects. One group engaged in supervised aerobic exercise for 45 minutes. The second experimental group engaged in sit-ups and push-ups for 45 minutes. The control group engaged in a supervised study session. Following the exposure, all subjects were told to wait in a room for the experimenter to return. During this period, they were hooked up to medical equipment monitoring their heart rate, muscle tension, respiration and blood pressure.

3.   Among the following examples, identify which correlations are positive, negative or zero.

      A.   Height and weight
      B.   Smoking and health
      C.   Studying and drop-out rates
      D.   SAT score and grade point average (GPA)
      E.   Education level and height
      F.   Smoking and education level
      G.   Alcohol intake and reaction time
      H.   Alcohol intake and automobile accidents
      I.   Delinquency and education level
      J.   Weight and schizophrenia

4.   After reviewing the ethical guidelines adopted by the American Psychological Association (APA), determine which of the following research practices are ethical or unethical and explain why.

      A.   Require psychology students to participate as subjects in a research study.
      B.   Tell subjects that once they begin a study as a research subject, they must continue until the research is complete.
      C.   Withhold information about the hypothesis and research purposes.
      D.   Deliberately misrepresent research purposes.
      E.   Use animals to check the side-effects of a drug thought to cure depression.
      F.   Carry out a study that causes discomfort in people after securing informed consent that includes full information about possible risks.

CHAPTER 3

Evolution, Genes, and Behavior

LEARNING OBJECTIVES

1. Describe the perspectives of behavior genetics and evolutionary psychology.

2. Distinguish among genes, chromosomes and DNA.

3. Describe how the basic elements of DNA affect the characteristics of the organism.

4. Describe both the simplest and more common types of inheritance and the role of dominant and recessive genes.

5. Summarize the heredity processes that account for genetic diversity.

6. Explain how natural selection accounts for many similarities among humans.

7. Explain the assumption that the mind develops as independent "modules."

8. Describe and cite evidence supporting Chomsky's position on language acquisition.

9. Explain sociobiologists' and evolutionary psychologists' views on mating and marriage.

10. Cite evidence for and against evolutionary approaches to mating and marriage.

11. Define and discuss the characteristics of heritability and describe how it is studied.

12. Explain set-point theory and other genetic and environmental influences on weight.

13. Summarize heritability estimates for intelligence and environmental factors that influence intelligence.

14. Summarize the debate and research explaining the differences in IQ between blacks and whites.

15. Describe the limitations and interpretation errors in behavioral-genetic studies.

16. Summarize the prevailing ideas about the role of nature and nurture in explaining similarities and differences among people.

CHAPTER CONCEPT MAP

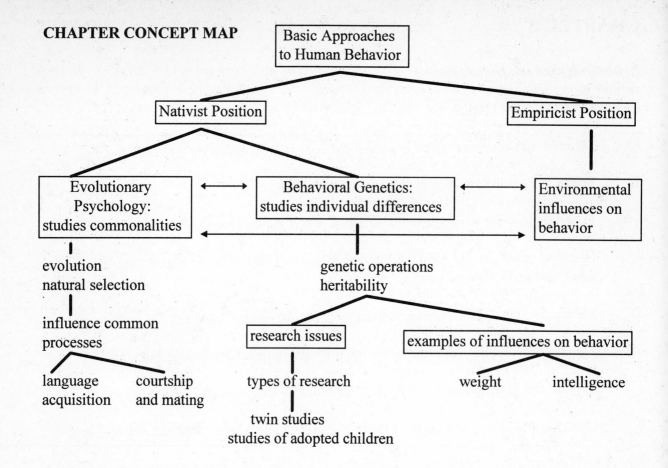

BRIEF CHAPTER SUMMARY

Chapter 3 examines the biological and evolutionary bases of behavior. Evolutionary psychology emphasizes the evolutionary mechanisms that might help explain commonalities in language learning, attention, perception, memory, sexual behavior, judgments, moral decision making, emotion and other aspects of human psychology. Genetic operations and the principle of natural selection contribute to the understanding of commonalities among humans. Language acquisition shares similar features across cultures, suggesting that this is an innate capacity. Evolutionary psychologists argue that certain social behaviors, such as courtship and mating, also have a biological base and serve an evolutionary function. A discussion of heritability helps explain differences among human beings. Heritability is used in an analysis of weight and intelligence, two characteristics on which human beings differ. Common misuses of heritability are discussed, along with the difficulties and complexities of behavioral-genetic research. The complexities of human behavior do not allow for simple "either-or" explanations, and the chapter demonstrates the need to be able to tolerate uncertainty in the exploration of the origins of human behavior.

PREVIEW OUTLINE AND REVIEW QUESTIONS

Before you read the chapter, review the preview outline and the Learning Objectives for each section of the text. Develop additional questions of your own based on key concepts and terms and write them in the designated spaces. Answer all questions as you read the text.

SECTION 1 - WHAT'S IN A GENE? (PP. 79-84)

I.   **WHAT'S IN A GENE?**
    A.   **How can we explain human differences?**
        1.   Nativists - looked to genes and inborn characteristics or nature
        2.   _____ - looked to learning, experience or nurture
        3.   Current position recognizes interaction of heredity and environment
    B.   **Definition and characteristics of genes**
        1.   Definition - basic units of _____
        2.   Characteristics
            a.   Located on _____ (found in all cells in the body)
                (1)   Each sperm and egg cell contains 23 chromosomes
                (2)   At conception, the fertilized egg contains 23 chromosomes from each or 23 pairs
                (3)   One pair of chromosomes determines anatomical sex
                    (a)   On this pair, the X chromosome is donated from the mother's egg because all eggs carry only an X
                    (b)   Either an X (female) or a Y (male) is contributed from the father's sperm since sperm can carry an X or a Y and this chromosome determines gender
            b.   Chromosomes consist of strands of _____; genes consist of small segments of this DNA
            c.   Each chromosome contains thousands of different genes
                (1)   Taken together, all genes are called the human _____
    C.   **How elements of DNA affect characteristics of the organism**
        1.   Each gene has _____ basic elements or bases of DNA (A,T,C, G)
        2.   They are arranged in a particular order, which influences amino acids, which influence proteins, which influence all structures and biochemical characteristics of the organism
    D.   **Inheritance and the search for genes that contribute to specific traits**
        1.   Most traits depend on more than one pair of genes, which makes tracking down the genetic contributions to a trait very difficult
        2.   _____ studies - look at genes located close together that may be inherited together across generations
        3.   Finding genes for specific disorders raises various ethical questions

E. **Individual genetic make up and the consequences of genetic patterns**
1. Each human has a unique genetic pattern
2. _____ of potential chromosome combinations exist
   a. Each sperm- or egg-producing cell has potential to produce millions of different chromosome combinations
   b. Genes can _____ or change spontaneously during formation of a sperm or egg
   c. Small segments of genetic material can "cross over" (exchange places) between members of a chromosome pair
3. Even same genes may have different outcomes in different organisms
4. Environment can influence functioning of genes

Answer these Learning Objectives while you read Section 1.

1. Describe the perspectives of behavior genetics and evolutionary psychology.

2. Distinguish among genes, chromosomes and DNA.

3. Describe how the basic elements of DNA affect the characteristics of the organism.

4. Describe both the simplest and more common types of inheritance and the role of dominant and recessive genes.

5. Summarize the heredity processes that account for genetic diversity.

Write the questions that you have formulated below and answer them while you read.

A. _____

B. _____

II.   OUR HUMAN HERITAGE: THE GENETICS OF SIMILARITY
    A.   Evolution - General characteristics
        1.   Definition: A change in the gene _____ within a population over many generations
        2.   Why do frequencies change?
            a.   Genetic variations arise as genes spontaneously mutate
            b.   Principle of natural _____
                (1)   As individuals with a genetically influenced trait become more successful at surviving and reproducing, their genes will become more common and may spread
                (2)   Those with traits not as adaptive will die before reproduction and their genes will become extinct
        3.   Approach of _____ psychology
            a.   Asks what challenges humans faced in prehistoric past and draws inferences about behaviors that might have evolved to solve survival problems - evaluates the inferences using empirical studies
            b.   Assumes the human mind evolved as a collection of specialized _____ to handle specific survival problems
            c.   Causes critics to worry that all behaviors will be seen as biological
    B.   Innate human characteristics
        1.   Common evolutionary history explains universal abilities, traits such as sucking and grasping, the attraction to novelty, and the motive to explore
        2.   Evolutionary psychologists speculate that other behaviors that might have been historically useful, could be influenced by inherited tendencies
    C.   Capacity for language
        1.   _____ - the study of the psychology of language
        2.   Syntax - rules that make up the grammar of a language
        3.   Noam _____ - changed thinking about how language is acquired
            a.   Not learned bit by bit, but with language acquisition device, or "mental module" in the brain
            b.   Children learn surface structure - the way a sentence is spoken, and _____ structure - the meaning of a sentence
            c.   Arguments to support Chomsky's position
                 (1)   Children everywhere go through similar stages of language development - born with a universal grammar
                (2)   Children combine words in ways adults would not, so they could not be simply imitating
                (3)   Adults do not consistently correct children's syntax
                (4)   Even profoundly retarded children acquire language

4. Some psychologists are returning to the learning model, but most accept Chomsky's idea that the faculty for language is biologically based

5. Current thinking - language depends on both _____ readiness and _____ experience

D.   Courtship and mating

1. The evolutionary viewpoint has been strongly influenced by _____ which contends that nature has selected psychological traits and social customs that aid individuals in propagating their genes

2. Males and females have faced different survival and mating problems, which has led to differences in behaviors according to sociobiologists

   a. Males profit by competing

   b. Males profit from inseminating as many females as possible

   c. Females need to choose the best genes, since their childbearing is limited and they have a large investment in each pregnancy

   d. Females pick males with status and resources

3. Cross-cultural support exists for the presence of these behaviors in humans

4. Critics of evolutionary approach

   a. Though behaviors between humans and animals may be similar, the origins of these behaviors may not be

   b. Many species defy stereotypes

   c. Among humans, sexual behavior is _____ and changeable

E.   Debate in this area has to do with the relative power of biology and culture

Answer these Learning Objectives while you read Section 2.

6. Explain how natural selection accounts for many similarities among humans.

7. Explain the assumption that the mind develops as independent "modules."

8. Describe and cite evidence supporting Chomsky's position on language acquisition.

9. Explain sociobiologists' and evolutionary psychologists' views on mating and marriage.

10. Cite evidence for and against evolutionary approaches to mating and marriage.

Write the questions that you have formulated below and answer them while you read.

A. _____

B. _____

SECTION 3 - OUR HUMAN DIVERSITY: THE GENETICS OF DIFFERENCE (PP. 96-110) AND
SECTION 4 - IN PRAISE OF HUMAN VARIATION (PP. 111-113)

III. **OUR HUMAN DIVERSITY: THE GENETICS OF DIFFERENCE**
    A.   **Definition of** _____: the proportion of the total variance in a trait that is attributable to genetic variation within a group
    B.   **The heritability hunt**
        1.   Facts about heritability
            a.   "Heritable" does not mean the same thing as _____
            b.   Heritability estimates apply only to variations in a particular group, not to individuals
            c.   Even highly heritable traits can be modified by the _____
            d.   Heritable behavioral traits are usually influenced by _____ genes
        2.   Ways to study heritability
            a.   Must study people whose degree of genetic similarity is known
            b.   Researchers study those who share either genes or environments
                (1)   _____ children
                (2)   _____ twins reared apart
                (3)   Fraternal twins
    C.   **Body weight and shape**
        1.   Weight not directly related to food intake
        2.   Set-point theory - _____ mechanism programmed to keep a body at a genetically influenced set point
            a.   Genetically programmed basal _____ rate interacts with fat cells and hormones to keep people at their set point
            b.   Studies suggest a genetic variation in hormone-like substances
        3.   Size/weight differences explained in part by genetic differences
        4.   _____ factors influencing weight include diet, exercise, culture
    D.   **Origins of Intelligence**
        1.   Intelligence is measured as an IQ score - from early days of testing
            a.   IQ = mental age divided by _____ age and multiplied by 100
            b.   This method had problems - now IQs computed from tables
            c.   Distribution of scores approximates a bell-shaped curve
        2.   Concept of IQ is controversial and IQ tests are criticized
        3.   Variations within groups
            a.   Variations in IQ scores are partly heritable; on average, studies find heritability to be about _____
            b.   Environmental influences on IQ: parental care, _____, exposure to toxins, mental stimulation, individual experiences, stressful family circumstances, parent-child interactions

4. Variations between groups
    a. Comparisons have been used to justify discrimination
    b. Group differences in IQ have been used to support eugenics
    c. Problems with and conclusions from between-group studies
        (1) Heritability estimates based on differences within group cannot be used to compare differences between groups
        (2) Black-white IQ differences influenced by environment
5. Interpreting behavioral-genetic research
    a. Goal - to determine the _____ of the variance in a trait that can be accounted for by genetic differences
    b. Problems
        (1) Measures of environmental influences are crude
        (2) Environments of separated twins and adopted children are often _____ to those of their twin or birth parents
        (3) Interactions between genes and environments overlooked
        (4) Heritability is confused with permanence

IV. IN PRAISE OF HUMAN VARIATION
    A. Heredity and environment interact to produce most human qualities
    B. The fitness of a species depends on its _____

Answer these Learning Objectives while you read Sections 3 and 4.

11. Define and discuss the characteristics of heritability and describe how it is studied.

12. Explain set-point theory and other genetic and environmental influences on weight.

13. Summarize heritability estimates for intelligence and environmental factors influencing intelligence.

14. Summarize the debate and research explaining black-white differences in IQ.

15. Describe the limitations and interpretation errors in behavioral-genetic studies.

16. Summarize the prevailing ideas about the role of nature and nurture in explaining similarities and differences among people.

Write the questions that you have formulated below and answer them while you read.

A. _____

B. _____

FLASH CARDS

Cut the following chart along the borders and test yourself with the resulting flash cards.

3.1 NATIVIST	3.6 GENES	3.11 DOMINANT/RECESSIVE GENES
3.2 EMPIRICIST	3.7 CHROMOSOMES	3.12 LINKAGE STUDIES
3.3 BEHAVIORAL GENETICS	3.8 DNA (DEOXYRIBONUCLEIC ACID)	3.13 MUTATE
3.4 EVOLUTIONARY PSYCHOLOGY	3.9 GENOME	3.14 EVOLUTION
3.5 SOCIOBIOLOGY	3.10 BASES	3.15 NATURAL SELECTION

3.11 Pairs of genes determine the expression of a trait; when a dominant and recessive gene are paired, the trait on the dominant-gene will show.	3.6 The functional units of heredity; they are composed of DNA and specify the structure of proteins.	3.1 Psychologists who emphasized nature or genes and inborn characteristics, in attempting to explain human differences.
3.12 Genetic studies that look for patterns of inheritance of genetic markers in large families in which a particular condition is common.	3.7 Rod-shaped structures, contained within every body cell, that carry the genes.	3.2 Psychologists who emphasized nurture or learning and experience in attempting to explain human differences.
3.13 The ability of genes to spontaneously change during formation of a sperm or an egg, due to an "error" in copying the original DNA sequence.	3.8 The molecule in the chromosomes that transfers genetic characteristics by way of coded instructions for the structure of proteins.	3.3 An interdisciplinary field of study concerned with the genetic bases of behavior and personality.
3.14 A change in gene frequencies within a population over many generations.	3.9 The full set of genes in each cell of an organism.	3.4 A field that emphasizes evolutionary mechanisms that help explain human commonalities in many areas of functioning.
3.15 Evolutionary process in which individuals with genetically influenced traits that are adaptive survive and reproduce.	3.10 The four basic elements of DNA contained within each gene and identified by the letters A, T, C and G, and numbering in the thousands.	3.5 An interdisciplinary field that emphasizes evolutionary explanations of social behavior in animals and human beings.

3.16 CHARLES DARWIN	**3.21 UNIVERSAL GRAMMAR**	**3.26 FRATERNAL (DIZYGOTIC) TWINS**
3.17 LANGUAGE	**3.22 OVER-REGULARIZATIONS**	**3.27 SET-POINT THEORY**
3.18 SYNTAX	**3.23 CRITICAL PERIOD (FOR LANGUAGE ACQUISITION)**	**3.28 INTELLIGENCE QUOTIENT (IQ)**
3.19 SURFACE STRUCTURE/ DEEP STRUCTURE	**3.24 HERITABILITY**	**3.29 MENTAL AGE**
3.20 LANGUAGE ACQUISITION DEVICE	**3.25 IDENTICAL (MONOZYGOTIC) TWINS**	**3.30 SOCIAL DARWINISM**

3.26 Twins who develop from two separate eggs fertilized by different sperm. They are no more alike genetically than any two siblings.	3.21 Children everywhere seem to go through similar stages of linguistic development.	3.16 British naturalist who first formulated in general terms the principle of natural selection.
3.27 A theory that a genetically-influenced weight range is maintained by a homeostatic mechanism regulating intake, fat reserves, and metabolism.	3.22 A type of error children make when grammatical rules have been learned but not the exceptions.	3.17 A system that combines meaningless elements, such as sounds or gestures, into structured utterances that convey meaning.
3.28 A measure of intelligence originally computed by dividing mental age by chronological age and multiplying by 100; it is now derived from norms.	3.23 A period, possibly from ages 1 to 5, when there is a biological readiness to learn language.	3.18 The rules that make up the grammar of a language.
3.29 A child's level of intellectual development relative to other children's; was a measure used originally to compute a person's IQ.	3.24 Estimate of the proportion of the total variance in a trait within a group, attributable to genetic differences among those in the group.	3.19 Identified by Chomsky, surface structure is the way a sentence is actually spoken; deep structure refers to the meaning of a sentence.
3.30 A theory that the prevailing social order reflects the "survival of the fittest." This was used to justify oppression and atrocities.	3.25 Twins born when a fertilized egg divides into two parts that develop into separate embryos.	3.20 According to Chomsky, the human brain has a "mental module" for language that allows children to develop language.

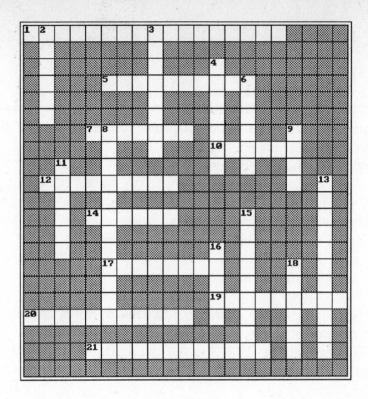

ACROSS

1. The psychology of language
5. The position that emphasizes the role of learning and experience in attempting to explain human differences
7. Linguist who argued that the human brain contains a language acquisition device
10. The full set of genes in each cell of an organism
12. An environmental influence on intelligence
14. British naturalist who formulated the principle of natural selection
17. System that combines meaningless elements into utterances that convey meaning
19. A change in gene frequencies over many generations
20. Type of twins born when a fertilized egg divides into two parts that develop into separate embryos
21. A characteristic that IQ tests attempt to measure

DOWN

2. The rules that make up the grammar of a language
3. The position that emphasizes genes and inborn characteristics in attempting to explain differences
4. Type of study that looks for patterns of inheritance in large families
6. Influence on intelligence
8. Estimate of the proportion of the variance in a trait within a group that is attributable to genetic differences among individuals
9. Type of structure that refers to the meaning of a sentence
11. How genes change spontaneously
13. Rod-shaped structures, within every cell, that carry the genes
15. Type of twins who develop from two separate eggs
16. The functional units of heredity
18. A social behavior that may be influenced by evolution

PRACTICE TEST 1

1. Nativists and empiricists
    A. agree with sociobiologists.
    B. are both evolutionary psychologists.
    C. disagree about the relative importance of nature and nurture in explaining human differences.
    D. developed the field of behavioral genetics.

2. Evolutionary psychology and sociobiology
    A. are branches of behavioral genetics.
    B. both focus on evolutionary influences on behaviors.
    C. have very little in common.
    D. emphasize the role of the environment.

3. Dr. Ricardo is studying how evolutionary mechanisms might help explain commonalities in language learning, attention, perception. He is a(n)
    A. behavioral geneticist.   B. sociobiologist.
    C. evolutionary psychologist.   D. empiricist.

4. Genes are
    A. rod-shaped structures found in every cell of the body.
    B. thread-like strands that make up chromosomes.
    C. one of the four basic elements of DNA.
    D. the basic units of heredity.

5. Chromosomes are
    A. rod-shaped structures found in every cell of the body.
    B. located on genes.
    C. one of the four basic elements of DNA.
    D. the basic units of heredity.

6. The full set of genes contained in each cell is the
    A. DNA.   B. chromosome.
    C. genome.   D. basis.

7. The father's sperm contributes a(n) _____ chromosome, which determines an offspring's sex.
   A.   X   B.   Y
   C.   X or Y   D.   XX

8. Most human traits depend on
   A.   more than one pair of genes.
   B.   a single pair of genes.
   C.   one gene.
   D.   between 5 and 10 pairs of genes.

9. In search of a genetic marker for Huntington's disease, researchers studied large families in which this condition was common. This type of study is called a(n)
   A.   case study.   B.   linkage study.
   C.   evolutionary study.   D.   family research.

10. Billions of genetically different offspring are possible because of the millions of chromosome combinations that each sperm- or egg-producing cell can produce, in combination with the genes' ability to _____ spontaneously.
   A.   divide   B.   multiply
   C.   split   D.   mutate

11. Within each gene, elements of DNA are arranged in a particular order which specifies the sequence of amino acids, which influences the synthesis of particular proteins which affects structural and biochemical characteristics of the organism. This describes
   A.   linkage studies.
   B.   how genes affect characteristics of the organism.
   C.   how genes mutate.
   D.   how natural selection occurs.

12. As gene frequencies change within a population over generations, certain genetically influenced characteristics become more or less common. This refers to
   A.   evolution.   B.   natural selection.
   C.   sociobiology.   D.   heritability.

13. A way to explain WHY gene frequencies change is the idea that individuals with traits that are adaptive in an environment will stay alive to reproduce, and over generations their genes will become more common. This describes
   A.   evolution.   B.   natural selection.
   C.   sociobiology.   D.   heritability.

14. Psycholinguists suggest that by applying rules that make up the grammar of language, we are able to understand and produce new sentences correctly. These rules are called

A. surface structure.
B. overregularizations.
C. syntax.
D. mental modules.

15. Chomsky's contribution to the understanding of language acquisition was the idea that

A. language is learned bit by bit, as one might learn a list of U.S. presidents.
B. there is a critical period for learning language.
C. children go through different stages of language development.
D. language is too complex to learn bit by bit, so there must be a "mental module" in the brain that allows young children to develop language.

16. Which of the following supports Chomsky's position on language acquisition?

A. Children everywhere go through similar stages of linguistic development.
B. Children combine words in ways adults never would, which rules out imitation.
C. Even children who are profoundly retarded acquire language.
D. All of the above support Chomsky's position on language acquisition.

17. Which of the following reflects the sociobiological view on mating and marriage?

A. Marriage and mating behaviors have been learned through reinforcements.
B. Males and females have faced different kinds of survival and mating problems and have evolved differently in aggressiveness and sexual strategies.
C. Socialization accounts for differences in mating behaviors.
D. None of the above reflect the sociobiological position.

18. "It pays for males to compete for access to fertile females and to try to inseminate as many females as possible because females can conceive and bear only a limited number of offspring, it pays for them to be selective and look for the best mate." This reflects the position of

A. outdated psychologists.
B. an empiricist.
C. sociobiology.
D. Chomsky.

19. Critics of the evolutionary approach cite which of the following positions to support their view?

A. Though humans and animals may engage in similar behaviors, the motives or origins of the behaviors differ.
B. Not all animal and human behavior conforms to the sexual stereotypes.
C. Among human beings, sexual behavior is extremely varied and changeable.
D. All of the above are arguments used by critics of the evolutionary approach.

20. Heritability
    A. estimates the proportion of difference in a trait that is attributable to genetic variation within a group.
    B. is equivalent in meaning to the term genetic.
    C. estimates the proportion of a trait that is attributable to genes in an individual.
    D. estimates the proportion of difference in a trait that is attributable to genetic variation between groups.

21. To study the heritability of a particular trait, which groups of people are studied?
    A. adopted children and twins   B. unrelated people
    C. biological mothers and daughters D. husbands and wives

22. Set-point theory suggests that
    A. a genetically influenced weight range is maintained by a homeostatic mechanism that regulates food intake, fat reserves and metabolism.
    B. in almost all cases, being overweight is caused by overeating.
    C. obesity is an indicator of emotional disturbance.
    D. weight is not influenced by genes but by learned behaviors.

23. Heritability estimates of intelligence for children and adolescents
    A. are very low since IQ is shaped primarily by environmental influences.
    B. vary widely but they have an average of .50.
    C. have an average of .90
    D. have an average of .10

24. Which of the following is a flaw in genetic theories of black-white differences in IQ?
    A. Blacks and whites do not grow up, on average, in the same kind of environment.
    B. Because of racial discrimination and de facto segregation, black children receive less encouragement and opportunities than whites.
    C. Heritability estimates based on one group (whites) are used to estimate the role heredity plays in differences between groups.
    D. All of the above are flaws.

25. Which of the following is NOT a limitation in behavioral-genetic studies?
    A. Measures of environmental influences are crude.
    B. The statistics used to calculate estimates are often inaccurate.
    C. Interactions between genetic factors and the environment are overlooked.
    D. Heritability is confused with permanence.

PRACTICE TEST 2

1.   Dr. Schmidt is interested in cross-cultural similarities in language acquisition. She thinks that evolution might help explain these similarities. She is a(n)
      A.   behavior geneticist.   B.   evolutionary psychologist.
      C.   empiricist.   D.   sociobiologist.

2.   The position of behavioral geneticists and evolutionary psychologists is related to
      A.   the nativist position, which focuses on learning and experience.
      B.   the empiricist position, which focuses on learning and experience.
      C.   nativism, which focuses on genes and inborn characteristics.
      D.   the empiricist position, which focuses on genes and inborn characteristics.

3.   Which statement describes the relationship between genes, chromosomes and DNA?
      A.   Genes, the basic unit of heredity, are located on chromosomes, which consist of strands of DNA. Genes consist of small segments of DNA molecules.
      B.   Genes are composed of chromosomes and DNA.
      C.   Chromosomes, the basic unit of heredity, direct the genes and the DNA.
      D.   DNA houses both genes and chromosomes in its rod-shaped structures.

4.   Which of the following describes how the basic elements of DNA within each cell affect characteristics of the organism?
      A.   DNA affects characteristics of the organism directly.
      B.   The process by which DNA affects the organism is unknown.
      C.   The basic elements are arranged in a particular order, which is a chemical code that specifies the sequence of amino acids, which influences protein synthesis, which affects the characteristics of the organism.
      D.   The basic elements direct specific genes that influence particular traits.

5.   Dr. Sayeed is trying to track down the genetic contributions to eye color. Which of the following is likely to be true?
      A.   Because it is a simple trait, probably a single pair of genes is responsible.
      B.   Most human traits, even simple ones, depend on more than one pair of genes.
      C.   She can locate the gene or genes through using a high resolution microscope.
      D.   She will have to map the entire human genome.

6. Which of the following hereditary processes contributes to genetic diversity?
    A. Genes can spontaneously change, or mutate.
    B. Sperm- or egg-producing cells have the potential to produce millions of different chromosome combinations.
    C. Small segments of genetic material can exchange places between members of a chromosome pair.
    D. All of the above account for genetic diversity.

7. "Characteristics that increase survival, and hence the opportunity to reproduce, will become more common over many generations." This reflects the theory of
    A. natural selection.   B. evolution.
    C. dominant genes.   D. heritability.

8. To handle survival problems in the prehistoric past, the human mind evolved as a collection of specialized _____ for certain behavioral tendencies.
    A. instincts   B. modules
    C. mutations   D. intuition

9. Like attraction to novelty and the motive to explore and manipulate things, evolutionary psychologists suggest that language and mating practices
    A. reflect our common evolutionary history.
    B. are learned behaviors.
    C. are examples of social Darwinism.
    D. differ across cultures.

10. "Lee gave the ball to Lynne," and "Lynne received the ball from Lee" have
    A. the same surface structure.
    B. different deep structures.
    C. the same surface and deep structures.
    D. the same deep structure.

11. Though they are learning different languages, Lana from Morocco, Ayse from Turkey and Paulo from Italy are going through similar stages of language development and combine words in ways that adults never would. This supports the conclusion that
    A. language is learned in bits and pieces.
    B. the syntax of all languages is remarkably similar.
    C. the brain contains a language acquisition device that allows children to develop language if they are exposed to an adequate sampling of speech.
    D. language acquisition is primarily the result of imitation of speech.

12. The sexually promiscuous male and the coy and choosy female
    A.   are outdated stereotypes.
    B.   are learned through the socialization process.
    C.   have evolutionary origins according to sociobiologists.
    D.   are common behaviors among most human beings.

13. "A male scorpionfly that coerces a female into copulation can hardly have the same 'motives' as a human male." This quote represents
    A.   one of the criticisms of the evolutionary approach to sex differences.
    B.   evidence supporting the evolutionary approach to sex differences.
    C.   the idea that similar behaviors among different species may have the same origins.
    D.   the theory that animal and human behavior conform to sexual stereotypes.

14. Heritability can be used to estimate
    A.   IQ differences between whites and Asians.
    B.   IQ differences among Harvard graduates.
    C.   how much of an individual's IQ is determined by heredity.
    D.   exactly which genes are responsible for intelligence.

15. Which of the following is consistent with the facts about heritability?
    A.   Heritability means the same thing as genetic.
    B.   Height can be dramatically affected by diet.
    C.   About fifty per cent of an individual's personality is due to heredity.
    D.   Research is being conducted to locate THE math gene.

16. Dr. Wood is studying the heritability of schizophrenia. The type of study that would accomplish this best would be a study of
    A.   monozygotic twins reared apart.
    B.   monozygotic twins reared together.
    C.   dizygotic twins reared together.
    D.   siblings reared together.

17. Dr. Cane's brother weighs much more than he does although he eats much less. How can this best be explained?
    A.   His brother is not honest about how much he eats.
    B.   Set-point theory explains this.
    C.   His brother has a faster metabolic rate.
    D.   Dr. Cane has more fat cells.

18. Set point is to _____ as thermostat is to _____.
    A. basal metabolic rate; furnace
    B. fat cells; temperature
    C. weight; furnace
    D. genes; temperature

19. Pete is adopting a child whose biological parents have low IQs. Pete asks whether this child is also likely to have a low IQ. Which of the following is the best response?
    A. The child is also quite likely to have a low IQ, since heritability of IQ is high.
    B. The IQs of the child's biological parents are irrelevant, since environmental influences outweigh heritability.
    C. While IQ is at least in part heritable, environmental influences can have a great impact; however, it is impossible to make predictions about any individual.
    D. Nothing is known about the heritability of IQ.

20. Richard wants to positively influence the IQ of his daughter as much as possible. To do this, he should
    A. provide good nutrition.
    B. remove environmental toxins.
    C. provide opportunities for mental stimulation.
    D. All of the above

21. Children fathered by black and white American soldiers in Germany after World War II, and reared in similar German communities by similar families, did not differ significantly in IQ. This study
    A. supports genetic theories explaining black-white IQ differences.
    B. refutes genetic theories explaining black-white IQ differences.
    C. has been criticized for methodological errors.
    D. demonstrates the IQ superiority of blacks over whites.

22. Two pots of tomatoes were planted with seeds of identical quality. One pot used enriched soil and one pot used impoverished soil. A comparison of the plants from each of these pots is analogous to
    A. comparing the IQs of two Asian-Americans from similar socioeconomic backgrounds, communities and school systems.
    B. looking for a genetic explanation of IQ differences between blacks and whites.
    C. comparing the IQs of two siblings.
    D. None of the above

23. Measures of environmental influences are crude; environmental and genetic factors interact; even highly heritable traits can be modified. These statements are
    A.   widely considered in the interpretation of behavioral-genetic studies.
    B.   inaccurate.
    C.   often overlooked or confused in the interpretation of behavioral-genetic studies.
    D.   controversial.

24. Although IQ is a predictor of success in schooling, schooling also has a substantial effect on IQ. This reflects the fact that
    A.   IQ test scores are not very reliable.
    B.   IQ is primarily influenced by the environment.
    C.   IQ cannot be predicted.
    D.   even highly heritable traits can be modified.

25. Which of the following statements best summarizes the prevailing ideas about the role of nature and nurture in explaining similarities and differences among people?
    A.   Heredity determines some characteristics and environment determines others.
    B.   It is likely that in time we will find genetic explanations for most behaviors.
    C.   Heredity and environment always interact to produce a unique mixture of qualities; once present, they blend and become indistinguishable.
    D.   We really know very little about the relative contributions of each on any given trait.

PRACTICE TEST 3

1 A. You are working in a drug treatment program. You hear many clients in this program describe their alcoholic family backgrounds and state their belief that their alcoholism is genetic. Using information about genes, chromosomes and DNA, give a general description of how this might be possible.

B. You attend a lecture in which an author of a self-help book on alcoholism says that alcoholism is fifty percent inherited and, therefore, if you have an alcoholic parent, you have a fifty percent chance of becoming an alcoholic. Discuss the problems with these statements using the facts about heritability.

C. If you wanted to search for the genes associated with alcoholism, describe the type of study you would conduct and how you would go about collecting your data.

2. Using the approach of evolutionary psychology, expand on the idea that the following characteristics were inherited because they were useful during the history of our species (they had an evolutionary function). Explain how they might have been useful in adapting.

A. the feeling of disgust
B. intuition
C. self-concept
D. kinship
E. male promiscuity
F. female selectivity

3. Compare Chomsky's position with an earlier position on the acquisition of language and use arguments to support this view.

4. A. Describe a study that you would design to evaluate the heritability of intelligence. Describe your conclusions about both hereditary and environmental influences on intelligence. What cautionary statements would you make about the heritability estimate?

B. Based on your findings, you are to make recommendations to a federal panel to convened to develop a parental training program for low income families to help them promote intellectual development in their children. Discuss the recommendations you would make to the panel.

CHAPTER 4

Neurons, Hormones, and the Brain

LEARNING OBJECTIVES

1. List and describe the features and functions of the central and peripheral nervous systems.

2. Distinguish between the somatic and autonomic nervous systems.

3. Describe biofeedback.

4. Distinguish between the sympathetic and parasympathetic nervous systems.

5. Describe the structure of a neuron and explain how impulses are transmitted from one neuron to another.

6. Describe the roles of neurotransmitters and endorphins.

7. Describe the functioning of hormones, specifically those in which psychologists are especially interested.

8. List and describe techniques psychologists use to study brain functions.

9. List and describe the location and function of each of the major portions of the brain.

10. Summarize the functions of the brain's two hemispheres and explain their relationship.

11. Explain localization of function and compare that with the theory that information is distributed across large areas of the brain.

12. Summarize the evidence on whether there are sex differences in the brain and how any differences might affect behavior.

13. Describe the effect of experience on brain development.

CHAPTER CONCEPT MAP

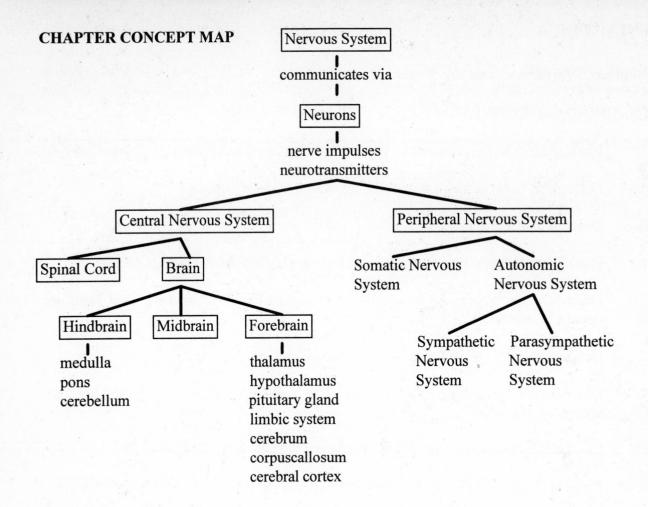

BRIEF CHAPTER SUMMARY

Chapter 4 reviews the nervous system. The central nervous system is composed of the brain and spinal cord. It receives incoming messages from the senses, processes that information, and sends output to the muscles and organs. The nerves in the rest of the body are part of the peripheral nervous system, which is composed of the somatic nervous system and the autonomic nervous system. The autonomic nervous system is made up of the sympathetic and parasympathetic nervous systems. The nervous system is made up of nerve cells--or neurons. A neuron is made up of dendrites, a cell body, and an axon, which ends in axon terminals. A neural message goes from the beginning to the end of a neuron via an electrical impulse. Neurons communicate with other neurons through chemicals called neurotransmitters. They are released by one neuron and temporarily received by another at the synapse, a tiny space between two neurons. Different brain structures and their functions are discussed, along with general issues about how the brain processes information.

PREVIEW OUTLINE AND REVIEW QUESTIONS

Before you read the chapter, review the preview outline and the Learning Objectives for each section of the text. Develop additional questions of your own based on key concepts and terms and write them in the designated spaces. Answer all questions as you read the text.

SECTION 1 - THE NERVOUS SYSTEM: A BASIC BLUEPRINT (PP. 117-122)

I. **THE NERVOUS SYSTEM: A BASIC BLUEPRINT**
    A. **The central nervous system**
        1. Functions - receives, processes, interprets and stores incoming information; sends out messages to muscles, glands, internal organs
        2. Parts - brain and _____ _____ (an extension of the brain)
    B. **The _____ nervous system** - nervous system outside brain and spinal cord
        1. Functions
            a. _____ neurons - bring input from skin, muscles, organs
            b. Motor neurons - carry output to muscles, glands and organs
        2. Divisions
            a. _____ nervous system
                (1) Nerves connected to sensory receptors
                (2) Nerves connected to skeletal muscles - voluntary action
            b. Autonomic nervous system - works automatically
                (1) Functions: regulates blood vessels, glands, organs
                (2) Divisions: _____/parasympathetic nervous systems
                (3) Biofeedback - helps people control autonomic responses

Answer these Learning Objectives while you read Section 1.

1. List/describe features and functions of the central and peripheral nervous systems.

2. Distinguish between the somatic and autonomic nervous systems.

3. Describe biofeedback.

4. Distinguish between the sympathetic and parasympathetic nervous systems.

Write the questions that you have formulated below and answer them while you read.

A. _____

B. _____

SECTION 2 - COMMUNICATION IN THE NERVOUS SYSTEM: NUTS AND BOLTS (PP. 122-130)

II. **COMMUNICATION IN THE NERVOUS SYSTEM**
  A. **Components of the nervous system**
    1. Neurons - _____ cells that communicate to, from or inside the CNS
    2. Glial cells - hold neurons in place, nourish, insulate neurons
    3. Nerves - individual neurons in peripheral nervous system collected together
  B. **The structure of the neuron**
    1. Dendrites - receive messages from other neurons, transmit to cell body
    2. Cell body - keeps the neuron alive, determines whether to fire
    3. _____ - transmit messages away from cell body to other neurons
      a. End in branches or axon terminals
      b. Many axons insulated by fatty material or myelin sheath
  C. **How neurons communicate**
    1. Synapses = axon terminal + synaptic _____ (small space between one axon and next dendrite) + receiving dendrite
      a. Billions of neurons may connect at a synapse
      b. Synaptic connections continue to be formed throughout life
    2. Neural impulses - how neurons communicate
      a. Wave of _____ voltage, called action potential, moves down axon to end of axon terminal, called synaptic end bulb
      b. Synaptic end bulb releases synaptic vesicles (sacs in the end bulb) containing _____ or neurotransmitters (transmitters)
      c. Transmitters cross the synaptic cleft and briefly lock into sites of the receiving dendrites
      d. They can excite or _____ the firing of the receiving neuron
      e. Receiving neuron averages the excitatory and inhibitory incoming messages to determine if it reaches firing threshold
      f. Neurons either fire or do not fire (all or none); the strength of firing does not alter
  D. **Chemical Messengers in the nervous system**
    1. Neurotransmitters: Versatile couriers
      a. _____ have been identified, more are being found
      b. Each binds only to certain types of receptor sites
      c. Levels that are too high or too low related to problems
      d. Each neurotransmitter plays many roles and functions overlap
      e. Cause and effect between neurotransmitters and behavior unclear
      f. Some better understood neurotransmitters and some of their effects
        (1) Serotonin - sleep, mood, and more
        (2) Dopamine - movement, learning, memory, emotion

   (3) Acetylcholine - muscle action, memory, emotion

   (4) Norepinephrine - heart rate, learning, memory

   (5) GABA - inhibitory neurotransmitter

   (6) Glutamate - excitatory neurotransmitter

 2. _____: The brain's natural opiates

  a. Produce effects similar to natural opiates; reduce pain, promote pleasure as well as other behaviors

  b. Most _____ - influence actions of neurotransmitters

  c. Levels increase during stress or fear response

 3. Hormones: Long-distance messengers

  a. Substances produced in one part of the body but affect another

  b. Originate in _____ glands that release hormones into the bloodstream, which carries them to other organs and cells

  c. Affected by and affect nervous system functions

  d. Hormones of particular interest to psychologists

   (1) _____ - affects appetite

   (2) Melatonin - regulates biological rhythm

   (3) Adrenal hormones - involved in arousal responses and produced by the adrenal glands which are composed of

    (a) cortex - an outer layer producing cortisol

    (b) _____ - inner core which produces epinephrine and norepinephrine

   (4) Sex hormones - all occur in both sexes

    (a) Androgens (i.e. testosterone) - masculinizing

    (b) _____ - feminizing

    (c) Progesterone - maintenance of uterine lining

Answer these Learning Objectives while you read Section 2.

5. Describe the structure of a neuron and how impulses are transmitted from one neuron to another.

6. Describe the roles of neurotransmitters and endorphins.

7. Describe the functioning of hormones in which psychologists are especially interested.

Write the questions that you have formulated below and answer them while you read.

A. _____

B. _____

SECTION 3 - EAVESDROPPING ON THE BRAIN (PP. 130-133)

III. **EAVESDROPPING ON THE BRAIN** - METHODS FOR STUDYING THE BRAIN
   A. **Researchers study the brains of those who have experienced disease or injury**
   B. _____ **method** - damaging or removing section of brain in animals and then observing the effects
   C. **Electrode methods** - detect electrical activity of the neurons
      1. Electroencephalogram (EEG)
         a. Brain _____ recording
         b. Incorporates computer technology
            (1) Yields picture of brain activity patterns associated with specific events
            (2) Computers help to analyze evoked potentials
      2. Needle _____
         a. Thin wires inserted into the brain to record electrical activity and to stimulate the brain
         b. Microelectrodes - fine wires that can be inserted into single cells
   D. **Positron-Emission Tomography - PET scan**
      1. Records biochemical changes in the brain as they occur
      2. Utilizes a _____ glucose-like substance
      3. Used to diagnose abnormalities or to learn about normal brain activity
   E. **Magnetic Resonance Imaging (MRI)**
      a. Uses _____ fields and radio frequencies
      b. Used for both diagnosing disease and studying normal brains
   F. **Other techniques** - include combining EEG and MRI technology

Answer this Learning Objective while you read Section 3

8. List and describe techniques psychologists use to study brain functions.

Write the questions that you have formulated below and answer them while you read.

A. _____

B. _____

SECTION 4 - A TOUR THROUGH THE BRAIN (PP. 133-140)

IV. **A TOUR THROUGH THE BRAIN**
- A. **The hindbrain: Vital functions**
  1. Brain _____ - located at base of skull; old part of brain
     - a. Medulla - regulates breathing and heart rate; automatic functions
     - b. Pons - regulates sleeping, waking, and dreaming
  2. Reticular _____ system - network of neurons, extends upward and connects with higher brain areas; screens information, arousal, alertness
  3. Cerebellum - regulates balance and coordination of muscle movement
- B. **The midbrain: Important way stations** - neural tracts running to and from the upper and lower portions of the brain
- C. **The forebrain: Emotions, memory and thought**
  1. _____ - directs incoming sensory messages to higher centers
     - a. Sense of smell is the only sense bypassing the thalamus
     - b. Information about smell goes to the olfactory bulb
  2. Hypothalamus - associated with _____, such as hunger, thirst, emotion, sex and reproduction, body temperature and the autonomic nervous system
  3. Pituitary gland - "master gland" governed by hypothalamus
  4. Limbic system - loosely interconnected structures involved in emotions
     - a. Amygdala - evaluates sensory information to determine its importance
     - b. _____ - "gateway to memory;" memory storage for future use
  5. Cerebrum - higher forms of thinking
     - a. Divided into two halves or cerebral hemispheres
       - (1) Right hemisphere in charge of left side of the body
       - (2) Left hemisphere in charge of right side of the body
       - (3) Each hemisphere has somewhat different tasks and talents
     - b. Connected by band of fibers called _____ callosum
     - c. Covered by layer of densely packed cells - cerebral cortex
       - (1) Grayish appearance = gray matter
       - (2) Contains three-fourths of all cells in the brain
       - (3) Divided into four regions
         - (a) _____ lobes - contain the visual cortex
         - (b) Parietal lobes - contain somatosensory cortex, which receives information about pressure, pain, touch and temperature from all over the body
         - (c) Temporal lobes - contain auditory cortex
         - (d) Frontal lobes - contain the motor cortex; responsible for making plans, taking initiative and thinking creatively

(4) Contains _____ areas - responsible for higher mental processes
    (a) The prefrontal lobe contains association areas
    (b) Association areas involve personality, social judgment, and the ability to set goals and make and carry out plans
    (c) Aid in the normal expression of emotions
    (d) Involved in helping us determine the proper order of behaviors and knowing when to stop

Answer this Learning Objective while you read Section 4.

9. List and describe the location and function of each of the major portions of the brain.

Write the questions that you have formulated below and answer them while you read.

A. _____

B. _____

SECTION 5 - THE TWO HEMISPHERES OF THE BRAIN (PP. 140-145) AND
SECTION 6 - TWO STUBBORN ISSUES IN BRAIN RESEARCH (PP. 146-153)

V.   THE TWO HEMISPHERES OF THE BRAIN
    A.   Split brains: A house divided
        1.   Corpus callosum, which connects the cerebral hemispheres in the case of normal brains, is severed
        2.   This surgery is performed in animal studies and for some human conditions
        3.   Effects
            a.   Split-brain patients are able to lead normal lives
            b.   Effects on perception and memory are observable under experimental conditions
    B.   Differentiation of function in normal brains
        1.   _____ hemisphere handles language for nearly all right-handed people and a majority of left-handers
            a.   Broca's area - speech _____
            b.   Wernicke's area - meaning and language comprehension
        2.   Left side more active than right during some logical, symbolic and sequential tasks, such as math
    C.   A question of dominance
        1.   Many researchers believe the left side is dominant because cognitive skills, including rational and analytic abilities, originate here
        2.   Others point to abilities of the right hemisphere: superior visual-____ abilities, appreciation of art and music; some researchers claim it is holistic and intuitive
    D.   In real life, the two hemispheres cooperate
VI.   TWO STUBBORN ISSUES IN BRAIN RESEARCH
    A.   How specialized are separate brain parts?
        1.   Localization of _____ - old theory that reflects the belief that different brain parts perform different jobs
            a.   For over 150 years research has supported in many ways
            b.   Continues to be the guiding principle in brain theories
        2.   Minority view - information is distributed across large areas of the brain - _____ theories
            a.   One approach says that the average pattern of cell activity throughout the brain is important - the brain works like an orchestra
            b.   Another approach compares brain functioning to holography
            c.   These approaches can explain the brain's plasticity and flexibility
        3.   Most likely a combination of both is true - parts of an event are localized, parts are distributed

B. **Are there "his" and "hers" brains?**
   1. Efforts to identify male-female differences have reflected biases
   2. Two questions must be asked:
      a. Are male and female brains physically different?
         (1) _____ differences have been found in animal brains
         (2) Human sex differences more elusive
            (a) Many changing findings, many contradictory findings
            (b) Many different conclusions drawn
      b. If there are brain differences, what do they mean for the behavior of men and women in real life?
         (1) Many sex differences that are discussed are stereotypes
         (2) Some sex differences are shrinking, others have been exaggerated
C. **Considerations when thinking about the brain**
   1. Brain organization - the proportion of brain cells found in any part of the brain; varies from person to person
   2. Experience constantly influences the brain
      a. Affects the brain _____
      b. Affects brains organization

Answer these Learning Objectives while you read Sections 5 and 6.

10. Summarize the functions of the brain's two hemispheres and explain their relationship.

11. Explain localization of function and compare that with the theory that information is distributed across large areas of the brain.

12. Summarize the evidence on whether there are sex differences in the brain and how any differences might affect behavior.

13. Describe the effect of experience on brain development.

Write the questions that you have formulated below and answer them while you read.

A. _____

B. _____

FLASH CARDS

Cut the following chart along the borders and test yourself with the resulting flash cards.

4.1 NEUROPSYCHOLOGY	**4.8 SOMATIC NERVOUS SYSTEM**	**4.15 DENDRITES**
4.2 CENTRAL NERVOUS SYSTEM	**4.9 AUTONOMIC NERVOUS SYSTEM**	**4.16 CELL BODY**
4.3 SPINAL CORD	**4.10 BIOFEEDBACK**	**4.17 AXON**
4.4 REFLEX	**4.11 SYMPATHETIC NERVOUS SYSTEM**	**4.18 AXON TERMINALS**
4.5 PERIPHERAL NERVOUS SYSTEM	**4.12 PARASYMPATHETIC NERVOUS SYSTEM**	**4.19 NERVE**
4.6 SENSORY NERVES	**4.13 NEURON**	**4.20 MYELIN SHEATH**
4.7 MOTOR NERVES	**4.14 GLIAL CELLS**	**4.21 SYNAPTIC CLEFT**

4.15 Branches on a neuron that receive information from other neurons and transmit it toward the cell body.	**4.8** The subdivision of the peripheral nervous system that connects to sensory receptors and skeletal muscles.	**4.1** The field of psychology concerned with the neural and biochemical bases of behavior and mental processes.
4.16 The part of the neuron that keeps it alive and determines whether it will fire.	**4.9** The subdivision of the peripheral nervous system that regulates the internal organs and glands.	**4.2** The portion of the nervous system consisting of the brain and spinal cord.
4.17 Extending fiber of a neuron that conducts impulses away from the cell body and transmits them to other neurons.	**4.10** A technique for controlling bodily functions by attending to an instrument that monitors the function and signals changes in it.	**4.3** A collection of neurons and supportive tissue running from the base of the brain down the center of the back, protected by a column of bones.
4.18 Branches at the end of the axon into which the axon divides.	**4.11** The subdivision of the autonomic nervous system that mobilizes bodily resources and increases the output of energy during arousal responses.	**4.4** An automatic response to a stimulus.
4.19 A bundle of nerve fibers (axons and sometimes dendrites) in the peripheral nervous system.	**4.12** The subdivision of the autonomic nervous system that operates during relaxed states and conserves energy.	**4.5** All portions of the nervous system outside the brain and spinal cord; it includes sensory and motor nerves.
4.20 A fatty insulating sheath surrounding many axons.	**4.13** A cell that conducts electrochemical signals; the basic unit of the nervous system. Also called a nerve cell.	**4.6** Nerves in the peripheral nervous system that carry sensory messages toward the central nervous system.
4.21 A minuscule space where the axon terminal of one neuron nearly touches a dendrite or the cell body of another.	**4.14** Cells that hold neurons in place, insulate neurons and provide them with nutrients.	**4.7** Nerves in the peripheral nervous system that carry messages from the central nervous system to muscles, glands and internal organs.

4.22 SYNAPSE	4.29 ENDORPHINS	4.36 ADRENAL HORMONES
4.23 ACTION POTENTIAL	4.30 NEUROMODULATORS	4.37 ADRENAL CORTEX AND MEDULLA
4.24 SYNAPTIC END BULB	4.31 HORMONES	4.38 CORTISOL
4.25 SYNAPTIC VESICLES	4.32 ENDOCRINE GLANDS	4.39 EPINEPHRINE
4.26 NEUROTRANSMITTER	4.33 NEUROENDOCRINE SYSTEM	4.40 NOREPINEPHRINE
4.27 RECEPTOR SITES	4.34 INSULIN	4.41 SEX HORMONES (ANDROGENS, ESTROGENS, PROGESTERONE)
4.28 EXCITATORY AND INHIBITORY EFFECTS	4.35 MELATONIN	4.42 ELECTRODES

4.36 Produced by the adrenal glands, they are involved in emotion and responses to stress. Each adrenal gland has a cortex and a medulla.	**4.29** Neuromodulators that are similar in structure and action to opiates. They are involved in pain reduction, pleasure, and memory.	**4.22** The site where transmission of a nerve impulse occurs; it includes the synaptic end bulb, synaptic cleft, receptor sites.
4.37 Each adrenal gland has an outer layer called the cortex and an inner core or medulla.	**4.30** Chemical messengers in the nervous system that increase or decrease the action of specific neurotransmitters.	**4.23** A neural impulse; a wave of electrical voltage that travels down a transmitted axon; an exchange of differently charged ions across the axon wall.
4.38 An adrenal hormone produced by the cortex, or outer layer, of the adrenal gland. It increases blood-sugar levels and enhances energy.	**4.31** Chemical substances, secreted by organs called glands, that affect the functioning of other organs.	**4.24** The button-like tip of the axon terminals that contain tiny sacs filled with molecules of a chemical substance.
4.39 Adrenal hormone produced by the inner core or medulla of the adrenal gland. It activates the sympathetic nervous system.	**4.32** Internal organs that produce hormones and release them into the bloodstream.	**4.25** Tiny sacs in the end bulb that contain a few thousand molecules of a chemical substance called a neurotransmitter.
4.40 Adrenal hormone produced by the medulla, or inner core of the adrenal gland. It affects heart rate, learning and memory.	**4.33** The parts of the nervous and endocrine systems that interact.	**4.26** A chemical substance that is released by a transmitting neuron at the synapse and that alters the activity of a receiving neuron.
4.41 Regulate the development and functioning of reproductive and sex organs and stimulate the development of sex characteristics.	**4.34** A hormone produced by the pancreas that plays a role in the body's use of glucose (a sugar) and affects appetite.	**4.27** Special molecules in the membrane of the receiving neuron to which the transmitter molecules bind briefly.
4.42 A method for studying the brain that detects and records electrical activity.	**4.35** A hormone secreted by the pineal body which is a small gland deep within the brain that appears to regulate biological rhythms.	**4.28** The effects of the transmitter molecules on the receiving cells are either voltage shifts in a positive or negative direction.

4.43 ELECTRO-ENCEPHALOGRAM	**4.50 RETICULAR ACTIVATING SYSTEM (RAS)**	**4.57 PITUITARY GLAND**
4.44 PET SCAN	**4.51 CEREBELLUM**	**4.58 LIMBIC SYSTEM**
4.45 MRI (MAGNETIC RESONANCE IMAGING)	**4.52 MIDBRAIN**	**4.59 AMYGDALA**
4.46 HINDBRAIN	**4.53 FOREBRAIN**	**4.60 HIPPOCAMPUS**
4.47 BRAIN STEM	**4.54 THALAMUS**	**4.61 CEREBRUM**
4.48 MEDULLA	**4.55 OLFACTORY BULB**	**4.62 CEREBRAL HEMISPHERES**
4.49 PONS	**4.56 HYPOTHALAMUS**	**4.63 CORPUS CALLOSUM**

4.57 A small endocrine gland at the base of the brain that releases many hormones and regulates other endocrine glands.	4.50 A dense network of neurons found in the core of the brain stem; arouses the cortex and screens incoming information.	4.43 A recording of neural activity detected by electrodes.
4.58 A group of brain areas involved in emotional reactions and motivated behavior.	4.51 A brain structure that regulates movement and balance.	4.44 A method for analyzing biochemical activity in the brain, using injections of a radioactive, glucose-like substance.
4.59 A brain structure involved in the arousal and regulation of emotion; it may play a role in the association of memories formed in different senses.	4.52 Contains neural tracts running from upper and lower parts of the brain; receives visual information and is involved in eye movements.	4.45 A method for studying body and brain tissue that uses magnetic fields and special radio receivers.
4.60 A brain structure thought to be involved in the storage of new information in memory.	4.53 Brain structure involved in complex behaviors, such as thought, memory and emotions. Contains many brain structures.	4.46 Part of the brain that controls reflexive or automatic behaviors. Consists of the brain stem, medulla, pons, RAS and cerebellum.
4.61 Largest brain structure, consisting of the upper part of the forebrain; in charge of most sensory, motor, and cognitive processes in humans.	4.54 The brain structure that relays sensory messages to the cerebral cortex.	4.47 The part of the brain at the top of the spinal cord; responsible for automatic functions such as heartbeat and respiration.
4.62 The two halves of the cerebrum.	4.55 The switching station for the sense of smell.	4.48 A structure in the brain stem responsible for certain automatic functions, such as breathing and heart rate.
4.63 The bundle of nerve fibers connecting the two cerebral hemispheres.	4.56 Brain structure involved in emotions and drives vital to survival, such as fear, hunger, thirst, reproduction; regulates the autonomic nervous system.	4.49 A structure in the brain stem involved in, among other things, sleeping, waking, and dreaming.

4.64 LATERALIZATION	4.71 AUDITORY CORTEX	4.78 WERNICKE'S AREA
4.65 CEREBRAL CORTEX	4.72 FRONTAL LOBES	4.79 CEREBRAL DOMINANCE
4.66 OCCIPITAL LOBES	4.73 MOTOR CORTEX	4.80 LOCALIZATION OF FUNCTION
4.67 VISUAL CORTEX	4.74 ASSOCIATION CORTEX	4.81 PLASTICITY
4.68 PARIETAL LOBES	4.75 PREFRONTAL CORTEX	4.82 PHRENOLOGY
4.69 SOMATOSENSORY CORTEX	4.76 "SPLIT-BRAIN" SURGERY	4.83 HOLISTIC THEORIES
4.70 TEMPORAL LOBES	4.77 BROCA'S AREA	4.84 DISTRIBUTED THEORIES

4.78 Region in the left, temporal lobe that handles language meaning and comprehension.	**4.71** Contained in the temporal lobes, the auditory cortex processes sound.	**4.64** Specialization of the two cerebral hemispheres for particular psychological operations.
4.79 The left side of the brain has greater cognitive talents than the right hemisphere, therefore many researchers believe it is dominant.	**4.72** Regions of the cortex located toward the front of the brain that contains the motor cortex and are responsible for making plans and intuition.	**4.65** A collection of several thin layers of cells covering the cerebrum; largely responsible for higher functions.
4.80 Specialization of particular brain areas for particular functions.	**4.73** Section of the frontal lobe which issues orders to the muscles that produce voluntary movement.	**4.66** Regions of the cerebral cortex located at the back of the head that contain the visual cortex, where visual signals are processed.
4.81 Brain's ability to be flexible. For example, after brain damage, being able to learn new strategies to accomplish various tasks.	**4.74** Areas of the cortex in which no sensation occurs during electrical stimulation. They appear to be involved in higher mental processes.	**4.67** A section of the occipital lobe where visual signals are processed. Damage to the visual cortex can cause visual impairment.
4.82 An old, disproved theory of Joseph Gall that suggested personality traits were reflected in the development of different areas of the brain.	**4.75** An association area in the fowardmost part of the frontal lobe. Has to do with will, personality, judgment and making and carrying out plans.	**4.68** Regions of the cerebral cortex located at the top of the brain that contain the somatosensory cortex.
4.83 Theories that argue against localization of function or the idea of specialization.	**4.76** Surgery performed on animals for experiments and on humans in the case of illness that involves severing the corpus callosum.	**4.69** A section of the parietal lobe that receives information about pressure, pain, touch and temperature from all over the body.
4.84 As opposed to localization of function, the belief that information is distributed across large areas of the brain.	**4.77** Region in the left, frontal lobe that handles speech production.	**4.70** Regions of the cerebral cortex located above the ears, that are involved in memory, perception, emotion and language and audition.

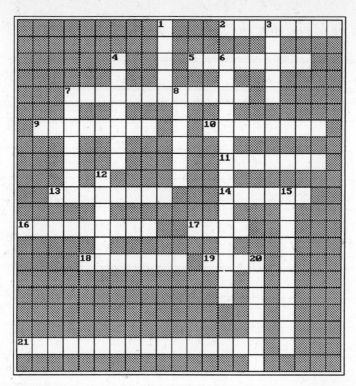

ACROSS

2. Part of limbic system involved in arousal and regulation of emotion
5. Receives information from other neurons
7. Regulates autonomic nervous system
9. Lobe that contains the somatosensory cortex
10. Theories suggesting that information is distributed across large areas of the brain
11. Site where transmission of a nerve impulse from one neuron to another occurs
13. Largest brain structure
14. Layer of cells covering the cerebrum
16. Brain structure involved in complex behaviors such as thought
17. Conducts impulses away from the cell body
18. Hormone produced by the pancreas
19. Structure in brain stem involved in waking, sleeping and dreaming
21. Chemical released by neuron at synapse

DOWN

1. Region in left, frontal lobe that handles speech production
3. Cells that hold neurons in place
4. Region of the cortex that contains the motor cortex
6. Field concerned with the neural bases of behavior and mental processes
7. Chemicals secreted by the glands
8. System containing brain areas involved in emotions and motivated behaviors
12. Basic unit of the nervous system
15. Neuromodulator similar to opiates
20. Neurons that carry messages toward the central nervous system

Complete this chart by identifying the function that corresponds to the brain structure listed in the left column.

BRAIN STRUCTURE	FUNCTION
HINDBRAIN	
Medulla	
Pons	
Reticular Activating System	
Cerebellum	
MIDBRAIN	
FOREBRAIN	
Thalamus	
Hypothalamus	
Olfactory Bulb	
Pituitary Gland	
Limbic System	
Amygdala	
Hippocampus	
Cerebrum	
Left Cerebral Hemisphere	
Right Cerebral Hemisphere	
Corpus Callosum	
Cerebral Cortex	
Occipital Lobes	
Temporal Lobes	
Parietal Lobes	
Frontal Lobes	

PRACTICE TEST 1

1. The function of the central nervous system is
   A. to receive, process and interpret incoming information.
   B. to send out messages to muscles.
   C. to send out messages to glands and organs.
   D. all of the above.

2. The peripheral nervous system
   A. is made up of the brain and spinal cord.
   B. handles the central nervous system's input and output.
   C. depends exclusively on sensory neurons.
   D. depends exclusively on motor neurons.

3. The _____ nervous system is part of the peripheral nervous system.
   A. somatic   B. sympathetic
   C. autonomic   D. all of the above

4. One function of the somatic nervous system is to
   A. carry information from the senses to the CNS and from the CNS to the skeletal muscles.
   B. carry information to the glands and organs.
   C. control the sympathetic and parasympathetic nervous systems.
   D. process information in the brain.

5. The sympathetic nervous system handles _____ responses, while the parasympathetic nervous system governs _____ responses.
   A. voluntary; involuntary   B. involuntary; voluntary
   C. arousal; relaxing   D. sensory; motor

6. Biofeedback has been used to help people
   A. control their temper.
   B. learn to speak after a stroke.
   C. learn to control involuntary autonomic responses such as blood pressure.
   D. treat depression.

7. The autonomic nervous system is involved with
   A. voluntary responses.
   B. the nerves connected to the senses and skeletal muscles.
   C. involuntary responses such as the regulation of blood vessels and glands.
   D. only sensory nerves.

8.   Neurons
      A.   are the basic units of the nervous system.
      B.   are held in place by glial cells.
      C.   transmit electrical messages throughout the nervous system.
      D.   are characterized by all of the above.

9.   The three main parts of the neuron are the
      A.   dendrites, cell body and axon.
      B.   axon, dendrites and synapse.
      C.   synapse, impulse and cleft.
      D.   myelin sheath, dendrites and synapse.

10.   The _____ receive messages from other neurons, while the _____ carry
      messages on to other neurons or to muscle or gland cells.
      A.   cell bodies; dendrites
      B.   dendrites; axons
      C.   axons; dendrites
      D.   myelin sheaths; cell bodies

11.   The cell body
      A.   determines whether the neuron should fire.
      B.   receives incoming impulses from other neurons.
      C.   speeds the conduction of the neural impulse.
      D.   connects with the synapse.

12.   What occurs at the synapse?
      A.   The electrical charge jumps from the synaptic end bulb across the synaptic cleft
            to the dendrites of the next neuron.
      B.   The axon terminals contact the dendrites of the next neuron and neurotransmitters
            are transferred.
      C.   Synaptic vesicles in the synaptic end bulb release neurotransmitters into the
            synaptic cleft, and they lock into receptor sites of receiving dendrites.
      D.   Scientists are studying the process because the exact mechanism is unknown.

13. How do neurotransmitters affect the post-synaptic neuron?
   A. They cause a change in the electrical potential, exciting the neuron and causing it to fire.
   B. They cause a change in the electrical potential, either exciting or inhibiting the next neuron.
   C. They cause a change in the electrical potential, inhibiting the neuron and stopping it from firing.
   D. They do not make contact with the next neuron; they stay in the synapse.

14. Mood, memory, well-being, Alzheimer's disease, depression, sleep, appetite, pain and temperature regulation are all influenced by
   A. dopamine.   B. neurotransmitters.
   C. endorphins.   D. all of the above.

15. _____ are neuromodulators that influence pain and pleasure.
   A. dopamine   B. serotonin
   C. insulin   D. endorphin

16. _____ are chemicals that are released directly into the bloodstream, which then carries them to organs and cells that may be far from their point of origin.
   A. Neurotransmitters   B. Endorphins
   C. Hormones   D. Neuromodulators

17. Androgen, estrogen and progesterone are three types of
   A. sex hormones.   B. neurotransmitters.
   C. neurons.   D. neuromodulators.

18. The _____ is a method for analyzing biochemical activity in the brain that uses injections containing a harmless radioactive element.
   A. MRI (magnetic resonance imaging)
   B. PET scan (positron-emission tomography)
   C. EEG (electroencephalogram)
   D. EP (evoked potentials)

19. The three major subdivisions of the brain are the
   A. cortex, cerebrum and corpus callosum.
   B. spinal cord, brain and peripheral nervous system.
   C. thalamus, hypothalamus and limbic system.
   D. hindbrain, midbrain and forebrain.

20. The four distinct lobes of the cortex are the
    A.   occipital, parietal, temporal and frontal lobes.
    B.   sensory, auditory, visual and motor lobes.
    C.   hind, mid, fore and association lobes.
    D.   front, back, side and top lobes.

21. The _____ has deep crevasses and wrinkles that enable it to contain billions of neurons without requiring people to have the heads of giants.
    A.   corpus callosum   B.   cerebral cortex
    C.   cerebellum   D.   hypothalamus

22. Which of the following summarizes the different hemispheric functions?
    A.   The left brain is more active in logic and the right brain is associated with visual-spatial abilities.
    B.   The left brain is more active in artistic and intuitive tasks, and the right brain is more involved in emotional and expressive abilities.
    C.   The left brain has visual-spatial abilities, while the right brain is more involved in artistic and creative activities.
    D.   The right brain is more dominant and the left brain is more subordinate.

23. Localization of function refers to the fact that
    A.   personality traits are reflected in different areas of the brain.
    B.   information is distributed across large areas of the brain.
    C.   different brain parts perform different jobs and store different sorts of information.
    D.   brain processes are like holography.

24. The issue of whether there are sex differences in the brain is controversial because
    A.   evidence of anatomical sex differences in humans is contradictory.
    B.   findings have flip-flopped as a result of the biases of the observers.
    C.   even if anatomical differences exist, we do not know what they mean.
    D.   all of the above reasons.

25. Which of the following best describes the affect of experience on brain development?
    A.   Different brain structures can grow with continued use.
    B.   Learning causes new neurons to develop.
    C.   Learning results in new synaptic connections.
    D.   New axons are continuously developing.

PRACTICE TEST 2

1. The _____ receives, processes, interprets and stores incoming information from the senses and sends out messages destined for the muscles, glands, and internal organs. The _____ handles its input and output.
   A. central nervous system; peripheral nervous system
   B. peripheral nervous system; autonomic nervous system
   C. sympathetic nervous system; parasympathetic nervous system
   D. peripheral nervous system; central nervous system

2. _____ nerves carry messages from the receptors in the sense organs to the spinal cord and brain, and _____ nerves carry orders from the central nervous system to the muscles, glands and organs.
   A. Voluntary; involuntary
   B. Motor; sensory
   C. Sensory; motor
   D. Autonomic; sympathetic

3. As you are driving along, you hear the sound of tires screeching and then see a car hit another car. The sounds and sights are carried to your brain via the
   A. autonomic nervous system.
   B. somatic nervous system.
   C. sympathetic nervous system.
   D. central nervous system.

4. Which of the following examples accurately describes the types of output associated with the somatic and autonomic nervous systems?
   A. The somatic nervous system is involved when you turn off a light.
   B. The autonomic nervous system is involved when your heart races after a scare.
   C. The somatic nervous system is involved when you write your name.
   D. all of the above

5. Dr. Miller is training you to control your blood pressure by monitoring it with a device that delivers a signal to you whenever it drops. This is called
   A. a PET scan.   B. biofeedback.
   C. phrenology.   D. an EEG.

6. Sympathetic is to _____ as parasympathetic is to _____.
   A.   arousal; relaxation   B.   autonomic; somatic
   C.   relaxation; arousal   D.   somatic; autonomic

7. The path of a neural impulse is
   A.   axon, cell body, neuron, dendrite.
   B.   dendrite, cell body, axon, axon terminals.
   C.   dendrite, axon, axon terminals, cell body.
   D.   neuron, cell body, dendrite, axon.

8. Neurons are like catchers and batters. The _____ are like catchers because they receive information; the _____ are like batters because they send on the message.
   A.   dendrites; axons   B.   cell bodies; axons
   C.   axons; dendrites   D.   dendrites; glials

9. When a neural impulse reaches the tip of the axon terminal,
   A.   the neuron fires.
   B.   synaptic vesicles in the synaptic end bulb release neurotransmitters that cross the synaptic cleft and lock into receptor sites on the post-synaptic neuron.
   C.   the synaptic end bulb sends an electrical current into the dendrites of the next neuron.
   D.   the synaptic end bulb locks into the receptor sites on the post-synaptic dendrites.

10. During Dr. Wisch's hospital rounds, he meets with patients who are suffering with Alzheimer's disease, Parkinson's disease and severe depression. To understand these disorders better, he looks to the role of
    A.   hormones.   B.   endorphins.
    C.   neurotransmitters.   D.   melatonin.

11. Serotonin, dopamine, acetylcholine and norepinephrine are
    A.   adrenal hormones.   B.   endorphins.
    C.   sex hormones.   D.   neurotransmitters.

12. During a dangerous situation, pain sensations are reduced. This reduction of pain is due to an increase in
    A.   testosterone levels.
    B.   endorphin levels.
    C.   androgen levels.
    D.   insulin levels.

13. What do insulin and melatonin have in common with androgen and estrogen?
    A. They are all neurotransmitters.
    B. They are all sex hormones.
    C. They are all adrenal hormones.
    D. They are all hormones.

14. For a recording of brain wave patterns, a(n) _____ device would be used. To find out what parts of the brain are normally active while listening to music, a(n) _____ device would be used.
    A. magnetic resonance imaging; electroencephalogram
    B. electroencephalogram; positron-emission tomography
    C. positron-emission tomography; needle electrode
    D. positron-emission tomography; magnetic resonance imaging

15. Hindbrain is to _____ as forebrain is to _____.
    A. way stations; vital functions
    B. vital functions; way stations
    C. emotions, memory and thought; vital functions
    D. vital functions; emotion, memory, and thought

16. The condition of being "brain dead" refers to the loss of the higher functions of the _____, but the person remains alive due to the functions of the _____.
    A. cortex; medulla   B. pons; medulla
    C. thalamus; cortex   D. hypothalamus; pons

17. Shondra is sitting at her desk trying to study psychology. The stereo is on too loud and is distracting her, so she decides to turn it down. While singing along with the music, she crosses the room, reaches out to the stereo and turns it off. Which brain structure is most directly involved when Shondra reaches out to turn off the stereo?
    A. amygdala   B. thalamus
    C. cerebellum   D. pons

18. In question 17, which brain structure is most directly involved when Shondra listens to the music?
    A. cerebellum   B. limbic system
    C. hippocampus   D. auditory cortex

19. In question 17, which brain structure is most directly involved when Shondra remembers information contained in the psychology text?
    A. hypothalamus   B. hippocampus
    C. thalamus   D. parietal lobe

101

20. In question 17, which brain structure is involved when Shondra sings?
   A. Broca's area
   B. left brain
   C. frontal lobe
   D. all of the above

21. Reed just missed being in a bad car accident. Immediately following the incident, his heart was racing, his palms were sweaty and he felt terrified. Which of the following was involved in these responses?
   A. autonomic nervous system
   B. limbic system
   C. pituitary gland
   D. all of the above

22. If Lucy is like most people, her _____ is most involved when she calculates a math problem and her _____ is most active when she reads a map.
   A. right brain; left brain
   B. left brain; right brain
   C. corpus callosum; cerebellum
   D. amygdala; thalamus

23. Distributed is to specialized as _____ is to _____.
   A. holistic; localized
   B. right brain; left brain
   C. creative; intuitive
   D. none of the above

24. Some of the controversy surrounding the idea of sex differences in the brain centers around
   A. the reasons that male brains are more localized.
   B. whether anatomical differences exist and if they do, what they mean.
   C. the reluctance to publicize the unpopular finding that female brains have greater capacity.
   D. all of the above.

25. Throughout life, new learning results in the establishment of new synaptic connections in the brain, with stimulating environments producing the greatest changes. Conversely, some unused synaptic connections are lost as cells or their branches die and are not replaced. This indicates that the brain
   A. is more lateralized than scientists once thought.
   B. continues to develop and change in response to the environment.
   C. develops new brain cells on a regular and ongoing basis.
   D. is more holistic than scientists once thought.

PRACTICE TEST 3

1. You are sitting at your desk trying to study for a test you are very nervous about, and a you can focus on is the stereo playing in the other room. You get up, go to the other room and turn down the stereo. Beginning with the external stimuli (the sound) and ending with your movement to the other room, describe what happens in terms of:

   A.   from the standpoint of a single neuron
   B.   the brain structures that are involved, in sequence
   C.   the nervous system involvement

2. For each description indicate the brain structure most likely to be involved and state whether it is found in the hindbrain, midbrain or forebrain.

   A.   Dr. Smith inserts an electrode into a structure within the brain. As this electrode is activated, the person sweats and shivers, feels hungry and thirsty, and sometimes even seems angry and sexually aroused.
   B.   A computer-enhanced image has enabled a research team to observe the flow of information within the nervous system. While watching this flow, the researchers notice that incoming sensory messages are relayed through this center before finally reaching their destination in the cerebral hemispheres.
   C.   As a result of a serious automobile accident, Fred's ability to make plans and show initiative were seriously impaired.
   D.   Bjorn's great grandmother has had a serious stroke. As a result, she is unable to speak, though she appears to understand and respond non-verbally to what is being said.
   E.   Tiffany's elderly neighbor is showing signs of memory loss.
   F.   Mary has been unable to continue as a gymnast since the lower rear area of her brain was damaged in a car accident. All tasks requiring balance or coordinated movements are beyond Mary's capacities.

3. As a result of mixing tranquilizers and alcohol, Helen has become what is called "brain dead," and though she does not respond to people, she continues to live without any life-sustaining equipment. Describe which parts of her brain have been damaged and which parts continue to function?

descriptions that follow, cortical functions are disrupted in various ways. From the ptions identify the cortical structures and state their functions.

Removing a tumor from an area just behind her forehead has dramatically altered Denise's personality. Previously outgoing and warm, she is now hostile and needs prodding to get anything done.

Lately Ralph has been experiencing tingling sensations in various body parts and he sometimes "forgets" where his hands and fingers are. Tests reveal a growth near the surface of the brain just under the center of his head.

C.   Hazan has a large blind spot in his visual field and doctors have eliminated the possibility of eye and optic nerve problems.

5.   In the examples below, identify whether the phenomena are primarily related to the functioning of the right hemisphere, the left hemisphere, or both.

A.   Ken is being tested for school placement. Part of the test involves putting puzzle pieces together so they form geometric shapes. Ken performs well.

B.   Another portion of the test involves reading simple sentences aloud. Ken garbles the words and says them in an improper sequence.

C.   A third portion of the test requires Ken to respond to sets of photographs, each set containing five pictures of a person posed identically except for facial expression.

D.   The last portion of the test assesses manual dexterity in the nondominant arm and hand. Because Ken is left-handed, he is required to perform all sorts of mechanical tasks with his right hand. He fails this part of the test.

E.   What overall conclusion might be reached about Ken's hemispheric functioning?

CHAPTER 5

Body Rhythms and Mental States

LEARNING OBJECTIVES

1. Define consciousness and the biological rhythms often associated with states of consciousness.

2. Describe circadian rhythms, including how they are studied and how they may be desynchronized.

3. Discuss examples of ultradian and infradian rhythms and distinguish endogenous rhythms from those caused by external factors.

4. Summarize the evidence on whether emotional symptoms associated with "PMS" are tied to the menstrual cycle.

5. Summarize theories about the biological functions of sleep.

6. Distinguish between rapid eye movement (REM) and non-REM periods in sleep and describe the four stages of non-REM sleep.

7. Summarize the principles of the psychoanalytic, problem-solving, information-processing and activation-synthesis theories of dreaming.

8. List the types of psychoactive drugs that can alter states of consciousness and describe their physical and behavioral effects.

9. List and explain the factors that influence the effects of psychoactive drugs.

10. Define hypnosis and describe it as an altered state and as a form of role playing.

11. Describe some problems with "hypnotically-refreshed" memories.

CHAPTER CONCEPT MAP

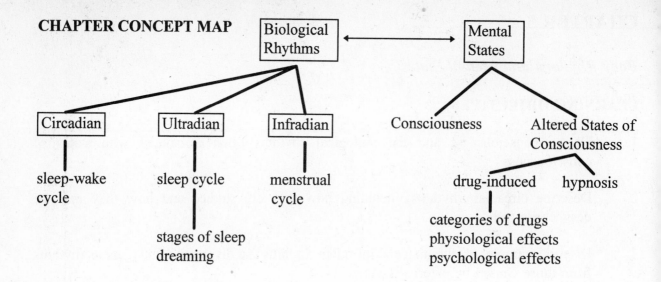

BRIEF CHAPTER SUMMARY

Chapter 5 examines biological rhythms and states of consciousness. There are three types of endogenous rhythms: circadian (occur once a day), ultradian (occur more than once a day) and infradian (occur less than once a day). During the sleep cycle, four stages of non-rapid eye movement (NREM) sleep alternate with rapid eye movement sleep (REM), on average, every 90 minutes during the night. Dreaming is more likely to occur during REM sleep. Though the purpose of dreams is not really known, psychologists have proposed several explanations. While endogenous biological rhythms can influence our states of consciousness, drugs also can alter consciousness. Different categories of drugs are described, along with their physiological and psychological effects. Hypnosis is considered by some to be an altered state of consciousness. An alternative view of hypnosis is that it is a social cognitive process.

PREVIEW OUTLINE AND REVIEW QUESTIONS

Before you read the chapter, review the preview outline and the Learning Objectives for each section of the text. Develop additional questions of your own based on key concepts and terms and write them in the designated spaces. Answer all questions as you read the text.

SECTION 1 - BIOLOGICAL RHYTHMS: THE TIDES OF EXPERIENCE (PP. 157-171)

I.   **Biological rhythms: The tides of experience**
    A.   **Definitions**
        1.   _____ - awareness of oneself and the environment
        2.   Biological rhythms - the ebb and flow associated with bodily events
        3.   Endogenous rhythms - rhythms generated from within
            a.   _____ rhythms - occur every 24 hours
            b.   Infradian rhythms - occur less often than once a day
            c.   Ultradian rhythms - occur more often than once a day
    B.   **Circadian rhythms**
        1.   Exist in plants, animals, insects, and humans
        2.   Can be studied by isolating subjects from environmental time cues
        3.   Several "clocks" in the brain synchronized by overall coordinator or "super clock," in the suprachiasmatic nucleus in the hypothalamus
            a.   Synchrony influenced by neurotransmitters and hormones
            b.   _____ in the pineal gland responds to light and dark
        4.   Change in routine may cause internal _____
        5.   Cycles are affected by environmental factors; differ individually
    C.   **The menstrual cycle and other long-term rhythms** - infradian cycles
        1.   Menstruation
            a.   First half of the cycle, estrogen increases; midcycle, ovaries release egg, then progesterone increases; if conception does not occur, estrogen and progesterone decline
            b.   _____ syndrome introduced in 1970s
                (1)   No consistent support for any theory of PMS
                (2)   Physical and emotional symptoms not distinguished
                (3)   Considerable research evidence refutes the presence of emotional symptoms
        2.   Menopause
            a.   A discrepancy exists between beliefs about menopause and reality
            b.   Negativity related to attitude towards female reproductive processes
        3.   Male cycles - evidence on influence of testosterone is contradictory
        4.   Conclusion - few of either sex undergo personality shifts because of _____

D. **The rhythms of sleep** - ultradian rhythms which occur more than once a day
    1.   Theories about why we sleep
          a.   Sleep is recuperative
          b.   The brain requires sleep
    2.   The realms of sleep - sleep is not an unbroken state of rest
          a.   Ultradian cycle occurs, on average, every 90 minutes
               (1)   Rapid eye movement (REM) periods are characterized by
                    (a)   Active brain waves resembling wakefulness
                    (b)   Limp muscles
                    (c)   Dreams
               (2)   4 Non-REM stages, each deeper than the previous
                    (a)   1 - small, irregular brain waves; light sleep
                    (b)   2 - high-peaking waves called sleep spindles
                    (c)   3 - _____ waves begin
                    (d)   4 - mostly delta waves and deep sleep
               (3)   After stage 4 the cycle reverses and REM sleeps recurs following stage 1
               (4)   REM and non-REM sleep _____ throughout the night
               (5)   The purpose of REM sleep is unclear

Answer these Learning Objectives while you read Section 1.

1.   Define consciousness and the biological rhythms associated with states of consciousness.

2.   Describe circadian rhythms; how they are studied and how they may be desynchronized.

3.   Discuss examples of ultradian and infradian rhythms and distinguish endogenous rhythms from those caused by external factors.

4.   Summarize the evidence on emotional symptoms associated of "PMS".

5.   Summarize theories about the biological functions of sleep.

6.   Distinguish between rapid eye movement (REM) and non-REM periods in sleep and describe the four stages of non-REM sleep.

Write the questions that you have formulated below and answer them while you read.

A.   _____

B.   _____

II.   EXPLORING THE DREAM WORLD
   A.   **Characteristics of dreams**
      1.   REM dreams are more _____ than non-REM dreams
      2.   _____ dreams - dreams in which people know they are dreaming
         a.   Dissociation occurs - dreaming and observing part of consciousness
         b.   Some have learned to produce lucid dreams and control them
   B.   **Theories of dreams**
      1.   Dreams as _____ wishes
         a.   Freud - "royal road to the unconscious;" all dreams meaningful
            (1)   Manifest content - what we experienced and remember
            (2)   _____ content - hidden, symbolic; the unconscious wishes
         b.   Many people disagree with Freud's interpretations
      2.   Dreams as problem solving
         a.   Reflect ongoing _____ of waking life
         b.   Convey true meaning not symbols
      3.   Dreams as information processing
         a.   Act as snippets of sorting, scanning and sifting process
         b.   REM periods help people assimilate and integrate new information and experiences, according to some researchers
         c.   Associated with consolidation of memories
      4.   Dreams as interpreted brain activity
         a.   Activation-_____ theory
            (1)   Dreams are the result of neurons firing spontaneously in the lower brain
            (2)   Dreams are not meaningful, but the _____ tries to make sense of them
         b.   Critics say dreams are a modification of waking state
   C.   **Conclusion - no single theory explains all facets of dreaming**

Answer this Learning Objectives while you read Section 2.

7.   Summarize the principles of the psychoanalytic, problem-solving, information-processing and activation-synthesis theories of dreaming.

Write the questions that you have formulated below and answer them while you read.

A.   _____

B.   _____

III. **CONSCIOUSNESS-ALTERING DRUGS**
   A. **Classifying drugs**
      1. Definition - _____ drug - substance affecting perception, mood, thinking, memory or behavior by changing the body's biochemistry
      2. Classified according to effects on central nervous system
         a. Stimulants - speed up activity in central nervous system; includes cocaine, amphetamines, nicotine, caffeine
         b. Depressants - slow down activity in central nervous system; include alcohol, tranquilizers, barbiturates
         c. Opiates - mimic endorphins; include opium, morphine, heroine, methadone
         d. Psychedelics - alter _____; include LSD, mescaline, psilocybin
         e. Anabolic steroids and Marijuana - don't fit other classifications
   B. **The physiology of drug effects**
      1. Can increase, decrease, prevent reabsorption, block _____
      2. Can produce cognitive or emotional effects
      3. Repeated use of certain drugs can cause permanent brain damage
      4. Some lead to _____ (needing more over time) and withdrawal (symptoms upon removal of the drug)
   C. **The psychology of drug effects**
      1. Depend on a person's physical condition, experience with the drug, environmental setting, and _____ _____
      2. Alcohol can provide an excuse for violent or other behavior
      3. How we _____ the effects of drugs is important and is learned
      4. Distinction between drug abuse and use
   D. **Distinction between legal and illegal drugs is arbitrary**

Answer these Learning Objectives while you read Section 3.

8. List the types of psychoactive drugs and describe their physical and behavioral effects.

9. List and explain the factors that influence the effects of psychoactive drugs.

Write the questions that you have formulated below and answer them while you read.

A. _____

B. _____

SECTION 4 - THE RIDDLE OF HYPNOSIS (PP. 186-193)

IV. **THE RIDDLE OF HYPNOSIS**
   A. **Definition** - heightened state of _____ or responsiveness
   B. **Characteristics**
       1. Not a sleeping state; person is fully aware and remembers the experience
       2. Cannot force people to do something they don't want to do
       3. Most people can respond
       4. Can be _____ to do unacceptable things, as is the case with drug-induced states
       5. Has application in medicine and psychology
   C. **Hypnosis as an altered state**
       1. Traditionally considered an _____ state because it involves dissociation; one part of mind operates independently from another as a hidden observer
       2. Controversial - no way to verify
           a. Powers often overblown or poorly supported
           b. Appearance of being hypnotized could be _____
           c. There is evidence that suggestion alone produces same results
   D. **Hypnosis as a social-cognitive process**
       1. Playing the _____ of a hypnotized person without faking
       2. This role, like others, is so engrossing, it's done without intent
       3. Some tests can penetrate the role
       4. Hypnotized people use active _____ strategies to stay in role
           a. They try their best to meet the demands
           b. They use imagination and fantasy to comply
       5. Studies on hypnotic age regression support the role-playing theory
           a. Confusion of fact and speculation
           b. Boosts amount of information remembered, but can be inaccurate
   E. **Conclusion** - it is doubtful that it is an altered state

Answer these Learning Objectives while you read Section 4.

10. Define hypnosis and describe it as an altered state and as a form of role playing.

11. Describe some problems with "hypnotically-refreshed" memories.

Write the questions that you have formulated below and answer them while you read.

A. _____

B. _____

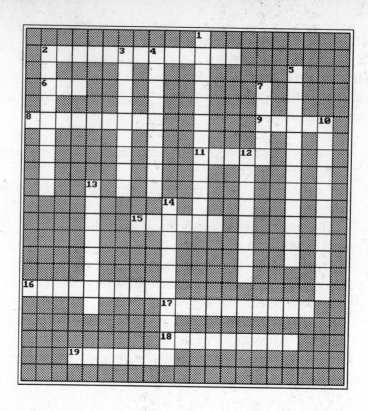

ACROSS

2. awareness of the environment and of one's own existence
6. sleep periods characterized by eye movement
8. most widely used illicit drug in the U.S.
9. dream in which the dreamer is aware of dreaming
11. large, slow brain waves, characteristic of relaxed wakefulness
15. dream content that expresses unconscious wishes symbolically
16. symptoms that occur when someone addicted to a drug stops taking it
17. activity in the lower part of the brain that causes dreams
18. increased resistance to a drug's effects with continued use
19. drugs that relieve pain and produce euphoria

DOWN

1. ebbing and flowing of hormones in females over roughly a 28-day period
2. biological rhythm of about 24 hours
3. biological rhythm exemplified by birds flying south
4. biological rhythm exemplified by the sleep cycle
5. drugs capable of influencing mood, perception, cognition, behavior
7. wave characteristic of stage 3 and stage 4 sleep
10. slows down activity in the central nervous system
12. a condition in which a person is focused and extremely responsive to suggestion
13. synthetic derivatives of testosterone
14. speeds up central nervous system activity

FLASH CARDS

Cut the following chart along the borders and test yourself with the resulting flash cards.

5.1 CONSCIOUSNESS	5.8 FREE-RUNNING	5.15 REM SLEEP
5.2 STATES OF CONSCIOUSNESS	5.9 MELATONIN	5.16 NON-REM SLEEP
5.3 BIOLOGICAL RHYTHM	5.10 INTERNAL DESYNCHRONIZATION	5.17 ALPHA WAVES
5.4 ENDOGENOUS	5.11 MENSTRUAL CYCLE	5.18 DELTA WAVES
5.5 CIRCADIAN RHYTHM	5.12 "PREMENSTRUAL SYNDROME"	5.19 LUCID DREAMS
5.6 INFRADIAN RHYTHM	5.13 MENOPAUSE	5.20 DISSOCIATION
5.7 ULTRADIAN RHYTHM	5.14 SEASONAL AFFECTIVE DISORDER	5.21 PSYCHOANALYTIC THEORY OF DREAMS

5.15 Sleep periods characterized by eye movement, loss of muscle tone and dreaming.	5.8 In a typical study of circadian rhythms, subjects sleep, eat and work whenever they wish. Self-imposed schedule.	5.1 The awareness of the environment and of one's own existence, sensations and thoughts.
5.16 Periods of fewer eye movements that alternate with REM sleep in an ultradian cycle; there are 4 stages of non-REM sleep.	5.9 A hormone secreted by the pineal gland; it is involved in the regulation of circadian rhythms.	5.2 Distinctive and discrete patterns in the functioning of consciousness, characterized by particular modes of perception, thought, memory or feeling.
5.17 Relatively large, slow brain waves characteristic of relaxed wakefulness.	5.10 When a person's normal routine changes, circadian rhythms may be thrown out of phase with one another.	5.3 A periodic, more or less regular fluctuation in a biological system; may or may not have psychological implications.
5.18 Slow, regular brain waves characteristic of stage 3 and stage 4 sleep.	5.11 The ebbing and flowing of hormones in females over roughly a 28-day period; related to reproduction.	5.4 Generated from within rather than as a result of external events.
5.19 A dream in which the dreamer is aware of dreaming.	5.12 A cluster of symptoms associated with the days preceding menstruation that has come to be thought of as an "illness" and given this label.	5.5 A biological rhythm with a period (from peak to peak or trough to trough) of about 24 hours.
5.20 Separation of consciousness into distinct parts.	5.13 The midlife cessation of menstruation, which is brought on when the ovaries stop producing estrogen and progesterone.	5.6 A biological rhythm that occurs less frequently than once a day.
5.21 Freudian approach that dreams are the "royal road to the unconscious." All dreams have meaning related to our wishes and desires.	5.14 Depression that occurs in winter, when periods of daylight are short, and improves every spring, as daylight increases.	5.7 A biological rhythm that occurs more frequently than once a day.

5.22 MANIFEST CONTENT OF DREAMS	5.29 STIMULANTS	5.36 TOLERANCE
5.23 LATENT CONTENT OF DREAMS	5.30 DEPRESSANTS	5.37 WITHDRAWAL SYMPTOMS
5.24 PROBLEM-SOLVING APPROACH TO DREAMS	5.31 SEDATIVES	5.38 HYPNOSIS
5.25 INFORMATION-PROCESSING APPROACH TO DREAMS	5.32 OPIATES	5.39 HIDDEN OBSERVER
5.26 ACTIVATION-SYNTHESIS THEORY OF DREAMS	5.33 PSYCHEDELICS	5.40 SOCIAL-COGNITIVE STRATEGIES
5.27 ALTERED STATES OF CONSCIOUSNESS	5.34 ANABOLIC STEROIDS	5.41 DELAYED AUDITORY FEEDBACK
5.28 PSYCHOACTIVE DRUGS	5.35 MARIJUANA	5.42 REFRESHED MEMORIES

5.36 Increasing resistance to a drug's effects with continued use; larger doses are required to produce effects once made by smaller ones.	**5.29** Drugs that speed up activity in the central nervous system.	**5.22** Part of the psychoanalytic theory of dreams; the aspects of the dreams that we consciously experience and may remember upon wakening.
5.37 Physical and psychological symptoms that occur when someone addicted to a drug stops taking it.	**5.30** Drugs that slow down activity in the central nervous system.	**5.23** Part of the psychoanalytic theory of dreams; the unconscious wishes and thoughts being expressed symbolically in our dreams.
5.38 A condition in which attention is focused and a person is extremely responsive to suggestion.	**5.31** Another term for depressants, because they usually make a person feel calm or drowsy, and may reduce anxiety and tension.	**5.24** Theory that dreams reflect the ongoing emotional preoccupations of waking life.
5.39 The altered state theory of hypnosis states that dissociation occurs; one part of the person goes along with the suggestions while the other is an observer.	**5.32** Drugs derived from the opium poppy that relieve pain and commonly produce euphoria.	**5.25** The theory that dreaming is an opportunity for mental housekeeping; dreams are snippets from a process of sorting, scanning and sifting.
5.40 Theory that states that the hypnotized person is playing the part of a hypnotized person; analogous to other roles we play in life.	**5.33** Consciousness-altering drugs that produce hallucinations, change thought processes or disrupt the normal perception of time and space.	**5.26** The theory that dreaming results from the cortical synthesis and interpretation of neural signals from activity in the lower part of the brain.
5.41 A research technique in which words are played through earphones with a half-second delay to subjects while they read the same words.	**5.34** Synthetic derivatives of testosterone. Unclear whether they are psychoactive.	**5.27** A deliberately produced state of consciousness that differs from ordinary wakefulness or sleep.
5.42 Memories that are "refreshed" by hypnosis; great likelihood that they are pseudomemories.	**5.35** Most widely used illicit drug in the U.S. The active ingredient is tetrahydrocannabinol (THC).	**5.28** A drug capable of influencing perception, mood, cognition or behavior.

PRACTICE TEST 1

1.   Being aware of one's own existence is
     A.   a psychological problem.   B.   a philosophical dilemma.
     C.   the definition of consciousness.   D.   an altered state.

2.   Geraldo goes to sleep by 11:00 p.m. and awakens at 7:00 a.m. This cycle is a(n)
     A.   infradian rhythm.   B.   circadian rhythm.
     C.   nocturnal rhythm.   D.   ultradian rhythm.

3.   The seasonal migration of birds is an example of
     A.   a circadian rhythm.   B.   an infradian rhythm.
     C.   an ultradian rhythm.   D.   a diurnal rhythm.

4.   Rhythms that continue in the absence of all external time cues are called
     A.   endogenous rhythms.   B.   exogenous rhythms.
     C.   indigenous rhythms.   D.   none of the above.

5.   Periods of dreaming and nondreaming occur during the night in
     A.   a circadian rhythm.   B.   an infradian rhythm.
     C.   an ultradian rhythm.   D.   a diurnal rhythm.

6.   Which of the following can desynchronize circadian rhythms?
     A.   an overseas trip   B.   switching shifts at work
     C.   going on daylight savings time   D.   all of the above

7.   Premenstrual syndrome
     A.   has been experienced by a majority of women according to scientific studies.
     B.   has been questioned, particularly its association with emotional symptoms.
     C.   has been widely documented and confirmed in scientific studies.
     D.   is a diagnosable psychological disorder.

8.   The relationship between menstruation and intellectual performance is
     A.   absent.
     B.   that women perform intellectual tasks best at the start of the cycle.
     C.   that women perform intellectual tasks best at the middle of the cycle.
     D.   that women perform intellectual tasks best near the end of the cycle.

9. Sleep is necessary
   A. because of its recuperative properties.
   B. because the brain requires sleep.
   C. to repair cells and remove waste products from the muscles.
   D. for all of the above reasons.

10. The brain waves that occur when you first go to bed and relax are called
    A. alpha waves.   B. delta waves.
    C. beta waves.   D. gamma waves.

11. REM sleep is called paradoxical sleep because
    A. dreams are often paradoxical and they occur most often in REM sleep.
    B. the brain is extremely active but the body is devoid of muscle tone.
    C. people are easily awakened, even though it is a deep sleep.
    D. the brain is very calm and inactive, but the body is quite active.

12. After the first 30 to 45 minutes of sleep, you have progressed from stage 1 sleep to stage 4 sleep. After this, you
    A. go into a prolonged non-REM period.
    B. enter REM sleep.
    C. progress back up the ladder from stage 4 to stage 3 to stage 2 to stage 1.
    D. go back to stage 1 and continue through the four stages all night.

13. The most vivid dreams occur during
    A. the menstrual cycle.   B. REM sleep.
    C. stage 1 sleep.   D. non-REM sleep.

14. Which hypothesis suggests that dreams result from cortical attempts to interpret spontaneous neural activity?
    A. information-processing   B. psychoanalytic
    C. activation-synthesis   D. problem-solving

15. According to the _____ hypothesis, dreams express our unconscious desires.
    A. information-processing hypothesis   B. psychoanalytic hypothesis
    C. activation-synthesis hypothesis   D. problem-solving hypothesis

16. When Ruth dreams, she is in the dream, but also observing the dream and controlling what happens in it. Ruth is experiencing
    A. nightmares.   B. manifest dreams.
    C. lucid dreams.   D. REM dreams.

17. Which of the following are psychoactive drugs?
    A. tobacco
    B. opium
    C. caffeine
    D. all of the above

18. Psychoactive drugs work primarily by affecting
    A. brain structures.
    B. bodily rhythms.
    C. neurotransmitters.
    D. blood flow to the brain.

19. Alcohol, tranquilizers and sedatives are examples of
    A. opiates.
    B. depressants.
    C. psychedelics.
    D. stimulants.

20. When Micky began using drugs, he used only a small amount. After six months, he required more and more to achieve the same effect. Micky experienced
    A. withdrawal.
    B. brain damage.
    C. tolerance.
    D. mental set.

21. Hank and Bill both used the same amount of cocaine, but they each had different reactions. Which of the following differences between them might account for this?
    A. physical condition
    B. expectations for the drug
    C. prior experience with cocaine
    D. all of the above

22. Research on "hypnotically refreshed" memories suggests that
    A. "age regression" allows one to remember childhood experiences accurately.
    B. under hypnosis, people can recall events from earlier lives.
    C. these memories are often vivid but inaccurate.
    D. memory errors decrease under hypnosis.

23. Those who say hypnosis is a(n) _____ believe that hypnosis involves role-playing.
    A. altered state
    B. deliberate deception
    C. social-cognitive process
    D. none of the above

24. Those who believe that hypnosis is an altered state argue that
    A. altered states involve dissociation, which occurs during hypnosis.
    B. the powers of hypnosis are overblown.
    C. suggestion alone can produce the same results.
    D. all of the above are true.

25. Hypnosis is defined as
    A. an act.
    B. an altered state.
    C. a heightened state of suggestibility.
    D. a cognitive process.

PRACTICE TEST 2

1.   Jim likes to get drunk and smoke marijuana because this enables him to see himself and the world differently. This motive is consistent with which of the following statements about consciousness?
    A.   Consciousness is awareness of one's bodily changes or rhythms.
    B.   Consciousness is awareness of oneself and the environment.
    C.   Consciousness is directly related to changes in brain wave patterns.
    D.   Consciousness is a philosophical issue that cannot be defined.

2.   What is the relationship between consciousness and bodily rhythms?
    A.   Consciousness can vary with bodily rhythms.
    B.   Changes in consciousness direct changes in bodily rhythms.
    C.   Bodily rhythms can change but consciousness does not.
    D.   Consciousness and bodily rhythms are unrelated.

3.   As part of a research study, Bob is living in a comfortable room with a V.C.R. and stereo, but there are no windows, clocks or sounds coming in from outside. He is told to eat, sleep and work whenever he feels like doing so. This type of study is used to
    A.   examine sensory deprivation.
    B.   examine the affect of daylight on depression.
    C.   explore endogenous circadian rhythms.
    D.   attempt to modify infradian rhythms.

4.   Ursula's job requires that she change shifts often. She is likely to experience
    A.   internal desynchronization.
    B.   internal synchronization.
    C.   a need for less sleep.
    D.   external desynchronization.

5.   Which of the following is an example of an infradian rhythm?
    A.   hibernation of bears   B.   stages of sleep
    C.   sleep-wake cycle   D.   all of the above

6.   Which of the following is an example of an ultradian rhythm?
    A.   stomach contractions   B.   hormone level fluctuations
    C.   appetite for food   D.   all of the above

7. Menstrual cycle research on hormones and mood shifts suggests that
    A.   for most people, hormones are reliably and strongly correlated with mood.
    B.   hormonal shifts cause mood shifts.
    C.   mood changes cause hormonal shifts.
    D.   no causal relationship has been established between hormonal shifts and moods.

8. Which of the following conclusions reflects the findings on premenstrual symptoms?
    A.   The idea of mood swings as a prementrual symptom has been questioned since men and women don't differ in the number of mood swings they experience in a month.
    B.   For most women, the relationship between cycle stage and symptoms is weak.
    C.   There is no reliable relationship between cycle stage and work efficiency.
    D.   All of the above have been found.

9. Theories about the biological functions of sleep include to facilitate
    A.   bodily restoration and brain function.
    B.   psychic healing.
    C.   providing a time for dreaming.
    D.   all of the above.

10. One reason why people are likely to be dreaming when the alarm goes off is because as the night progresses, REM periods _____
    A.   get longer.   B.   get shorter.
    C.   become more intense.   D.   occur at more regular intervals.

11. Joe is a subject in a sleep study. When his brain emits occasional short bursts of rapid, high-peaking waves, he is in which stage of sleep?
    A.   stage 1   B.   stage 3
    C.   stage 2   D.   stage 4

12. In what type of sleep is Joe's body totally limp, but his brain wave pattern is active?
    A.   paradoxical sleep   B.   dream sleep
    C.   REM sleep   D.   all of the above

13. Pat had an upsetting disagreement with her father before going to sleep and she dreamt about her brother. The theory of dreams as _____ suggests the latent content is about her father.
    A.   problem solving theory   B.   unconscious wishes
    C.   information processing   D.   activation-synthesis

14. Which theory suggests that neurons in Pat's brain stem are spontaneously firing and her cortex is simply trying to make sense of the neuronal activity?
    A. dreams as problem solving theory   B. dreams as unconscious wishes
    C. dreams as information processing   D. activation-synthesis theory

15. Which theory suggests that Pat's dream reflects her desire to talk to her brother?
    A. dreams as problem solving theory   B. dreams as unconscious wishes
    C. dreams as information processing   D. activation-synthesis theory

16. Drug classifications are based on
    A. the legality of a drug.
    B. whether a drug is addictive.
    C. the effects of a drug on the central nervous system.
    D. all of the above.

17. Though cocaine is a(n) _____, heroine is a(n) _____, and marijuana is a(n) _____, they can all produce euphoria.
    A. stimulant; psychedelic; depressant
    B. amphetamine; opiate; psychedelic
    C. psychedelic; stimulant; unclear category
    D. stimulant; opiate; unclear category

18. Bruno smokes four packs of cigarettes and drinks nine cups of coffee a day. He
    A. is using drugs.   B. is relying on stimulants.
    C. may feel excited and confident.   D. all of the above

19. Drugs can affect neurotransmitters by
    A. increasing or decreasing them at the synapse.
    B. eliminating them altogether.
    C. mutating their chemical formula.
    D. all of the above.

20. Half of all men arrested for assaulting their wives claim to have been drinking at the time of the assault, yet most of these men did not have enough alcohol in their bloodstreams to qualify as legally intoxicated. Of the factors that influence drug effects, which does this represent?
    A. physical condition   B. environmental setting
    C. mental set   D. experience with the drug

21. Rick and Dick had the same amount to drink, yet Rick cannot walk a straight line and Dick seems fine. Which of the following might explain this difference?
    A. Rick was very upset about an argument he'd had with Nick before the party.
    B. Dick drank while watching T.V. at home with a friend, while Rick was at a party.
    C. Dick grew up drinking with meals and does not think about alcohol use as a way to get drunk, while Rick sees it as a way to blow off steam.
    D. all of the above

22. Hypnosis and drugs can be used in a similar fashion to
    A. justify letting go of inhibitions.
    B. dissociate.
    C. hallucinate.
    D. alter neurotransmitter levels.

23. Susan, who is normally very modest, is removing her clothes under hypnosis. How might this be explained, according the theory that hypnosis is a social-cognitive process?
    A. She is in an altered state.
    B. She has dissociated.
    C. She is playing the role of a hypnotized person.
    D. She has relinquished control to the hypnotist.

24. Which of the following evidence argues against the credibility of age regression?
    A. Subjects who were age regressed as part of a study could not accurately recall their favorite comforting object from age three.
    B. Subjects in a study did not know basic facts about the time period in which they were supposed to have lived in a previous life.
    C. When people are regressed to an earlier age, brain wave patterns do not resemble those of children.
    D. all of the above

25. "Hypnotically refreshed" memories
    A. are generally quite accurate.
    B. should always be believed.
    C. often contain many errors.
    D. are always inaccurate.

PRACTICE TEST 3

1.   Identify which type of rhythm each example represents and explain why.
     A.   hunger
     B.   mating behavior in dogs and cats
     C.   fatigue
     D.   sexual behavior in human beings
     E.   concentration
     F.   full moons

2.   Dr. Irving is conducting a survey on premenstrual syndrome (PMS). Of the 100 subjects who responded to the survey, 70% indicated that they experience PMS on a regular basis. Compare these findings to the research in the text that argues against PMS and answer the following questions:
     A.   How was PMS defined? What symptoms were included and why is this important?
     B.   What are some of the problems with the self-reporting of PMS symptoms?
     C.   Describe possible influences of expectations and attitudes toward menstruation on the results of the survey.
     D.   Describe the results of research findings from studies that did not reveal their true purpose.

3.   For the ninth grade science project, Megan kept a detailed diary of her sleep experiences during a one-month interval. The information obtained and her conclusions are submitted below. Using actual evidence related to sleep, comment on each of these claims.

     A.   During the period of the study, I awakened myself once during each night at different times. Each time I woke myself up, I felt the same as when I wake up in the morning. This indicates that sleep actually is the same kind of thing all through the night.
     B.   I was allowed to stay up all night twice. It was really hard to keep my eyes open at around 4:00 a.m., but by 6:00 a.m. I felt wide awake. This suggests that the loss of sleep is invigorating.
     C.   After missing sleep two nights in a row, I felt like going to bed extra early the next day. This indicates that we need to catch up on our rest.
     D.   Even though I felt O.K. after missing sleep for two nights, I got a "D" on an exam at school. This suggests that maybe sleep loss has more effects than I thought!
     E.   During the time of the study, I had two dreams and my sister had five. This indicates that we only dream several times a month.

4.   Gretchen had a dream that she and her husband had gone horse back riding. He was far ahead of her and, though she was riding as fast as she could, she was unable to catch up. Eventually she lost her way and was unsure where she was going. She dismounted her horse and found that she was in a beautiful valley, and she stopped there and felt very peaceful. Identify which theory would give each of the following interpretations of this dream.

A.   This dream has little significance or meaning. It represents the attempt of the cortex to make sense of random neuronal firing in the brainstem.

B.   This dream has little significance. It represents the brain's mental housekeeping. It is sorting, scanning and sifting new information into "wanted" and "unwanted" categories.

C.   The dream has great significance. It is likely to be a dream about Gretchen's unresolved relationship with her father. She has always felt abandoned by him and could never win his attention or affection, which she has always deeply desired.

D.   The dream has to do with Gretchen's concern that she cannot keep up with her husband's pace. He always has more energy than she does and although she tries, what she would most like to do is "get off the merry-go-round," relax, and take life easier.

5.   For each type of drug listed below, indicate the following: 1) the type of drug, 2) the common effects of the drug, and 3) the result of abusing the drug.

A.   alcohol
B.   tranquilizers
C.   morphine
D.   amphetamines
E.   cocaine
F.   LSD
G.   marijuana

CHAPTER 6

Sensation and Perception

LEARNING OBJECTIVES

1. Distinguish between sensation and perception.

2. Distinguish between anatomical and functional codes in the nervous system.

3. Define psychophysics, absolute and difference thresholds and signal detection theory.

4. Explain sensory adaptation, sensory deprivation, sensory overload and selective attention.

5. List the characteristics of light waves and their correspondence to the visual experience.

6. Identify the parts of the eye and describe how they convert light to vision.

7. Discuss two theories of color vision and how they relate to stages of processing.

8. Explain how form, distance and depth perception occur.

9. List and explain visual constancies and distinguish them from visual illusions.

10. List the characteristics of sound waves and their correspondence to loudness, pitch and timbre.

11. Identify the parts of the ear and describe how they convert sound to hearing.

12. List and explain the factors that affect gustation (taste) and olfaction (smell).

13. List the four skin senses.

14. Describe the gate-control theory of pain and recent research in the physiology of pain.

15. Describe the internal senses of kinesthesis and equilibrium.

16. Summarize the evidence for innate abilities in perception and describe the psychological and cultural influences on perception.

17. Discuss the evidence on the effectiveness of "subliminal perception" tapes and ESP.

CHAPTER CONCEPT MAP

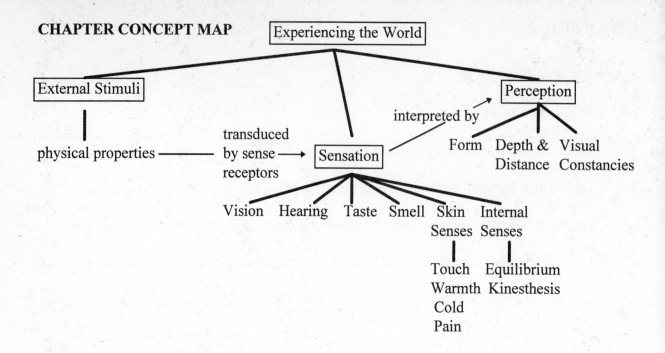

BRIEF CHAPTER SUMMARY

Chapter 6 examines the processes of sensation and perception and the relationship between them. The process of transduction changes physical energy into neural energy through the sense receptors. The physical characteristics of the stimuli correspond to psychological dimensions of our sensory experience. The general processes of vision, hearing, taste, smell, pain, equilibrium and kinesthesis are reviewed. Once sensation has occurred, the process of organizing and interpreting the sensory information, called perception, begins. Perceptual strategies, including depth and distance strategies, visual constancies and form perception strategies, are described. Some perceptual abilities appear to be inborn, while others are influenced by psychological, environmental and cultural factors. Conscious and nonconscious processes are examined. Extrasensory perception is critically evaluated.

PREVIEW OUTLINE AND REVIEW QUESTIONS

Before you read the chapter, review the preview outline and the Learning Objectives for each section of the text. Develop additional questions of your own based on key concepts and terms and write them in the designated spaces. Answer all questions as you read the text.

SECTION 1 - OUR SENSATIONAL SENSES (PP. 197-206)

I.   **OUR SENSATIONAL SENSES**

     A.   **Definitions**

         1.   _____ - the detection and encoding of changes in physical energy caused by environmental or internal events

         2.   Sense _____ - cells that detect such changes; located in the sense organs and internal body tissues

         3.   Perception - processes that organize and interpret sensory impulses; assembling sensory experience into meaningful patterns

     B.   **The riddle of separate sensations** - How we can explain separate sensations

         1.   Introduction to the senses

             a.   There are ____ widely known senses and other lesser known senses

             b.   All senses evolved to help us survive

         2.   _____ - begins with stimulus, converts stimulus energy into electrical impulses that travel along nerves to the brain

         3.   Encoding the electrical messages - the nervous system uses two kinds of codes

             a.   _____ codes

                 (1)   Doctrine of specific _____ energies - signals received by the sense organs stimulate different nerve pathways, which terminate in different areas of the brain

                 (2)   Does not fully explain separate sensations because skin senses aren't clearly linked to distinct nerve pathways or variations (i.e. color) within a sense

             b.   Functional codes

                 (1)   Particular receptors fire or are inhibited from firing in the presence of certain stimuli

                 (2)   Codes relate to which cells, how many, and the rate and pattern of firing

     C.   **Measuring the senses**

         1.   Psychophysics - how the _____ properties of stimuli are related to our psychological experience of them

         2.   Absolute _____

a. The smallest amount of energy a person can detect reliably (50 percent of the time)

b. The senses can pick up only a narrow band of physical energies

3. _____ threshold

a. The smallest difference in stimulation that a person can detect reliably (50 percent of the time); also called just noticeable difference (j.n.d.)

b. Weber's Law - when a person compares two stimuli, the size of the change necessary to produce a just noticeable difference is a constant _____ of the original stimulus

4. Signal detection theory

a. Accounts for _____ bias (tendency to say yes or no to a signal)

b. Separates sensory processes (the intensity of the stimulus) from the _____ process (influenced by observer's response bias)

D. **Sensory Adaptation**

1. Decline in sensory _____ occurs when a stimulus is unchanging; nerve cells temporarily stop responding

2. Sensory deprivation studies

a. When sensory experiences removed subjects became edgy, disoriented, confused, restless and had hallucinations

b. Early studies overexaggerated negative reactions

3. Brain requires minimum stimulation to function normally

E. **Sensory overload**

1. "Cocktail party phenomenon" - blocking out unimportant sensations

2. Selective _____ - protects us from being overwhelmed with sensations

Answer these Learning Objectives while you read Section 1.

1. Distinguish between sensation and perception.

2. Distinguish between anatomical and functional codes in the nervous system.

3. Define psychophysics, absolute and difference thresholds and signal detection theory.

4. Explain sensory adaptation, sensory deprivation, sensory overload and selective attention.

Write the questions that you have formulated below and answer them while you read.

A. _____

B. _____

II.   VISION

    A.   What we see

        1.   Stimulus for vision is _____, which travels in waves

        2.   Characteristics of light _____

            a.   Hue - color that is related to wavelength

            b.   Brightness - intensity, corresponds to _____ and wavelength

            c.   Saturation - colorfulness - complexity of the range of wavelengths

        3.   _____ dimensions of visual experience - hue, brightness, saturation

        4.   Physical properties of light - wavelength, intensity, complexity

    B.   An eye on the world - Parts of the eye

        1.   Cornea - front part of the eye; protects the eye and bends light rays toward

        2.   Lens - located behind the cornea; focuses light by changing curvature

        3.   Iris - _____ that control the amount of light that gets into the eye

        4.   Pupil - round opening surrounded by iris; widens and dilates to let light in

        5.   Retina - visual _____ located in the back of the eye

            a.   Parts of retina

                (1)   Two types of receptors

                    (a)   Rods: sensitive to light, not to color

                    (b)   Cones: see color, but need more light to respond

                (2)   Fovea - center of retina, sharpest vision, contains only cones

            b.   Processing visual information

                (1)   Rods and cones connect to _____ neurons, which connect to ganglion cells, which converge to form _____ nerve, which carries information out of the eye to the brain

                (2)   Optic nerve - leaves the eye at optic disc - no rods or cones

                (3)   Dark _____ - time it takes to adjust to dim illumination

    C.   Why the visual system is not a camera

        1.   Eyes are not a _____ recorder of external world; neurons build picture

        2.   Information about a stimulus is contained in the frequency, pattern or rhythm with which the cells fire

    D.   How we see color

        1.   Trichromatic theory

            a.   _____ mechanisms in the visual system, each sensitive to a range of wavelengths, interact to produce other colors

            b.   This approach applies to the first level of processing in the retina

            c.   Retina contains three types of _____: one responds to blue, another to green, another to red; these combine to make all colors

        2.   Opponent-process theory

            a.   Treats pairs of colors as if they are opposing

        b.   Second stage of color processing in the bipolar and ganglion cells of the retina and neurons in the thalamus (opponent process cells)

        c.   They turn off to one wavelength in a pair and on to the other

   3.   Two-stage theories is not yet a complete explanation for color vision

E.   **Constructing the visual world**

   1.   Visual perception - the mind interprets the retinal image and constructs the world using information from other senses

   2.   Form perception - Gestalt strategies for building perceptual units include: figure/ground distinction, _____, closure, similarity and continuity

   3.   Depth and distance perception - object's location inferred from distance or depth cues

        a.   Binocular cues - dependent on information from both _____

            (1)   Changes in angle of convergence of the image seen by each eye provide distance cues

            (2)   Retinal _____ - differing retinal images of same object to infer depth and distance

        b.   _____ cues - cues that do not depend on using both eyes include: interposition, linear perspective and relative size

   4.   Visual constancies

        a.   The perception of objects as unchanging though the sensory patterns they produce are constantly shifting

        b.   Visual constancies - shape, _____, brightness, color and size

   5.   Visual illusions - systematic errors that provide hints about perception

Answer these Learning Objectives while you read Section 2.

5.   List the characteristics of light waves and their correspondence to the visual experience.

6.   Identify the parts of the eye and describe how they convert light to vision.

7.   Discuss two theories of color vision and how they relate to stages of processing.

8.   Explain how form, distance and depth perception occur.

9.   List and explain visual constancies and distinguish them from visual illusions.

Write the questions that you have formulated below and answer them while you read.

A.   _____

B.   _____

SECTION 3 - HEARING (PP. 218-222)

III. HEARING
  A. **What we hear**
    1. Stimulus for sound is a wave of pressure created when an object vibrates, which causes molecules in a transmitting substance to move
    2. Characteristics of sound _____
      a. Loudness - intensity of a wave's pressure; corresponds to amplitude; also affected by pitch - measured in decibels
      b. Pitch - frequency (and intensity) of wave; measured in hertz
      c. Timbre - _____ of wave; the distinguishing quality of a sound
    3. Psychological properties of sound - loudness, pitch, timbre
    4. _____ properties of sound waves - amplitude, frequency, complexity are
  B. **An ear on the world - the process of hearing**
    1. Sound wave passes into the outer ear through a canal to strike the eardrum
    2. Eardrum vibrates at the same _____ and amplitude as the wave
    3. The wave vibrates three small bones in the inner ear; the third bone pushes on a membrane that opens into the inner ear which contains the cochlea
    4. The cochlea contains the organ of _____, the actual organ of hearing
    5. Organ of Corti contains the receptor cells called cilia, or hair cells, which are imbedded in the _____ membrane stretching across the cochlea
    6. Pressure causes movement in the basilar membrane; the hair cells initiate a signal to the auditory nerve, which carries the message to the brain
    7. The pattern of movement of the basilar membrane influences the pattern and frequency of how the neurons fire, which determines the what is heard
  C. **Constructing the auditory world**
    1. Perception is used to organize patterns of sounds to construct meaning
    2. Strategies include figure/ground, proximity, _____, similarity, closure
    3. Loudness is a distance cue; using both ears helps estimate direction

Answer these Learning Objectives while you read Section 3.

10. List the characteristics of sound waves and their correspondence to loudness, pitch, timbre.

11. Identify the parts of the ear and describe how they convert sound to hearing.

Write the questions that you have formulated below and answer them while you read.

A. _____

B. _____

IV.   OTHER SENSES
- A.   **Taste: Savory sensations**
  1.   _____ stimulate receptors on tongue, throat and roof of mouth
     - a.   Papillae - bumps on tongue, contain taste buds
     - b.   Replaced every 10 days - number declines with age
  2.   Four basic tastes: salty, _____, bitter, sweet
     - a.   Each taste produced by a different type of chemical
     - b.   Each can be perceived wherever there are receptors
     - c.   Flavors are a combination of the four, but unclear how this occurs
     - d.   Natural tastes - preference for _____, dislike for bitter
     - e.   Taste is heavily influenced by smell, culture, individual differences
- B.   **Smell: The sense of scents**
  1.   Receptors are specialized neurons (5 million) in a mucous membrane in upper part of nasal passage that respond to chemical molecules in the air
  2.   Not well understood - no agreement on which smells are basic; there may be a _____ different receptor types
  3.   Signals travel from receptors to olfactory bulb in the _____
  4.   Probably evolved because it aids survival; contributes to sexual chemistry
     - a.   _____ - chemicals released by one member of a species that affect other members
     - b.   Involved in animal behavior - role is less clear in humans
  5.   Odor preferences influenced by culture, context and experience
- C.   **Senses of the skin**
  1.   Skin protects innards, helps identify objects, involved in intimacy, serves as boundary
  2.   Skin senses include: _____, warmth, cold and pain
     - a.   No correspondence between four sensations and types of receptors
     - b.   Focus is on neural codes in skin senses
  3.   Pain differs in that removal of stimulus doesn't always terminate sensation
     - a.   _____ theory of pain: to experience pain sensation, impulses must pass a "gate" to central nervous system
     - b.   The gate = neurons that either transmit or block pain message
     - c.   Chronic pain results when fibers that close the gate are damaged
     - d.   One explanation for phantom pain
       - (1)   Impulses responsible for closing gate were removed during amputation
       - (2)   Another theory: once pain-producing activity starts in the brain, it continues without further impulses

    e. Pain involves release of chemicals, including substance P, at pain site and in spinal cord and brain

    f. _____ prevent pain fibers from releasing substance P

D. The environment within

  1. Kinesthesis - tells us about location and movement of body parts using pain and pressure receptors in joints

  2. Equilibrium - gives information about body as a whole using three semicircular canals in the inner ear

Answer these Learning Objectives while you read Section 4.

12. List and explain the factors that affect gustation (taste) and olfaction (smell).

13. List the four skin senses.

14. Describe the gate-control theory of pain and recent research in the physiology of pain.

15. Describe the internal senses of kinesthesis and equilibrium.

Write the questions that you have formulated below and answer them while you read.

A. _____

B. _____

**SECTION 5 - PERCEPTUAL POWERS: ORIGINS AND INFLUENCES (PP. 229-233)
AND SECTION 6 - PUZZLES OF PERCEPTION (PP. 233-240)**

V.   **PERCEPTUAL POWERS: ORIGINS AND INFLUENCES**
    A.   **Inborn abilities and perceptual lessons**
        1.   Studies with _____ show that experience during a critical period may ensure survival of skills present at birth
        2.   Research concludes that infants born with many perceptual abilities
            a.   Visual cliff experiment shows depth _____ by two months of age
            b.   Taste and smell preferences, ability to localize sound present early
        3.   Evidence from those who regain sensation later in life
    B.   **Psychological and _____ influences on perception**
        1.   Needs, beliefs, emotions, _____ (perceptual set)
VI.   **PUZZLES OF PERCEPTION**
    A.   **Conscious and nonconscious perception**
        1.   Evidence exists for perceptual processing without awareness (blindsight)
        2.   A visual stimulus of which one is not aware can influence responses
        3.   Evidence for nonconscious processes in memory, thinking, decision making
        4.   Real world implications small - little evidence for subliminal persuasion
    B.   **Extrasensory perception: Reality or illusion?**
        1.   Four categories of ESP or (Psi) experiences: telepathy, clairvoyance, precognition, _____ experiences
        2.   Evidence or coincidence?
            a.   Most comes from unreliable _____ accounts
            b.   Studies under controlled conditions by parapsychologists
                (1)   Some positive results found but there were methodological problems and results were not replicated
                (2)   Conclusion is that there is no supporting scientific evidence

Answer these Learning Objectives while you read Sections 5 and 6.

16.   Summarize the evidence for innate abilities in perception and describe the psychological and cultural influences on perception.

17.   Discuss the evidence on the effectiveness of "subliminal perception" tapes and ESP.

Write the questions that you have formulated below and answer them while you read.

A.   _____

B.   _____

FLASH CARDS

Cut the following chart along the borders and test yourself with the resulting flash cards.

6.1 SENSATION	6.8 FUNCTIONAL CODES	6.15 SENSORY DEPRIVATION
6.2 SENSE RECEPTORS	6.9 PSYCHOPHYSICS	6.16 SELECTIVE ATTENTION
6.3 SENSE ORGANS	6.10 ABSOLUTE THRESHOLD	6.17 HUE
6.4 PERCEPTION	6.11 DIFFERENCE THRESHOLD OR J.N.D.	6.18 BRIGHTNESS
6.5 TRANSDUCTION	6.12 WEBER'S LAW	6.19 SATURATION
6.6 ANATOMICAL CODES	6.13 SIGNAL DETECTION THEORY	6.20 COMPLEXITY OF LIGHT
6.7 DOCTRINE OF SPECIFIC NERVE ENERGIES	6.14 SENSORY ADAPTATION	6.21 AMPLITUDE

6.15 The absence of normal levels of sensory stimulation.	**6.8** A second way the nervous system processes different sensations; certain receptors and neurons fire only in the presence of certain sorts of stimuli.	**6.1** The detection or direct experience of physical energy in the external or internal environment due to stimulation of receptors in the sense organs.
6.16 The focusing of attention on selected aspects of the environment and the blocking out of others.	**6.9** The area of psychology concerned with the relationship between physical properties of stimuli and sensory experience.	**6.2** Specialized cells that convert physical energy in the environment into electrical energy that can be transmitted as nerve impulses to the brain.
6.17 The dimension of visual experience specified by color names and related to the wavelength of light.	**6.10** The smallest quantity of physical energy that can be reliably detected by an observer.	**6.3** The eyes, ears, tongue, nose, skin and internal body tissues; contain the sense receptors.
6.18 Lightness or luminance; the dimension of visual experience related to the amount of light emitted from or reflected by an object.	**6.11** The smallest difference in stimulation that can be reliably detected by an observed when two stimuli are compared. Also called just noticeable difference.	**6.4** The process by which the brain organizes and interprets sensory information.
6.19 Vividness or purity of color; the dimension of visual experience related to the complexity of light waves.	**6.12** A law of psychophysics stating that the change necessary to produce a j.n.d. is a constant proportion of the original stimulus.	**6.5** The conversion of one form of energy to another. Sensory receptors are biological transducers.
6.20 Refers to the number of different wavelengths contained in light from a particular source.	**6.12** A psychophysical theory that divides the detection of a sensory signal into a sensory process and a decision process.	**6.6** One way the nervous system processes different sensations; different senses stimulate different nerve pathways to different brain areas.
6.21 Maximum height of a wave.	**6.14** The reduction or disappearance of sensory responsiveness that occurs when stimulation is unchanging or repetitious.	**6.7** A description of anatomical coding; signals received by the sense organs stimulate different nerve pathways, which go to different brain areas.

6.22 WAVELENGTH	6.29 OPTIC NERVE	6.36 BINOCULAR CUES
6.23 RETINA	6.30 FEATURE DETECTORS	6.37 RETINAL DISPARITY
6.24 RODS	6.31 TRICHROMATIC THEORY	6.38 MONOCULAR CUES
6.25 CONES	6.32 OPPONENT-PROCESS THEORY	6.39 PERCEPTUAL CONSTANCY
6.26 FOVEA	6.33 NEGATIVE AFTERIMAGE	6.40 PERCEPTUAL ILLUSION
6.27 DARK ADAPTATION	6.34 GESTALT PRINCIPLES	6.41 AUDITION
6.28 GANGLION CELLS	6.35 FIGURE AND GROUND	6.42 LOUDNESS

6.36 Visual cues to depth or distance requiring two eyes.	6.29 Formed by a bundle of axons of the ganglion cells; carries information out from the back of the eye and on to the brain.	6.22 The distance between the crests of a wave.
6.37 The slight differences in lateral separation between two objects as seen by the left eye and the right eye.	6.30 Cells in the visual cortex that are sensitive to specific features of the environment.	6.23 Neural tissue lining the back of the eyeball's interior that contains the receptors for vision.
6.38 Visual cues to depth or distance that can be used by one eye alone.	6.31 A theory of color perception that proposes three mechanisms in the visual system, each sensitive to a certain range of wavelengths.	6.24 Visual receptors that respond to dim light but are not involved in color vision.
6.39 The accurate perception of objects as stable or unchanged despite changes in the sensory patterns they produce.	6.32 A theory of color perception that assumes the visual system treats pairs of colors as opposing or antagonistic.	6.25 Visual receptors involved in color vision.
6.40 An erroneous or misleading perception of reality.	6.33 When we stare at a particular hue, we see a different color when we look away; a sort of neural rebound effect.	6.26 The center of the retina where vision is sharpest and contains only cones.
6.41 The sense of hearing.	6.34 Visual perception uses some Gestalt psychology principles including proximity, closure, similarity, and continuity.	6.27 A two-stage process by which visual receptors become maximally sensitive to dim light.
6.42 The dimension of auditory experience related to the intensity of a pressure wave.	6.35 The Gestalt idea that the visual field is organized into a figure, which stands out from the rest of the environment, and a formless background.	6.28 Neurons in the retina of the eye that gather information from receptor cells (via bipolar cells); their axons make up the optic nerve.

6.43 PITCH	**6.50 PAPILLAE**	**6.57 EQUILIBRIUM**
6.44 FREQUENCY OF A SOUND WAVE	**6.51 TASTE BUDS**	**6.58 SEMICIRCULAR CANALS**
6.45 TIMBRE	**6.52 OLFACTION**	**6.59 THE VISUAL CLIFF**
6.46 COCHLEA	**6.53 PHEROMONES**	**6.60 PERCEPTUAL SET**
6.47 BASILAR MEMBRANE	**6.54 GATE-CONTROL THEORY OF PAIN**	**6.61 SUBLIMINAL PERCEPTION**
6.48 AUDITORY NERVE	**6.55 PHANTOM PAIN**	**6.62 EXTRASENSORY PERCEPTION**
6.49 GUSTATION	**6.56 KINESTHESIS**	**6.63 PARAPSYCHOLOGY**

6.57 The sense of balance.	6.50 Knob-like elevations on the tongue containing taste buds.	6.43 The dimension of auditory experience related to the frequency of a pressure wave; height or depth of a tone.
6.58 Sense organs in the inner ear that contribute to equilibrium by responding to rotation of the head.	6.51 Nests of taste receptor cells.	6.44 The number of times per second that a sound wave cycles through a peak and low point.
6.59 A device used in research to ascertain if babies have depth perception; the "cliff" is a pane of glass covering a shallow and a deep surface.	6.52 The sense of smell.	6.45 The distinguishing quality of a sound; the dimension of auditory experience related to the complexity of the pressure wave.
6.60 A habitual way of perceiving, based on expectations.	6.53 Odorous chemical substances released by one member of a species that affect the physiology or behavior of other members.	6.46 A snail-shaped, fluid-filled organ in the inner ear containing the receptors for hearing.
6.61 The perception of messages that are below sensory thresholds.	6.54 The theory that the experience of pain depends on whether pain impulses get past a neurological "gate" in the spinal cord to the brain.	6.47 The receptors (hair cells) of the cochlea are embedded in this membrane, which stretches across the interior of the cochlea.
6.62 The hypothesized system for sending and receiving messages about the world without relying on the usual sensory channels.	6.55 Pain that continues to be felt that seemingly comes from an amputated limb, breast or internal organ that has been surgically removed.	6.48 The fibers that carry the signal from the auditory receptors to the brain.
6.63 The study of purported psychic phenomena, such as ESP and mental telepathy.	6.56 The sense of body position and movement of body parts; also called kinesthesia.	6.49 The sense of taste.

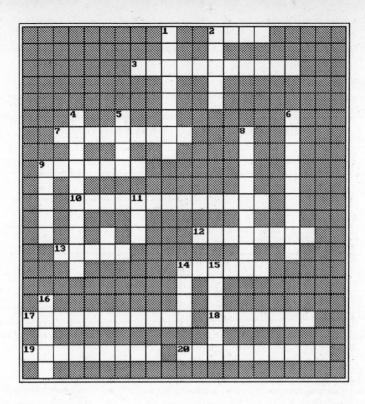

ACROSS

2. a skin sense and an internal sense
3. sense of body position and movement of body parts
7. detection of physical energy due to stimulation of receptors in the sense organs
9. snail-shaped, fluid-filled organ
10. the relationship between physical properties of stimuli and sensory experience
12. hearing
13. center of retina where vision is sharpest
14. contains receptors for vision
17. allows us to see objects as unchanged despite changes in the sensory patterns they produce
18. receptor for hearing imbedded in this membrane
19. cells that convert physical energy in the environment into neural energy
20. odorous chemical substances

DOWN

1. neurons in the retina that gather information from receptor cells
2. height or depth of a tone
4. process of organizing and interpreting sensory information
5. it has amplitude and frequency
6. taste
8. smell
9. visual receptors involved in color
11. dimension of vision related to wavelength of light
14. visual receptors that respond to dim light
15. the distinguishing quality of a sound
16. two ways the nervous system processes different sensations

Complete the following charts on vision and audition and on perceptual strategies

VISION AND AUDITION

SENSE	RECEPTORS AND THEIR LOCATIONS	PHYSICAL PROPERTIES OF THE STIMULUS	PSYCHOLOGICAL DIMENSIONS OF THE SENSORY EXPERIENCE
VISION			
AUDITION			

PERCEPTUAL STRATEGIES

PERCEPTUAL STRATEGY	DEFINITION	GIVE EXAMPLE
FORM PERCEPTION Proximity		
Closure		
Similarity		
Continuity		
DEPTH AND DISTANCE Retinal Disparity		
Interposition		
Linear Perspective		
VISUAL CONSTANCIES Shape		
Location		
Brightness		
Color		

PRACTICE TEST 1

1. The neural encoding of changes in physical energy is called
   A. perception.
   B. transduction.
   C. sensation.
   D. sensory adaptation.

2. The eyes, ears, tongue, nose, skin and internal body tissues all contain
   A. anatomical codes.
   B. functional codes.
   C. sense receptors.
   D. sense organs.

3. Perception differs from sensation in that
   A. perception allows us to organize and interpret sensations.
   B. perception is the raw data coming in from the senses.
   C. sensation is an organizing and interpretive process, perception is not.
   D. perception can be measured, sensations cannot.

4. Which theory argues that light and sound produce different sensations because they stimulate different brain parts?
   A. signal detection theory
   B. Weber's Law
   C. doctrine of specific nerve energies
   D. opponent-process theory

5. Which of the following best accounts for the fact that light and sound produce different sensations due to the specific cells that are firing, how many are firing, the rate at which they are firing and the patterning of each cell's firing?
   A. anatomical codes
   B. functional codes
   C. doctrine of specific nerve energies
   D. feature detectors

6. Signal detection theory takes into account
   A. observers' response tendencies.
   B. sensory differences among species.
   C. the role of feature detectors.
   D. which cells are firing, how many cells are firing and the rate at which they fire.

7. As a research subject, Betsy is asked to compare lights within several pairs of lights and indicate whether one is brighter than the other. Betsy is being asked to detect
   A. the absolute threshold.
   B. the j.d.n.
   C. the difference threshold.
   D. Weber's Law.

8. Researchers have found that sensory deprivation may
   A. lead to confusion and grouchiness.
   B. produce a restless, disoriented feeling.
   C. cause hallucinations.
   D. cause all of the above.

9. Maria enjoys the wonderful smells from the kitchen when she first arrives at her mother's house, but after a while, she no longer notices them. What accounts for this?
   A. sensory adaptation
   B. selective attention
   C. absolute thresholds
   D. difference thresholds

10. In class, Jonah is completely focused on the professor's words, though there are noises and distractions all around him. This is best accounted for by
    A. sensory adaptation.
    B. selective attention.
    C. sensory deprivation.
    D. sensory overload.

11. Humans experience the wavelength of light as
    A. hue or color.
    B. brightness.
    C. saturation or colorfulness.
    D. wave complexity.

12. The fovea contains
    A. only rods.
    B. only cones.
    C. an equal number of rods and cones.
    D. more rods than cones.

13. The visual receptors are located in the
    A. cornea.
    B. pupil.
    C. lens.
    D. retina.

14. The optic nerve connects
    A. rods and cones.
    B. the cornea with the brain.
    C. the pupil and the lens.
    D. the retina with the brain.

15. Which theory of color vision best explains negative afterimages?
    A. trichromatic theory
    B. opponent-process theory
    C. doctrine of specific nerve energies
    D. Weber's Law

16. Which Gestalt strategy would explain why you see $$$AAA### as three groups of figures instead of nine separate figures?
    A. closure
    B. figure-ground
    C. continuity
    D. similarity

17. The slight difference in sideways separation between two objects as seen by the left eye and the right eye is called
    A.   a binocular cue.   B.   a depth cue.
    C.   retinal disparity.   D.   all of the above.

18. As you watch a door opening, its image changes from rectangular to trapezoidal, yet you continue to think of the door as rectangular. What explains this phenomenon?
    A.   perceptual constancy   B.   retinal disparity
    C.   monocular depth cues   D.   selective attention

19. Pitch is the dimension of sound related to the
    A.   amplitude of a pressure wave.
    B.   frequency of a pressure wave.
    C.   distinguishing quality of a sound.
    D.   complexity of a pressure wave.

20. The part of the ear that plays the same role in hearing as the retina plays in vision is called the
    A.   cochlea.   B.   eardrum.
    C.   organ of Corti.   D.   auditory nerve.

21. When you bite into a piece of bread or an orange, the taste is a result of
    A.   a combination of the four basic tastes: salty, sour, bitter and sweet.
    B.   a combination of the four basic tastes: salty, smooth, pungent and sweet.
    C.   the activation of specific taste receptors.
    D.   the taste receptors located in a specific part of the tongue.

22. The skin senses are
    A.   tickle, temperature, touch and pain.
    B.   tickle, itch, tingle and burn.
    C.   touch, warmth, cold and pain.
    D.   warmth, heat, cool and cold.

23. Under certain circumstances people do not experience pain, although they have experienced an event that normally causes pain. What theory best explains this?
    A.   gate-control theory
    B.   mind over matter theory
    C.   phantom pain theory
    D.   the release of substance P

24. Malga can touch her finger to her nose with her eyes shut. What allows her to do this?
   A. substance P   B. kinesthesis
   C. equilibrium   D. ESP

25. Which group is studied to evaluate whether perceptual abilities are inborn?
   A. cats
   B. people who first gained sensation as an adult
   C. babies and infants
   D. all of the above

PRACTICE TEST 2

1. Sensation is to perception as neural message is to _____.
   A. encoding
   B. meaning
   C. reception
   D. transduction

2. Anatomical and functional codes
   A. explain why we see light and hear sound.
   B. explain how we experience different sensations.
   C. explain why light and sound produce different sensations.
   D. explain all of the above.

3. _____ stimulate different nerve pathways, which go to different places in the brain, while focusing on the number, rate and pattern of the firing of particular cells in response to certain stimuli describes the functioning of _____.
   A. anatomical codes; functional codes
   B. neural codes; cellular codes
   C. functional codes; anatomical codes
   D. psychophysics; transduction

4. A series of barely audible tones is being played to Ethan. The researcher wants to know which is the softest tone that Ethan can reliably hear. This is called the
   A. difference threshold.
   B. absolute threshold.
   C. j.n.d.
   D. partial threshold.

5. The researcher presents Ethan with some trials in which there is no tone presented. She is interested in knowing how often Ethan thinks he hears something when no tone is presented, as compared to how often he thinks he hears something when a weak tone is presented. This type of information is used in
   A. calculating difference thresholds.
   B. determining absolute thresholds.
   C. signal detection theory.
   D. calculating just noticeable differences.

6. Which of the following describes what happens in sensory adaptation?
   A. receptors get "tired" and temporarily stop responding
   B. nerve cells high up in the sensory system temporarily switch off
   C. you no longer smell a gas leak that you noticed when you first entered the house
   D. all of the above

7. Hue is to brightness as
   A. wavelength is to amplitude.   B. complexity is to wavelength.
   C. amplitude is to frequency.   D. frequency is to complexity.

8. Hue, brightness and saturation are all _____ dimensions of visual experience, whereas wavelength, intensity and complexity are all _____ properties of visual experience.
   A. physical; psychological   B. temporary; permanent
   C. complex; simple   D. psychological; physical

9. The cornea, lens, iris and pupil are part of the _____, whereas the rods and cones are the _____
   A. eye; sense organ.   B. retina; eye ball.
   C. sense organ; receptors.   D. receptors; retina.

10. Rods are to cones as
    A. bright light is to dim light.   B. the iris is to the pupil.
    C. black and white vision is to color vision.   D. none of the above.

11. In a softball game, Rocio has made it to third base. When Elena pitches she must watch the batter and Rocio out of the corner of her eye. Watching Rocio requires her to use
    A. cones.   B. rods.
    C. both rods and cones.   D. the optic disc.

12. Which theory of color vision suggests that one type of cone responds to blue, another to green and a third to red?
    A. doctrine of specific nerve energies   B. opponent-process theory
    C. trichromatic theory   D. feature detector theory

13. The fact that you see the words written on a page and pay little attention to the paper they are written on is an illustration of what aspect of our perceptual powers?
    A. figure-ground discrimination   B. color constancy
    C. shape constancy   D. depth perception

14. The fact that tomatoes look smaller and smaller as you look down the rows of your vegetable garden demonstrates which monocular depth cue?
    A. interposition   B. retinal disparity
    C. linear perspective   D. light and shadow

150

15. . Pitch is to timbre as
    A.   intensity is to amplitude.   B.   complexity is to intensity.
    C.   frequency is to complexity.   D.   amplitude is to frequency.

16. What makes a note played on a flute sound different from the same note played on an oboe?
    A.   loudness   B.   saturation
    C.   timbre   D.   pitch

17. Rods and cones are to vision as the _____ is/are to hearing.
    A.   cilia or hair cells   B.   eardrum
    C.   basilar membrane   D.   cochlea

18. The cilia are imbedded in the _____ of the _____.
    A.   cochlea; auditory nerve   B.   basilar membrane; cochlea
    C.   eardrum; cochlea   D.   cochlea; basilar membrane

19. Which of the following might explain why Aiko does not like foods with a bitter taste?
    A.   cultural differences
    B.   supertaste for bitter substances
    C.   evolutionary reasons
    D.   all of the above

20. How does the sense of smell differ from the sense of vision and taste?
    A.   Smell does not have receptor cells.
    B.   Vision and taste have limited numbers of basic cell types, smell may have as many as a thousand.
    C.   Smell uses anatomical coding and not functional coding while vision and taste use both.
    D.   There are fewer basic smells than basic tastes or colors.

21. Which of the following examples uses all of the skin senses?
    A.   After laying in the hot sun, Kathy's skin burned as she felt the pressure of the cool shower.
    B.   Herb became very warm as he ran five miles on a summer day.
    C.   Carol felt her muscles ache as she felt the pressure of the massage.
    D.   Mori hurt her knee when she fell off her bike.

22. After Ceasar ate many chile peppers, they seemed to burn his tongue less than they did at first. This effect is due to the
   A. release of endorphins on the tongue.
   B. release of substance P on the tongue.
   C. depletion of substance P.
   D. closing of the pain gate in the brain.

23. Calan is trying to balance on her left leg while holding her right foot with her left hand. Her ability to balance relies on the sense of _____, and her ability to grab her foot relies on the sense of _____.
   A. equilibrium; kinesthesis
   C. kinesthesis; equilibrium
   C. touch; equilibrium
   D. coordination: touch

24. Baby Huey is placed on a board in the middle of a glass covering both a shallow surface and a deep one (a visual cliff). His mother beckons to him to cross over both sides of the "cliff." This study is trying to
   A. evaluate visual acuity in babies.
   B. evaluate attachment in babies.
   C. determine whether depth perception is inborn.
   D. evaluate learned cues on distance perception.

25. There is considerable evidence that a simple visual stimulus can affect a person's responses to a task even when the person has no awareness of seeing the stimulus. What conclusions can we reach about subliminal perception?
   A. There are dramatic implications for real world applications.
   B. Real world implications are limited.
   C. Subliminal persuasion has been used successfully in marketing.
   D. Subliminal perception is an excellent learning tool.

PRACTICE TEST 3

1. Explain the phenomena listed below in terms of the concept listed after it.

    A. Roberta is shopping at a flea market and has just refused to buy a scarf because the salesperson is charging $10 and she saw it at another stall for $8.00. Later that week, she is shopping for a new car and does not think anything about spending an extra $2.00 for a car. Discuss this as an analogy of Weber's Law.

    B. A nurse notices that patients perform more poorly on auditory tests - tests or auditory thresholds - when they are tired as a result of losing sleep. Analyze the effects of their performance using signal detection theory.

    C. John is looking all over for his glasses when his wife points them out at the top of his head. Explain this using principles of sensory adaptation.

    D. Malcolm is studying for a test in psychology while the T.V. is blaring and his roommate is on the phone in the same room. Discuss this in relation to sensory overload.

2. Starting with a light wave, describe what happens to that wave from the environment to the brain, including all relevant structures.

3   Assume you are developing a color-generating device that will reproduce the colors in the human color spectrum. Explain what colors you need and why, according to the two theories of color vision listed below.

    A. Trichromatic theory
    B. Opponent-process theory

4. You are watching a monitor depicting sound waves. Describe what changes in the sound would accompany the modifications indicated below.

    A. The sound waves remain constant except for their height, which is increasing.
    B. The wave frequency is changing.
    C. Waves of different types are being increasingly mixed together.

5. In each of the examples below, identify and describe the Gestalt principle involved.

    A.   People scattered on a beach appear to be in clusters.
    B.   A sequence of dots on a canvas appear to form a face.
    C.   People crowded on a soccer field appear to be two different teams and referees.
    D.   A wall seems to be continuous even though vines block sections from view.

6. Psychological factors can influence what we perceive and how we perceive it. Identify the psychological factors that could influence the following perceptions.

    A.   You had an argument with your sister. As you are walking home from school, she drives past you. You saw her look at you but figured that she did not stop because she is angry with you.
    B.   You think that your neighbor is an unethical character. One day you see him entering his house during the day and you are certain that he is sneaking around so no one will see him.
    C.   You are expecting your best friend to come visit you and you are very excited. Every time you hear something, you run to the door, sure that there was a knock.

CHAPTER 7

Learning

LEARNING OBJECTIVES

1. Identify the two types of conditioning shown by behaviorists to explain human behavior.

2. List and explain the four components of classical conditioning.

3. List and explain the four principles of classical conditioning.

4. Compare the traditional and recent views of how associations are formed between unconditioned and conditioned stimuli.

5. Describe both the impact of classical conditioning on everyday life, and the therapeutic technique of counterconditioning.

6. Compare and contrast the principles of operant and classical conditioning.

7. List and explain the three types of consequences a response can lead to and distinguish between positive and negative reinforcement and primary and secondary reinforcement.

8. Describe shaping, extinction, stimulus generalization and stimulus discrimination in operant conditioning.

9. Distinguish between continuous and intermittent schedules of reinforcement and describe the four types of intermittent reinforcement schedules.

10. Describe how superstitions might be learned according to operant conditioning.

11. List and discuss six limitations of punishment as a way of controlling behavior and state a more effective strategy.

12. Describe a token economy and distinguish between intrinsic and extrinsic reinforcers, and discuss the effects of extrinsic reinforcers on motivation.

13. Explain social learning theory and compare it to conditioning models of learning.

14. Compare and contrast cognitive approaches and behavioral approaches.

CHAPTER CONCEPT MAP

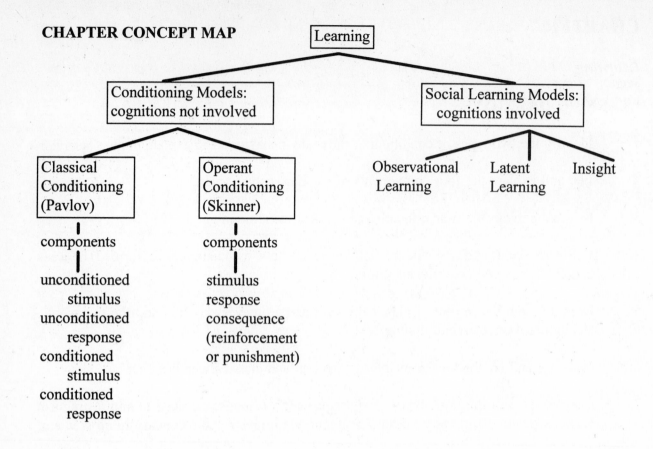

BRIEF CHAPTER SUMMARY

Chapter 7 explores how we learn or make permanent changes in our behaviors due to experience. Two broad types of learning are explored: conditioning models and cognitive-social learning models. Both conditioning models suggest that learning is acquired through simple associations without the involvement of mental processes. Classical conditioning explains how we learn involuntary behaviors, such as fears and preferences. Operant conditioning explains that we learn voluntary behaviors as a result of the favorable or unfavorable consequences of our actions. Social learning models expand behavioral principles to recognize the role that mental processes play in the acquisition of new behaviors. Observational learning, latent learning and insight are types of social learning.

PREVIEW OUTLINE AND REVIEW QUESTIONS

Before you read the chapter, review the preview outline and the Learning Objectives for each section of the text. Develop additional questions of your own based on key concepts and terms and write them in the designated spaces. Answer all questions as you read the text.

SECTION 1 - CLASSICAL CONDITIONING: NEW REFLEXES FROM OLD (PP. 245-254)

I.   **CLASSICAL CONDITIONING: NEW REFLEXES FROM OLD**
  A.   **Definitions**
    1.   Learning - any relatively _____ change in behavior that occurs due to experience
    2.   Behaviorism - the view that behavior should be explained in terms of _____ events rather than hypothetical mental processes
    3.   Terminology
      a.   Unconditioned stimulus (US) - stimulus eliciting a _____ response
      b.   Unconditioned response (UR) - response that is automatically produced
      c.   Conditioned stimulus (CS) - when a _____ stimulus comes to elicit a conditioned response after being paired with a US
      d.   Conditioned response (CR) - response that is elicited by a CS
    4.   Learning occurs when a neutral stimulus is regularly paired with a US and the neutral stimulus becomes a CS, which elicits a CR that is similar to the original, unlearned one
    5.   Later psychologists said that, for learning to occur, it is not enough to pair the stimuli, the neutral stimulus must reliably signal the unconditioned one
  B.   **Principles of classical conditioning**
    1.   Extinction - repeating the conditioned stimulus without the _____ stimulus, the conditioned response disappears
    2.   Spontaneous recovery - after a response has been extinguished, it may spontaneously _____ after the passage of time with exposure to the conditioned stimulus
    3.   Higher-order conditioning - a neutral stimulus can become a conditioned stimulus by being paired with an already established _____
    4.   Stimulus _____ - after a stimulus becomes a conditioned stimulus for some response, other, similar stimuli may produce the same reaction
    5.   Stimulus discrimination - different responses are triggered by stimuli that resemble the conditioned stimulus in some way

C. **Classical conditioning in real life**

1. Examples of behaviors learned through classical conditioning include taste preferences, love, fears (little Albert example), addictions (able to explain tolerance and overdosing)

2. Therapy techniques that have developed include counterconditioning and systematic _____

3. Some things may be more easily learned because of a _____ predisposition based on evolutionary considerations

Answer these Learning Objectives while you read Section 1.

2. List and explain the four components of classical conditioning.

3. List and explain the four principles of classical conditioning.

4. Compare the traditional and recent views of how associations are formed between unconditioned and conditioned stimuli.

5. Describe both the impact of classical conditioning on everyday life, and the therapeutic technique of counterconditioning.

Write the questions that you have formulated below and answer them while you read.

A._____

B._____

**SECTION 2 - OPERANT CONDITIONING: THE CARROT AND THE STICK
(PP. 255-274)**

II.   **OPERANT CONDITIONING: THE CARROT AND THE STICK**
   A.   **History of operant conditioning**
      1.   Introduced at the turn of the century
      2.   Thorndike's law of _____ - behavior is controlled by its consequences
      3.   B.F.Skinner's extensions of the theory
         a.   Behavior is explainable by looking outside the individual not inside
         b.   Behavior _____ by the environment; humans have no free will
   B.   **Reinforcers and punishers: A matter of consequence**
      1.   Central idea of operant conditioning is that behavior becomes more or less likely depending on its _____
      2.   A response can lead to three types of consequences: neutral consequences, _____ (increases the probability that the response it follows will recur), punishment (makes the response it follows less likely to recur)
      3.   Consequences are most effective when they capitalize on inborn tendencies or instinctive drift
   C.   **Positive and negative reinforcers**
      1.   Reinforcers - always increase the likelihood of a response punishers
         a.   Positive reinforcement - something pleasant occurs
         b.   Negative reinforcement - something unpleasant is removed
      2.   Punishers - decrease the likelihood of a response
         a.   Positive punishment - something unpleasant occurs
         b.   Negative punishment - something pleasant is removed
   D.   **Primary and secondary reinforcers and punishers** - can be very powerful
      1.   Primary reinforcers satisfy _____ needs
      2.   Primary punishers are inherently unpleasant
      3.   Secondary reinforcers are reinforcing through association with other (possibly primary) reinforcers
      4.   Secondary punishers are punishing through association with other punishers
   E.   **Principles of operant conditioning**
      1.   Extinction - a previously learned response stops occurring because of the removal of the _____
      2.   Spontaneous recovery is the return of a response that has been extinguished
      3.   Immediate consequences are more effective than delayed consequences
      4.   Stimulus _____ - a response occurs to stimuli that resemble the stimuli present during the original learning
      5.   Stimulus discrimination - the ability to distinguish between similar stimuli and responding only to the one that results in the reinforcer

6. _____ stimulus is a signal whether a response will pay off; it is said to exert stimulus control over the response because it determines under what conditions the response will be reinforced

7. _____ of reinforcement - the pattern of delivery of reinforcements; can have powerful effects on rate, form and timing of behavior
   a. Continuous reinforcement - reinforcing a response each time it occurs
   b. Partial or _____ schedules - reinforcing only some responses
      (1) Ratio schedules - deliver reinforcement after a certain number of responses
         (a) Fixed-ratio schedules - reinforcement occurs after a fixed number of _____
         (b) Variable-ratio schedules - reinforcement occurs after some average number of responses, but the number varies from reinforcement to reinforcement
      (2) _____ schedules - deliver reinforcement after a certain amount of time has passed
         (a) Fixed-interval schedule - reinforcement occurs only if a fixed amount of time has passed since the previous reinforcer
         (b) Variable-interval schedule - reinforcement occurs only if a variable amount of time has passed since the previous reinforcer
   c. For a response to persist, it should be reinforced intermittently, which will make the response more difficult to _____

8. Shaping - method of getting a response in the first place by reinforcing behavioral tendencies in the right direction (_____ approximations), and then gradually reinforcing responses that are more similar to the desired response

9. Superstitious behaviors can be learned when coincidental behavior is reinforced

F. **Just deserts? The problems with punishment**
   1. Punishment is often administered _____ or in a state of rage
   2. The recipient often responds with anxiety, fear or rage
   3. Effects can be _____ and may depend on the presence of the punisher
   4. Most behavior is hard to punish immediately
   5. Punishment conveys little information about how to behave differently
   6. A punishment may be reinforcing because it brings attention

> 7.   Alternatives to punishment
>> a.   Give information about desirable behavior
>> b.   Try to extinguish the behavior
>> c.   Reinforce alternate behaviors that are desirable
> **G.**   **Putting operant principles to work**
>> 1.   Use of behavior modification programs such as token _____
>> 2.   People work for intrinsic as well as extrinsic reinforcers
>> 3.   Reinforcers can interfere with intrinsic motivation

Answer these Learning Objectives while you read Section 2.

1.   Identify the two types of conditioning shown by behaviorists to explain human behavior.

6.   Compare and contrast the principles of operant and classical conditioning.

7.   List and explain the three types of consequences a response can lead to and distinguish between positive and negative reinforcement and primary and secondary reinforcement.

8.   Describe shaping, extinction, stimulus generalization and stimulus discrimination in operant conditioning.

9.   Distinguish between continuous and intermittent schedules of reinforcement and describe the four types of intermittent reinforcement schedules.

10.   Describe how superstitions might be learned according to operant conditioning.

11.   List and discuss six limitations of punishment as a way of controlling behavior and state a more effective strategy.

12.   Describe a token economy and distinguish between intrinsic and extrinsic reinforcers, and discuss the effects of extrinsic reinforcers on motivation.

Write the questions that you have formulated below and answer them while you read.

A._____

B._____

III. **SOCIAL LEARNING THEORIES**
   A. **General characteristics of social learning theories**
      1. Disagree with the exclusion of _____ operations from behaviorism and focus on conditioning as sole explanation for behavior
      2. Similarities to behaviorism
         a. Agree with laws of conditioning
         b. Recognize importance of reinforcers and the environment
      3. Differences from behaviorism
         a. Include the importance of higher-level _____ processes
         b. Emphasize reciprocal determinism - the interaction between individuals and their environment
         c. Emphasize perceptions, assumptions, beliefs, expectations
   B. **Observational learning: The copycat syndrome**
      1. Vicarious conditioning occurs from observing a _____
      2. Supported by Bandura's studies
   C. **Cognitive processes: Peering into the "Black Box"**
      1. Tolman's experiment with latent learning
      2. Learning occurs that is not immediately expressed as a response
      3. Learning occurs without obvious reinforcement

IV. **COGNITIONS VERSUS CONNECTIONS: WHY DOES LEARNING OCCUR?**
   A. Tension between behaviorism and cognitive approaches
   B. Behaviorists explain insight in terms of prior _____ history
   C. Cognitive theorists say insight requires mentally combining previously learned responses in new ways

Answer these Learning Objectives while you read Sections 3 and 4.

13. Explain social learning theory explain and compare it to conditioning models of learning.

14. Compare and contrast cognitive approaches and behavioral approaches.

Write the questions that you have formulated below and answer them while you read.

A._____

B._____

FLASH CARDS

Cut the following chart along the borders and test yourself with the resulting flash cards.

7.1 LEARNING	**7.9 SPONTANEOUS RECOVERY**	**7.17 PUNISHMENT/ PUNISHERS**
7.2 BEHAVIORISM	**7.10 HIGHER-ORDER CONDITIONING**	**7.18 INSTINCTIVE DRIFT**
7.3 UNCONDITIONED STIMULUS (US)	**7.11 STIMULUS GENERALIZATION (IN CLASSICAL CONDITIONING)**	**7.19 POSITIVE REINFORCEMENT**
7.4 UNCONDITIONED RESPONSE (UR)	**7.12 STIMULUS DISCRIMINATION (IN CLASSICAL CONDITIONING)**	**7.20 NEGATIVE REINFORCEMENT**
7.5 CONDITIONED STIMULUS (CS)	**7.13 COUNTER-CONDITIONING**	**7.21 POSITIVE PUNISHMENT**
7.6 CONDITIONED RESPONSE (CR)	**7.14 OPERANT CONDITIONING**	**7.22 NEGATIVE PUNISHMENT**
7.7 CLASSICAL CONDITIONING	**7.15 LAW OF EFFECT (THORNDIKE)**	**7.23 PRIMARY REINFORCERS/ PUNISHERS**
7.8 EXTINCTION (IN CLASSICAL CONDITIONING)	**7.16 REINFORCEMENT/ REINFORCERS**	**7.24 SECONDARY (CONDITIONED) REINFORCERS/ PUNISHERS**

7.17 The process by which a stimulus or event weakens or reduces the probability of the response that it follows.	7.9 The reappearance of a learned response after its apparent extinction.	7.1 A relatively permanent change in behavior (or behavioral potential) due to experience.
7.18 The tendency of an organism to revert to an instinctive behavior over time; can interfere with learning.	7.10 In classical conditioning, a neutral stimulus becomes a CS through association with an already established CS.	7.2 An approach that emphasizes observable behavior and the role of the environment as a determinant of behavior.
7.19 A response is followed by a reinforcing stimulus and therefore, it becomes stronger or more likely to occur.	7.11 After conditioning, when a stimulus that resembles the conditioned stimulus elicits the conditioned response.	7.3 The classical-conditioning term for a stimulus that elicits a reflexive response in the absence of learning.
7.20 A response is followed by the removal of an unpleasant stimulus, increasing the likelihood it will recur.	7.12 The tendency to respond differently to two or more similar stimuli.	7.4 The classical-conditioning term for a reflexive response elicited by a stimulus in the absence of learning.
7.21 A response is followed by an unpleasant occurrence, decreasing the likelihood the response will recur.	7.13 Pairing a CS with a stimulus that elicits a response that is incompatible with an unwanted conditioned response.	7.5 A neutral stimulus that comes to elicit a conditioned response after association with an unconditioned stimulus.
7.22 A response is followed by the removal of a pleasant occurrence, decreasing the likelihood it will recur.	7.14 The process by which a response becomes more or less likely to occur, depending on its consequences.	7.6 The classical-conditioning term for a response that is elicited by a conditioned stimulus.
7.23 A stimulus that is inherently reinforcing or punishing.	7.15 A correct response gets "stamped in" by satisfying effects and unsatisfying effects "stamp out" behavior.	7.7 A neutral stimulus elicits a response through association with a stimulus that already elicits a similar response.
7.24 A stimulus that has reinforcing or punishing properties by association with other reinforcers or punishers.	7.16 The process by which a stimulus strengthens or increases the probability of the response it follows.	7.8 The disappearance of a learned response. In classical conditioning when the CS is no longer paired with the US.

7.25 SKINNER BOX	**7.33 FIXED-RATIO (FR) SCHEDULE**	**7.41 EXTRINSIC/INTRINSIC REINFORCERS**
7.26 EXTINCTION (IN OPERANT CONDITIONING)	**7.34 VARIABLE-RATIO (VR) SCHEDULE**	**7.42 BEHAVIORAL "ABCs"**
7.27 STIMULUS GENERALIZATION (IN OPERANT CONDITIONING)	**7.35 FIXED-INTERVAL (FI) SCHEDULE**	**7.43 SOCIAL LEARNING THEORIES**
7.28 STIMULUS DISCRIMINATION (IN OPERANT CONDITIONING)	**7.36 VARIABLE-INTERVAL (VI) SCHEDULE**	**7.44 RECIPROCAL DETERMINISM**
7.29 DISCRIMINATIVE STIMULUS	**7.37 SHAPING**	**7.45 OBSERVATIONAL (VICARIOUS) LEARNING**
7.30 STIMULUS CONTROL	**7.38 SUCCESSIVE APPROXIMATIONS**	**7.46 LATENT LEARNING**
7.31 CONTINUOUS REINFORCEMENT	**7.39 BEHAVIOR MODIFICATION**	**7.47 COGNITIVE MAP**
7.32 INTERMITTENT (PARTIAL) REINFORCEMENT	**7.40 TOKEN ECONOMY**	**7.48 INSIGHT**

7.41 Reinforcers that are (intrinsic) or are not (extrinsic) inherently related to the activity being reinforced.	7.33 An intermittent schedule of reinforcement in which reinforcement occurs only after a fixed number of responses.	7.25 A cage equipped with a device that delivers food into a dish when an animal makes a desired response.
7.42 A way to explain learning by specifying the antecedents (events preceding behavior), behaviors and consequences.	7.34 An intermittent schedule of reinforcement in which reinforcement occurs after a variable number of responses.	7.26 The disappearance of a learned response; it occurs in operant conditioning when a response is not reinforced.
7.43 Theories emphasizing observational learning, cognitive processes and motivating beliefs.	7.35 A reinforcement schedule in which reinforcement is delivered after a fixed period of time has elapsed.	7.27 A response that has been reinforced in the presence of one stimulus occurs in the presence of similar stimuli.
7.44 A person's qualities, the environment and a person's behaviors all mutually affect each other.	7.36 A reinforcement schedule in which a response is reinforced after a variable period of time has elapsed.	7.28 A response that occurs in the presence of one stimulus but not in the presence of similar, but different stimuli.
7.45 An individual learns new responses by observing the behavior of another rather than through direct experience.	7.37 An operant conditioning procedure in which successive approximations of a desired response are reinforced.	7.29 A stimulus that signals when a particular response is likely to be followed by a certain type of consequence.
7.46 A form of learning that is not immediately expressed in an overt response; occurs without obvious reinforcement.	7.38 In the procedure of shaping, behaviors are ordered in terms of increasing similarity to the desired response.	7.30 Control over the occurrence of a response by a discriminative stimulus.
7.47 A mental representation of the environment.	7.39 The application of conditioning techniques to teach new responses or reduce problematic behavior.	7.31 A reinforcement schedule in which a particular response is always reinforced.
7.48 A form of learning that appears to involve the sudden understanding of how a problem can be solved.	7.40 A technique in which tokens can be collected and exchanged for other reinforcers and used to shape behavior.	7.32 A reinforcement schedule in which a particular response is sometimes but not always reinforced.

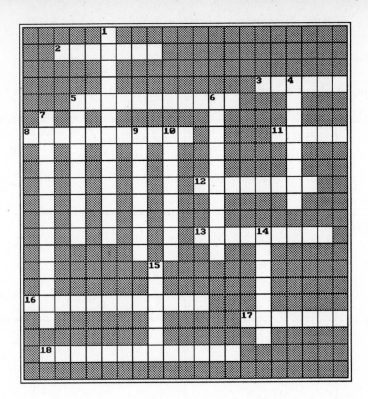

ACROSS

2. extended principles of operant conditioning
3. Russian physiologist associated with classical conditioning
5. depending on environmental conditions
8. emphasizes the study of observable behavior and the role of the environment as a determinant of behavior
11. type of schedule of reinforcement; can be either interval or ratio
12. the pattern in which reinforcers are delivered
13. types of learning involving mental processes
16. broad category of reinforcement schedules
17. an operant conditioning procedure
18. type of learning in which an individual learns new responses by observing another's behavior

DOWN

1. not depending on environmental conditions
4. type of schedule of reinforcement
5. conditioning also known as Pavlovian
6. weakening and eventual disappearance of a learned response
7. increases the probability of a response that it follows
9. a behavior
10. an event or change in the environment that causes, elicits, or leads to a response
14. learning that appears to occur in a flash
15. learning that is not immediately expressed

LEARNING THEORIES

Complete the following chart by providing responses under each model of learning.

	OPERANT CONDITIONING	CLASSICAL CONDITIONING	SOCIAL LEARNING THEORIES
INDICATE WHAT IS LEARNED			
GIVE EXAMPLES			
IDENTIFY KEY FIGURES			
LIST KEY TERMS			
LIST PRINCIPLES			

PRACTICE TEST 1

1.   Learning is
      A.   memorization of information.
      B.   acquisition of practical skills.
      C.   any relatively permanent change in behavior that occurs because of experience.
      D.   any relatively permanent change in behavior.

2.   A neutral stimulus becomes a conditioned stimulus by
      A.   preceding it with an unconditioned stimulus.
      B.   following it with an unconditioned stimulus.
      C.   pairing it with an conditioned response.
      D.   reinforcing it.

3.   Once a neutral stimulus becomes a conditioned stimulus, it
      A.   can elicit a conditioned response.
      B.   can elicit an unconditioned response.
      C.   elicits a voluntary response.
      D.   elicits none of the above.

4.   A loud, sudden clap behind a child causes the child to cry. The child's tears are called the
      A.   conditioned stimulus.   B.   unconditioned stimulus.
      C.   conditioned response.   D.   unconditioned response.

5.   If a stimulus similar to the conditioned stimulus is repeatedly presented without being followed by the unconditioned stimulus, it will stop evoking the conditioned response. The differential responses to the conditioned stimulus and the similar stimulus demonstrate
      A.   extinction.   B.   stimulus discrimination.
      C.   stimulus generalization.   D.   higher-order conditioning.

6.   If the CS is repeatedly presented without the US what will happen?
      A.   extinction   B.   stimulus discrimination
      C.   stimulus generalization   D.   higher-order conditioning

7.   _____ views state that a CR is learned simply because the CS and US occur close together in time, whereas _____ views suggest that information is conveyed by one stimulus about another.
      A.   Recent; traditional   B.   Social learning; traditional
      C.   Traditional; recent   D.   Classical; operant

8. Tastes and fears are examples of behaviors learned through
   A. operant conditioning.
   B. social learning.
   C. imitation.
   D. classical conditioning.

9. Peter was afraid of rabbits. John Watson and Mary Cover Jones presented a rabbit to Peter along with milk and crackers and eventually Peter could play with the rabbit. This technique is called
   A. operant conditioning.
   B. counterconditioning.
   C. spontaneous recovery.
   D. higher-order conditioning.

10. A difference between classical and operant conditioning is that
    A. classical conditioning does not involve consequences.
    B. classical conditioning involves reflexive responses.
    C. operant conditioning involves more complex responses than classical conditioning.
    D. all of the above are differences.

11. Voluntary behavior becomes more or less likely to occur depending on its consequences. This principle is at the core of
    A. classical conditioning.
    B. Pavlovian conditioning.
    C. operant conditioning.
    D. counter-conditioning.

12. In operant conditioning, a response may lead to one of three types of consequences. One consequence strengthens or increases the probability of the response that it follows. This consequence is known as
    A. neutral.
    B. reinforcement.
    C. punishment.
    D. higher-order conditioning.

13. When a stimulus or event that follows a response weakens it or makes it less likely to recur, it is called
    A. negative reinforcement.
    B. positive reinforcement.
    C. punishment.
    D. secondary reinforcement.

14. _____ is a primary reinforcement, whereas _____ is/are a secondary reinforcement.
    A. Food; money
    B. Food; water
    C. Money; grades
    D. Applause; food

15. Cindy's teacher tells her parents, "Cindy's misbehavior is just for attention. You should just ignore her and it should stop." Cindy's teacher is using what principle?
    A. primary reinforcement
    B. extinction
    C. stimulus generalization
    D. stimulus discrimination

16. You want your roommate to be neater. Though you've told her several times, she never manages to clean up. You've made a plan that every time she does any of the five things you've asked her to do, you will reward her on what she's done and overlook what she has not done. Eventually, you plan to give her the rewards only after she has done more of the tasks you want her to do. This plan is an example of which technique?
    A. primary reinforcement
    B. extinction
    C. shaping
    D. stimulus generalization

17. Receiving your pay check every Friday represents what type of reinforcement schedule?
    A. fixed-interval
    B. fixed-ratio
    C. variable-interval
    D. variable-ratio

18. You take a quiz on every chapter in psychology. Some chapters are covered in one class and some chapters require two classes. This is a _____ reinforcement schedule?
    A. fixed-interval
    B. fixed-ratio
    C. variable-interval
    D. variable-ratio

19. You wear your "lucky sweater" whenever you have a test because you got an "A" on two tests while wearing that sweater. This is an example of
    A. a fixed-interval schedule.
    B. stimulus generalization.
    C. a learned superstition.
    D. none of the above.

20. One disadvantage of punishment is
    A. the effects of punishment are enduring.
    B. punishment conveys a great deal of information, sometimes too much to absorb.
    C. most behavior is too difficult to punish immediately.
    D. all of the above.

21. Although operant techniques have produced dramatic successes in real-world settings, some problems that can occur with behavior modification include
    A. the fact that extrinsic reinforcers may undermine intrinsic motivation.
    B. the possibility that it may crush creativity.
    C. a refusal to cooperate, since people perceive they are being manipulated.
    D. all of the above.

22. While at overnight camp, Jesse's counselor tells him that when campers make their beds, pass inspection and are on time for all activities, they get a chip. At the end of the week, they can turn their chips in for candy at the camp store. This is called
    A. reciprocal determinism.
    B. an example of classical conditioning in the real-world.
    C. a token economy.
    D. a variable-interval schedule of reinforcement.

23. Social learning theories differ from conditioning models of learning in that
    A. proponents study higher-level cognitive processes as well as environmental influences.
    B. social learning theories do not utilize discrimination and generalization.
    C. they are more scientific than conditioning models of learning.
    D. they focus almost exclusively on the use of primary reinforcers.

24. Which of the following are among the main influences identified by social learning theories?
    A. reciprocal determinism   B. observational learning
    C. perceptions and interpretations of events   D. all of the above

25. Cognitive models of learning believe that
    A. insight can be understood in terms of the organism's conditioning history.
    B. learning occurs as a result of reinforcers in combination with the influence of a person's attitudes, beliefs and expectations
    C. behavior can be explained in terms of "ABCs:" antecedents, behaviors and consequences.
    D. learning occurs because of the associations between stimuli and responses.

PRACTICE TEST 2

1. Classical is to operant as
   A. learning is to instinct.
   B. voluntary is to involuntary.
   C. involuntary is to voluntary.
   D. unlearned is to instinct.

2. Every time I open any can of food, my cat Luna, comes running. The food is
   A. an unconditioned stimulus.
   B. an unconditioned response.
   C. a conditioned stimulus.
   D. a conditioned response.

3. In the example in question 2, the can opener is
   A. an unconditioned stimulus.
   B. an unconditioned response.
   C. a conditioned stimulus.
   D. a conditioned response.

4. Behra was once bitten by a collie. He is now afraid of all dogs. His fear of dogs represents
   A. extinction.
   B. stimulus generalization.
   C. stimulus discrimination.
   D. spontaneous recovery.

5. Behra was once bitten by a collie. He now has a phobia of collies but is fine with other dogs. This is an example of
   A. extinction.
   B. stimulus generalization.
   C. stimulus discrimination.
   D. spontaneous recovery.

6. When Olimpia threw tantrums, her father spent a lot of time with her to calm her down. After a while, he began to ignore this behavior and eventually it lessened. Ignoring her behavior is an example of
   A. extinction.
   B. stimulus generalization.
   C. stimulus discrimination.
   D. spontaneous recovery.

7. Which of the following was most likely learned through classical conditioning?
   A. I once got sick on Chinese food and now I hate it.
   B. Since elementary school I've learned to raise my hand in class.
   C. After losing pay once, I learned to come to work on time.
   D. all of the above

173

8.   If, after conditioning little Albert to be afraid of rats, Watson had paired the rat with milk and cookies, he would have been using
       A.   extinction.   B.   stimulus generalization.
       C.   counter-conditioning.   D.   systematic desensitization.

9.   Extinction, stimulus generalization and stimulus discrimination are principles of
       A.   classical conditioning only.   B.   operant conditioning only.
       C.   classical and operant conditioning. D.   counter-conditioning.

10.   "Since you took out the garbage, you don't have to do the dishes." Which learning principle does this represent?
       A.   positive reinforcement   B.   punishment
       C.   negative reinforcement   D.   primary reinforcement

11.   "Since you came home after curfew, you are grounded." This represents
       A.   positive reinforcement.   B.   punishment.
       C.   negative reinforcement.   D.   primary reinforcement.

12.   "Since you got all A's, you get to go on vacation." This represents
       A.   positive reinforcement.   B.   punishment.
       C.   negative reinforcement.   D.   primary reinforcement.

13.   Not having to do the dishes and getting to take a vacation are
       A.   primary reinforcers.   B.   punishers.
       C.   secondary reinforcers.   D.   higher-order conditioning.

14.   Liza learned to raise her hand in class when she was in first grade. She has since raised her hand in all classrooms, for all teachers and in all the schools she has attended. Which principle of operant conditioning does this represent?
       A.   extinction   B.   stimulus generalization
       C.   stimulus discrimination   D.   shaping

15.   Liza now has Dr. Falk for a teacher and he likes a free atmosphere in which students speak when they please. He takes off points if students raise their hands. Though Liza continues to raise her hand in all her other classes, she no longer does so in Dr. Falk's class. Which principle of operant conditioning does this represent?
       A.   extinction   B.   stimulus generalization
       C.   stimulus discrimination   D.   shaping

16. When Jennifer throws a tantrum in the supermarket, her father tries to talk to her calmly or to ignore her behavior. Sometimes, he does not have the patience to be calm and he just gives her a cookie to quiet her down. He has put her on
    A.   a partial reinforcement schedule.
    B.   a variable schedule.
    C.   an intermittent reinforcement schedule.
    D.   all of the above.

17. What behavior can we expect in the future when Jennifer goes to the supermarket?
    A.   She will throw tantrums.
    B.   It will be difficult to get her to stop throwing tantrums.
    C.   Though she might not get a cookie each time, she will keep trying.
    D.   all of the above

18. One time Angus got a extra $20 from a money machine. Though it has never happened since, Angus keeps going to that machine whenever possible just in case the error is repeated. He is on a
    A.   continuous reinforcement schedule.
    B.   variable-interval schedule.
    C.   variable-ratio schedule.
    D.   fixed-ratio schedule.

19. A pigeon accidentally received food while hopping on one leg. Though hopping is not the behavior being reinforced, the pigeon continues to hop. What has occurred?
    A.   The pigeon has learned a superstitious behavior.
    B.   The pigeon has been negatively reinforced.
    C.   The pigeon is on a continuous reinforcement schedule.
    D.   none of the above

20. A prison has instituted a program to teach inmates problem-solving skills, life-coping skills and career training. This program addresses which problem related to punishment?
    A.   The effects of punishment may depend on the presence of the punisher.
    B.   Punishment may be reinforcing misbehavior because of the attention received.
    C.   Punishment conveys little information about how to behave differently.
    D.   Those who are punished often respond with anxiety, fear or rage.

21. Nick is a struggling artist who loves his work. He becomes well-known and people are now commissioning him to paint. He finds that his passion for his work has decreased. What has happened?
    A.   Intrinsic reinforcers have interfered with extrinsic reinforcers.
    B.   He has been put on a token economy and does not like it.
    C.   Extrinsic reinforcers have interfered with intrinsic motivation.
    D.   His love for his work has been extinguished through the absence of reinforcers.

22. Maggie is 16 years old and learning to drive. Though she has never driven before, she is able to put the key in the ignition, turn the starter and put the car into gear. Which of the following best explains these abilities?
    A.   Maggie's intelligence
    B.   observational learning
    C.   cognitive maps
    D.   the "ABCs" of learning

23. Mary is assertive, very ambitious, especially competent in handling money, and self-confident. She loves her new job and is experiencing great success. Her co-worker, Claudia who is sensitive to criticism, trusting, friendly and a little naive, is miserable in this setting. Which of the following best explains this difference?
    A.   cognitive mapping   B.   insight learning
    C.   latent learning   D.   reciprocal determinism

24. Tolman's experiments demonstrating latent learning showed that
    A.   learning can occur even though it may not be immediately expressed.
    B.   rats are capable of insight.
    C.   extrinsic reinforcement can reduce intrinsic motivation.
    D.   personality characteristics interact with environmental influences.

25. How do behaviorists explain insight?
    A.   It is a result of observational learning.
    B.   It is a result of an organism's prior learning history.
    C.   It is a result of latent learning.
    D.   It is a result of cognitive mapping.

PRACTICE TEST 3

1. In the following examples, identify the unconditioned stimulus, unconditioned response, conditioned stimulus and conditioned response.

   A. When your father is angry with you, he calls you by both your first and middle names. Every time you hear him call you that way, you become anxious.

   B. You keep your dog's leash in the front closet. Every time you go to get something out of the closet, Fido comes running excitedly and waits to go out.

   C. Your true love wears a certain perfume. Every time you smell that perfume, you feel happy inside.

   D. You had a terrifying car accident at the corner of Park Place and Main Street. Now every time you approach that corner, you feel anxious.

2. In the following examples identify the principles of classical conditioning.

   A. While caring for your friend's dog, you notice that it displays a cowering posture as you roll up a newspaper. You try this several more times with magazines or stacks of notebook paper and the dog displays the same behavior. You become convinced that this dog is generally afraid of rolled-up paper.

   B. Joan, a dog breeder, has been phobic about Doberman pinschers since one attacked her. After the attack, she felt tense and apprehensive whenever she walked by a Doberman, even if the dog was in a cage or on a leash though she was never uncomfortable with any other type of dog. Recently she has been experiencing a change in her feelings toward Dobermans. She was given four Doberman puppies to sell and since being around them for several months, she is no longer fearful of Dobermans.

   C. At a red light, Bob and Fred automatically tensed and felt chills when they heard the screech of tires behind them. Later, while watching a car race, Bob remarked that the screeching of tires was having little effect on them then.

   D. After Bill got food poisoning from roast chicken, he vowed he would never return to that restaurant nor would he ever eat chicken again. All he wanted was to go home and eat his mother's cooking. As he entered the kitchen, he became nauseated when he saw the turkey sitting on the table.

3. Using operant conditioning, identify whether the consequences in the following examples are positive or negative reinforcement, or positive or negative punishment. Indicate the probable effects of the consequences, according to operant theories of learning.

    A. A buzzer sound continues until a seat belt is fastened.
    B. Whenever Joe picks up a cigarette, his roommate complains and insults him.
    C. Whenever Warren does the dishes, his girlfriend compliments and kisses him.
    D. Whenever Fred skis down the most difficult slopes, he always has a bad fall.

4. Identify the problem or problems in the following examples and, using principles of learning theories, suggest the changes needed.

    A. Ten-year-old Sara is expected to keep her room clean. Her parents check her room weekly and in the past year, her room was clean on 20 occasions. Sara's parents praised her lavishly on 10 of those occasions that her room was clean and on the other 10 occasions, Sara received no reinforcement. This technique has not been working well since on any given day, the room is likely to be a mess.

    B. Baby Ari is not yet sleeping through the night. Every time the baby cries, one of his parents picks him up. His parents decide that after checking to make sure the baby is O.K., they will just let him cry. Ari cries and cries for five nights in a row. On the first four nights, his parents kept to their agreement, but on the fifth night, they couldn't stand it any longer and picked him up. Now Ari is crying more than ever.

    C. Sue is always in trouble in class. Her teacher has tried everything he knows to make her behave: talking to her privately, having her stay after class, and scolding her in public. Regardless of what he does, her misbehavior continues.

5. Below is a description using punishment. Identify the problems demonstrated in this example and suggest a more effective approach.

A parent discovers crayon marks and scribbling on a recently painted wall. Tommy, 18-months-old, is angrily pulled from the playpen, brought before the wall, and harshly told, "No! No! No!", and given a sharp slap on the back of his hand. He is still crying when placed in the crib for a nap. Things become quiet for a time, and then the sound of movement is heard. A quick check shows Tommy is not in his crib. A search locates Tommy in the office room. He has doodled in various places with pens and pencils from the desk.

6. Identify the schedule of reinforcement that is being used in each example.

    A.   Pop quizzes
    B.   Quizzes after every chapter
    C.   Quizzes every Monday
    D. $10 for every A

7. Describe similarities and differences between cognitive and behavioral models of learning.

CHAPTER 8

Thinking and Intelligence

LEARNING OBJECTIVES

1.   Define thinking.

2.   Define and distinguish among concepts, propositions and cognitive schemas.

3.   Distinguish among subconscious processes, nonconscious processes and mindless conscious processing.

4.   Distinguish among inductive, deductive and dialectical reasoning, and between informal and formal reasoning.

5.   List and describe the stages of reflective judgment, according to studies by King and Kitchener.

6.   Discuss six types of cognitive bias that can influence reasoning.

7.   Discuss the role of heuristics in problem solving.

8.   Define and explain the g factor in intelligence.

9.   Distinguish between the psychometric approach and cognitive approaches to intelligence.

10.   Discuss the objectives, uses and criticisms of IQ tests.

11.   Describe the components of Sternberg's theory of intelligence and discuss whether these components are measured on most intelligence tests.

12.   Describe Gardner's theory of multiple intelligences.

13.   Describe factors other than intelligence that contribute to achievement.

14.   Discuss the cognitive abilities found in nonhuman animals.

CHAPTER CONCEPT MAP

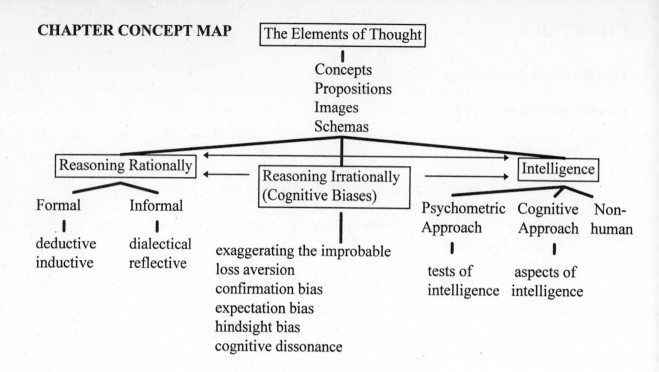

The Elements of Thought

Concepts
Propositions
Images
Schemas

Reasoning Rationally

Reasoning Irrationally
(Cognitive Biases)

Intelligence

Formal   Informal

deductive   dialectical
inductive   reflective

exaggerating the improbable
loss aversion
confirmation bias
expectation bias
hindsight bias
cognitive dissonance

Psychometric   Cognitive   Non-
Approach   Approach   human

tests of   aspects of
intelligence   intelligence

BRIEF CHAPTER SUMMARY

Chapter 8 examines the elements and processes of thinking. Concepts, propositions, schemas and images are all elements of thought. Deductive and inductive reasoning are types of formal reasoning that are useful for well-specified problems that have a single correct answer. Dialectical reasoning and reflective judgment are types of formal reasoning that are useful for more complex problems that require critical thinking. Several cognitive biases affect rational thinking and cause cognitive errors and distortions. Intelligence is a characteristic that is difficult to define but is related to one's ability to think. Theorists examine intelligence from two approaches: the psychometric approach, which attempts to measure intelligence through tests, and the cognitive approach, which examines the aspects or domains of intelligence. Intellectual achievement as measured by test scores is heavily influenced by such factors as motivation and attitude. Finally, psychologists have been interested in the cognitive abilities of nonhumans. Whether animals have language has been studied and debated; both sides of this issue are discussed.

PREVIEW OUTLINE AND REVIEW QUESTIONS

Before you read the chapter, review the preview outline and the Learning Objectives for each section of the text. Develop additional questions of your own based on key concepts and terms and write them in the designated spaces. Answer all questions as you read the text.

SECTION 1 - THOUGHT: USING WHAT WE KNOW (PP. 287-292)

I.   **THOUGHT: USING WHAT WE KNOW**
- A.   **Definition - thinking is the mental _____ of information**
- B.   **The elements of _____**
  - 1.   Concepts - a mental _____ that groups objects, relations, activities, abstractions or qualities having common properties
    - a.   Concepts formed through direct contact with objects, situations or contact with symbols (words, maps, graphs, pictures, gestures)
    - b.   _____ concepts - those with a moderate number of instances
    - c.   Prototype - most representative example of a concept
  - 2.   _____ - units of meaning made up of concepts that express a unitary idea
  - 3.   Cognitive schemas - _____ that are linked together in networks of knowledge, associations, beliefs and expectations
  - 4.   Mental images - mental representations formed through any of the senses
- C.   **How conscious is thought?**
  - 1.   Subconscious processes - _____ of awareness but can be made conscious; include many automatic routines
  - 2.   _____ processes - outside of awareness but affect behavior; intuition
  - 3.   Mindlessness - acting, speaking, making decisions out of habit

Answer these Learning Objectives while you read Section 1.

1.   Define thinking.

2.   Define and distinguish among concepts, propositions and cognitive schemas.

3.   Distinguish among subconscious processes, nonconscious processes and mindless conscious processing.

Write the questions that you have formulated below and answer them while you read.

A._____

B._____

II.   **REASONING RATIONALLY**
   A.   **Reasoning** - _____ mental activity that involves operating on information in order to reach conclusions; drawing inferences from observations or facts
   B.   **Deductive and inductive reasoning** - the information you need for drawing conclusions is specified clearly and there is a single right answer
      1.   _____ reasoning - if the premises are true, the conclusion must be true
      2.   Inductive reasoning - the conclusion does not necessarily follow from the premises, though the premises support the conclusion; requires drawing conclusions from past experience
   C.   **Dialectical reasoning and reflective judgment** - information may be incomplete; many viewpoints compete; no established problem-solving procedures
      1.   _____ reasoning - ability to evaluate opposing points of view; requires more than inductive and deductive logic
      2.   _____ judgment - critical thinking; the ability to evaluate and integrate evidence, relate evidence to theory or opinion, and reach and defend conclusions
      3.   General outline of seven cognitive stages of King and Kitchener
         a.   _____ stages - assume a correct answer exists and is knowable through the senses or from authorities; don't distinguish between knowledge and belief, or belief and evidence
         b.   Middle or quasi-_____ stages - recognize that some things can't be known with certainly, but unsure how to deal with this
         c.   Last stages of reflective judgment - understand that knowing is an active process of _____; some judgments more valid than others

Answer these Learning Objectives while you read Section 2.

4.   Distinguish among inductive, deductive and dialectical reasoning, and between informal and formal reasoning.

5.   List and describe the stages of reflective judgment, according to studies by King and Kitchener.

Write the questions that you have formulated below and answer them while you read.

A._____

B._____

III.   CONFRONTING OUR COGNITIVE BIASES
-   **A.   Problem-solving strategies**
    1.   _____ - a method guaranteed to produce a solution
    2.   _____ - rules of thumb that suggest a course of action without guaranteeing an optimal solution
-   **B.   Exaggerating the** _____; influenced by the availability _____ (the visibility of instances of unlikely occurrences)
-   **C.   _____ aversion** - making decisions based on avoiding loss
-   **D.   _____ bias** - paying attention to information that confirms what we believe while ignoring information that opposes our beliefs
-   **E.   Biases due to expectations**
-   **F.   The hindsight bias** - believing that an outcome was known all along
-   **G.   Cognitive** _____ - state of tension that occurs when a person simultaneously holds two cognitions that are psychologically inconsistent or holds a belief that is inconsistent with the person's behavior
    1.   Conditions under which people most likely to reduce dissonance
        a.   When people feel they have _____ made a decision
        b.   When people feel the decision is important and irrevocable
        c.   When people feel personally responsible for negative consequences
        d.   When people put a lot of _____ into a decision and the results are less than they hoped for; justification of effort
    2.   Limitations exist with dissonance theory
    3.   The motive for consistency can lead to irrational decisions in some cases
-   **H.   Factors that reduce cognitive biases**
    1.   When people have some _____ in an area
    2.   When decisions have real-life consequences
    3.   When people understand the bias

Answer these Learning Objectives while you read Section 3.

6.   Discuss six types of cognitive bias that can influence reasoning.

7.   Discuss the role of heuristics in problem solving.

Write the questions that you have formulated below and answer them while you read.

A._____

B._____

IV.   **INTELLIGENCE**
   A.   **Disagreements exist on the nature of intelligence**
      1.   Factor _____ is a procedure used to identify which abilities underlie performance on certain tasks on an intelligence test
      2.   Some believe in a general ability, or g factor, underlying all other abilities
   B.   **Measuring intelligence: The psychometric approach**
      1.   Focus on people's performance on standardized mental tests
         a.   Types of tests
            (1)   _____ - measure skills and knowledge that have been taught
            (2)   _____ test - measures ability to acquire skills and knowledge
      2.   Binet's brainstorm: a test to identify slow learners
         a.   Measured a child's _____ age (MA) - intellectual development relative to other children's
         b.   Scoring system compared mental age to _____ age (CA) to yield intelligence quotient (IQ)
         c.   Recognized the test sampled intelligence - didn't measure everything covered by the term and should not be confused with intelligence itself
         d.   Brought to the U.S. and established norms for U.S. children
      3.   _____ developed test for adults (Wechsler Adult Intelligence Scale or WAIS) and children (Wechsler Intelligence Scale for Children or WISC)
         a.   Used different scoring system
         b.   Produced general IQ and scores on verbal and nonverbal subtests
         c.   Both have been revised
      4.   Problems with the tests and their use in the United States
         a.   Tests used for different purposes in France and in the United States
         b.   Overlooked _____ and experience differences prevalent in the U.S. population which resulted in the tests favoring certain groups
         c.   Seen by test-givers as revealing the limits of a child's potential
      5.   Culture-_____ and culture-_____ tests
         a.   Tried to address biases present in other IQ tests
         b.   Culture-free tests - non-verbal tests
         c.   Culture-fair tests - tried to eliminate the influence of culture
         d.   Some suggest we should use the differences, not eliminate them
      6.   Beyond the IQ test - some conclusions
         a.   Tests have value but to be effective they must be used better
         b.   Educators must recognize the limits of the tests

                    (1)   Tests don't reveal problem-solving strategies or practical intelligence
                    (2)   When students do poorly, teachers must be willing to evaluate their teaching strategies
   C.   **Dissecting intelligence: The cognitive approach**
          1.   Emphasizes problem-solving strategies
          2.   Sternberg's _____ theory of intelligence - three aspects
                 a.   _____ intelligence - internal information-processing strategies; the only one measured by most IQ tests; involves metacognition, or the awareness of and ability to monitor and control one's cognitive processes
                 b.   Experiential intelligence - ability to transfer skills to a new situation
                 c.   _____ intelligence - practical application of intelligence; includes _____ knowledge, or strategies for success not formally taught
          3.   Domains of intelligence
                 a.   Traditional definitions focus on behaviors useful in the classroom
                 b.   Gardner's theory of multiple intelligences
                    (1)   Seven domains: linguistic, logical-mathematical, spatial, musical, bodily-kinesthetic, and _____ intelligence
                    (2)   These are independent talents and may have their own neural structure

Answer these Learning Objectives while you read Section 4.

8.   Define and explain the g factor in intelligence.

9.   Distinguish between the psychometric and cognitive approaches to intelligence.

10.   Discuss the objectives, uses and criticisms of IQ tests.

11.   Describe the components of Sternberg's theory of intelligence and discuss whether these components are measured on most intelligence tests.

12.   Describe Gardner's theory of multiple intelligences.

Write the questions that you have formulated below and answer them while you read.

A._____

B._____

V.   **ATTITUDES, MOTIVES, AND INTELLECT**
    A.   **Terman study** - showed that _____ was determining factor in life success
    B.   **Study by Stevenson and colleagues**: Asian vs. American students
        1.   American parents more likely than Asian parents to believe math ability was innate; Asian teachers saw studying hard as the key to success
        2.   American parents had _____ standards for performance and for schools
        3.   American students had more conflicting demands on their time
        4.   American students did not value education as much as Asian students

VI. **ANIMAL MINDS** - cognitive ethology studies cognitive processes in nonhuman animals
    A.   **Language and cognition**
        1.   Primary ingredient in human cognition is language
        2.   Criteria for language
            a.   Meaningfulness - adequate ability to refer to things, ideas, feelings
            b.   _____ - permits communication about objects not present
            c.   Productivity - rules allow infinite number of utterances created on the spot
    B.   **Do animals have language?**
        1.   They communicate, but using above criteria, they don't have language
        2.   Early efforts to teach language had good success followed by skepticism
        3.   Newer research better controlled; has found that animals communicate
            a.   Use signs, symbols, some understanding of words and sentences, spontaneous communication, learning without formal training
            b.   Some evidence nonprimates can acquire aspects of language
        4.   Meaning of the studies questioned; concerns about anthropomorphism and anthropocentrism

Answer these Learning Objectives while you read Sections 5 and 6.

13.   Describe factors other than intelligence that contribute to achievement.

14.   Discuss the cognitive abilities found in nonhuman animals.

Write the questions that you have formulated below and answer them while you read.

A._____

B._____

FLASH CARDS

Cut the following chart along the borders and test yourself with the resulting flash cards.

8.1 THINKING	**8.8 SUBCONSCIOUS PROCESSES**	**8.15 INDUCTIVE REASONING**
8.2 CONCEPT	**8.9 NONCONSCIOUS PROCESSES**	**8.16 INFORMAL REASONING**
8.3 BASIC CONCEPT	**8.10 MINDLESSNESS**	**8.17 FORMAL REASONING**
8.4 PROTOTYPICAL INSTANCE	**8.11 REASONING**	**8.18 DIALECTICAL REASONING**
8.5 PROPOSITION	**8.12 PREMISE**	**8.19 REFLECTIVE JUDGMENT**
8.6 COGNITIVE SCHEMA	**8.13 DEDUCTIVE REASONING**	**8.20 PREREFLECTIVE STAGES**
8.7 MENTAL IMAGE	**8.14 SYLLOGISM**	**8.21 QUASI-REFLECTIVE STAGES**

8.15 A form of reasoning in which the premises provide support for a certain conclusion, but the conclusion may still be false.	8.8 Mental processes occurring outside of conscious awareness but accessible to consciousness when necessary.	8.1 The mental manipulation of information stored in the form of concepts, images or propositions.
8.16 The kind of reasoning likely to be found on an intelligence test. The needed information is specified and there is a single correct answer.	8.9 Mental processes occurring outside of and not available to conscious awareness.	8.2 A mental category that groups objects, relations, activities, abstractions or qualities having common properties.
8.17 The type of reasoning problem in which information may be incomplete and complex, and there is no clearcut solution.	8.10 Mental inertia; conscious thinking but not thinking hard; making decisions out of habit rather than consideration of the information.	8.3 Concepts that have a moderate number of instances and that are easier to acquire than those having few or many instances.
8.18 A process in which opposing facts or ideas are weighed and compared, with a view to determining the best solution.	8.11 The drawing of conclusions or inferences from observations, facts or assumptions.	8.4 Instances that are most representative of a concept.
8.19 Critical thinking; the ability to evaluate and integrate evidence, relate it to a theory or opinion and reach a conclusion.	8.12 A series of observations or propositions.	8.5 A unit of meaning that is made up of concepts and expresses a unitary idea.
8.20 The early stages of reflective thought. Those in this stage assume that a correct answer exists and it can be obtained through the senses.	8.13 A form of reasoning in which a conclusion follows necessarily from certain premises; if the premises are true, the conclusion is true.	8.6 An integrated mental network of knowledge, beliefs and expectations concerning a particular topic or aspect of the world.
8.21 The middle stages of reflective thought. Those in this stage recognize that some things cannot be known with certainty.	8.14 A simple argument consisting of two premises and a conclusion.	8.7 A mental representation that mirrors or resembles an object.

8.22 REFLECTIVE STAGES	8.29 COGNITIVE DISSONANCE	8.36 APTITUDE TESTS
8.23 ALGORITHM	8.30 JUSTIFICATION OF EFFORT	8.37 MENTAL AGE
8.24 HEURISTICS	8.31 INTELLIGENCE	8.38 INTELLIGENCE QUOTIENT (IQ)
8.25 AVAILABILITY HEURISTIC	8.32 FACTOR ANALYSIS	8.39 STANFORD-BINET INTELLIGENCE TEST
8.26 LOSS AVERSION	8.33 G FACTOR	8.40 WECHSLER ADULT INTELLIGENCE TEST (WAIS)
8.27 CONFIRMATION BIAS	8.34 PSYCHOMETRIC APPROACH TO INTELLIGENCE	8.41 WECHSLER INTELLIGENCE SCALE FOR CHILDREN (WISC)
8.28 HINDSIGHT BIAS	8.35 ACHIEVEMENT TESTS	8.42 CULTURE-FREE TESTS

8.36 Tests designed to measure your ability to acquire skills or knowledge in the future.	8.29 A state of tension that occurs when a person simultaneously holds two cognitions that are inconsistent.	8.22 The last stages of reflective thought in which a person becomes capable of reflective judgment.
8.37 A measure of mental development expressed in terms of the average mental ability at a given age.	8.30 The harder you work to achieve a goal, the more you will value the goal, even if the goal isn't so great after all.	8.23 A problem-solving strategy guaranteed to produce a solution, even if the user does not know how it works.
8.38 A measure of intelligence originally computed by dividing a person's mental age by his or her chronological age and multiplying by 100.	8.31 An inferred characteristic, usually defined as the ability to profit from experience, acquire knowledge, think abstractly, act purposefully, adapt to changes.	8.24 A rule of thumb that suggests a course of action or guides problem solving but does not guarantee an optimal solution.
8.39 The adaptation of Binet's intelligence test for American children. The test was revised by Stanford psychologist, Lewis Terman.	8.32 A statistical method for analyzing test scores. Clusters of highly correlated scores are assumed to measure the same underlying trait or ability.	8.25 The tendency to judge the probability of a type of event by how easy it is to think of examples or instances.
8.40 An intelligence test designed by David Wechsler expressly for adults; developed two decades after the Stanford-Binet test.	8.33 A general intellectual ability assumed by some theorists to underlie various specific mental abilities and talents.	8.26 People making decisions try to avoid or minimize risks and losses.
8.41 An intelligence test designed by David Wechsler for children. It yields a general IQ score and specific scores for different abilities.	8.34 The traditional approach to intelligence that focuses on how well people perform on standardized mental tests.	8.27 The tendency to look for or pay attention only to information that confirms one's belief.
8.42 Tests designed to eliminate culture bias in testing by eliminating the influence of culture. These tests were usually non-verbal.	8.35 Tests designed to measure skills and knowledge that have been explicitly taught.	8.28 The tendency to overestimate one's ability to have predicted an event once the outcome is known; the "I knew it all along" phenomenon.

8.43 CULTURE-FAIR TESTS	**8.50 CONTEXTUAL INTELLIGENCE**	**8.57 ANTHROPOMORPHISM**
8.44 LEARNING DISABILITY	**8.51 TACIT KNOWLEDGE**	**8.58 ANTHROPOCENTRISM**
8.45 PRACTICAL INTELLIGENCE	**8.52 METACOGNITION**	**8.59 CONVERGENT THINKING**
8.46 COGNITIVE APPROACH TO INTELLIGENCE	**8.53 THEORY OF MULTIPLE INTELLIGENCES**	**8.60 DIVERGENT THINKING**
8.47 TRIARCHIC THEORY OF INTELLIGENCE	**8.54 EMOTIONAL INTELLIGENCE**	**8.61 MENTAL SET**
8.48 COMPONENTIAL INTELLIGENCE	**8.55 COGNITIVE ETHOLOGY**	**8.62 INTRINSIC MOTIVATION**
8.49 EXPERIENTIAL INTELLIGENCE	**8.56 CRITERIA FOR LANGUAGE**	**8.63 EXTRINSIC MOTIVATION**

8.57 The tendency to falsely attribute human qualities to nonhuman beings.	8.50 An aspect of intelligence in the triarchic theory; refers to the application of intelligence and the ability to take different contexts into account.	8.43 Tests designed to eliminate culture bias in intelligence tests. Their aim was to incorporate knowledge and skills common to many cultures.
8.58 The tendency to think that human beings have nothing in common with other animals.	8.51 Strategies for success that usually are not formally taught.	8.44 A problem with a specific mental skill, such as reading or arithmetic, without having a general intellectual impairment.
8.59 Type of thinking involving following a particular set of steps that are expected to converge on one correct solution.	8.52 The knowledge or awareness of one's own cognitive processes.	8.45 The ability to behave intelligently in real life; reveals itself in the ordinary behavior of average citizens; may be unrelated to IQ scores.
8.60 Type of thinking in which side alleys are explored and several possible solutions are generated; associated with creative thinking.	8.53 Gardner's theory suggesting that there are actually seven relatively independent domains of talent.	8.46 Emphasizes the strategies people use when thinking about problems and arriving at a solution.
8.61 A tendency to solve new problems using the same heuristics, strategies and rules that have worked in the past.	8.54 Two domains in Gardner's theory that include intrapersonal and interpersonal intelligence.	8.47 A theory of intelligence developed by Sternberg that identifies three aspects of intelligence: componential, experiential and contextual.
8.62 Motivation that includes a sense of accomplishment, intellectual fulfillment, the satisfaction of curiosity and the love of the activity.	8.55 The study of cognitive processes in nonhuman animals.	8.48 An aspect of intelligence in the triarchic theory; includes information-processing strategies involved in intelligent thinking.
8.63 Motivation that is prompted by external gains such as money, fame, attention or the wish to avoid punishment.	8.56 Meaningfulness, displacement, productivity.	8.49 An aspect of intelligence in the triarchic theory; includes the ability to transfer skills to new situations and to cope well with novelty.

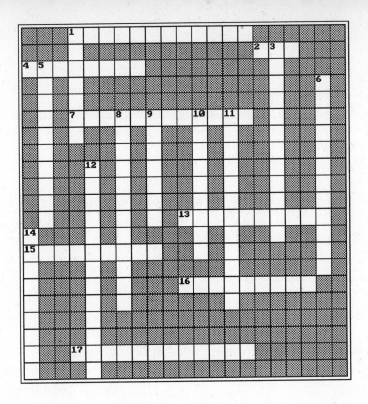

ACROSS

1. cognitive bias in which one only looks for information that agrees with one's beliefs
2. solving new problems using the same heuristics that have worked in the past
4. mental manipulation of information
7. units of meaning made up of concepts
13. tension from holding two inconsistent beliefs
15. drawing conclusions from observations, facts, assumptions
16. type of reasoning in which a conclusion follows necessarily from certain premises
17. type of intelligence in Sternberg's theory

DOWN

1. mental category that groups things by common properties
3. aspect of intelligence that includes the ability to transfer skills to new situations
5. rules of thumb suggesting a course of action
6. an inferred characteristic
8. instances that are most representative of a concept
9. integrated mental networks
10. reasoning in which premises provide support for a certain conclusion, but the conclusion may still be false
11. mental processes occurring outside of and not available to conscious awareness
12. the knowledge or awareness of one's own cognitive processes
14. theory of intelligence identifying three aspects of intelligence

PRACTICE TEST 1

1. The ability to think
   A. is defined as the mental manipulation of information.
   B. frees you from the confines of the immediate present.
   C. allows for the mental manipulation of internal representations of objects, activities and situations.
   D. incorporates all of the above.

2. A mental category that groups things that have common properties is called a
   A. concept.   B. symbol.
   C. proposition.   D. schema.

3. Relationships between concepts are expressed by
   A. super concepts.   B. symbols.
   C. propositions.   D. schemas.

4. What are propositions linked together in complex networks?
   A. basic concepts   B. mental images
   C. prototypes   D. cognitive schemas

5. Knitting, typing and driving a car are performed by using
   A. subconscious processes.   B. mindlessness.
   C. nonconscious processes.   D. none of the above.

6. Nonconscious processes refer to
   A. processes that can be brought into consciousness when necessary.
   B. decisions that are made without thinking very hard.
   C. processes that are outside awareness but affect behavior.
   D. the practice of operating on information in order to reach conclusions.

7. "All cats have fur. This animal is a cat. Therefore, it has fur." This is an example of
   A. deductive reasoning.   B. dialectical reasoning.
   C. inductive reasoning.   D. divergent thinking.

8. Inductive reasoning
   A. is used when the premises provide support for the conclusion, but the conclusion still could be false.
   B. is often used in scientific thinking.
   C. allows for a specific conclusion.
   D. incorporates all of the above.

9. When information is incomplete or many viewpoints compete, it is necessary to use
   A. informal reasoning.
   B. formal reasoning.
   C. inductive reasoning.
   D. deductive reasoning.

10. For complicated problems in real life, it is best to use
    A. dialectical reasoning.
    B. informal reasoning.
    C. reflective judgment.
    D. all of the above.

11. When asked about his views on abortion, Carl responds, "That's what I was brought up to believe." According to Kitchener and King, he is in the _____ stage of reflective thought.
    A. quasi-reflective
    B. prereflective
    C. reflective judgment
    D. none of the above

12. People are more likely to take risks
    A. for a potentially more rewarding solution than for a smaller sure gain.
    B. if the risks are perceived as a way to avoid loss.
    C. when the results are explained in terms of lives saved not lives lost.
    D. none of the above.

13. Which of the following helps to explain the popularity of lotteries and why people buy earthquake insurance?
    A. confirmation bias
    B. loss aversion
    C. exaggerating the improbable
    D. hindsight bias

14. Unless your coursework is totally determined for you, you probably use _____ to decide what courses to take.
    A. an algorithm
    B. a heuristic
    C. deductive reasoning
    D. hindsight

15. The g factor refers to
    A. a general ability that underlies all specific abilities.
    B. a technique using factor analysis.
    C. the psychometric approach to intelligence.
    D. all of the above.

16. The psychometric approach to intelligence focuses on
    A. culture-free and culture-fair tests.
    B. how well people perform on standardized mental tests.
    C. those with learning disabilities.
    D. strategies people use when problem solving.

17. Dr. Bell is more interested in how students arrive at their answers on IQ tests than in their scores. This represents
   A. the psychometric approach to intelligence. B. the triarchic theory.
   C. the cognitive approach to intelligence. D. practical intelligence.

18. Which of the following is one of the criticisms of IQ tests?
   A. Tests are used to "track" people rather than identify strengths and weaknesses.
   B. Tests favor some children over others.
   C. Test-users have thought that tests reveal the limits of a child's potential.
   D. all of the above

19. Componential, experiential, and contextual refer to
   A. Gardner's domains of intelligence. B. aspects of metacognition.
   C. the triarchic theory of intelligence. D. divergent thinking.

20. Which of the following are measured on most intelligence tests?
   A. experiential intelligence B. componential intelligence
   C. contextual intelligence D. all of the above

21. Gardner's theory best explains which of the following?
   A. "idiot savants" B. gifted people
   C. retarded people D. people of average intelligence

22. Gardner's theory suggests that there is/are
   A. three types of intelligence.
   B. seven, relatively independent, intelligences.
   C. seven, highly overlapping, intelligences.
   D. a single, overall intelligence called a g factor

23. Based on the studies comparing Asian and American school children, which of the following contributes to achievement?
   A. whether skills are seen as innate or learned
   B. standards for performance
   C. expectation for involvement in outside activities
   D. all of the above

24. Cognitive ethology refers to the study of cognitive processes in
   A. humans.
   B. children.
   C. the elderly.
   D. nonhumans.

25. Which of the following summarizes the current thinking on language ability in nonhumans?

    A.   Nonhumans are able to use the basics of language.

    B.   Though animals have greater cognitive abilities than is often thought, scientists are divided on this issue.

    C.   Animals do not demonstrate any of the aspects of human language.

    D.   Only primates (chimpanzees and gorillas) have shown any type of language abilities.

PRACTICE TEST 2

1. Which of the following represents some type of thinking?
   A. looking over your transcript to see what courses you still need
   B. knitting a sweater
   C. having a solution "pop into your mind"
   D. all of the above

2. Which concept is most basic?
   A. footwear   B. high heels
   C. shoes   D. clothing

3. Concept is to proposition as
   A. category is to story.   B. category is to relationship.
   C. relationship is to category.   D. model is to relationship.

4. "Professors are intelligent, serious and absent-minded." This represents a
   A. concept.   B. proposition.
   C. cognitive schema.   D. mental image.

5. Intuition is an example of
   A. a subconscious process.   B. a nonconscious process.
   C. mindlessness.   D. a conscious process.

6. Processes that are automated, such as typing or driving, are called _____, whereas making decisions without stopping to analyze what we are doing makes use of _____.
   A. subconscious processes; nonconscious processes
   B. mindlessness; subconscious processes
   C. nonconscious processes; mindlessness
   D. subconscious processes; mindlessness

7. Dr. Rey does not give "A"s. You are taking Dr. Rey's class. You probably will not get an "A". This is an example of
   A. formal reasoning.   B. inductive reasoning
   C. logic.   D. all of the above.

8. Dialectical is to deductive as
   A. deductive is to inductive.   B. formal is to informal.
   C. informal is to formal.   D. dialectic is to reflective.

9. What type of reasoning should Raoul use to decide what to do about his failing marriage?
   A. inductive
   B. dialectical
   C. deductive
   D. all of the above

10. The problem in Raoul's marriage is that his wife is unhappy with their traditional roles. Despite the fact that his marriage might fail, Raoul is unwilling to try anything different. He says "This is the way I was brought up to believe marriages should be." He is in the _____ stage of reasoning, according to King and Kitchener's model.
    A. prereflective
    B. quasi-reflective
    C. reflective
    D. oral

11. During a financial consultation, Ms. Brandt suggests investment strategies for the Washington's retirement plan. The strategy is based on
    A. formal logic.
    B. reflective judgment.
    C. a heuristic.
    D. none of the above.

12. Though Allison lives comfortably in a city with a high crime rate, she is afraid to visit California because of a potential earthquake. Which cognitive bias does this represent?
    A. loss aversion
    B. exaggerating the improbable
    C. cognitive dissonance
    D. biases due to expectations

13. Harry and Larry are in a very boring class. It is a required course for Harry, but Larry chose to take this course and it is too late to withdraw. What is likely to happen?
    A. Harry is likely to try to reduce dissonance by saying he likes the class.
    B. Larry is likely to try to reduce dissonance by saying he likes the class.
    C. Larry is not likely to experience any dissonance.
    D. Both are likely to experience dissonance.

14. Gardner's theory takes the opposite point of view of which approach to intelligence?
    A. factor analysis
    B. triarchic approach
    C. componential approach
    D. g factor

15. The Stanford-Binet and the Wechsler tests represent which approach to intelligence?
    A. psychometric approach
    B. triarchic approach
    C. cognitive approach
    D. all of the above

16. The psychometric approach to intelligence is to the cognitive approach as
    A. problem solving is to test scores.
    B. test scores are to problem solving.
    C. the triarchic theory is to the theory of multiple intelligences.
    D. the g factor is to triarchic theory.

17.   Stephanie is strong in componential intelligence. She should do well on
       A.   conventional mental tests.   B.   recognizing a problem.
       C.   selecting good problem-solving strategies. D.   all of the above.

18.   Though Emily has never travelled overseas before, she is coping well with and adapting
       well to new situations on her trip to Europe. Which type of intelligence is involved?
       A.   componential   B.   contextual
       C.   experiential   D.   metacognitive

19.   How did the use of Binet's test change when it was brought to America?
       A.   The advantages of individualized testing were lost.
       B.   The test was no longer used to bring slow learners up to average.
       C.   The tests were used to "track" people according to their presumed "natural" ability.
       D.   All of the above occurred.

20.   As an item on an intelligence test, asking whether the "Emperor" concerto was written by
       Beethoven, Mozart, Back, Brahms or Mahler represents which problem with this kind of
       test?
       A.   IQ tests are seen as revealing the limits of a child's potential.
       B.   Low scoring children do not get the attention or encouragement they need.
       C.   The tests favor children from certain backgrounds.
       D.   The tests are sex biased.

21.   The fact that people with brain damage often lose one of several mental abilities without
       losing their competence in others supports
       A.   Sternberg's theory.   B.   Gardner's theory.
       C.   Terman's theory.   D.   none of the above

22.   According to Gardner, actors, athletes, and dancers use _____, whereas having
       insight into oneself and others requires the use of _____.
       A.   logical-mathematical intelligence; spatial intelligence
       B.   spatial intelligence; emotional intelligence
       C.   bodily-kinesthetic intelligence; emotional intelligence
       D.   interpersonal intelligence; logical intelligence

23.   Jacob's IQ score is in the upper one percent of the distribution, yet he continues to get
       "C"s in school. What might explain this?
       A.   low contextual intelligence   B.   poor practical intelligence
       C.   low motivation   D.   mild brain damage

24. Based on Stevenson and his colleagues' study comparing the performances of Asian and American students in school, what kinds of recommendations would you make to the school board for improving student achievement?
     A.   Change the attitudes of teachers, students and parents regarding the roles of hard work versus innate talent in math achievement.
     B.   Help parents to increase their standards and expectations for students.
     C.   Reduce outside activities and help students to focus more on school.
     D.   all of the above

25. Kanzi can use a sign to represent food that is not present in the room. This represents which feature of language?
     A.   meaningfulness   B.   productivity
     C.   displacement   D.   creativity

PRACTICE TEST 3

1. List a prototype for each of the concepts listed below.
   A. clothing
   B. animal
   C. pet
   D. relative

2. In each of the following examples, indicate what type of reasoning is most suitable for each problem and explain why.

   A. A navigator must determine the ship's position from the knowledge of a standard formula and the position of the North Star.
   B. A psychologist must determine if nonconformity facilitates creativity.
   C. A scientist must decide whether to pursue a career in teaching or research.
   D. A couple must decide if they are going to have a child.

3. Identify the cognitive biases in each of the following situations.
   A. Richard would rather drive 1,000 miles than fly because it is safer.
   B. Not only did you choose to go to this party 45 minutes away, but you convinced three other friends to go along. Even though no one is enjoying the party, you say you are having a good time.
   C. Jane doesn't want to get married and John does. When discussing the issue, Jane brings up only troubled relationships she knows of and cannot think of any of the happy relationships.

4. In the following examples identify what type of intelligence is being described, according to Sternberg's theory and according to Gardner's theory.
   A. Dr. Morris can go into a big organization and quickly identify the problem and select effective strategies for its solution.
   B. Dr. Mira works with people in psychotherapy and knows which strategies are working and when she needs to try something different.
   C. Regardless of what group of people Nicholas finds himself with, he is able to quickly adjust to the situation, handle himself appropriately and feel comfortable with himself.

5. Do animals have cognitive abilities? Make a case for and against this question.

CHAPTER 9

Memory

LEARNING OBJECTIVES

1. Discuss the reconstructive nature of memory and the implications for legal cases.

2. Compare recognition, recall and priming, and explicit and implicit memory.

3. Describe the information-processing approach to memory and explain its components, including the role of cognitive schema.

4. Describe the "three-box model" of memory and explain its components.

5. Describe the parallel distributed processing model of memory.

6. Discuss the role of sensory memory, including icons and echoes.

7. Describe the processes and limitations of short-term memory (STM), and list and discuss ways STM can be expanded.

8. Describe the characteristics of long-term memory (LTM), and explain how information is organized.

9. Distinguish between procedural and declarative memories and between semantic and episodic memories.

10. Explain the limitations of the three-box model in accounting for the serial position effect.

11. Describe techniques for keeping information in short-term memory and for transferring information to long-term memory.

12. Summarize current findings about the physiological processes involved in memory.

13. List and discuss theories of why forgetting occurs.

14. Discuss hypotheses about why childhood amnesia occurs.

15. Describe the relationship between a person's "life story" and actual memories.

CHAPTER CONCEPT MAP

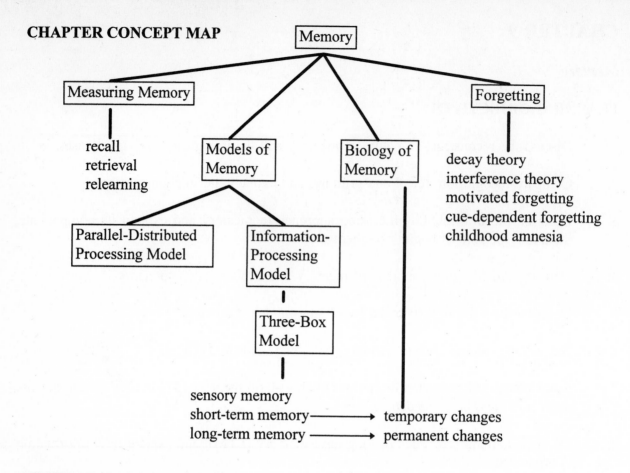

BRIEF CHAPTER SUMMARY

Chapter 9 examines the nature of memory. Memory does not record events like a video camera to be replayed at a later time. Rather, our memories incorporate outside information into our recollections so that what we recall is a reconstruction of events and not necessarily a memory of them. Memory is tested using the recall, retrieval and relearning methods. There are two prominent models of memory: the information-processing model, which compares memory processes to computer processes, and the parallel-distributed processing model, which states that knowledge is represented as connections among thousands of processing units operating in parallel. The three-box model, an information-processing model, suggests that there are three types of memory: sensory memory, short-term memory and long-term memory. Psychologists are interested in knowing what kinds of brain changes take place when we store information. Research examines memory and its relationship to neurons, brain structures and hormones. There are several different theories to explain why we forget. They include the decay theory, interference theory, the theory of motivated forgetting, cue-dependent forgetting and theories about childhood amnesia

PREVIEW OUTLINES AND REVIEW QUESTIONS

Before you read the chapter, review the preview outline and the Learning Objectives for each section of the text. Develop additional questions of your own based on key concepts and terms and write them in the designated spaces. Answer all questions as you read the text.

SECTION 1 - RECONSTRUCTING THE PAST (PP. 327-336)

I. **RECONSTRUCTING THE PAST**
   A. **Definition** - memory is the capacity to retain and _____ information
   B. **The manufacture of memory** - a _____ process
      1. Process of reconstruction seen in patients with _____ amnesia - inability to form lasting memories for new events and facts
      2. Other information is integrated into memories and can't be distinguished
      3. Some information can be recalled, but not necessarily all
      4. No evidence that all memories last forever; they can be wiped out by new information or become inaccessible
      5. _____ memories - memories of emotional events that seem photographic are not always complete or accurate
      6. Remembering is an _____ process; recalling and organizing information
   C. **The eyewitness on trial**
      1. People fill in missing pieces from memories, so eyewitness testimony can be incorrect
      2. Recollection of past events influenced by the way a question is asked
      3. Studies on children's testimony describe the conditions under which a child might be suggestible
         a. When the child is very _____
         b. When the child is influenced by other children's stories
         c. When the child has a desire to please an interviewer; will change answers if questions are repeated
         d. When the child is pressured by adults

Answer this Learning Objective while you read Section 1.

1. Discuss the reconstructive nature of memory and the implications for legal cases.

Write the questions that you have formulated below and answer them while you read.

A._____

B._____

SECTION 2 - TAKING MEMORY'S MEASURE (PP. 336-338)
SECTION 3 - MODELS OF MEMORY (PP. 338-343)

II.   **TAKING MEMORY'S MEASURE**
       A.   **Ways to measure _____ memory (conscious recollection)**
           1.   Recall - the ability to retrieve information that is not present
           2.   _____ - the ability to identify information you already knew
           3.   Relearning (or savings) - the ability to relearn information already learned
       B.   **Priming - a way to measure _____ memory**
III.   **MODELS OF MEMORY**
       A.   **Information processing models are based on computers**
           1.   Remembering begins with _____ information for brain storage
               a.   Not an exact replica of experience, changed to fit existing schema
               b.   Information stored as units of meaning, auditory and visual images
               c.   Some encoding is _____, others require effort to encode
           2.   After encoding, next step is storage (maintenance of memory over time)
           3.   After storage, then retrieval (recovery of stored memory)
       B.   **Three-box model - interacting systems required for information-processing**
           1.   _____ memory - retains incoming information for a second or two
           2.   Short-term memory (STM) - holds limited amount for about 30 seconds
           3.   Long-term memory (LTM) - accounts for longer storage
       C.   **Parallel _____ processing model - rejects information-processing models**
           1.   Maintains that memory is different than a computer; processes information simultaneously
           2.   Considers knowledge to be connections among thousands of units

Answer these Learning Objectives while you read Sections 2 and 3.

2.   Distinguish among recognition, recall, priming and between explicit and implicit memory.

3.   Describe the information-processing approach to memory and explain its components

4.   Describe the "three-box model" of memory and explain its components.

5.   Describe the parallel distributed processing model of memory.

Write the questions that you have formulated below and answer them while you read.

A._____

B._____

SECTION 4 - THE THREE BOX MODEL (PP. 343-350)

IV.   **THE THREE BOX MODEL**
- A.   **Fleeting impressions: Sensory memory** (entryway of memory)
  - 1.   Includes separate memory subsystems called sensory _____
  - 2.   Stores information as _____ images (icons) and auditory images (echoes)
  - 3.   Acts as a holding bin until we select items for attention
- B.   **Memory's work area: Short-term memory** (working memory)
  - 1.   Holds information up to about 30 seconds as an encoded representation
  - 2.   Transfers information to LTM or information decays and is lost
  - 3.   Holds information retrieved from _____ for temporary use
  - 4.   Holds seven (plus or minus two) chunks of information
- C.   **Final Destination: Long-term memory**
  - 1.   Organizes information according to _____ categories, sound and form
  - 2.   Contents of long-term memory
    - a.   _____ memories - knowing how
    - b.   Declarative memories - knowing that
      - (1)   Semantic memories - internal representations of the world
      - (2)   _____ memories - representations of experienced events
  - 3.   Transfer of information from short-term to long-term memory is a riddle
  - 4.   Serial position effect
    - a.   This model has been used to explain recency and _____ effects
    - b.   Cannot fully explain serial position effect

Answer these Learning Objectives while you read Section 4.

6.   Discuss the role of sensory memory, including icons and echoes.

7.   Describe the processes and limitations of STM, and discuss ways STM can be expanded.

8.   Describe the characteristics of LTM, and explain how information is organized.

9.   Distinguish among procedural, declarative, semantic and episodic memories.

10.   Explain the limitations of the three-box model in accounting for the serial position effect.

Write the questions that you have formulated below and answer them while you read.

A._____

B._____ _____

SECTION 5 - HOW TO REMEMBER (PP. 350-353) AND
SECTION 6 - THE BIOLOGY OF MEMORY (PP. 353-358)

V.   **HOW TO REMEMBER**
    A.   **Rehearsal (review or practice)**
    B.   **Techniques**
        1.   _____ rehearsal - maintains in STM but doesn't lead to LTM retention
        2.   _____ rehearsal (elaboration of encoding) - interacting with items
        3.   Deep processing (processing of _____) - analysis of meaning
        4.   Mnemonics - strategies for encoding, storing and retaining information
VI.   **THE BIOLOGY OF MEMORY**
    A.   **Changes in _____ and synapses**
        1.   STM retention does not involve permanent _____ changes but changes neuron's ability to release _____
        2.   LTM changes involve permanent structural changes in the brain
            a.   Long-term _____ occurs - synaptic pathways get more excitable
            b.   Two main and several minor physical changes cause this
            c.   Time required for physical changes to occur in LTM is _____
    B.   **Locating memories**
        1.   Unclear whether neuronal changes are localized or _____
        2.   Particular brain structures responsible for certain types of memories
            a.   Formation of declarative memories involve _____ and parts of the temporal lobe cortex (not necessarily involved in storage)
            b.   Procedural memories involves the amygdala, cerebellum
            c.   Different brain involvement for _____ and explicit memory tasks
    C.   **Hormones and memory**
        1.   May be involved in _____ or intense memories
        2.   Regulate or modulate the storage of information
        3.   Conclusion - moderate emotional arousal important in memory

Answer these Learning Objectives while you read Sections 5 and 6.

11.   Describe techniques to keep information in STM and to transfer it to LTM.

12.   Summarize current findings about the physiological processes involved in memory.

Write the questions that you have formulated below and answer them while you read.

A._____

B._____

VII.   **WHY WE FORGET**
   A.   **The decay theory** - memories _____ with time; doesn't apply well to LTM
   B.   **New memories for old** - new information wipes out old information
   C.   **Interference**
      1.   Retroactive interference - new information interferes with old
      2.   _____ interference - old information interferes with new
   D.   **Motivated forgetting** - Freud said painful memories blocked from consciousness
   E.   **Cue-dependent forgetting** - forgetting due to lack of retrieval cues
      1.   Retrieval cues important for remembering
      2.   Cues may work by getting us into the right area of memory
      3.   Context or mental/physical states can be retrieval cues (state-dependent memory)
VIII.   **AUTOBIOGRAPHICAL MEMORIES: THE WAY WE WERE**
   A.   **Childhood amnesia: The missing years** - the inability to remember things from the first years of life
      1.   May occur because hippocampal or cortical areas involved in LTM storage not well developed for some years after birth
      2.   Cognitive scientists explain it as lack of emergence of cognitive self
      3.   Cognitive and information processing abilities differ between children and adults making it difficult to reconstruct early events
   B.   **Memory and narrative: The stories of our lives**
      1.   Narratives are a unifying theme to organize the events of our lives
      2.   Narratives rely on memory, which is constructed
      3.   Implicit theories about how things work guide our stories

Answer these Learning Objectives while you read Sections 7 and 8.

13.   List and discuss theories of why forgetting occurs.

14.   Discuss hypotheses about why childhood amnesia occurs.

15.   Describe the relationship between a person's "life story" and actual memories.

Write the questions that you have formulated below and answer them while you read.

A._____

B._____

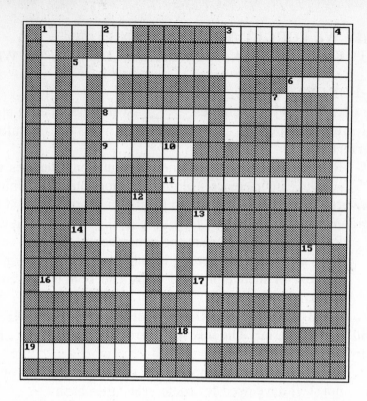

ACROSS

1. capacity to retain and retrieve information
3. type of memory that includes general knowledge, facts, rules
5. ability to identify previously encountered material
6. items that help us find specific information
8. maintenance of material over time
9. ability to retrieve and reproduce from memory previously encountered material
11. stories people live by
14. system of memory involved in the retention of information for brief periods
16. loss of ability to remember
17. memories for personally experienced events
18. the effect of improved ability to recall items at the beginning of a list
19. type of interference

DOWN

1. strategies and tricks for improving memory
2. the addition, deletion and changing of elements in ways that help make sense of information
3. memory system that momentarily preserves extremely accurate sensory images
4. memory becomes durable; the process by which long-term memory becomes stable
5. the recovery of stored material
7. level of processing of information
10. memory system with a theoretically unlimited capacity
12. type of amnesia
13. type of memory for the performance of actions
15. forgetting over time

FLASH CARDS

Cut the following chart along the borders and test yourself with the resulting flash cards.

9.1 MEMORY	9.8 RECOGNITION	9.15 PROPOSITION
9.2 RECONSTRUCTION OF MEMORY	9.9 RELEARNING METHOD	9.16 EFFORTFUL ENCODING
9.3 ANTEROGRADE AMNESIA	9.10 IMPLICIT MEMORY	9.17 AUTOMATIC ENCODING
9.4 FLASHBULB MEMORIES	9.11 PRIMING	9.18 STORAGE
9.5 LEADING QUESTIONS	9.12 INFORMATION-PROCESSING MODELS	9.19 RETRIEVAL
9.6 EXPLICIT MEMORY	9.13 ENCODING	9.20 "THREE-BOX MODEL"
9.7 RECALL	9.14 COGNITIVE SCHEMA	9.21 PARALLEL DISTRIBUTED PROCESSING MODELS (PDP)

9.15 Similar to sentences, but they express unitary ideas and are made up of abstract concepts rather than words.	9.8 The ability to identify previously encountered material.	9.1 The capacity to retain and retrieve information, the mental structures that account for this capacity and the material that's retained.
9.16 A type of encoding that requires effort; necessary for certain types of information, such as school work.	9.9 A method for measuring retention that compares the time required to relearn material with the time used in the initial learning.	9.2 The addition, deletion and changing of elements in ways that help make sense of information and events.
9.17 A type of encoding that occurs without effort; certain types of information, such as location in time and space, occur effortlessly.	9.10 Unconscious retention in memory, as evidenced by the effect of a previous experience or information on current thoughts or actions.	9.3 The inability to form lasting memories for new events and facts.
9.18 The maintenance of material over time; the second step in information-processing models of remembering.	9.11 A method for measuring implicit memory.	9.4 Vivid, detailed recollections of the circumstances in which one learned of a surprising event, or of the event itself.
9.19 The recovery of stored material; the third step in information-processing models of remembering.	9.12 Models for understanding memory that liken the mind to an information processor or computer.	9.5 Questions posed in a manner that directs the response in a particular way; can influence what is remembered.
9.20 An information-processing model of memory that proposes three separate systems: sensory, short- and long-term memory.	9.13 The conversion of information into a form that can be stored in and retrieved from memory.	9.6 Conscious, intentional recollection of an event or an item of information.
9.21 A memory model in which knowledge is represented as connections among thousands of networking units working in parallel.	9.14 An integrated network of knowledge, beliefs and expectations concerning a particular topic.	9.7 The ability to retrieve and reproduce from memory previously encountered material.

9.22 NEURAL NETWORKS	9.29 SHORT-TERM MEMORY	9.36 DECLARATIVE MEMORIES
9.23 ARTIFICIAL INTELLIGENCE	9.30 WORKING MEMORY	9.37 SEMANTIC MEMORIES
9.24 SENSORY MEMORY	9.31 CHUNKS	9.38 EPISODIC MEMORIES
9.25 SENSORY REGISTERS	9.32 LONG-TERM MEMORY (LTM)	9.39 SERIAL-POSITION EFFECT
9.26 ICONS	9.33 SEMANTIC CATEGORIES	9.40 PRIMACY EFFECT
9.27 ECHOES	9.34 TIP-OF-THE-TONGUE STATE	9.41 RECENCY EFFECT
9.28 PATTERN RECOGNITION	9.35 PROCEDURAL MEMORIES	9.42 REHEARSAL

9.36 Memories of facts, rules, concepts and events ("knowing that"); they include semantic and episodic memories.	9.29 Part of the three-box memory model; a limited capacity memory system involved in the retention of information for brief periods.	9.22 A model for computers that attempts to imitate the brain's grid of densely connected neurons. Units are linked together in webs.
9.37 Memories of general knowledge, including facts, rules, concepts and propositions.	9.30 Short-term memory; called this because it also is used to retrieve information from long-term memory for temporary use.	9.23 Interdisciplinary field that relates software to hardware to attempt to simulate the human mind.
9.38 Memories for personally experienced events and the contexts in which they occurred.	9.31 Meaningful units of information; they may be comprised of smaller units.	9.24 A memory system that momentarily preserves extremely accurate images of sensory information.
9.39 The tendency for recall of the first and last items on a list to surpass recall of items in the middle of the list.	9.32 Part of the three-box memory model; the memory system involved in the long-term storage of information.	9.25 Subsystems of sensory memory. Most memory models assume a separate register for each sensory modality.
9.40 The tendency for items at the beginning of a list to be recalled best.	9.33 Words or concepts are thought to be organized in LTM according to the word category to which they belong.	9.26 Visual images held in sensory memory for about a half second.
9.41 The tendency for items at the end of a list to be recalled best.	9.34 Condition in which an item is near recall; characteristics about the item can often be recalled, such as words similar in meaning or sound.	9.27 Auditory images held in sensory memory for up to two seconds.
9.42 The review or practice of material.	9.35 Memories for the performance of actions or skills ("knowing how").	9.28 The preliminary identification of a stimulus on the basis of information already contained in long-term memory.

9.43 MAINTENANCE REHEARSAL	9.50 CONSOLIDATION	9.57 RETRIEVAL CUES
9.44 ELABORATIVE REHEARSAL	9.51 DECAY THEORY	9.58 CONTEXTUAL CUES
9.45 DEEP PROCESSING	9.52 RETROACTIVE INTERFERENCE	9.59 STATE-DEPENDENT MEMORY
9.46 SHALLOW PROCESSING	9.53 PROACTIVE INTERFERENCE	9.60 CHILDHOOD (INFANTILE) AMNESIA
9.47 MNEMONICS	9.54 MOTIVATED FORGETTING (REPRESSION)	9.61 NARRATIVES
9.48 LONG-TERM POTENTIATION	9.55 RETROGRADE AMNESIA	9.62 IMPLICIT THEORY
9.49 LONG-TERM DEPRESSION	9.56 CUE-DEPENDENT FORGETTING	9.63 "REMINISCENCE BUMP"

9.57 Items of information that can help us find the specific information we're looking for.	9.50 The process by which a long-term memory becomes durable and stable.	9.43 Rote repetition of material in order to maintain its availability in memory.
9.58 Cues that were present at the time you learned a new fact or had a certain experience are apt to be useful as retrieval aids.	9.51 The theory that information in memory eventually disappears if it is not reactivated; applies more to STM than to LTM.	9.44 Association of new information with already stored knowledge to make the new information memorable.
9.59 The tendency to remember something when one is in the same physical or mental state as during the original learning or experience.	9.52 Forgetting that occurs when recently learned material interferes with the ability to remember similar material stored previously.	9.45 In the encoding of information, the processing of meaning rather than simply the physical features of a stimulus.
9.60 The inability to remember events and experiences that occurred in the first two or three years of life.	9.53 Forgetting that occurs when previously stored material interferes with the ability to remember similar, more recently learned material.	9.46 In the encoding of information, the processing of the physical or sensory features of a stimulus.
9.61 Stories people compose to make sense of their lives; they organize the events of people's lives and give them meaning.	9.54 Forgetting because of a desire to eliminate awareness of painful, embarrassing or otherwise unpleasant experiences.	9.47 Strategies and tricks for improving memory, such as the use of a verse or formula.
9.62 Ideas (often never expressed) about how much certain traits or beliefs can change.	9.55 Loss of ability to remember events or experiences that occurred before some particular point in time.	9.48 A long-lasting increase in the strength of synaptic responsiveness, thought to be a biological mechanism of long-term memory.
9.63 As we age, certain periods of our lives stand out; old people remember more from adolescence and early adulthood than from midlife.	9.56 The inability to retrieve information stored in memory due to a lack of sufficient cues for recall.	9.49 A condition in which some cells become less responsive.

PRACTICE TEST 1

1.   The reconstructive nature of memory refers to
   A.   the alteration of remembered information to help make sense of it.
   B.   the capacity to retain and retrieve information.
   C.   the ability to retrieve from memory previously encountered material.
   D.   vivid, detailed recollections of circumstances.

2.   Eyewitness testimony is influenced by
   A.   the fact that the details of events are often inferred rather than observed.
   B.   memory errors that increase when the races suspect and witness differ.
   C.   the wording of questions.
   D.   all of the above.

3.   What type of memory is measured by multiple-choice tests?
   A.   recall   B.   relearning
   C.   recognition   D.   procedural

4.   Unconsciously remembered material that continues to have an effect on actions is
   A.   semantic memory.   B.   implicit memory.
   C.   explicit memory.   D.   declarative memory.

5.   Comparing the mind to a computer and speaking in terms of inputs and outputs reflects the
   A.   parallel distributed processing model of memory.
   B.   cognitive model of memory.
   C.   information-processing model of memory.
   D.   connectionist model of memory.

6.   According to information-processing models of memory, we
   A.   process information like neurons in the brain.
   B.   develop a system of neural networks.
   C.   encode information and then integrate it into existing cognitive schema.
   D.   demonstrate all of the above.

7.   According to the "three-box" model, which is the first step in memory?
   A.   short-term memory   B.   retrieval
   C.   storage   D.   sensory memory

8. Which of the following is not a basic memory process?
    A. encoding
    B. retrieval
    C. storage
    D. perception

9. Which model maintains that knowledge is represented in the brain as connections among thousands of interacting processing units that are distributed in a vast network and operate in parallel?
    A. "three box" model
    B. information-processing model
    C. parallel distributed processing model
    D. all of the above

10. In what way does the parallel distributed processing (PDP) model differ from the information-processing model?
    A. The PDP model suggests there are only two systems of memory rather than three.
    B. The PDP model rejects the notion that the brain can be modeled after a computer.
    C. The PDP model suggests that information is processed bit by bit, sequentially.
    D. The PDP model suggests that the brain can be likened to a computer.

11. Auditory images in sensory memory are referred to as
    A. echoes.
    B. traces.
    C. icons.
    D. schema.

12. Which of the following describes the function of sensory memory?
    A. It holds information that has been retrieved from LTM for temporary use.
    B. It acts as a holding bin until we select items for attention.
    C. It retains information for up to 30 seconds.
    D. It aids in the retrieval of information from short-term memory.

13. By most estimates, information can be kept in STM for _____ without rehearsal?
    A. one half to two seconds
    B. up to 10 seconds
    C. up to 30 seconds
    D. up to 5 minutes

14. One way to increase the amount of information held in STM is to
    A. group information into chunks.
    B. form echoes and icons.
    C. reduce interference.
    D. use all of the above methods.

15. Which of the following best describes the limits of the capacity of long-term memory?
    A. It can hold from five to nine pieces of information.
    B. It can hold up to 100 pieces of information.
    C. There are no limits to what it can hold.
    D. Its capacity is not yet known.

16. How is information organized in long-term memory?
    A. by semantic category only
    B. by the way words look or sound
    C. by semantic category and by the way words look or sound
    D. none of the above

17. Learning to type, swim or drive is a function of which type of memory?
    A. semantic   B. episodic
    C. procedural   D. declarative

18. Your recollection of specific information for this test is an example of
    A. procedural memory.   B. episodic memory.
    C. semantic memory.   D. implicit memory.

19. Which of the following represents the limitations of the "three-box" model in accounting for the serial position effect?
    A. The primacy effect occurs under conditions when, theoretically, it should not.
    B. The recency effect persists even beyond the time STM should have been emptied.
    C. The primacy effect does not occur in animals.
    D. There is no serial position effect in animals.

20. Which method is the least likely to transfer information from STM to LTM?
    A. maintenance rehearsal   B. deep processing
    C. elaborative rehearsal   D. elaboration of encoding

21. Which of the following describes brain changes in long-term memory?
    A. Some permanent structural changes in the brain occur.
    B. In studies with rats, dendritic growth occurs.
    C. In studies with rats, more synaptic connections are made.
    D. all of the above

22. Decay theory does not seem to explain forgetting in long-term memory as evidenced by the fact that
    A. it is not uncommon to forget an event from years ago while remembering what happened yesterday.
    B. it is not uncommon to forget an event from yesterday while remembering what happened years ago.
    C. people who took Spanish in high school did not do well on Spanish tests 30 years later.
    D. people generally don't remember high school algebra by the time they go to college.

23. Which of the following is NOT an explanation advanced to explain forgetting?
   A. interference
   B. motivated forgetting
   C. the idea that new memories can wipe out old information
   D. explicit forgetting

24. Why is it difficult to remember events earlier than the third or fourth year of life?
   A. The brain systems involved in memory take up to three or four years to develop.
   B. Adults use different schema than children.
   C. Children use different encoding methods than adults.
   D. all of the above

25. Which of the following best describes the relationship between a person's "life story" and actual memories?
   A. Both are quite accurate.
   B. Only memories are accurate.
   C. Both involve some reconstruction.
   D. Only life stories are accurate.

PRACTICE TEST 2

1.   Why does the tendency to reconstruct memories present a particularly serious problem in
      the courtrooms?
      A.   Witnesses will lie to cover their memory errors.
      B.   Reconstructed memories are almost always wrong.
      C.   Witnesses who have reconstructed testimony will fail lie detector tests.
      D.   Witnesses sometimes can't distinguish between what they actually saw and what
            they have reconstructed.

2.   Memories are unintentionally reconstructed in order to
      A.   fit into existing cognitive schemas.
      B.   make a story more believable or interesting.
      C.   achieve a specific goal.
      D.   cover memory deficits.

3.   Multiple choice is to essay as
      A.   recall is to relearning.   B.   recall is to recognition.
      C.   priming is to recall.   D.   recognition is to recall.

4.   As a subject in a memory study, you are shown a list of words. Later, you are asked to
      complete word stems with the first word that comes to mind. You are being tested for
      A.   relearning.   B.   implicit memory.
      C.   explicit memory.   D.   priming.

5.   "When we are exposed to information, we convert it so the brain can process and store
      it. As we process it, the information is integrated with what we already know." This
      statement reflects the
      A.   parallel distributed processing model.   B.   connectionist model.
      C.   information-processing model.   D.   cognitive model.

6.   Which of the following best represents the parallel distributed processing model?
      A.   The human brain does not operate like your average computer.
      B.   The human brain performs many operations simultaneously, not sequentially.
      C.   Knowledge is not propositions; it is connections among thousands of interacting
            units distributed in a vast network and all acting in parallel.
      D.   all of the above

7. Why does the parallel distributed processing model reject the computer metaphor?
    A. Unlike computers, the brain does not process information sequentially.
    B. The brain is not as complex as a computer.
    C. Unlike the brain, computers process information in a parallel manner.
    D. The brain recognizes bits of information, rather than patterns all at once.

8. Pattern recognition occurs
    A. during the storage of information in short-term memory.
    B. during the transfer of information from short-term memory to long-term memory.
    C. during the transfer of information from sensory memory to short-term memory.
    D. while in long-term memory.

9. You call information and ask the number of your favorite restaurant. How long do you have to dial the number before you forget?
    A. 10 seconds   B. up to 10 minutes
    C. up to 30 seconds   D. 3 to 5 minutes

10. What could you do to extend the time that you remember this information?
    A. maintenance rehearsal   B. deep processing
    C. elaborative rehearsal   D. all of the above

11. Short-term memory is to long-term memory as
    A. an oven is to a kitchen.
    B. episodic memory is to declarative memory.
    C. a loading dock is to a warehouse.
    D. an echo is to an icon.

12. Which of the following helps transfer information from short-term memory to long-term memory?
    A. deep processing   B. chunking
    C. elaborative rehearsal   D. all of the above

13. Information is stored by subject, category and associations in
    A. the sensory register.   B. short-term memory.
    C. the sensory memory.   D. long-term memory.

14. You recall from Chapter 7 that B.F. Skinner was involved in the development of operant conditioning. Which type of memory does this represent?
    A. declarative   B. semantic
    C. explicit   D. all of the above

15. Semantic and episodic memories
    A. are types of declarative memories.
    B. are types of implicit memories.
    C. are examples of procedural memories.
    D. exhibit the primacy effect.

16. How does the "three-box" model account for the recency effect?
    A. Recent items are recalled because they have the best chance of getting into LTM.
    B. Short-term memory is empty when recent items are entered.
    C. At the time of recall, recent items are still in short-term memory and have not been dumped yet.
    D. all of the above

17. A list of words has been read to you. You are retested on them one hour later and find that you recall more words at the end of the list. This demonstrates
    A. the primacy effect.
    B. a problem with the explanation provided by the "three-box" model of the recency effect.
    C. ways to extend the length of time information can remain in short-term memory.
    D. the effects of sensory memory.

18. The best way to get information into long-term memory is by using
    A. maintenance rehearsal.
    B. elaborative rehearsal.
    C. repetition.
    D. all of the above.

19. Physiologically, short-term memory involves changes in _____, whereas long-term memory involves _____
    A. the neuron's ability to release neurotransmitters; permanent structural changes in the brain.
    B. permanent structural changes in the brain; changes in the neurons
    C. the hippocampus; the cortex
    D. long-term potentiation; changes in the neuron's ability to release neurotransmitters

20. Synaptic responsiveness
    A. is influenced by long-term memory.
    B. increases are known as long-term potentiation.
    C. increases during the formation of long-term memories.
    D. incorporates all of the above.

21. Pat learned to speak Italian at home as a child. Now when she studies Spanish, she can recall only the Italian words. This is an example of
    A. retroactive interference.
    B. motivated forgetting.
    C. proactive interference.
    D. decay.

22. The idea that you will remember better if you study for a test in the same environment in which you will be tested is an example of
   A. state-dependent memory.
   B. elaborated rehearsal.
   C. cue-dependent memory.
   D. deja-vu.

23. Jocelyn is convinced that she remembers an event that occurred when she was six months old. This is impossible because
   A. parts of the brain are not well developed for some years after birth.
   B. cognitive processes are not in place at that age.
   C. at that age encoding is much less elaborate.
   D. all of the above are reasons.

24. What might explain Jocelyn's early memory?
   A. She has incorporated into her memories stories she has heard from that time.
   B. She is confused or lying.
   C. Certain people have early memory capacity and she may be someone with that ability.
   D. She has intentionally constructed a memory.

25. What is meant by Gerbner's observation that "our species is unique because we tell stories and live by the stories we tell?"
   A. Human beings are creative and imaginative.
   B. Human beings compose stories to make sense of their lives and these narratives then have a profound influence on how they live their lives.
   C. Human beings are basically self-deceptive.
   D. Human beings are natural story-tellers.

PRACTICE TEST 3

1. Identify and describe the three basic processes involved in the capacity to remember.

2. Imagine that you watched a baseball game yesterday and presently retain many details about the game. According to the "three-box" theory, what kind of sequence have such details followed?

3. The home team brings in a new pitcher in the fifth inning. In each situation below, suggest the type of memory most likely to be the prime determinant.

    A. Her warm-up style indicates the fluid and coordinated movements of an experienced athlete.
    B. After several batters are walked, she tells the umpire that the calls are no better this week than last week.
    C. As the third batter steps up, the pitcher indicates to the umpire that improper attire is being worn.

4. Written descriptions of a fight on a school bus have been collected from several students. Explain below how memory processes are likely to influence the various descriptions.

5. While searching the attic, Henry discovers his senior-year diary, written over 30 years ago and not seen since.
    A. According to decay theory, what will have been forgotten and why?
    B. The first page contains the title "Happy Times as a Senior." He tries hard to remember but is not successful until he begins reading a description of his homeroom. This triggers a flood of memories. What variable related to forgetting best explain this experience.
    C. Henry finds another section entitled "Worst Times as a Senior." He is sure there were very few but begins to change his mind as he reads. This time there is no flood of memories, but many descriptions of unhappy moments. Henry wonders whether he was overly imaginative or whether senior year was pretty awful. What variables that influence memory best explain this?

6. For finals week, you had to be prepared for exams in english, math, spanish, italian, and history. How should the sequence of study be arranged to minimize the possibility of interference?

CHAPTER 10

Emotion

LEARNING OBJECTIVES

1.   Describe the components involved in the experience of emotion.

2.   Explain the James-Lange theory of emotions.

3.   Describe the role of facial expressions in emotional experience.

4.   Summarize evidence about the origin of emotion in the brain.

5.   List and discuss the physiological changes that accompany emotional experiences.

6.   Define and discuss the two-factor theory of emotion.

7.   Explain through the use of examples how cognitive processes can affect emotions.

8.   Summarize the conclusions of research related to the historic mind-body conflict.

9.   Distinguish between primary and secondary emotions and describe contradictory views on primary emotions.

10. Discuss how culture can influence the experience and expression of emotion.

11. Compare and contrast emotional experience and expression in men and women.

CHAPTER CONCEPT MAP

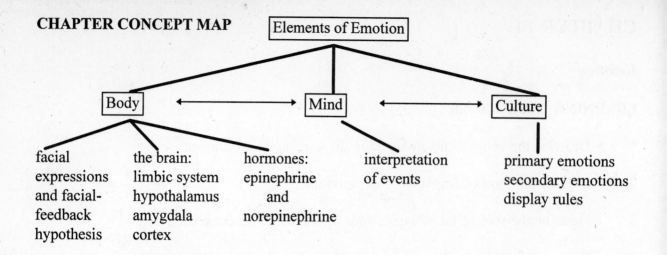

BRIEF CHAPTER SUMMARY

Chapter 10 explores the elements of emotions. Emotions have a physical component that involves facial expressions, brain involvement and hormonal activity. The physiological component does not result directly in the experience of emotion. Events are interpreted, and our perception of events influences our emotional experience. The final element that influences our emotions and their expression is culture. Cultural rules govern how and when emotions may be expressed. Researchers have searched for primary, or universal, emotions. The search for primary emotions is controversial among those who feel that culture influences even biologically based emotions. The research on gender differences in emotions suggests that men and women experience similar emotions, though they differ somewhat in their physiological responses and their perceptions and expectations about emotional experiences.

PREVIEW OUTLINE AND REVIEW QUESTIONS

Before you read the chapter, review the preview outline and the Learning Objectives for each section of the text. Develop additional questions of your own based on key concepts and terms and write them in the designated spaces. Answer all questions as you read the text.

SECTION 1 - ELEMENTS OF EMOTION 1: THE BODY (PP. 375-383)

I. **ELEMENTS OF EMOTION 1: THE BODY**
    A.   **Historical approaches to emotion**
          1.   Early philosophers thought there were four basic body fluids or _____
          2.   James-____ theory - events triggers bodily responses and emotions follow
    B.   **The face of emotion**; facial muscles tied to autonomic nervous system
          1.   Ekman's cross-cultural work: identified _____ universal expressions
          2.   Neuro-cultural theory - face muscle physiology and cultural variations
          3.   Facial-_____ hypothesis - when you feel angry because you are frowning
    C.   **Emotion and the brain**
          1.   Source of basic emotions in _____ system, hypothalamus, amygdala
          2.   Cortex allows us to override emotional response triggered by amygdala
          3.   Two _____ express different emotions; left=positive, right=negative
    D.   **The energy of emotion - hormones influence changes in action readiness**
          1.   Epinephrine and norepinephrine activate _____ nervous system
          2.   Most emotions cause similar physiological reactions; some are distinct

Answer these Learning Objectives while you read Section 1.

1. Describe the components involved in the experience of emotion.

2. Explain the James-Lange theory of emotions.

3. Describe the role of facial expressions in emotional experience.

4. Summarize evidence about the origin of emotion in the brain.

5. List and discuss the physiological changes that accompany emotional experiences.

Write the questions that you have formulated below and answer them while you read.

A._____

B._____

SECTION 2 - ELEMENTS OF EMOTION 2: THE MIND (PP. 383-391)

II.   **ELEMENTS OF EMOTION 2: THE MIND**
- A.   **How thoughts create emotions** - the meaning people give to events
  1. _____ _____ theory of emotion - emotion depends on physiological arousal and cognitive interpretation of events
  2. Explanations of events predicts emotion better than events themselves
  3. Aspects of a person's _____ influence the experience of depression
     - a. Internality - negative feelings attributed to internal causes
     - b. _____ - the reasons for the feelings are seen as permanent
     - c. Control - is there something one can do to change things
  4. Many emotions distinguished by particular thoughts or perceptions
  5. Emotions are complex; occur in _____ but studied separately
  6. People who experience emotions more intensely think in a certain way
     - a. _____ events
     - b. Pay selective attention to the emotion-provoking aspects
     - c. Overgeneralize
- B.   **The mind-body connection** - historically thinking and feeling were considered separate processes but new research suggests otherwise
  1. Emotions and cognitions _____ and change in the course of human development, and so do their interconnections
  2. Relationships between _____ and emotion work in both directions
  3. Cognitions need not be conscious and voluntary to create emotions; there are different levels of cognitive processing and awareness
  4. Both emotion and cognition can be "rational" or "irrational"

Answer these Learning Objectives while you read Section 2.

6. Define and discuss the two-factor theory of emotion.

7. Explain through the use of examples how cognitive processes can affect emotions.

8. Summarize the conclusions of research related to the historic mind-body conflict.

Write the questions that you have formulated below and answer them while you read.

A._____

B._____

SECTION 3 - ELEMENTS OF EMOTION 3: THE CULTURE (PP. 391-395)

III. ELEMENTS OF EMOTION 3: THE CULTURE
  A. Cultural differences exist in norms, norm violations, language for emotions
  B. The varieties of emotion
     1. _____ approach to the concept of emotion - basic-level emotions that people everywhere consider core examples
        a. Learned these earliest, followed by less prototypical and more culture-specific emotions
        b. Effort to identify _____ emotions (those experienced universally): List varies some, but usually includes: fear, anger, sadness, joy, surprise, disgust, contempt
        c. Secondary emotions are more _____-specific
     2. Many think searching for primary emotions is misleading and masks the influence of culture on all emotions
        a. What is considered basic or primary is influenced by culture
        b. Whether emotions are considered universal depends on whether focus is on _____ elements or cultural _____
        c. In general sense, emotions evoked by same situations
  C. The communication of emotion
     1. _____ rules - the cultural rules that govern how and when emotions may be expressed
        a. Tell us what to do when we are feeling an emotion
        b. Tell us how and when we should show an emotion we don't feel - called emotion _____
     2. Display rules of a culture are learned automatically like language

Answer these Learning Objectives while you read Section 3.

9. Distinguish between primary and secondary emotions and describe contradictory views on primary emotions.

10. Discuss how culture can influence the experience and expression of emotion.

Write the questions that you have formulated below and answer them while you read.

A._____

B._____

SECTION 4 - PUTTING THE ELEMENTS TOGETHER: THE CASE OF EMOTION AND GENDER (PP. 395-401)

IV. PUTTING THE ELEMENTS TOGETHER: EMOTION AND GENDER

    A. The experience of emotion
        1. Not much evidence for gender differences
        2. Both sexes equally likely to experience similar feelings

    B. The physiology of emotion
        1. Men are _____ physiologically reactive than women, which might explain their greater discomfort with conflict in marriages
        2. May be due to more sensitive and reactive _____ nervous systems
        3. Men more likely than women to rehearse negative thoughts

    C. Cognitions that generate emotions
        1. Differences exist in perceptions and expectations that generate emotions
        2. Same situation may be interpreted differently producing different emotions

    D. Nonverbal communication
        1. Factors determining sensitivity to emotional signals
            a. The _____ of the sender and the receiver
            b. How well the two people know each other
            c. Who has the _____ - less powerful can read more powerful better
            d. The _____ rules for emotional expression - women permitted to express certain emotions while men expected to control them
        2. Sensitivity to emotional signals often depends on context not gender

    E. Conclusions
        1. Cultural differences greater than gender differences
        2. Situational variables determine emotional expressiveness more than gender
        3. Gender differences in _____ work begin early
        4. Finding gender differences in emotion depends on how emotionality is defined, the individual, the situation, the particular emotion, and the culture

Answer this Learning Objective while you read Section 4.

11. Compare and contrast emotional experience and expression in men and women.

Write the questions that you have formulated below and answer them while you read.

A._____

B._____

FLASH CARDS

Cut the following chart along the borders and test yourself with the resulting flash cards.

10.1 EMOTION	10.7 NOREPINEPHRINE	10.13 CONTROL
10.2 JAMES-LANGE THEORY	10.8 AROUSAL	10.14 PROTOTYPES AND EMOTION
10.3 FACIAL-FEEDBACK HYPOTHESIS	10.9 TWO-FACTOR THEORY OF EMOTION	10.15 PRIMARY EMOTIONS
10.4 AMYGDALA	10.10 COGNITIONS AND DEPRESSION	10.16 SECONDARY EMOTIONS
10.5 LIMBIC SYSTEM	10.11 INTERNALITY	10.17 DISPLAY RULES
10.6 EPINEPHRINE	10.12 STABILITY	10.18 EMOTION WORK

10.13 An interpretation of events that increases feelings of depression. Refers to the belief that one has no control over the situation.	10.7 Along with epinephrine, activates the sympathetic nervous system to produce a state of arousal that allows the body to respond quickly.	10.1 State of arousal involving facial and bodily changes, brain activation, cognitive appraisals, subjective feelings and tendencies toward action.
10.14 Emotions that people everywhere consider core examples of the category "emotion."	10.8 A level of energy that allows the body to respond quickly and is associated with various bodily changes.	10.2 The theory, proposed by William James and Carl Lange, that emotion results from the perception of one's own bodily reactions.
10.15 Emotions that are considered to be universal and biologically based. They include fear, anger, sadness, joy, surprise and disgust.	10.9 The theory that emotions depend on both physiological arousal and a cognitive interpretation of that arousal.	10.3 The notion that the facial muscles send messages to the brain, identifying the emotion a person feels.
10.16 Emotions that are either "blends" of primary emotions or specific to certain cultures.	10.10 Certain interpretations of events make a person respond to various situation with greater degrees of sadness or depression.	10.4 Structure in the limbic system that evaluates sensory information for its emotional importance.
10.17 Social and cultural rules that regulate when, how and where a person may express (or suppress) emotions.	10.11 An interpretation of events that increases depression. Refers to the belief that the cause of the emotion is a part of one's personality.	10.5 From an evolutionary standpoint, an old part of the brain that is the source of our basic emotions.
10.18 Expression of an emotion, often because of a role requirement, that one does not really feel.	10.12 An interpretation of events that increases depression. Refers to the belief that the emotion is permanent rather than temporary.	10.6 Activates the sympathetic nervous system to produce a state of arousal that allows the body to respond quickly. Provides the feeling of emotion.

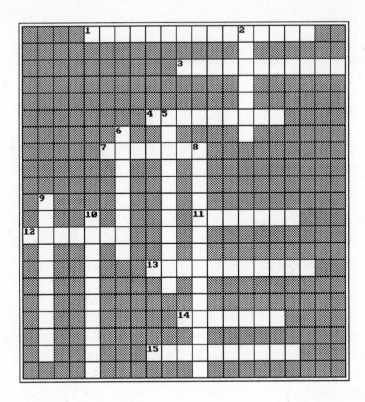

ACROSS

1. hypothesis that facial muscles send messages to the brain
3. theory that emotions result from the perception of one's own bodily reactions
4. emotions that are "blends" of other emotions and are specific to certain cultures
7. state of arousal involving facial and bodily changes, brain activation, cognitive appraisals, subjective feelings and tendencies toward action
11. emotions considered universal
12. the belief that one has none of this can increase feelings of depression
13. the belief that the cause of negative emotions lies within
14. level of energy that allows the body to respond quickly
15. beliefs that can influence emotions

DOWN

2. social and cultural rules that regulate when, how and where a person may express emotions.
5. activates the sympathetic nervous system; provides the feeling of emotion
6. structure that evaluates sensory information
8. activates the sympathetic nervous system
9. theory that emotions depend on both physiological arousal and a cognitive interpretation of that arousal
10. core examples of the category "emotion"

PRACTICE TEST 1

1.   The elements of emotion include
   A.   the face and body.   B.   the mind.
   C.   the culture.   D.   all of the above.

2.   Which of the following is <u>NOT</u> one of the bodily aspects of emotion?
   A.   the mind   B.   the face
   C.   the brain   D.   hormones

3.   "We feel sorry because we cry and angry because we strike." This reflects the
   A.   two-factor theory.   B.   James-Lange theory.
   C.   neuro-cultural theory.   D.   facial-feedback hypothesis.

4.   Ekman's studies found that
   A.   there are 15 universal facial expressions of emotion.
   B.   there are really no universal facial expressions of emotion because of the different
         meaning each culture attaches to the expressions.
   C.   there are six basic facial expressions of emotion and evidence for a seventh.
   D.   all facial expressions are learned.

5.   That certain emotions are registered on the face
   A.   evolved to help us communicate with others and ourselves.
   B.   helps teach young children which emotions are appropriate.
   C.   can cause problems for those who do not wish their emotions to be known.
   D.   is a direct result of display rules and emotion work.

6.   "When I clenched my jaw and knitted my brows, I suddenly felt angry." This reflects the
   A.   two-factor theory.   B.   prototype theory.
   C.   facial-feedback hypothesis.   D.   James-Lange theory.

7.   Voluntary facial expressions seem to affect
   A.   the autonomic nervous system.   B.   the involuntary nervous system.
   C.   the heart rate and breathing.   D.   all of the above.

8. A limitation of the role of facial expressions in the experience of emotion includes
   A.   the fact that facial expressions communicate states other than emotion.
   B.   the fact that people do not always wear their emotions on their faces.
   C.   the fact that there is no way to "peek under the mask" of what people choose to display.
   D.   all of the above.

9. The part of the brain that is able to process immediate perceptions of danger or threat is the
   A.   left cerebral hemisphere.   B.   frontal lobe.
   C.   amygdala.   D.   cerebellum.

10. The _____ can override the response described in question 9 with a more accurate appraisal of the situation.
    A.   limbic system   B.   cortex
    C.   temporal lobe   D.   corpus callosum

11. The _____ is the source of our basic emotions and an old brain part from an evolutionary standpoint.
    A.   limbic system   B.   cortex
    C.   temporal lobe   D.   corpus callosum

12. Your grandfather had a stroke and he is more angry, fearful and depressed than he was before the stroke. What might explain this personality change?
    A.   He may have experienced damage to the right cerebral hemisphere.
    B.   He may have experienced damage to the left cerebral hemisphere.
    C.   He may have experienced damage to the medulla.
    D.   He may have experienced damage to norepinephrine-producing neurons.

13. You are terrified and are experiencing a state of arousal. Which of the following is involved?
    A.   the sympathetic nervous system   B.   the autonomic nervous system
    C.   the involuntary nervous system   D.   all of the above

14. _____ activates the sympathetic nervous and causes the feeling of an emotion.
    A.   Epinephrine   B.   Dopamine
    C.   Norepinephrine   D.   Serotonin

15. One function of arousal appears to be that it
    A.   prepares the body to cope with danger or threat.
    B.   exhausts and calms the body.
    C.   responds to all emotional states with the same pattern.
    D.   makes one feel nauseated and seek protection.

16. Which is(are) involved in the physiological experience of emotion?
    A.   hypothalamus and limbic system   B.   cerebral hemispheres
    C.   autonomic nervous system   D.   all of the above

17. The two-factor theory suggests that both
    A.   facial features and the limbic system are necessary to experience emotion.
    B.   physiological arousal and cognitive interpretation are involved in emotion.
    C.   primary and secondary emotions are necessary to experience emotion.
    D.   display rules and emotion work are involved in emotional experiencing.

18. Chris and Joan pass their friend Joel, who hardly acknowledges them. Chris feels hurt
    while Joan feels worried about Joel. This demonstrates the role of
    A.   the physiology of emotion.   B.   the interpretation of events.
    C.   the importance of facial features.   D.   all of the above.

19. Hannah thinks she is lonely because she is unattractive and does not know how to make
    friends. This demonstrates the _____ aspect of interpretation.
    A.   stability   B.   control
    C.   internality   D.   depression

20. Which of the following reflects a research finding about the relationship between thinking
    and feeling?
    A.   Both emotion and cognition can be "rational" or "irrational."
    B.   Cognitions need not be voluntary to create emotions.
    C.   The relationship between cognition and emotion works in both directions.
    D.   all of the above

21. Primary emotions
    A.   indicate that in all cultures certain behaviors are considered acceptable.
    B.   include emotions that are morally superior.
    C.   are thought to be experienced universally.
    D.   incorporate all of the above.

22. Which of the following represents the position of those who disagree with the search for primary emotions?
    A. There is little agreement in what most people think of as primary.
    B. There is a cultural influence on every aspect of emotional experience.
    C. Some emotions may be "basic" in some cultures and not in others.
    D. all of the above

23. Primary emotions are _____, whereas secondary emotions are _____.
    A. universal; culture-specific   B. desirable; undesirable
    C. culture specific; subculture-specific D. agreed upon; controversial

24. In terms of gender differences in the experiencing of emotion, research suggests that
    A. women experience more emotions more often.
    B. women and men experience similar emotions equally often.
    C. men experience more emotions more often.
    D. the evidence is very contradictory.

25. Where are gender differences in emotion found?
    A. There are some physiological difference in response to conflict.
    B. There are differences in the perceptions and expectations that generate certain emotions.
    C. There are different display rules.
    D. all of the above

PRACTICE TEST 2

1.   Though Terri's heart is racing, she tries to act appropriately as she goes to the stage to receive the award she feels she has earned. As she smiles, she notices she feels better. What elements of emotion are represented in this example?
        A.   face and body, mind, culture
        B.   physiological arousal and interpretation
        C.   brain, nervous system and hormones
        D.   emotion work, display rules and nonverbal behavior

2.   As Sabia sits in the dentist chair, she notices her hands are trembling. After that, she feels anxious. This is an example of
        A.   primary emotions.   B.   the James-Lange theory.
        C.   the facial-feedback hypothesis.   D.   the theory of humors.

3.   Ekman's cross-cultural studies on facial expressions suggest
        A.   certain facial expressions are universal in their emotional meaning.
        B.   people from different cultures can recognize the emotions in pictures of people who are entirely foreign to them.
        C.   that in the cultures they studied most people recognized the emotional expressions portrayed by people in other cultures.
        D.   all of the above.

4.   Dr. Varga is smiling.   Based on the research, what can you conclude about what she feels?
        A.   She is feeling happy.
        B.   She is experiencing a primary emotion.
        C.   You cannot be sure what she is feeling since facial expressions can communicate states besides emotions.
        D.   She is experiencing something positive, though you cannot be sure what.

5.   The longer Dr. Varga smiles, the more her mood improves. What best accounts for this?
        A.   two-factor theory   B.   James-Lange theory
        C.   theory of primary emotions   D.   facial-feedback hypothesis

6. Identify one hypothesis that has been advanced to explain why smiling, yoga and meditation all might improve mood.
   A. They "turn on" parts of the hindbrain.
   B. They all make people feel better about themselves.
   C. They all tap into primary emotions.
   D. They might lower brain temperature, which affects the release of neurotransmitters.

7. You feel a tap on your shoulder outside the dorm at night. What brain structure helps you to evaluate whether this is a dangerous situation?
   A. limbic system   B. cortex
   C. amygdala   D. all of the above

8. Left hemisphere is to _____ as right hemisphere is to _____.
   A. anger; laughing   B. laughing; joking
   C. laughing; anger   D. anger; tears

9. My heart is beating, I'm hyperventilating and my pupils are dilated. Which of the following is involved in this response?
   A. epinephrine   B. adrenal glands
   C. norepinephrine   D. all of the above

10. Benjamin was angry that his friends forgot his 21st birthday until he was surprised by a large party. His feelings of anger and surprise
    A. corresponded to the same pattern of autonomic activity.
    B. corresponded to distinct patterns of autonomic activity.
    C. were different levels of the same emotion.
    D. involved different nervous systems.

11. According to the two-factor theory of emotion, if you are physiologically aroused and don't know why,
    A. you will not feel a need to explain the changes in your body.
    B. your interpretations of events will not produce a true emotion.
    C. you will try to label your feeling, using interpretation of events around you.
    D. you will become irritable and angry.

12. In a series of experiments, students reported occasions in which they had succeeded or failed on an exam. Researchers found that the students' emotions were most closely associated with
   A. whether they had passed or failed the exam.
   B. their explanations for their success or failure.
   C. other peoples' perceptions of their performance.
   D. past experiences with success or failure.

13. Certain events set the stage for loneliness, but the course of loneliness depends on
   A. how long the individual has lived alone.
   B. how the individual interprets and reacts to these events over time.
   C. how often the individual interacts with other people.
   D. age, because loneliness increases as we get older.

14. Which of the following statements is likely to make a person feel more lonely?
   A. "I'm no good at making friends. I've always been that way and there's nothing much I can do about it."
   B. "The people in this city are so unfriendly."
   C. "This has been a terrible period in my life, I've had such bad luck lately."
   D. "She will probably refuse, but I'm going to invite a colleague over."

15. If someone insults you, you are more likely to feel very angry, very quickly if you are
   A. watching a romantic comedy.   B. listening to a quiet flute.
   C. lying on a sofa.   D. at a noisy, crowded concert.

16. Who among the following is likely to feel things most intensely?
   A. Fran always thinks about what she might feel like in a similar situation.
   B. Stan tends to focus on the most upsetting aspect of information.
   C. Dan tends to make mountains out of molehills.
   D. They all have characteristics of people who feel things intensely.

17. Which of the following examples reflects one of the research findings about the mind-body connection?
   A. As we age, cognitive appraisals and emotions become more complex.
   B. You decide a friend intentionally stood you up for lunch and you are angry; because you are angry, you won't listen to his explanation.
   C. You believe that airplanes are safe and at the same time feel worried about flying.
   D. all of the above

18. Schadenfreude, hagaii and isin are all examples of
    A. primary emotions.   B. emotion work.
    C. secondary emotions.   D. prototypes.

19. Primary emotions are thought to
    A. differ in each culture.
    B. be experienced universally.
    C. result in similar behaviors in different cultures.
    D. be blends of secondary emotions.

20. Culture can affect
    A. what people feel emotional about.
    B. how particular emotions might be expressed.
    C. the meaning of expressions of emotion.
    D. all of the above.

21. "Being emotional" refers to
    A. an internal emotional state.   B. nonverbal expressiveness.
    C. how an emotion is displayed.   D. all of the above.

22. Dr. White objects to the notion that it is useful to search for primary emotions. Why?
    A. Different emotions are more fundamental in different cultures.
    B. Culture influences all emotional responding, even emotions that are biologically based.
    C. Most people don't agree on which emotions are really primary.
    D. all of the above

23. Which of the following is an example of emotion work?
    A. A flight attendant gets angry at a passenger when he is rude.
    B. A bill collector expresses sympathy for a person in debt.
    C. An employee conveys cheerfulness, though his boss is demanding unreasonable deadlines.
    D. A scientist smiles after receiving an award for her recent research.

24. Which of the following statements is true?
    A. Women feel emotions more often and more intensely than men.
    B. Men are more likely than women to reveal negative emotions, such as sadness and fear.
    C. Men and women are fairly similar in how often they experience normal, everyday emotions.
    D. Powerful people are more sensitive to subordinates' nonverbal signals than vice versa.

25. Riessman questioned the assumption that men suffer less than women when relationships end, because she found that many divorced men
    A. admitted to being depressed a lot of the time.
    B. claimed they felt very sad for quite a long time.
    C. were expressing grief in acceptably "masculine" ways, such as frantic work and heavy drinking.
    D. expressed their unhappiness by staying in bed or talking about their unhappiness with friends and family.

PRACTICE TEST 3

1.   A.   While enacting a role, performers sometimes report being lost in the feelings they are depicting. How might this be explained by the facial-feedback hypothesis?

        B.   Successful negotiators and gamblers are often described as having poker faces. What does such a phenomenon indicate about the outward expression of emotion?

        C.   Emotion work is the acting out of emotions the person does not truly feel. From the standpoint of facial expression and body language, how might this concept be defined?

        D.   Body language is specific to cultures and is not good as a universal indicator of emotions. However, when facial expression is the clue, the ability to identify emotions universally rises dramatically. How might Charles Darwin explain this?

2.   A.   A nurse looks in on a patient shortly before surgery. The patient's heart rate and blood pressure are elevated, breathing is rapid, the pupils are dilated and the patient appears flushed. The nurse concludes that the patient is fearfully anticipating the surgery. What physiological mechanism produces the pattern observed by the nurse?

        B.   The nurse tries to reassure the patient but he laughs and denies feeling nervous. In fact, the patient is not very cooperative and the nurse begins to feel irritated but continues to attempt to be comforting and pleasant. Explain the patient and the nurse's behavior in terms of emotion work and display rules.

        C.   What areas of the brain enable the nurse and patient to recognize and interpret the nature of their feelings?

3.   Larry, Curly and Moe all got a grade of 75 on a test, yet they each had different reactions to the grade. Larry felt disappointed and depressed. Curly felt relieved that he passed, though he didn't feel particularly happy or sad about the grade. Moe felt extremely happy. Using information about the influence of interpretations on feelings, identify expectations, surrounding events and interpretations of each student's emotional responses.

4. Mary was given a surprise party for her 40th birthday. As each gift was being opened, Mary felt the following: shocked, then touched, by the pet caterpillar from her young daughter; delighted at the earrings from her sister; warmly amused at the cane, laxatives and contributions for a facelift that came from neighbors; insulted and angry over the "girdle for burgeoning hips" from her cousin; and irritated by the insensitivity of her husband's gift of a vacuum cleaner. Regardless of her true feelings, Mary warmly expressed gratitude and appreciation after each gift, and no one except her younger sister sensed Mary's true feelings. When the guests departed, Mary's husband began to assemble the vacuum cleaner. One look at Mary's face made it clear that she was angry. After prodding, Mary heatedly revealed that her own husband might have been more thoughtful. To her surprise, another package was produced. It contained 40 beautifully arranged exotic flowers from all over the world. Mary's husband had sent out for the flowers and arranged them himself, but confessed that he was too embarrassed to give this gift in front of the guests. Mary confessed that she really wanted to punch her cousin. The next day Mary's younger sister called and was virtually perfect in guessing Mary's true feeling about each gift.

A. Why did Mary find it important to express gratitude for each gift?

B. What type of performance is illustrated when Mary feigns gratitude for gifts that disturb her?

C. Mary's husband easily sees anger on her face. Why isn't this surprising?

D. Mary privately displays aggressive feelings toward her cousin. Her husband privately displays sensitivity and tenderness. What cultural mechanisms contribute to such behavior?

E. What advantages does Mary's younger sister have over the other guests when reading Mary's feelings?

F. Examine Mary's reactions to each gift and think about why she felt as she did. Which reactions tend to result from a process of interpretation that involves culturally determined meanings?

CHAPTER 11

Motivation

LEARNING OBJECTIVES

1. Define motivation and distinguish between drives based on physiological needs and those that are learned.

2. Discuss the need for affiliation as a source of human motivation.

3. Describe the importance of contact comfort in early life and the research findings on attachment.

4. List and explain three categories or theories describing varieties or styles of love.

5. Summarize the findings from biological research on the sexual behavior of men and women.

6. List and explain intrapsychic, interpersonal and cultural factors that influence the sexual attitudes and behaviors of men and women.

7. Discuss the motivational factors involved in rape and unwanted sexual behavior.

8. Describe traditional and current approaches to understanding the origins of sexual orientation.

9. List and explain the internal and external forces that motivate people to work and to succeed.

10. Distinguish between the need for achievement and the need for power.

11. List and discuss three types of motivational conflicts.

12. Summarize Maslow's hierarchy of needs and discuss whether motives can be ranked.

CHAPTER CONCEPT MAP

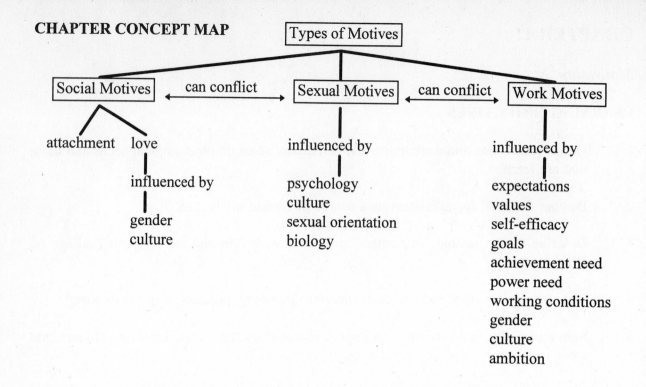

BRIEF CHAPTER SUMMARY

Chapter 11 describes three categories of motives: social motives, sexual motives and work motives. Attachment can develop between children and caregivers and between adults. Three approaches to studying love are described. The attachment theory of love is based on Ainsworth's studies of attachment styles in infants. The chapter discusses gender differences in love and reports that no gender differences have been found in the desire for attachment, but some other differences have been found by researchers. The biological, psychological and cultural influences on sexual motives are discussed. Kinsey introduced the scientific study of sex, which was continued by Masters and Johnson. Coercive sex, or rape, is considered an act of dominance or aggression rather than an act motivated by sexual desire. Different theories that attempt to explain sexual orientation are reviewed. These theories reach the conclusion that sexual orientation is a result of the interaction of biology, culture, learning and circumstances. The motive to work is influenced by internal factors, such as one's expectations, values, self-efficacy, needs for achievement and power, and by external factors, such as working conditions.

PREVIEW OUTLINE AND REVIEW QUESTIONS

Before you read the chapter, review the preview outline and the Learning Objectives for each section of the text. Develop additional questions of your own based on key concepts and terms and write them in the designated spaces. Answer all questions as you read the text.

SECTION 1 - THE SOCIAL ANIMAL: MOTIVES FOR CONNECTION (PP. 405-415)

I. **THE SOCIAL ANIMAL: MOTIVES FOR CONNECTION**
   A. **Definition** - motivation is an _____ process within a person or animal that causes that organism to move toward a goal
   B. **Approaches to motivation**
       1. Drive theory - early approach which was later rejected
       2. Current approach emphasizes unique human aspirations
   C. **Attachment**
       1. Two types
           a. Children to caregivers
           b. Between adults
       2. Need for _____ - the motive to be with others
       3. Emotional attachment begins with early physical attachment
           a. Harlow studies - showed need for _____ comfort
           b. Bowlby maintains contact provides sense of security and trust
       4. Stranger anxiety and _____ anxiety develop between seven and nine months and last until middle of second year; experienced by all children
       5. Ainsworth - evaluated attachment with the "strange situation" studies
           a. Mother leaves baby in a room with stranger and the baby's reaction is observed with mother, with stranger and alone
           b. Identified three _____ categories
               (1) securely attached - cries when she leaves, happy upon return
               (2) insecurely attached
                   (a) avoidant - not caring about the mother
                   (b) anxious/_____ - baby protests when mother leaves, resists when she returns
           c. Maintains that mother's treatment of infant in first months of life establishes attachment style
           d. Problems with the research
               (1) Ignores _____ differences
               (2) Other studies find no relationship between varieties of maternal responsiveness and children's attachment patterns
               (3) Patterns can be influenced by life changes
               (4) Ignores influence of other caregivers

     (5) Behavior can be conditioned
    e. Subsequent research agrees that early care is important

D. **Love**
   1. The varieties of love
    a. Passionate and _____ love
    b. Lee's six styles of loving: ludus (game-playing); eros (romantic); storge (affectionate); mania (possessive); pragma (pragmatic) and agape (unselfish)
    c. _____ theory of love
     (1) Adult styles originate in infant-parent relationship
     (2) Research supports Ainsworth's three attachment styles in adults: secure, _____, ambivalent
     (3) Research supports that some styles of love better suited to stable, satisfying relationships than others
   2. Gender, culture and love
    a. No evidence that one sex loves more than the other
    b. Many studies have found no gender differences in desire for attachment or _____
    c. Gender differences that have been found
     (1) Women more _____ and less ludic
     (2) Men and women differ in how they express love
     (3) These differences influenced by gender role expectations
     (4) Gender differences changing some as women's roles change

Answer these Learning Objectives while you read Section 1.

1. Define motivation and distinguish between drives based on physiological needs and those that are learned.

2. Discuss the need for affiliation as a source of human motivation.

3. Describe the importance of contact comfort in early life and the research findings on attachment.

4. List and explain three categories or theories describing varieties or styles of love.

Write the questions that you have formulated below and answer them while you read.

A._____

B._____

II.   THE EROTIC ANIMAL: MOTIVES FOR SEX
    A.   **The biology of desire** - limited influence on sexual motivation
        1.   _____ levels implicated in sexual motivation
        2.   Scientific sex research began by _____, furthered by Masters and Johnson
    B.   **The psychology of desire**
        1.   Motivations for sex are varied
        2.   Motives for rape - primarily an act of _____ and aggression
            a.   Mixture of motives for rape
            b.   Characteristics of sexually aggressive male: hostile and _____
            c.   Gender differences in the perception of coercion
    C.   **The culture of desire** - sexual motivation and behavior occur in a context
        1.   Kissing, arousal and orgasm affected by _____
        2.   Sexual practices and behavior highly variable across cultures
        3.   Sexual behavior shaped by gender roles and sexual scripts
        4.   Three kinds of sexual scripts
            a.   _____ scripts - culture's requirements for proper sexual behavior
            b.   Interpersonal scripts - rules of behavior developed by a couple
            c.   Intrapsychic scripts - develop out of a person's unique history
    D.   **The riddle of sexual orientation**
        1.   Some researchers say sexual orientation has a biological basis
        2.   Psychological theories have not been supported
        3.   Interaction of biology, _____, experiences, and opportunities

Answer these Learning Objectives while you read Section 2.

5.   Summarize biological research findings on the sexual behavior of men and women.

6.   List and explain intrapsychic, interpersonal and cultural factors that influence the sexual attitudes and behaviors of men and women.

7.   Discuss the motivational factors involved in rape and unwanted sexual behavior.

8.   Describe old and new approaches to understanding the origins of sexual orientation.

Write the questions that you have formulated below and answer them while you read.

A._____

B._____

III.   THE COMPETENT ANIMAL: MOTIVES TO WORK
   A.   The effects of motivation on work
      1.   The influence of expectation and _____
         a.   Work harder if success expected; creates a self-fulfilling prophecy
         b.   Work harder if something is valued
      2.   The influence of goals and competence - helplessness or _____
         a.   Those motivated by goals give up more easily
         b.   Those motivated by learning and mastery see failure as learning
         c.   Goal attainment enhances competence, which is highly motivating
         d.   Competence based on _____ - one's ability to accomplish
      3.   The need for achievement
         a.   Early studies by McClelland using the Thematic Apperception Test
         b.   Differences between those with high and low need for achievement
         c.   Two varieties of achievement motive; _____ (unconscious) motive and explicit (self-aware) motive
      4.   The need for power - desire to dominate and _____ others
         a.   Gender differences in distribution of power not in motivation
         b.   High need for power related to leadership
   B.   The effects of work on motivation
      1.   Working conditions
         a.   Aspects of work influence many aspects of workers' satisfaction
         b.   High income does not increase work motivation, rather how and when money is paid influences work motivation
      2.   Teamwork - often raises _____ and job satisfaction
      3.   Gender, culture and ambition
         a.   Achievement highly related to opportunity
         b.   Glass ceiling for women and minorities

Answer these Learning Objectives while you read Section 3.

9.   Explain the internal and external forces that motivate people to work and to succeed.

10.   Distinguish between the need for achievement and the need for power.

Write the questions that you have formulated below and answer them while you read.

A._____

B._____

IV.   **WHEN MOTIVES CONFLICT**
A.   **Four kinds of motivational conflicts**
1.   Approach-_____ - equal attraction to two or more goals
2.   Avoidance-avoidance - when you dislike two alternatives
3.   Approach-_____ - when one activity has a positive and negative aspect
a.   Attraction and repulsion strongest when nearest the goal
b.   Makes this type difficult to resolve
4.   Multiple approach-avoidance - several possible choices each containing advantages and disadvantages
B.   **Consequences of high levels of conflict and ambivalence**
1.   Some internal conflict inevitable
2.   Unresolved conflict has physical and emotional cost
3.   Associated with anxiety, depression, headaches and other symptoms
C.   **Maslow's hierarchy of _____**
1.   Survival needs at the bottom, self-actualization needs at the top
2.   Lower need must be met before higher needs can be addressed
3.   Popular theory but unsupported by _____
a.   People experience many needs simultaneously
b.   Those whose lower needs are met do not necessarily go on to meet higher needs
c.   Higher needs may overcome lower needs
4.   We each develop our own hierarchy

Answer these Learning Objectives while you read Section 4.

11.   List and discuss three types of motivational conflicts.

12.   Summarize Maslow's hierarchy of needs and discuss whether motives can be ranked.

Write the questions that you have formulated below and answer them while you read.

A._____

B._____

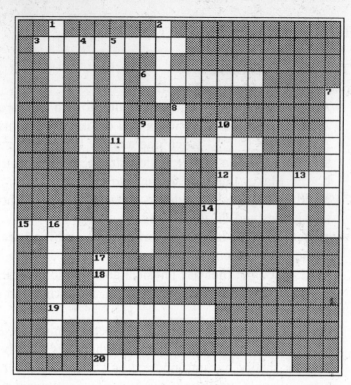

ACROSS

3. causes an organism to move toward a goal
6. cooperative groups working together
11. emotional tie between babies and their caregivers
12. attachment style in which babies seem indifferent to the mother
14. a central, motivating belief reflecting important goals and ideals
15. a type of ceiling that is a barrier to promotion
18. a kind of love characterized by affection and trust
19. a type of motive studied using the Thematic Apperception Test
20. The belief that one is capable of producing desired results

DOWN

1. motives that develop in the context of family, environment and culture
2. learned motive to dominate or influence others
4. unconscious motives
5. motive to associate with other people
7. reward
8. attachment style in which babies cry when mother leaves and are happy upon mother's return
9. type of anxiety babies experience between seven and nine months
10. type of anxiety babies experience when mothers leave the room
13. attachment style in which babies protest when mother leaves but resist contact upon her return
16. half of an internal conflict in which one is attracted to one aspect of a choice
17. expectations that are taught about what to consider sexy

FLASH CARDS

Cut the following chart along the borders and test yourself with the resulting flash cards.

11.1 MOTIVATION	**11.8 SECURE ATTACHMENT**	**11.15 STORGE**
11.2 SOCIAL MOTIVES	**11.9 AVOIDANT ATTACHMENT**	**11.16 MANIA**
11.3 NEED FOR AFFILIATION	**11.10 ANXIOUS/AMBIVALENT ATTACHMENT**	**11.17 PRAGMA**
11.4 ATTACHMENT	**11.11 PASSIONATE LOVE**	**11.18 AGAPE**
11.5 CONTACT COMFORT	**11.12 COMPANIONATE LOVE**	**11.19 ATTACHMENT THEORY OF LOVE**
11.6 STRANGER ANXIETY	**11.13 LUDUS**	**11.20 GENDER ROLES**
11.7 SEPARATION ANXIETY	**11.14 EROS**	**11.21 SEXUAL SCRIPTS**

11.15 One of six styles of loving characterized by Lee; affectionate, friendly love.	11.8 An attachment style identified by Ainsworth; babies who cry or protest if a parent leaves and welcome the parent when he or she returns.	11.1 An inferred process within a person or animal causing that organism to move toward a goal.
11.16 One of six styles of loving characterized by Lee; possessive, dependent, "crazy" love.	11.9 An attachment style identified by Ainsworth; babies who do not seem to care if the mother leaves them and who seek little contact with her.	11.2 In contrast to biological drives, these motives are learned and develop in the context of family, environment and culture.
11.17 One of six styles of loving identified by Lee; logical, pragmatic love.	11.10 An attachment style identified by Ainsworth; babies who protest when the mother leaves the room but resist contact upon her return.	11.3 The motive to associate with other people, as by seeking friends, moral support, contact comfort or companionship.
11.18 One of six styles of loving identified by Lee; unselfish love.	11.11 A kind of love characterized by a turmoil of intense emotions. This kind of love is often highly sexualized and often feels unstable.	11.4 The deep emotional tie that babies and children develop for their primary caregivers, and their distress at being separated from them.
11.19 The theory that adult styles of love originate in the infant-parent attachment. Like Ainsworth's babies, adults can be secure, avoidant, anxious.	11.12 A kind of love characterized by affection and trust. This kind of love feels calm, stable and reliable and is not necessarily sexualized.	11.5 The need for touching; the Harlows first demonstrated this need in primates with their classic experiment.
11.20 A set of rules and norms that define socially approved attitudes and behavior for men and women.	11.13 One of six styles of loving identified by Lee; game-playing love.	11.6 Many babies between seven and nine months of age become wary or fearful of strangers.
11.21 Learned during childhood and adolescence, they teach boys and girls what to consider erotic or sexy, and how to behave during dating.	11.14 One of six styles of loving identified by Lee; romantic or passionate love.	11.7 Many babies between seven and nine months of age become attached to a primary caregiver and show distress if she or he leaves the room.

11.22 CULTURAL SCRIPTS	11.29 LEARNING GOALS	11.36 WORKING CONDITIONS
11.23 INTERPERSONAL SCRIPTS	11.30 SELF-EFFICACY	11.37 INCENTIVE PAY
11.24 INTRAPSYCHIC SCRIPTS	11.31 NEED FOR ACHIEVEMENT	11.38 TEAMWORK
11.25 EXPECTATIONS AND VALUES	11.32 THEMATIC APPERCEPTION TEST	11.39 "GLASS CEILING"
11.26 SELF-FULFILLING PROPHECY	11.33 IMPLICIT ACHIEVEMENT MOTIVES	11.40 APPROACH-APPROACH CONFLICT
11.27 VALUE	11.34 EXPLICIT ACHIEVEMENT MOTIVES	11.41 AVOIDANCE-AVOIDANCE CONFLICT
11.28 PERFORMANCE GOALS	11.35 NEED FOR POWER	11.42 APPROACH-AVOIDANCE AND MULTIPLE APPROACH-AVOIDANCE CONFLICT

11.36 Aspects of work, such as fringe benefits, complexity of daily tasks, pace, pressure and how routine or varied work is; affect workers' attitudes.	**11.29** A type of goal concerned with mastery and increasing competence and skills. Failure is seen as information that will help a person improve.	**11.22** The larger culture's requirements for proper sexual behavior. The scripts differ from culture to culture.
11.37 The strongest monetary motivator; bonuses given upon completion of a goal and not as an automatic part of salary.	**11.30** The belief that one is capable of producing, through one's own efforts, desired results (such as mastering new skills and reaching goals).	**11.23** The rules of behavior that a couple develops in the course of their relationship. The scripts differ depending on the relationship.
11.38 Cohesive, cooperative groups working together on a project. Often raises workers' motivation and job satisfaction.	**11.31** A learned motive to meet personal standards of success and excellence in a chosen area (often abbreviated nAch).	**11.24** Scenarios for ideal or fantasized sexual behavior that develop out of a person's unique history.
11.39 A barrier to promotion that is so subtle as to be transparent, yet strong enough to prevent advancement.	**11.32** A test consisting of a series of ambiguous pictures about which the test taken must make up a story. Used to evaluate achievement needs.	**11.25** One's certainty about success (expectations) and how much one wants a goal (values) influences how hard a person will work to reach a goal.
11.40 Type of conflict in which you are equally attracted to two or more possible activities or goals.	**11.33** Unconscious motives that predict sustained achievement over time due to the pleasure derived from achievement itself.	**11.26** An expectation that comes true because of the tendency of the person holding it to act in ways to confirm it.
11.41 Type of conflict which requires you to choose between "the lesser of two evils;" when you dislike two alternatives.	**11.34** Self-aware motives that predict how a person will behave in a specific situation, because of immediate incentives and rewards.	**11.27** A central motivating belief reflecting the fundamental goals and ideals that are important to the person.
11.42 Type of conflict in which one activity or goal has both a positive and a negative aspect or many advantages and disadvantages (multiple).	**11.35** A learned motive to dominate or influence others.	**11.28** A type of goal that is concerned with doing well, being judged highly and avoiding criticism.

PRACTICE TEST 1

1. An inferred process within a person or animal that causes that organism to move toward a goal is called
   A.   energy.
   B.   incentive.
   C.   motivation.
   D.   the need for achievement.

2. Hunger and thirst are _____, while achievement and affiliation are _____
   A.   drives; needs.
   B.   biological; unlearned.
   C.   unlearned; learned.
   D.   learned; biological.

3. Social motives are
   A.   biological.
   B.   unlearned.
   C.   learned.
   D.   primary.

4. The motive to be with others, make friends, cooperate, and love is the need for
   A.   achievement.
   B.   contact comfort.
   C.   attachment.
   D.   affiliation.

5. The deep emotional tie that babies and children develop for their primary caregivers, and their distress at being separated from them, is called
   A.   attachment.
   B.   affiliation.
   C.   contact comfort.
   D.   security.

6. Harry and Margaret Harlow's studies, in which infant rhesus monkeys ran to soft, terry cloth "mothers" when they were frightened or startled, demonstrated the need for
   A.   affiliation.
   B.   food.
   C.   contact comfort.
   D.   love.

7. Babies who are well fed and sheltered but who are not touched and held show
   A.   retarded emotional and physical development.
   B.   moodiness.
   C.   no problems as long as they are well treated.
   D.   anger.

8. "I try to keep my lover a little uncertain about my commitment to him/her" is a statement that represents which type of love?
   A.   passionate love
   B.   insecure
   C.   ludus
   D.   eros

9. Which of the following is NOT one of the theories of love discussed in the text?
    A. passionate love and companionate love
    B. friendship love, parent-child love, romantic love
    C. ludus, eros, storge, mania, pragma, agape
    D. secure, avoidant, anxious/ambivalent

10. Adult love styles originate in a person's first and most important "love relationship," the infant-parent attachment. Which approach to love does this describe?
    A. affiliation theory   B. Lee's theory
    C. attachment theory of love   D. narrative theory of love

11. Kinsey made which of the following observations about biological differences in sexual behavior between men and women?
    A. Males and females are alike in their basic anatomy and physiology.
    B. Males and females differ in frequency of masturbation and orgasm.
    C. Females have a lesser "sexual capacity."
    D. all of the above

12. Which of the following was a finding of Masters and Johnson?
    A. Male and female arousal and orgasms are remarkably similar.
    B. Orgasms are physiologically the same, regardless of the source of stimulation.
    C. Women's capacity for sexual response infinitely surpasses that of men.
    D. all of the above

13. Which of the following is true about gender differences in motives for sex?
    A. Motives for sex are generally quite similar.
    B. People rarely have sex when they don't want to.
    C. Women engage in sex when they don't want to but men do not.
    D. none of the above

14. Which characteristics were found more often in sexually aggressive males?
    A. a history of violence and psychological problems
    B. poor communication and feelings of insecurity
    C. hostile attitudes and sexual promiscuity
    D. a history of being abused and family problems

15. Motivation for rape includes which of the following?
    A. sexual outlet   B. power and anger at women
    C. crossed signals   D. psychological disturbance

16. Kissing, sexual arousal and orgasm are
    A. natural behaviors.   B. biologically based behaviors.
    C. highly influenced by culture and learning.   D. normal behaviors.

17. The fact that boys are motivated to impress other males with their sexual experiences and girls are taught not to indulge in sexual pleasure demonstrates the effects of
    A. interpersonal scripts.   B. cultural scripts.
    C. intrapsychic scripts.   D. sexual orientation.

18. Which of the following best describes current thinking about the origins of sexual orientation?
    A. Most research supports a genetic basis.
    B. Dominant mothers and absent/passive fathers contribute to male homosexuality.
    C. Brain differences between heterosexuals and homosexuals explains sexual orientation.
    D. Sexual identity and behavior involve an interaction of biology, culture, experiences and opportunities.

19. Which of the following represents an argument against biological explanations of sexual orientation?
    A. Women's sexual experiences are often "fluid."
    B. Most gay men and lesbians do not have a close gay relative.
    C. Subject selection problems have existed in studies on brain differences.
    D. all of the above

20. Which of the following motivations influences peoples' work habits?
    A. their expectation and values   B. how competent they feel
    C. the type of goals they have   D. all of the above

21. Stacey is studying to be a master violin maker. When she makes a mistake she feels she has learned useful information about what to do next time. She knows that this process will take time and that she must be patient. She is motivated by
    A. performance goals.   B. learning and mastery goals.
    C. self-efficacy.   D. all of the above.

22. People who dream about becoming rich and famous probably have a high need for _____, while those who dream about being a leader and influencing others are probably high in the need for _____.
    A. power; manipulation.   B. achievement; power.
    C. power; achievement.   D. none of the above

23. Great leaders have
    A. used power for social goals rather than personal ambition.
    B. used their personal ambition for the greater good.
    C. been high in the need for affiliation, achievement and power.
    D. tried to suppress their power motivation in favor of affiliation.

24. You want to have Chinese food for dinner but you also have a craving for Italian food. This represents a(n)
    A. approach-approach conflict.   B. avoidance-avoidance conflict.
    C. approach-avoidance conflict.   D. no lose situation.

25. Research on Maslow's hierarchy of needs
    A. has supported the idea that motives are met in a hierarchy.
    B. has not supported any aspect of this theory.
    C. has found that it is true that lower needs must be met first but that once these needs are met, all people do not necessarily go on to meet the higher needs.
    D. has found that very few people go on to meet the higher needs.

PRACTICE TEST 2

1. Susan has no energy for studying. Whenever she tries, she falls asleep. She does, however, feel very energetic when asked to go to a movie. Which aspect of motivation does this demonstrate?
   A. reducing a state of physical deprivation   B. satisfying of a biological need
   C. moving toward a goal   D. fulfilling a drive

2. Affiliation, attachment, achievement, love and power are examples of
   A. unlearned motives.   B. social motives.
   C. primary motives.   D. all of the above.

3. Jerry needs a lot of solitude and "space," while Harry needs friends and family around as much as possible. They differ on
   A. the need for affiliation.   B. attachment needs.
   C. the need for contact comfort.   D. love style.

4. Lucia's mom is not very comfortable with physical affection. Although she loves Lucia and takes good care of her, she does not hold or cuddle her. In contrast, her dad likes to hug and cuddle. Based on Harlow's experiments, to which parent would Lucia be most likely to go to when she is upset?
   A. her mom   B. her dad
   C. either   D. impossible to say

5. Which of the following supports the findings of the Harlow studies?
   A. Babies who are adequately fed and sheltered but deprived of touch show retarded emotional and physical development.
   B. Emotional and physical symptoms occur in adults who are "undertouched."
   C. Patients find even mild touching by nurses comforting and reassuring.
   D. all of the above

6. Baby Huey cries for his mother to pick him up, yet when she does, he wants to be put back down. According to Ainsworth's studies, Huey exhibits a(n)
   A. avoidant attachment style.   B. ambivalent attachment style.
   C. secure attachment style   D. psychological problem.

7. Which of the following is <u>NOT</u> considered a problem with Ainsworth's research on infant attachment?
   - A. Some babies are insecurely attached because they are temperamentally difficult.
   - B. Some studies have found no relationship between maternal responsiveness and children's attachment.
   - C. The "strange situation" used to measure attachment is not scientific enough.
   - D. The influence of caregivers besides the mother was not considered.

8. Which type of love does the following personal ad represent? "Passionate male seeking companion who likes to have romantic dinners by candlelight, take moonlit walks on the beach and read poetry together."
   - A. pragma
   - B. eros
   - C. ludus
   - D. storge

9. Victoria knows what she wants in a man. He must be good looking, have a good job, want to have at least two children and have a college education. This represents which type of love?
   - A. ludus
   - B. storge
   - C. agape
   - D. pragma

10. Which types of love styles would be most likely to make the best match?
    - A. avoidant-avoidant
    - B. ludic-ludic
    - C. secure male-anxious female
    - D. avoidant female-anxious male

11. Studies of men who have been chemically castrated, women who are taking androgens, and women who kept diaries of their sexual activity while having their hormone levels measured support
    - A. the role of cognitive interpretations on sexual motivation.
    - B. the role of cultural scripts on sexual motivation.
    - C. the role of testosterone on sexual motivation.
    - D. all of the above.

12. The biological researchers have made important contributions to our understanding of the sexual behavior of men and women, including
    - A. identifying the biological differences between men and women.
    - B. identifying the similarities between men and women in their basic anatomy and in their arousal responses and orgasms.
    - C. identifying how sexual responses vary among individuals according to age, experience, and culture.
    - D. identifying how strongly peoples' subjective experiences of orgasm correlate with their physiological responses.

13. Jason may have sex when he doesn't want to because _____, whereas Jennifer may be sexual when she doesn't want to because _____
    A. he feels obligated; of peer pressure.
    B. of peer pressure; she feels guilty.
    C. he feels guilty; of inexperience.
    D. it is easier than having an argument; of peer pressure.

14. In a large-scale sex survey, 22.8 percent of the women said they had been forced by men to do something sexually that they did not want to do, but only 2.8 percent of the men said that they ever had forced a woman into a sexual act. How might this be explained?
    A. Men are in denial about their sexual behavior.
    B. What many women experience as coercion is not seen as such by many men.
    C. Women tend to overexaggerate these experiences.
    D. Women say "no," but they mean "yes."

15. Of the following men, the one who is most likely to be sexually aggressive is
    A. a man with a psychiatric disorder.
    B. a man who has not had a sexual encounter in many months.
    C. a man who had his first sexual experiences early and has had many partners.
    D. a man who adores women.

16. Talking about sexual responses and motivations in a college class is embarrassing for Maia, who is from Morocco. She feels she should not be listening to this kind of information, particularly in a public place with males present. This is an example of
    A. interpersonal scripts.   B. intrapsychic scripts.
    C. cultural scripts.   D. social scripts.

17. Neha's parents are from India though she was raised in the U.S. What feels comfortable to her and her boyfriend conflicts strongly with her parents ideas about acceptable behavior for females. She is experiencing a conflict between
    A. interpersonal and intrapsychic scripts.
    B. gender roles and sexual scripts.
    C. interpersonal and cultural scripts.
    D. cultural scripts and gender roles.

18. Felicia was a heterosexual for many years and has recently fallen in love with another woman. Felicia's situation argues against
    A. psychological explanations of sexual orientation.
    B. biological explanations of sexual orientation.
    C. cultural explanations of sexual orientation.
    D. the idea that sexual orientation is a choice.

19. Which of the following explanations for homosexuality has been supported by research?
    A.   bad mothering, absent fathering   B.   parental role models
    C.   homosexuals have a mental disorder   D.   none of the above

20. The person who is more likely to work hard is
    A.   someone who expects to succeed.   B.   someone with a high salary.
    C.   someone who has performance goals.   D.   someone very competent.

21. Expectations, values, goals and the need for achievement show the effects of
    _____, whereas working conditions and opportunity show the effects of
    _____.
    A.   motivation on work; work on motivation
    B.   work on motivation; motivation on work
    C.   external forces; internal forces
    D.   none of the above

22. Julie has been passed over for a promotion several times and each time a male has been
    hired. Based on research, which is the most likely explanation?
    A.   Her managing style is different from the approach taken by men.
    B.   The "glass ceiling" limits her opportunities.
    C.   She has less commitment to the job than a man would.
    D.   She has poorer self-esteem and feelings of competence than men.

23. The person most likely to become a great leader is someone
    A.   high in personal ambition.
    B.   with a high need to use power for social goals.
    C.   with a high need for power and personal ambition.
    D.   with a high commitment to social goals who does not need a lot of power.

4. Going to the dentist or having one's teeth fall out is an example of a(n) _____
    conflict; wanting to go out with Dan while continuing to date Stan is an example of a(n)
    _____ conflict; wanting to travel this summer but knowing if you do you will miss
    the summer with your friends is an example of a(n) _____ conflict.
    A.   avoidance-avoidance; approach-approach; approach-avoidance
    B.   approach-avoidance; approach-approach; avoidance-avoidance
    C.   approach-approach; avoidance-avoidance; approach-avoidance
    D.   approach-avoidance; approach-approach; approach-approach

25. People like Mahatma Ghandi and Martin Luther King, Jr. show that people
    A.   can choose higher needs over lower ones.   B.   make their own hierarchies.
    C.   may have many needs simultaneously.   D.   may do all of the above.

PRACTICE TEST 3

1. Donna is a college student. Her work and her household responsibilities are completed and she finds herself with free time. She decides to do the following: call her friend, visit her boyfriend, do an extra credit assignment and work on an extra project for her job. Describe the influence of motives on her behaviors.

2. Write a personal ad for each of the six types of love styles described by Lee.

3. You are at a party and there is a debate about what "causes" homosexuality. On the one side, Lee says it is a choice that people freely make. Amy says that it is clearly biological. Describe the information that supports and refutes each of their positions. Also discuss the political implications of each point of view.

4. A. John is thinking about a major and is considering chemical engineering. He has a high achievement need and believes that only really bright people make it, and his scores are in the middle of the class performance range. John's father's firm will pay part of his tuition and provide a great job after graduation, but John still has self-doubts. How is John likely to respond?

   B. Weekly quizzes constantly remind Joe that he needs to do better in several courses. Whenever a poor quiz result is returned, Joe vows to do better and begins by trying to study endlessly. This never works for more than a day. Identify the problem with Joe's study goals and strategy.

   C. Many courses are relatively unstructured. Teachers do not monitor study and base grades on a small number of tests at designated times in the semester. Discuss the motivational complications related to feedback and working conditions associated with such courses.

5. Identify the type of conflict associated with each example below.

   A. Sarah couldn't decide whether to purchase a van or a sports car. Each had desirable qualities, but neither provided everything she wanted.

   B. Hank promised the counselor that this third switch between chemistry and physics would be the last. He dreaded both courses but had to take one to fulfill requirements.

   C. When the networks put her favorite shows on at the same time, Lucy bought a VCR so she could watch one program and record the other for later viewing.

   D. David, an avid fisherman, just met new neighbors who made his day. The neighbors agreed to clean his fish and split the catch. David loved landing the fish but couldn't do the cleaning because it made him nauseous.

CHAPTER 12

Theories of Personality

LEARNING OBJECTIVES

1. Define personality.

2. List and discuss the major trait theories of personality, including the five "robust (stable) factors."

3. Discuss the issue of heritability of personality and temperament, including cautionary considerations.

4. Compare and contrast the behavioral and cognitive social learning approaches to personality.

5. List and explain problems associated with the learning theories of personality.

6. Explain the basic principles of Freud's psychoanalytic approach to the study of personality and list the emphases shared by modern psychodynamic theories.

7. Describe the structure of the personality, according to Freud, and the seven defense mechanisms.

8. Describe the five psychosexual stages of personality development identified by Freud.

9. Discuss the challenges to psychoanalytic theory made by Jung, Horney, Adler, Erikson and the object-relations school.

10. Summarize the criticisms of psychodynamic theories.

11. Summarize the principles of humanistic psychology proposed by Maslow, Rogers, and May.

12. Describe how the sense of consistency of personality is enhanced by the private personality.

CHAPTER CONCEPT MAP

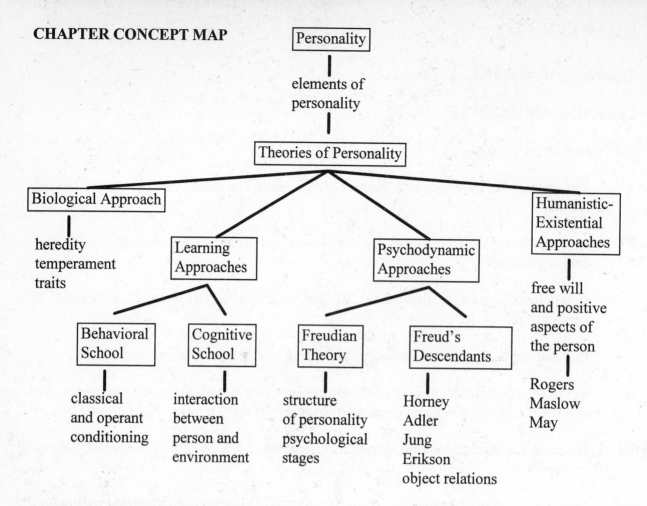

Personality

elements of personality

Theories of Personality

Biological Approach

heredity
temperament
traits

Learning Approaches

Psychodynamic Approaches

Humanistic-Existential Approaches

free will and positive aspects of the person

Rogers
Maslow
May

Behavioral School

classical and operant conditioning

Cognitive School

interaction between person and environment

Freudian Theory

structure of personality psychological stages

Freud's Descendants

Horney
Adler
Jung
Erikson
object relations

BRIEF CHAPTER SUMMARY

Chapter 12 defines personality and reviews the major theoretical approaches that have been advanced to explain its development. The biological approach looks to the heritability of certain traits and to the idea that there is a genetic basis to certain temperaments. The behavioral approach considers personality a collection of behaviors that have been conditioned through classical and operant conditioning. The cognitive social learning approach emphasizes the ability of the organism to regulate itself. Locus of control and self-efficacy are characteristics that have an important influence on how much control people believe they have over their lives. The psychodynamic approaches focus on the role of unconscious processes and the development of the id, ego and superego. Freud originally developed this approach, and other theorists have made modifications to his work. The humanist and existential approaches reject the negative and deterministic views of the psychoanalytic and behavioral approaches. These approaches focus on the positive aspects of humanity and the idea that human beings have free will and can shape their own destinies.

PREVIEW OUTLINE AND REVIEW QUESTIONS

Before you read the chapter, review the preview outline and the Learning Objectives for each section of the text. Develop additional questions of your own based on key concepts and terms and write them in the designated spaces. Answer all questions as you read the text.

SECTION 1 - THE ELEMENTS OF PERSONALITY (PP. 437-440)

I.   **THE ELEMENTS OF PERSONALITY**
    A.   **Definition** - distinctive and _____ pattern of behavior, thoughts, motives and emotions that characterizes an individual over time; this pattern reflects a particular constellation of _____
    B.   **Traits and trait theories**
        1.   Trait - characteristic assumed to describe a person across many situations
        2.   Allport's trait theory - individual traits make people unique
            a.   _____ traits - of overwhelming importance to an individual
            b.   Central (or global) traits - characteristic ways of behaving
            c.   Secondary traits - the more _____ aspects of personality
        3.   Cattell theory - studied traits using factor analysis and found 16 factors
            a.   Surface traits - those that are visible in a person's words or deeds
            b.   _____ traits - the underlying causes of surface traits
        4.   The "Big Five" traits - supported by research as robust or stable traits
            a.   Introversion versus extroversion
            b.   _____ or emotional instability - have negative affectivity
            c.   Agreeableness
            d.   Conscientiousness
            e.   Openness to experience

Answer these Learning Objectives while you read Section 1.

1.   Define personality.

2.   List and discuss the major trait theories of personality, including the five "robust (stable) factors."

Write the questions that you have formulated below and answer them while you read.

A._____

B._____

SECTION 2 - THE BIOLOGICAL TRADITION: YOU ARE WHAT YOU'RE BORN (PP. 440-445)

II. **THE BIOLOGICAL TRADITION: YOU ARE WHAT YOU'RE BORN**
    A. **Heredity, temperament and traits**
        1. _____ - relatively stable, characteristic styles of responding that appear in infancy and have some genetic basis
           a. Kagan's inhibited and uninhibited temperamental styles
           b. Inhibited temperaments respond with anxiety to novelty and change
           c. Some aspects of temperaments can lead to habits and mannerisms
        2. Heritability estimates of adult personality traits - regardless of the trait, heritability is around _____
           a. Some have reported high heritability estimates for specific behaviors
           b. Only environmental effects on personality come from nonshared experiences - _____ environment and parental child-rearing practices do not seem related to adult personality traits
    B. **Evaluating genetic theories**
        1. Measures of environmental factors are still _____ causing us to miss environmental influences and overestimate the role of heredity
        2. Separated twins used as subjects grow up in similar environments
        3. Temperaments are not _____ blueprints; less intense traits show less consistency over time
        4. Even those with intense traits are influenced by environmental interactions
        5. Diminishing effect of genes overtime

Answer this Learning Objective while you read Section 2.

3. Discuss the issue of heritability of personality and temperament, including cautionary considerations.

Write the questions that you have formulated below and answer them while you read.

A._____

B._____

SECTION 3 - THE LEARNING TRADITION: YOU ARE WHAT YOU DO (PP. 445-450)

III.   THE LEARNING TRADITION: YOU ARE WHAT YOU DO
   - A.   **The behavioral school**
     1. Radical behaviorists - personality is a set of habits that have been _____
     2. All behavior is learned through _____ and operant conditioning
     3. Mental states are subject to the laws of learning
   - B.   **The cognitive social-learning school**
     1. _____ learning and the role of models
     2. Cognitive processes of _____ and interpretation of events
     3. Motivating beliefs such as expectations and confidence
     4. Personality - habits and beliefs become self-regulated by thoughts, values
     5. Two personality traits that influence behavior
        - a. Locus of _____ (Rotter)
           - (1) People develop _____ and self-fulfilling prophecies
           - (2) Feelings or beliefs are as important as reinforcers
           - (3) Expectations about one's actions called locus of control
              - (a) _____ locus of control - people believe they control their own destinies
              - (b) External locus of control - people feel like victims
        - b. Self-efficacy - developing a sense of _____
           - (1) Experience in mastery and overcoming obstacles
           - (2) Vicarious experiences provided by models similar to oneself
           - (3) Encouragement and persuasion from others
           - (4) Judgments of one's own physiological state
   - C.   **Evaluating learning theories - criticisms**
     1. Imply people are malleable and _____, which misrepresents Skinner
     2. Environment and its process of influence too vaguely defined
     3. Researchers study one influence at a time; in life many interact at once

Answer these Learning Objectives while you read Section 3.

4. Compare and contrast behavioral and cognitive social learning approaches to personality.

5. List and explain problems associated with the learning theories of personality.

Write the questions that you have formulated below and answer them while you read.

A._____

B._____

SECTION 4 - THE PSYCHODYNAMIC TRADITION: YOU ARE WHAT YOU WERE (PP. 450-466)

IV. **THE PSYCHODYNAMIC TRADITION: YOU ARE WHAT YOU WERE**
   A. **The elements shared by all psychodynamic theories**
      1. Emphasize _____ intrapsychic dynamics
      2. Adult behavior determined primarily by early childhood experiences
      3. Psychological development occurs in fixed _____
      4. Unconscious fantasies and symbols are main motivators of personality
      5. Reliance on subjective methods of getting at the truth of a person's life
   B. **Freud and psychoanalysis - Freud's theory of personality**
      1. The structure of personality - made up of three systems that must balance
         a. The id - operates according to the _____ principle and contains the life or sexual (libido) instinct and death (aggressive) instincts
         b. The ego - referee between demands of id and society; reason
         c. The _____ - morality and rules of parents and society; consists of ego ideal (moral standards) and conscience (inner voice)
      2. Defense _____
         a. Used by ego to reduce anxiety when id wishes conflict with society
         b. They are unconscious and distort _____
         c. They are necessary to protect us from uncomfortable conflict
         d. Some defense mechanisms are: repression, _____, displacement, sublimation, reaction formation, regression, denial
      3. The development of personality occurs in five psychosexual stages
         a. The oral stage
         b. The anal stage - issue is _____
         c. The phallic or Oedipal stage - _____ emerges; identification with the same-sex parent; by the end of this stage, personality is formed
         d. The latency stage - sexual feelings subside
         e. The genital stage - beginning of mature adult sexuality
   C. **Freud's descendants**
      1. Karen Horney - challenged the notion of _____ and female inferiority
         a. Looked to women's status to explain feelings of inferiority
         b. Said Freud's view could be used to justify discrimination
      2. Alfred Adler - broke away and started his own school
         a. More _____ view of the human condition
         b. People strive for superiority to overcome childhood inferiority
      3. Carl Jung - biggest difference was the nature of the _____
         a. Collective unconscious contains the universal memory and history
         b. Concerned with _____ - symbolic images that appear in myths
         c. Perceived humans as more positively motivated than did Freud

4.   Erikson's psychosocial theory - personality develops throughout life
  a.   Identified eight stages of life, each with a crisis to be resolved
  b.   Stages include - trust versus mistrust; autonomy versus shame and doubt; initiative versus guilt; _____ versus inferiority; identity versus role confusion; intimacy versus isolation; generativity versus stagnation; ego integrity versus despair
  c.   Considered cultural and economic factors important influences
5. The object-relations school - emphasizes need for _____ and relationships
  a.   Object - a representation of the mother that the child introjects
  b.   Central tension is balance between _____ and connection
  c.   Children of both sexes identify with mother; males must separate

D.   **Evaluating psychodynamic theories**
1.   Projective tests developed to measure concepts, particularly the contents of the unconscious but they have poor reliability and validity
  a.   Thematic Apperception Test - uses ambiguous drawings
  b.   _____ Inkblot Test - uses patterns
2.   Criticisms
  a.   Some concepts finding empirical support but many are not testable
  b.   Principle of falsifiability violated - can't confirm or disprove ideas
  c.   Universal principles drawn from the experiences of selected patients
  d.   Theories based on the retrospective memories of patients

Answer these Learning Objectives while you read Section 4.

6.   Explain the basic principles of Freud's psychoanalytic approach to the study of personality and list the emphases shared by modern psychodynamic theories.

7.   Describe the structure of the personality, according to Freud, and defense mechanisms.

8.   Describe the five psychosexual stages of personality development identified by Freud.

9.   Discuss the challenges to psychoanalytic theory made by Jung, Horney, Adler, Erikson and the object-relations school.

10.   Summarize the criticisms of psychodynamic theories.

Write the questions that you have formulated below and answer them while you read.

A._____

B._____

SECTION 5 - THE HUMANIST AND EXISTENTIAL TRADITIONS: YOU ARE WHAT YOU BECOME (PP. 466-470) AND
SECTION 6 - THE PRIVATE PERSONALITY (PP. 470-473)

V. **THE HUMANIST AND EXISTENTIAL TRADITIONS**
    A.   **The inner experience**
        1.   Focus on phenomenology - a person's own sense of self and experience
        2.   Developed as a reaction against psychoanalysis and _____
        3.   Main theorists were Maslow, May and _____
        4.   Emphasized free _____, positive aspects of human beings and the dilemmas of human existence
    B.   **Carl Roger's approach**
        1.   Interested in the fully _____ person - based on the congruence between the self and the organism
        2.   Becoming fully functional requires _____ positive regard
        3.   Conditional love results in incongruence and unhappiness
    C.   **Rollo May** - brought aspects of _____ to American psychology
    D.   **Evaluating humanistic and existential theories**
        1.   Many assumptions cannot be _____
        2.   Closer to philosophy than science because of subjectivity
        3.   Add balance to psychology's view of personality

VI. **THE PRIVATE PERSONALITY**
    A.   **How stable or flexible is personality?**
        1.   Seems stable because of inner sense of continuity or private personality
        2.   Some qualities are _____ throughout life (temperaments, the Big Five personality traits); others are more changeable (attitudes, self-efficacy, locus of control, ambitions, interests)
    B.   **Conclusion** - personalities are a mixture of stability and change

Answer these Learning Objectives while you read Sections 5 and 6.

11.   Summarize the principles of humanistic psychology proposed by Maslow, Rogers, May.

12.   Describe how the sense of consistency of personality is enhanced by the private personality.

Write the questions that you have formulated below and answer them while you read.

A._____

B._____

FLASH CARDS

Cut the following chart along the borders and test yourself with the resulting flash cards.

12.1 PERSONALITY	12.8 NEUROTICISM	12.15 COGNITIVE SOCIAL LEARNING THEORY
12.2 TRAIT	12.9 AGREEABLENESS	12.16 SELF-HANDICAPPING STRATEGY
12.3 GORDON ALLPORT	12.10 CONSCIENTIOUSNESS	12.17 SELF-FULFILLING PROPHECY
12.4 RAYMOND CATTELL	12.11 OPENNESS TO EXPERIENCE	12.18 INTERNAL LOCUS OF CONTROL
12.5 FACTOR ANALYSIS	12.12 TEMPERAMENTS	12.19 EXTERNAL LOCUS OF CONTROL
12.6 "BIG FIVE" PERSONALITY TRAITS	12.13 HERITABILITY	12.20 SELF-EFFICACY
12.7 INTROVERSION/ EXTROVERSION	12.14 RADICAL BEHAVIORISM	12.21 SIGMUND FREUD

12.15 We acquire personality patterns as we learn to deal with the environment, and that personality and situation constantly influence each other.	12.8 One of the "Big Five" traits. Emotional instability; includes traits such as being anxious and unable to control impulses.	12.1 A distinctive and relatively stable pattern of behavior, thoughts, motives and emotions that characterizes an individual throughout life.
12.16 A strategy that uses anxiety as an excuse for poor performance, which allows a failure to be blamed on the handicap and not on ability.	12.9 The extent to which people are good-natured or irritable, gentle or headstrong, cooperative or abrasive, not jealous or jealous.	12.2 A descriptive characteristic of an individual, assumed to be stable across situations and time.
12.17 An expectation that comes true because of the tendency of those holding the expectation to act on it in certain ways.	12.10 The extent to which individuals are responsible or undependable; persevering or quit easily; steadfast or fickle; tidy or careless.	12.3 A trait theorist who said that members of a society share common traits. People have cardinal, central and secondary traits that make them unique.
12.18 An expectation that the results of one's actions are under one's own control.	12.11 Describes the extent to which people are imaginative, questioning, artistic, and capable of divergent (creative) thinking.	12.4 A trait theorist who used factor analysis to identify separate traits. He identified 16 factors necessary to describe personality.
12.19 An expectation that the results of one's actions are beyond one's control.	12.12 Characteristic styles of responding to the environment that are present in infancy and are assumed to be innate.	12.5 A statistical method for finding intercorrelations among measures. Highly correlated measures are assumed to be measuring the same thing.
12.20 The belief that one can accomplish what one sets out to do; involved with having a sense of one's competence.	12.13 Estimate of the proportion of the total variance in a trait within a group attributable to genetic differences among individuals in the group.	12.6 Five factors that are believed by many researchers to be able to describe personality. Not everyone agrees, but there is some consensus.
12.21 Originator of the theory of psychoanalysis: the first psychodynamic theory based on movement of psychological energy within the person.	12.14 Extreme type of behaviorism that holds the position that "personality" is an illusion.	12.7 Include such personality traits as being talkative or silent, sociable or reclusive, adventurous or cautious, shy or outgoing. One of the big five.

12.22 PSYCHOANALYSIS	**12.29 DISPLACEMENT**	**12.36 ID**
12.23 PSYCHODYNAMIC THEORIES	**12.30 SUBLIMATION**	**12.37 OEDIPUS COMPLEX**
12.24 INTRAPSYCHIC DYNAMICS	**12.31 REACTION FORMATION**	**12.38 IDENTIFICATION**
12.25 "PSYCHIC REALITY"	**12.32 REGRESSION AND FIXATION**	**12.39 KAREN HORNEY**
12.26 DEFENSE MECHANISMS	**12.33 DENIAL**	**12.40 ALFRED ADLER**
12.27 REPRESSION	**12.34 INTELLECTUALIZATION**	**12.41 INFERIORITY COMPLEX**
12.28 PROJECTION	**12.35 PSYCHOSEXUAL STAGES**	**12.42 CARL JUNG**

12.36 In psychoanalysis, the part of personality containing inherited psychological energy, particularly sexual and aggressive instincts.	12.29 People direct their emotions (especially anger) toward things, animals or other people that are not the real object of their feelings.	12.22 A theory of personality and a method of psychotherapy developed by Sigmund Freud; it emphasizes unconscious motives and conflicts.
12.37 In psychoanalysis, a conflict in which a child desires the parent of the other sex and views the same-sex parent as a rival; issue in the phallic stage.	12.30 When displacement serves a higher cultural or socially useful purpose, as in the creation of art or inventions.	12.23 Theories that explain behavior and personality in terms of unconscious energy dynamics within an individual.
12.38 Process by which the child adopts an adult's standards of morality, values and beliefs as his or her own.	12.31 The feeling that causes unconscious anxiety is transformed into its opposite in consciousness.	12.24 The movement of forces within the mind.
12.39 An early dissenter from Freud's theories; challenged Freud's notions of penis envy and female inferiority.	12.32 The halting of personality development (fixation) or the return to an earlier stage of development after a traumatic experience (regression).	12.25 The focus on fantasies and symbolic meanings of events as the unconscious mind perceives them.
12.40 Left Freud's circle to start his own school, which had a more positive view of the humans than Freud. Believed humans strove for superiority.	12.33 The refusal to admit that something unpleasant is happening or that forbidden emotions are being experienced.	12.26 Methods used by the ego to prevent unconscious anxiety or threatening thoughts from entering consciousness.
12.41 In Adlerian theory, individuals who are unable to accept their limitations and try to mask them by pretending to be strong.	12.34 Distancing oneself from anxiety by talking about emotions in a very rational manner.	12.27 A threatening idea, memory, or emotion is blocked from becoming conscious.
12.42 Left Freud's circle because of disagreement about the nature of the unconscious. Originally, one of Freud's closest friends.	12.35 The stages of personality development hypothesized by Freud; he believed that psychological development depended on sexual energy.	12.28 One's own unacceptable feelings are attributed to someone else.

12.43 COLLECTIVE UNCONSCIOUS	**12.50 RORSCHACH INKBLOT TEST**	**12.57 HUMANISTIC PSYCHOLOGY**
12.44 ARCHETYPES	**12.51 PHENOMENOLOGY**	**12.58 ABRAHAM MASLOW**
12.45 ERIK ERIKSON	**12.52 PLEASURE PRINCIPLE**	**12.59 CARL ROGERS**
12.46 IDENTITY CRISIS	**12.53 LIBIDO**	**12.60 ROLLO MAY**
12.47 OBJECT-RELATIONS SCHOOL	**12.54 EGO**	**12.61 PEAK EXPERIENCES**
12.48 PROJECTIVE TESTS	**12.55 REALITY PRINCIPLE**	**12.62 UNCONDITIONAL POSITIVE REGARD**
12.49 THEMATIC APPERCEPTION TEST	**12.56 SUPEREGO**	**12.63 EXISTENTIALISM**

12.57 A movement that rejected behavioral and psychoanalytic approaches; it focused on the positive aspects of human nature.	**12.50** A projective personality test that asks respondents to interpret abstract, symmetrical images.	**12.43** To Jung, the universal memories and the history of humankind, represented in the unconscious images and symbols of all people.
12.58 One of the leaders of humanistic psychology who said people strive for a life that is meaningful and challenging.	**12.51** The study of events as individuals experience them; in personality, the study of an individual's qualities from the person's own point of view.	**12.44** To Jung, universal, symbolic images that appear in myths, art, dreams and other expressions of the collective unconscious.
12.59 A humanist theorist who said that human beings need unconditional positive regard to become fully functioning and congruent.	**12.52** The principle that underlies the operation of the id by seeking to reduce tension, avoid pain and obtain pleasure.	**12.45** A psychoanalyst who proposed a theory of personality development from birth to death; his was called a psychosocial theory.
12.60 A humanist theorist who emphasized some of the difficult aspects of the human condition, including loneliness, anxiety and alienation.	**12.53** In psychoanalysis, the psychic energy that fuels the life or sexual instincts of the id.	**12.46** Based on Erikson's fifth stage, puberty, which sets off the crisis of identity versus role confusion. This describes the major conflict of adolescence.
12.61 Described by Maslow as rare moments of rapture caused by the attainment of excellence or the drive toward higher values.	**12.54** In psychoanalysis, the part of personality that represents reason, good sense and rational self-control.	**12.47** A psychodynamic approach that emphasizes the importance of the infant's first two years of life and the baby's formative relationships.
12.62 Hypothesized by Rogers as being necessary to become a fully functioning person; it involves love and support for the people we are.	**12.55** In psychoanalysis, the principle that underlies the operation of the ego; it reins in the id's desire for pleasure until a suitable outlet can be found.	**12.48** Psychological tests used to infer a person's motives and unconscious dynamics based on the person's interpretations of ambiguous stimuli.
12.63 A European philosophy that holds that human beings have freedom of choice, but the freedom can cause anxiety and despair.	**12.56** In psychoanalysis, the part of personality that represents conscience, morality and social standards.	**12.49** A projective personality test that asks respondents to interpret a series of drawings showing ambiguous scenes of people.

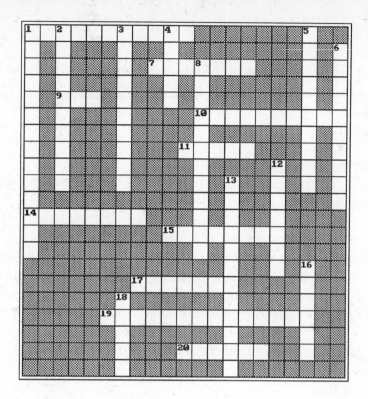

ACROSS

1. relatively stable pattern of behavior, thoughts, motives and emotions
7. a trait theorist who identified 16 factors he thought were necessary to describe personality
9. part of personality representing reason, good sense and self-control
10. psychological tests based on unconscious dynamics
11. founder of psychoanalysis
14. part of personality representing the conscience
15. locus of control in which one expects the results of one's actions to be under one's own control
17. complex that occurs in the phallic stage
19. the process by which the superego emerges
20. refusal to admit to oneself that something unpleasant is happening

DOWN

1. Freud's theory of personality and a method of psychotherapy
2. a way to block a threatening emotion from consciousness
3. universal, symbolic images
4. a descriptive characteristic of an individual
5. a movement within psychology that emphasized free will and the positive aspects of human nature
6. type of unconscious proposed by Jung
8. characteristic styles of responding present in infancy
12. inferiority _____
13. within the mind or self
16. introduced the idea of womb envy
18. introduced the idea of the inferiority complex

PRACTICE TEST 1

1. A distinctive and stable pattern of behavior, thoughts, motives and emotions that characterizes an individual over time is the definition of
   A. traits.
   B. temperament.
   C. personality.
   D. locus of control.

2. Allport's trait theory suggests there are
   A. cardinal, central and secondary traits.
   B. surface and source traits.
   C. sixteen factors.
   D. the "Big Five" traits.

3. The "Big Five" refers to
   A. the five main trait theories.
   B. five types of traits, including cardinal, central, secondary, surface and source.
   C. robust factors that are thought to be able to describe personality.
   D. five stages of personality development.

4. Jenny is always suspicious of others and thinks they are out to hurt her. This is an example of a
   A. cardinal trait.
   B. central trait.
   C. secondary trait.
   D. source trait.

5. Woody is a complainer and a defeatist. He always sees the sour side of life. This demonstrates which of the following "robust factors?"
   A. introversion
   B. depressiveness
   C. neuroticism
   D. disagreeableness

6. Studies on identical and fraternal twins have found the heritability of altruism to be about _____ and that of extroversion to be about _____.
   A. .80; .50
   B. .50; .80
   C. .30; .60
   D. .50; .50

7. The most controversial finding to come from the heritability studies on twins is the idea that
   A. the only environmental effects on personality come from nonshared experiences.
   B. environmental effects on personality come from only shared experiences.
   C. most personality traits are highly heritable.
   D. most personality traits are primarily a result of environmental influences.

8. Which of the following suggests caution about the heritability of personality?
   A. Less extreme temperaments show less consistency over time.
   B. Environmental measures are not very sensitive.
   C. The effects of genes diminish over time.
   D. all of the above

9. Radical behaviorists believe that personality is
   A. both influenced by and influences the environment in an unending chain.
   B. an illusion.
   C. a result of our thoughts, perceptions, feelings and interpretations of events.
   D. an interaction of the id, ego and superego.

10. Observational learning, perceptions and interpretations of events belong to
    A. the cognitive social learning school.   B. the radical behavioral school.
    C. the self-handicapping school.   D. none of the above.

11. According to the cognitive social learning school which two of the following traits are important to a person's ability to self-regulate his or her personality?
    A. neuroticism and openness to experience   B. expectancies and competence
    C. locus of control and self-efficacy   D. self-efficacy and extroversion

12. Which of the following is criticism of learning theories of personality?
    A. They are not testable.
    B. They are too heavily focused on genetics.
    C. They are not falsifiable.
    D. The environment is poorly defined.

13. Which of the following is NOT one of the shared elements among psychodynamic theories?
    A. an emphasis on environmental influences
    B. the assumption that adult behavior is determined primarily by childhood experiences
    C. a reliance on subjective rather than objective methods of getting at the truth of a person's life
    D. the belief that psychological development occurs in fixed stages

14. Which part of the personality would be likely to want to go for a pizza rather than study for a test?
    A. id   B. superego
    C. ego   D. ego ideal

15. The function of defense mechanisms is
    A. to make us look good in the eyes of other people.
    B. to protect ourselves from negative environmental consequences.
    C. to protect us from uncomfortable internal conflict.
    D. all of the above.

16. When the Ahern's brought home baby John, four-year-old Andy began acting like a baby himself by crawling around and wanting to drink out of a bottle. This is an example of
    A. regression.   B. identification.
    C. reaction formation.   D. projection.

17. The psychosexual stages of personality development identified by Freud are (in order)
    A. oral, anal, latency, phallic, genital.
    B. oral, phallic, anal, genital, latency.
    C. oral, anal, phallic, latency, genital.
    D. anal, phallic, genital, oral, latency.

18. According to Freud, the resolution of the _____ marks the emergence of the superego.
    A. anal stage   B. unconscious conflict
    C. Oedipus complex   D. latency stage

19. Horney disagreed with Freud about
    A. the nature of the unconscious.
    B. the notion of the inferiority complex.
    C. the notion that personality development continues into adult life.
    D. penis envy and female inferiority.

20. The idea that the human psyche contains the universal memories and history of mankind was contributed by
    A. Freud.   B. Jung.
    C. Erikson.   D. Horney.

21. The idea that the first two years of life are the most critical for the development of the core of personality because of the establishment of early attachments was suggested by
    A. Erikson.   B. Jung.
    C. the object-relations school.   D. Adler.

22. Which of the following is <u>NOT</u> one of the criticisms of psychodynamic theories?
   A. It violates the principle of falsifiability.
   B. It is based on retrospective memories.
   C. It is overly comprehensive; it tries to explain too much.
   D. It draws universal principles from studying selected patients.

23. Self, organism, congruence and unconditional positive regard are part of
   A. Roger's theory.   B. Maslow's theory.
   C. May's theory.   D. existential philosophy.

24. Humanism focuses on
   A. a person's own sense of self and experience.
   B. measurable traits.
   C. environmental influences.
   D. unconscious dynamics.

25. One reason that our personalities seem so consistent is because of
   A. our personality traits.   B. the consistency paradox.
   C. our private personality.   D. our unconscious processes.

1. Which of the following examples demonstrates the definition of personality?
    A.   Rick's bad mood must account for his outburst.
    B.   Ruth is as considerate and warm as always.
    C.   Ron used to be shy, but at camp he was quite outgoing.
    D.   Rene was very funny today.

2. Rudolph is a very suspicious person. He never trusts anyone and generally double checks whatever someone tells him. This is an example of which kind of trait?
    A.   cardinal   B.   secondary
    C.   central   D.   introversion

3. As part of a reference letter, Joe is described as a very positive person who is sociable, good-natured, responsible and imaginative. This description matches
    A.   traits cited by Cattell's theory.
    B.   the "Big Five" personalality traits.
    C.   cardinal traits as described by Allport.
    D.   the traits identified by factor analysis.

4. As a child, Petra was anxious and negative. She complained frequently about health problems even though she was not sick. As an adult, Petra will probably
    A.   outgrow these characteristics.
    B.   be equally likely to have the same characteristics or to change.
    C.   continue to have the same characteristics.
    D.   become even more negative and disturbed.

5. Your grandmother tells you that from the time you were born, you were a content infant and have continued to be throughout your childhood, but your sister has always been difficult right from the start. She is describing your
    A.   personalities.   B.   traits.
    C.   motives.   D.   temperaments.

6. Studies of twins have found that heritability for most traits is around .50. This means that
    A.   if one twin has a trait, there is a 50 percent chance the other twin will have the same trait.
    B.   most people have a 50 percent chance of having a given trait.
    C.   within a group about 50 percent of the variance in a trait is attributable to genes.
    D.   the differences between two groups of people can be explained.

7. Based on studies of twins, which of the following environmental factors would be expected to have the greatest influence on the personality of two siblings?
    A.   having the same parents
    B.   going to the same schools
    C.   having different extracurricular activities
    D.   having the same religious training

8. A study of Finnish twins, ages 18 to 59, found that the heritability of extroversion decreased from the late teens to the late twenties. What does this suggest?
    A.   Heritability of traits diminishes over time.
    B.   The influence of the environment increases over time.
    C.   For some traits, experiences at certain periods in life become more important.
    D.   all of the above

9. Christian has been told that his personality is aggressive, extroverted and conscientious. A behaviorist interpret this as
    A.   a description of his central traits.
    B.   a result of an interaction of his traits with the environment.
    C.   a collection of behavioral patterns.
    D.   none of the above.

10. Dr. Story tells Christian that his behavior is self-regulated and is shaped by thoughts, values, self-reflections and intentions. What approach does this represent?
    A.   behavioral   B.   trait
    C.   cognitive social learning   D.   radical behaviorism

11. "It seems the more I study, the worse I do. There's really no point to working hard in college because it doesn't seem to matter." This statement reflects
    A.   an internal locus of control.   B.   observational learning.
    C.   an external locus of control.   D.   self-handicapping.

12. Mr. Picks is conducting research on the effect of a teacher's reactions on students' self-efficacy. Which criticism of behaviorism applies to this research topic?
    A.   It is not testable.
    B.   It is not falsifiable.
    C.   Because there are many influences on self-efficacy, it is difficult to evaluate the effect of just one environmental influence at a time.
    D.   It is based on the retrospective memories of subjects.

13. Priscilla is having relationship problems. Which of the following approaches to her difficulties represents one of the shared elements of psychodynamic theories?
   A. The problems are a result of her interpretation of what is going on.
   B. The problems are a result of her previous relationship history.
   C. The problems result from the lack of unconditional positive regard.
   D. The problems are determined by experiences in her early childhood.

14. Jeff is very bossy and rigid. He is always watching the clock to see who is late and who leaves early. According to Freudian theory, Jeff
   A. overuses the defense of displacement.
   B. is too controlled by his superego.
   C. has too strong an ego.
   D. displays all of the above.

15. "I don't want to study; let's go get pizza." "If you go get pizza, you'll fail the test." "You owe it to your parents to get good grades." Which parts of the personality would make each of these statements, according to Freudian theory?
   A. id; ego; superego   B. id; superego; ego
   C. ego; id; superego   D. superego; id; ego

16. Les crusades against pornography because he feels that people have dirty minds and are oversexed. According to Freudian theory, Les is using the defense mechanism of
   A. displacement.   B. projection.
   C. reaction formation.   D. denial.

17. Johnny was aggressive as a child. He now plays professional football. This is an example of
   A. regression.   B. sublimation.
   C. reaction formation.   D. projection.

18. Max has just had his sixth birthday. Freud would expect that
   A. he has resolved the Oedipal complex.
   B. his personality pattern is basically formed.
   C. his superego has emerged.
   D. all of the above have occurred.

19. Adler is to Jung as
   A. womb envy is to persona.   B. archetype is to inferiority.
   C. anima is to animus.   D. inferiority is to archetype.

20. The fact that several basic archetypes appear in virtually every society supports which Jungian idea?
    A. penis envy   B. the strength of the ego
    C. psychosocial stages   D. the collective unconscious

21. Trust versus mistrust, autonomy versus shame and doubt and initiative versus guilt are proposed in the theory of _____ and are considered _____ that must be resolved.
    A. Horney; problems   B. Adler; complexes
    C. Erikson; crises   D. Freud; fixations

22. The object-relations school predicts that adult males will have problems permitting close attachments because
    A. their identities are based on <u>not</u> being like women, so they develop more rigid ego boundaries.
    B. their superegos are too strong.
    C. they have great difficulty resolving the Oedipus complex.
    D. all of the above.

23. Dr. West is studying depression. He has interviewed 50 subjects about their early lives and childhoods and he has identified common threads that fit an overall theory. This example represents which of the criticisms of psychodynamic theories?
    A. It violates the principle of falsifiability.
    B. It is a prospective study.
    C. It is based on the retrospective memories of subjects.
    D. People are seen as too malleable, like jellyfish.

24. How do the humanistic approaches differ from the behavioral and psychodynamic approaches?
    A. They focus on a person's own sense of self and experience.
    B. They focus on some of the more positive aspects of human nature.
    C. They believe that human beings have free will.
    D. all of the above

25. Josh found some letters he had written as a child and adolescent. As he read them, he recognized a sense of self and an identity that he still feels as an adult. This represents
    A. the consistency paradox.   B. the stability of traits.
    C. his private personality.   D. his genetic temperament.

PRACTICE TEST 3

1. Lynne is having fantasies of killing her husband or at least making him suffer. Over a long period, he has gotten drunk on a regular basis. Lynne well remembers her alcoholic father, who was never there when she needed him. She also remembers her mother, who suffered silently for years. Lynne swears this will not happen to her, but she can't seem to make anything change. She is hostile toward the children and her neighbors. Her husband is always repentant the next day, but his sorrow never lasts more than a week. Yet, Lynne can't make the final step of leaving.

    Identify which approach to personality each of the following set of comments represents.

    A. The perseverance of Lynne's mother is the significant determinant in this case. This taught Lynne that marriage was for better or for worse, but also that silence produces suffering. Lynne's pattern was acquired from an important role model.
    B. Aggressiveness is Lynne's outstanding characteristic and it dominates her actions and relationships with most people.
    C. Lynne's marriage to and anger with an alcoholic suggests many unresolved feelings toward her father. Her marriage to an alcoholic suggests her ongoing attachment to her father and the effort to resolve her issues with him. Her anger most likely is unresolved anger at her father. Her reluctance to leave reflects her desire to stay united with her father.
    D. Lynne is struggling with her choices. While marriage is important to her, she realizes that her husband's alcoholism is a source of despair. She is struggling with her values, principles, desires for growth and fulfillment and how they should influence her choices.

2. Bernard had studied for his psychology test, but before he was finished studying, he agreed to go partying with his friends and stayed out late. The test was very difficult and he found he did not know many of the answers. The class was crowded and a good student was sitting very close to him. It would have been very easy to look over at her paper. He was worried because this test grade would make a big difference on his final grade. He struggled with whether or not he should cheat. He decided not to cheat because he felt that he would have let his parents down if he did. Instead, he decided that this grade really didn't matter so much. He felt guilty about not having studied enough and about having considered cheating.

294

Indicate whether the id, ego or superego is involved in each of the following examples and explain the basis for your answer.

A. Bernard's studying for his test
B. Going out partying with his friends rather than studying
C. Wanting a good grade under any circumstance
D. Evaluating whether or not to cheat
E. Deciding not to cheat
F. Deciding that the grade did not matter so much
G. Feeling guilty about his behavior

3. Identify which defense mechanism each example represents.

A. A mother shows exaggerated concern and love for her children, even though she unconsciously feels trapped and frustrated by motherhood.
B. Bob often feels that other people don't like him and are talking behind his back.
C. Jack is unconsciously attracted to his sister-in-law and, though he seems to have no awareness of it, his sister-in-law senses these feelings.
D. Even after finding his lighter in the jacket worn the other day, Tony swears he never misplaces anything and someone must be playing a trick on him.
E. Whenever he is frustrated, Jack has a tantrum and destroys anything he can get his hands on.
F. The football coach loves to insult John and make him angry. Whenever he does this, the opposing team really suffers because then John begins to hit extra hard.

4. Suggest the most likely stage of fixation demonstrated in the descriptions provided below.

A. A husband has had long-term marital problems due to a continuing lack of interest in sex.
B. A chain smoker begins to eat whenever he becomes the least bit upset.
C. A young man is strongly attracted to much older women because of their protective, caring ways.
D. A young woman has all her CDs, tapes and the food in her cabinets organized alphabetically and the clothes in her closets are organized by color. The pencils on her desk all must be sharpened and her desk cleared off before she can work.

5. Below are criticisms of Freudian psychoanalysis. Identify which theorist would have been most likely to make each comment.

A. Freud focused on sex and aggression, when the really crucial need is to excel and be superior. People are attempting to resolve feelings of inferiority from childhood.

B. Freud saw the importance of the individual's past but failed to see the contribution of humanity's past. People have universal memories owing to the ancestry they share.

C. Freud misunderstood women. He believed they were motivated by envy for men when the true determining forces were social injustice and second-class treatment.

D. Freud emphasized a child's fear of the powerful father, but ignored the child's need for a powerful mother, especially during the baby's early years. He emphasized the dynamics of inner drives and impulses, but paid little attention to the child's relationship with others.

6. Consider the difference between the two learning schools by explaining how each would view the role of parents in personality formation.

7. Based on the three humanistic theorists, indicate how each thinker might account for a person's failure to reach his or her full potential.

8. Using the "Big Five" trait approach, indicate which set of traits would be most useful for describing each of the individuals described below.

A. Bob is stable, happy to meet people and well-liked. He has many friends and few worries.

B. Mary is neat, timely and dependable. She has relatively few interests or hobbies, but she is a good listener and is liked by her co-workers.

C. John complains constantly and worries about his health and his life in general. He reads widely and loves going to movies and to museums, but he always goes alone.

CHAPTER 13

Individual Development: Childhood and Adolescence

LEARNING OBJECTIVES

1.   List and discuss the stages of prenatal development.

2.   List harmful influences on prenatal development.

3.   List and discuss the motor and sensory capacities of newborns and infants.

4.   List and explain the fundamental principles of Piaget's theory of cognitive development.

5.   Describe the stages of Piaget's theory of cognitive development.

6.   Evaluate Piaget's theory of cognitive development.

7.   Describe the stages of language development.

8.   Distinguish between gender socialization and gender identity.

9.   List and discuss the explanations that have been given for sex-typing.

10.   Explain the principles of Kohlberg's theory of moral development and describe the stages.

11.   Summarize the criticisms of Kohlberg's theory of moral development.

12.   Discuss the "moral emotions" and their effect on moral development.

13.   List the various parental styles of child-rearing and discuss the effects of each.

14.   Summarize the factors that are associated with the most altruistic children.

15.   Describe the events that signal the onset of puberty in males and females and the relationship between age of onset and later adjustment.

16.   Summarize the evidence on the relationship between adolescence and emotional turmoil.

17.   Discuss the impact of childhood experience on adulthood.

CHAPTER CONCEPT MAP

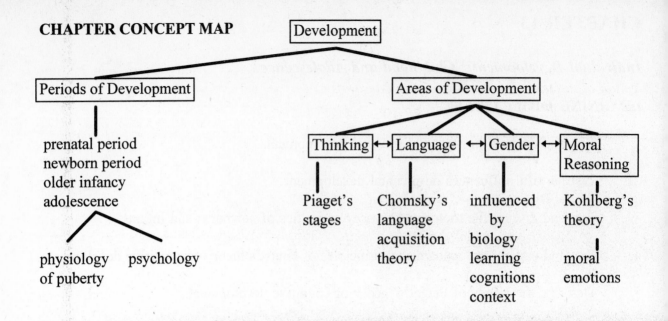

BRIEF CHAPTER SUMMARY

Chapter 13 describes the stages of prenatal development, which include the germinal stage, the embryonic stage and the fetal stage. The newborn is capable of processing information immediately, though there are many limitations to the newborn's abilities. According to Piaget's theory of cognitive development, thinking develops in four stages: the sensory-motor stage, the pre-operational stage, the concrete operations stage and the formal operations stage. While parts of Piaget's theory have been refuted, other parts have been confirmed. Ideas about language acquisition changed with the work of Noam Chomsky, who said that it does not appear that we acquire language in childhood strictly through a learning process, but rather, we have a mental module in the brain that is prepared to acquire language. Development of gender identity is complex, and many theories attempt to explain this phenomenon. Kohlberg's theory of moral reasoning is described along with a discussion of moral emotions and moral actions. Language, thinking, gender identity and moral reasoning are all areas of development that influence one another. Myths and realities of adolescent development are discussed. The physiology of puberty is described for males and females, along with the psychological issues of this period of development.

PREVIEW OUTLINE AND REVIEW QUESTIONS

Before you read the chapter, review the preview outline and the Learning Objectives for each section of the text. Develop additional questions of your own based on key concepts and terms and write them in the designated spaces. Answer all questions as you read the text.

SECTION 1 - FROM CONCEPTION TO THE FIRST YEAR (PP. 477-485)

I. **FROM CONCEPTION TO THE FIRST YEAR**
    A. **Definition and characteristics of development**
        1. The process of growth from a fetus to an adult including predictable changes in biological _____, physical structure, behavior and thinking
        2. Two approaches to development; gradual small steps or distinct stages
    B. **Prenatal development**
        1. Three stages
            a. _____ stage - fertilized egg (zygote) divides and attaches to the uterine wall; outside becomes placenta, inner part becomes embryo
            b. Embryonic stage - after implantation (about 2 weeks) to eighth week; embryo develops; _____ is secreted in males
            c. Fetal stage - after eighth week; development of organs and systems
        2. Teratogens - harmful influences that can cross the placental barrier
        3. Positive experiences - babies hear sounds in the last few months
    C. **The newborn child**
        1. Newborns have a series of reflexes; sensations are not fully developed
        2. Social skills - synchrony develops; three aspects to synchrony
    D. **The older infant** - rapid growth in first two years; biological capacities influenced by cultural expectations and customs

Answer these Learning Objectives while you read Section 1.

1. List and discuss the stages of prenatal development.

2. List harmful influences on prenatal development.

3. List and discuss the motor and sensory capacities of newborns and infants.

Write the questions that you have formulated below and answer them while you read.

A._____

B._____

SECTION 2 - COGNITIVE DEVELOPMENT (PP. 485-492)

II. **COGNITIVE DEVELOPMENT**
    A.   **The ability to think**
        1.   Piaget's theory - children understand and reason differently at different stages
        2.   Mental functioning depends on two biological processes: organization and _____, which takes two forms
            a.   Assimilation - fitting new information into present system of knowledge, beliefs, and _____ (categories of things and people)
            b.   _____ - must change or modify existing schemas to accommodate new information that doesn't fit
        3.   Piaget's cognitive stages
            a.   Sensory-motor stage - (birth to 2 years old)
                (1)   Infants learn through concrete actions
                (2)   Accomplish _____ permanence at around six months
                (3)   Object permanence begins representational thought - ability to use mental imagery and other symbolic systems
            b.   Preoperational stage - (ages 2 to 7)
                (1)   Abilities - can pretend
                (2)   Limitations - cannot _____ or use abstract principles (called operations), rely on "magical" reasoning, egocentric, lack conservation
                (3)   _____ operations stage (ages 6 or 7 to 11)
                (4)   Accomplishments - understand conservation, reversibility, cause and effect, identity, mathematical operations, serial ordering
                (5)   Thinking is still concrete, not abstract
            c.   Formal operations stage (ages 12 to adulthood)
                (1)   Beginning of _____ reasoning
                (2)   Can reason deductively, think about the future, problem-solve
        4.   Evaluating Piaget
            a.   Piagetian ideas that have been accepted
                (1)   New reasoning builds on previous abilities
                (2)   _____ of cognitive development hold up across cultures
                (3)   Children are not passive recipients of information; they interpret it
            b.   Challenges to Piagetian theory
                (1)   Shifts from stage to stage not as sweeping or clear cut
                (2)   Reasoning ability depends on content of problem and stage

          (3)   Children understand more than Piaget game them credit for

          (4)   Preschoolers are not as egocentric as Piaget thought, nor as fooled by appearances

                (a)   There may be two levels of perspective taking

                (b)   A theory of _____ has developed by age 4 or 5

          (5)   Children's cognitive development, like their biological development, occurs in a social and _____ context

B.   **The ability to speak**

    1.   An evolutionary adaptation of the human species

    2.   In first months, babies responsive to pitch, intensity and sound of language; people talk with more varied pitch and intonation - called _____

    3.   By 4 to 6 months, babies have learned many basic sounds of their language and over time lose ability to perceive speech sounds in another language

    4.   Between 6 months to one year, babies enter the _____ phase; infants become more familiar with the sound structure of their native language

    5.   Babies also develop gestures

    6.   Between 18 months and 2 years, two- and three-word combinations are produced; first combinations have a telegraphic quality

    7.   At same age they acquire new words at a rapid rate - a naming explosion

Answer these Learning Objectives while you read Section 2.

3.   List and discuss the motor and sensory capacities of newborns and infants.

4.   List and explain the fundamental principles of Piaget's theory of cognitive development.

5.   Describe the stages of Piaget's theory of cognitive development.

6.   Evaluate Piaget's theory of cognitive development.

7.   Describe the stages of language development.

Write the questions that you have formulated below and answer them while you read.

A._____

B._____

III.   GENDER DEVELOPMENT
A.   **Terminology**
1.   Sex - _____ and physiological attributes
2.   Gender - cultural and _____ attributes that children learn are appropriate for the sexes
3.   Gender _____ - fundamental sense of maleness or femaleness regardless of what one wears or does
4.   Gender socialization - called sex _____; the psychological process by which boys and girls learn what it means to be masculine or feminine
B.   **Biological factors**
1.   Biological and sociobiological theories believe some differences are inborn
2.   These researchers are critical of learning theories focusing on rewards because some characteristics are present regardless of rewards
C.   **Learning influences**
1.   Though learning principles can't account for all gender differences, systematic patterns of reinforcement do affect behavior
2.   Studies show aggression in boys and _____ abilities in girls rewarded
3.   Studies show parental attitudes and expectations influence older children
D.   **Gender schemas - focuses on cognitive abilities**
1.   Gender schemas divide people into _____ of male or female and all that is included in those categories - develops early
2.   Once gender schemas learned, children's behavior becomes more sex-typed
E.   **The specific situation - the social context**
1.   Certain _____ evoke sex-typed behavior
2.   A child's behavior depends on the gender of the playmate
3.   Sex-typed behaviors not as apparent when children are in single-sex groups
4.   Gender differences acquired in childhood do not necessarily _____

Answer these Learning Objectives while you read Section 3.

8.   Distinguish between gender socialization and gender identity.

9.   List and discuss the explanations that have been given for sex-typing.

Write the questions that you have formulated below and answer them while you read.

A._____

B._____

IV.   **MORAL DEVELOPMENT**
   A.   **Moral judgments: Reasoning about morality**
      1.   Piaget first formulated stages of moral reasoning in children
      2.   Kohlberg developed a new theory which states that there are three levels of moral reasoning which are _____ and occur in invariant order
         a.   Levels and stages
            (1)   Level 1 - preconventional morality
               (a)   Stage 1 - fear _____ for disobedience
               (b)   Stage 2 - in their best interest to obey
            (2)   Level 2 - conventional morality
               (a)   Stage 3 - based on trust, conformity and _____
               (b)   Stage 4 - a "law-and-order" orientation
            (3)   Level 3 - postconventional ("principled") morality
               (a)   Stage 5 - values and laws are relative and change
               (b)   Stage 6 - standard based on _____ human rights
         b.   Research finds stages 1, 5, and 6 are rare; stages 2, 3, and 4 develop _____ in many cultures
         c.   Limitations to the theory
            (1)   May reflect _____ ability rather than moral development favoring the educated and adults
            (2)   Some question the significance of the approach
            (3)   Moral reasoning depends on the situation - levels not fixed
         d.   Gilligan said according to Kohlberg's stages, males base moral reasoning on justice and females base moral reasoning on _____
            (1)   Most research finds no gender difference in moral reasoning
            (2)   Both genders use justice _and_ compassion in moral reasoning
   B.   **Moral emotions: Acquiring empathy, guilt and shame**
      1.   Capacity for moral feeling seems to be inborn
      2.   Children _____ parents' standards of good and bad behavior
      3.   Internalization begins with _____ - ability to feel good about another person's joy or bad about another person's unhappiness
         a.   Infants feel global empathy - general distress at another's misery
         b.   Toddlers have "_____" empathy - assume others feel as they do
         c.   By age two or three, children have empathy for another's feelings
         d.   By late childhood, can feel empathy for another's life condition
      4.   Shame -others have seen you doing something wrong and will like you less
      5.   _____ - when you have not lived up to your own internal standard
      6.   By the age of three or four, children judge their thoughts, feelings and behavior against the standards they know are "right"

C. Moral Action: Learning to behave morally

1. Learning theorists - actions learned from rewards, punishments and models
2. Parental methods of enforcing standards have effects on moral behavior
   a. Power _____
      (1) Threats, physical punishment, denial of privileges
      (2) Based on child's fear of punishment
      (3) Associated with a lack of moral feelings and behavior and negative outcomes for children
   b. Induction
      (1) More successful at teaching moral feelings and behavior
      (2) The parent appeals to the child's own _____, affection for others, and sense of responsibility
3. Baumrind's study finds three overall child-rearing styles and their results
   a. Authoritarian parents
      (1) Too much power, too little _____
      (2) Children have poorer social skills, self-esteem and school performance
   b. _____ parents
      (1) Nurturant but too little control and too few demands for mature behavior
      (2) Children are likely to be impulsive, immature, irresponsible and academically unmotivated
   c. Authoritative parents
      (1) Set clear disciplinary rules, set high but reasonable _____ and teach children how to meet them
      (2) Give emotional support and encourage two-way communication
      (3) Children have good self-control, high self-esteem and self-efficacy, are independent, mature, cheerful, helpful and thoughtful and do better in school
4. Parent's method of discipline interacts with child's temperament, _____ perceptions and context
5. Biggest influence on children's moral behavior is the _____ of others
6. Large-scale study finds the most altruistic children came from societies in which
   a. They are assigned many tasks
   b. They know that their work makes a genuine contribution
   c. Parents depend on the children's contributions
   d. Mothers have many responsibilities inside and outside the home
   e. Children respect parental authority

Answer these Learning Objectives while you read Section 4.

10.   Explain the principles of Kohlberg's theory of moral development and describe the stages.

11.   Summarize the criticisms of Kohlberg's theory of moral development.

12.   Discuss the "moral emotions" and their effect on moral development.

13.   List the various parental styles of child-rearing and discuss the effects of each.

14.   Summarize the factors that are associated with the most altruistic children.

Write the questions that you have formulated below and answer them while you read.

A._____

B._____

V.   **ADOLESCENCE**
  A.   **Definition** - period of development between _____, the age at which a person becomes capable of sexual reproduction, and adulthood
  B.   **The physiology of adolescence**: Puberty and the onset of reproductive capacity
    1.   Males
        a.   Reproductive glands stimulated to produce sperm from the testes
        b.   Produce higher levels of androgens than females
        c.   Nocturnal emissions, growth of tests, scrotum and penis occur
    2.   Females
        a.   Reproductive glands stimulated to produce eggs from the ovaries
        b.   Produce higher levels estrogens than males
        c.   Menstruation begins (called _____) and breasts develop
    3.   _____ responsible for secondary sex characteristics in both sexes
    4.   Timing of puberty significant; late maturers do better than early maturers
  C.   **The psychology of adolescence** and the process of individuation
    1.   Studies find that extreme turmoil and unhappiness are the exception
    2.   Three routes to adulthood identified
        a.   Those who have _____ emotional upsets
        b.   Those who have some difficulties and less stable self-esteem
        c.   About 20 percent have a tumultuous time; problems in background
VI. **CAN CHILDREN SURVIVE CHILDHOOD**
  A.   Events of the first year of life do not necessarily have permanent effects
  B.   The role of resilience in children of violent, abusive or alcoholic parents

Answer these Learning Objectives while you read Sections 5 and 6.

15.   Describe the events that signal the onset of puberty in males and females and the relationship between age of onset and later adjustment.

16.   Summarize the evidence on the relationship between adolescence and emotional turmoil.

17.   Discuss the impact of childhood experience on adulthood.

Write the questions that you have formulated below and answer them while you read.

A._____

B._____

FLASH CARDS

Cut the following chart along the borders and test yourself with the resulting flash cards.

13.1 MATURATION	**13.7 MOTOR REFLEXES**	**13.13 OPERATIONS**
13.2 GERMINAL STAGE	**13.8 SYNCHRONY**	**13.14 EGOCENTRIC THOUGHT**
13.3 EMBRYONIC STAGE	**13.9 ASSIMILATION**	**13.15 CONSERVATION**
13.4 FETAL STAGE	**13.10 ACCOMMODATION**	**13.16 THEORY OF MIND**
13.5 TERATOGENS	**13.11 OBJECT PERMANENCE**	**13.17 "MOTHERESE"**
13.6 FETAL ALCOHOL SYNDROME	**13.12 REPRESENTATIONAL THOUGHT**	**13.18 TELEGRAPHIC SPEECH**

13.13 In Piaget's theory, mental actions that are cognitively reversible.	13.7 Automatic behaviors that are necessary for survival.	13.1 The sequential unfolding of genetically governed behavior and physical characteristics.
13.14 Seeing the world only from one's own point of view; the inability to take another person's perspective.	13.8 The adjustment of one person's nonverbal behavior to coordinate with another's.	13.2 The first stage of prenatal development; the male sperm unites with the female egg, the zygote divides and attaches to the uterine wall.
13.15 The understanding that the physical properties of objects can remain the same even when their appearances change.	13.9 In Piaget's theory, the process of absorbing new information into existing cognitive structures, modifying them, if necessary, to fit.	13.3 The second stage of prenatal development; it occurs after implantation of the zygote is complete until the eighth week after conception.
13.16 A theory held by a child or adult about the way one's own mind and other peoples' minds work, and how people are affected by their beliefs.	13.10 In Piaget's theory, the process of modifying existing cognitive structures in response to experience and new information.	13.4 The third and final stage of prenatal development; from 8 weeks until birth; organs and systems further develop.
13.17 A manner in which most people speak to babies; their pitch is higher and more varied and the intonation is more exaggerated.	13.11 The understanding, which develops late in the first year of life, that an object continues to exist even when you can't see it or touch it.	13.5 External agents, such as a disease or chemical, that increase the risk of abnormalities in prenatal development.
13.18 A child's first combination of words, which omits (as a telegram did) unnecessary words.	13.12 The capacity for using mental images and other symbolic systems.	13.6 A pattern of physical and intellectual abnormalities in infants whose mothers drank an excessive amount of alcohol during pregnancy.

13.19 SEX VERSUS GENDER	13.25 POSTCONVENTIONAL STAGE OF MORAL REASONING	13.31 PERMISSIVE PARENTING STYLE
13.20 GENDER IDENTITY	13.26 EMPATHY AND ALTRUISM	13.32 AUTHORITATIVE PARENTING STYLE
13.21 GENDER SOCIALIZATION (SEX TYPING)	13.27 SHAME AND GUILT	13.33 PUBERTY
13.22 GENDER SCHEMA	13.28 POWER ASSERTION	13.34 MENARCHE
13.23 PRECONVENTIONAL STAGE OF MORAL REASONING	13.29 INDUCTION	13.35 "TURMOIL THEORY"
13.24 CONVENTIONAL STAGE OF MORAL REASONING	13.30 AUTHORITARIAN PARENTING STYLE	13.36 RESILIENCE

13.31 One of Baumrind's three child-rearing styles. This style is used by parents who are nurturant but exercise too little control and clear discipline.	13.25 The third stage of Kohlberg's theory of moral reasoning in which reasoning is based on universal human rights.	13.19 One term refers to the anatomical and physiological attributes; the other refers to the learned psychological and cultural attributes of the sexes.
13.32 One of Baumrind's three child-rearing styles. This style is used by parents who know how and when to discipline their children.	13.26 Moral emotions. One is the ability to feel bad about another's unhappiness and to feel good about another's joy. The other is concern for others.	13.20 The fundamental sense of being male or female, regardless of whether or not one conforms to the rules of sex typing.
13.33 The age at which a person becomes capable of sexual reproduction.	13.27 Moral emotions. One is a wound to the self-concept. The other is a result of feeling you have not lived up to your own internal standard.	13.21 The process by which children learn the behaviors, attitudes and expectations associated with being masculine or feminine in their culture.
13.34 The onset of menstruation.	13.28 A method of child-rearing in which the parent uses punishment and authority to correct the child's misbehavior.	13.22 A cognitive schema (mental network) of knowledge, beliefs, metaphors and expectations about what it means to be male or female.
13.35 A theory of adolescent development that holds that adolescent anguish and rebellion are necessary and inevitable.	13.29 A method of child-rearing in which the parent appeals to the child's own resources, abilities, sense of responsibility and feelings for others.	13.23 In Kohlberg's theory, the first stage of moral reasoning characterized by obedience based on fear of punishment or self-interest.
13.36 A characteristic of children who, as adults, do not experience specific and inevitable effects from painful or traumatic backgrounds.	13.30 One of Baumrind's three styles of child-rearing. This parenting style is related to the exercise of too much power and too little nurturance.	13.24 The second stage of Kohlberg's theory of moral reasoning characterized by reasoning based on trust, loyalty or "law and order."

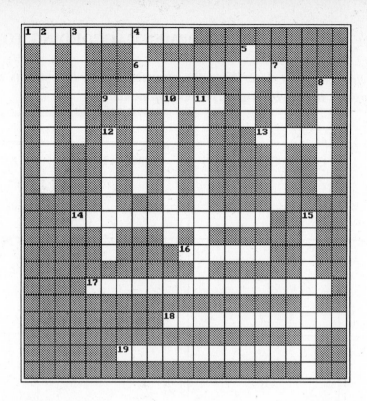

ACROSS

1. processes by which an organism grows from a fetus to an adult
6. agents that increase the risk of abnormalities in prenatal development
9. first stage of prenatal development
13. wound to the self-esteem
14. Piagetian process of modifying existing cognitive structures
16. developed a theory of cognitive development in children
17. type of thought involving the capacity for using mental images
18. understanding that physical properties of objects can remain the same even when their appearances change
19. child-rearing style that relies on the use of power

DOWN

2. seeing the world from only one's own point of view
3. the ability to feel bad and good about another person's circumstances
4. sequential unfolding of genetically governed behavior and physical characteristics
5. the third stage of prenatal development
7. the adjustment of one person's nonverbal behavior to coordinate with another's
8. the age at which a person becomes capable of sexual reproduction
10. child-rearing method in which child's own resources are appealed to
11. the process of absorbing new information into existing cognitive structures
12. onset of menstruation
15. mental actions that are cognitively reversible

STAGES OF COGNITIVE DEVELOPMENT ACCORDING TO PIAGET

Complete the following chart by describing the characteristics, limitations and achievements of each stage of Piaget's theory of cognitive development.

STAGE OF DEVELOPMENT	CHARACTERISTICS	LIMITATIONS	ACHIEVEMENTS
SENSORY-MOTOR STAGE			
PREOPERATIONAL STAGE			
CONCRETE OPERATIONS STAGE			
FORMAL OPERATIONS STAGE			

PRACTICE TEST 1

1. The order of the three stages of prenatal development is
   A. embryonic, germinal, fetal.
   B. germinal, fetal, embryonic.
   C. germinal, embryonic, fetal.
   D. fetal, germinal, embryonic.

2. During which stage of prenatal development do the eyes, ears, nose and mouth first develop?
   A. embryonic
   B. germinal
   C. fetal
   D. conception

3. Which of the following is a teratogen?
   A. coffee
   B. alcohol
   C. cigarettes
   D. all of the above

4. An infant touched on the cheek or corner of the mouth will turn in the direction he or she was touched and search for something to suck on. This is called the
   A. sucking reflex.
   B. rooting reflex.
   C. Moro reflex.
   D. Babinsky reflex.

5. During the first six to eight weeks, babies
   A. show a distinct preference for faces.
   B. show a distinct preference for curved lines over straight lines.
   C. can focus on parts of pictures.
   D. can track someone's location and movement.

6. Which of the following statements is true?
   A. Synchrony refers to the coordination of one person's behavior to another's.
   B. Newborns synchronize their behavior to adult speech, street noise, and tapping.
   C. Synchrony occurs in four stages.
   D. Synchrony is critical during the first year of life but unimportant later on.

7. The order of Piaget's stages of cognitive development is
   A. preoperational, sensory-motor, concrete operations, formal operations.
   B. concrete operations, preoperational, sensory-motor, formal operations.
   C. sensory-motor, preoperational, formal operations, concrete operations.
   D. sensory-motor, preoperational, concrete operations, formal operations.

8. Fitting new information into your present system of knowledge and beliefs is called
   A. assimilation.
   B. organization.
   C. accommodation.
   D. sensory-motor development.

9.   According to Piaget, during the concrete operations stage the child
      A.   thinks egocentrically.   B.   develops object permanence.
      C.   grasps conservation.   D.   can reason abstractly.

10.   Which of the following represents a challenge to Piaget's theory?
      A.   There seems to be no major shift from preoperational to concrete-operational
            thought.
      B.   Infants as young as 2-1/2 to 3-1/2 months are aware that objects continue to exist
            when masked by other objects.
      C.   Most 3- and 4-year-olds can take another person's perspective.
      D.   all of the above

11.   During the first months, babies are highly responsive to
      A.   normal adult talk.
      B.   the basic sounds of their native language.
      C.   the pitch, intensity and sound of language.
      D.   all of the above.

12.   "Mama here," "go 'way bug," and "my toy" are examples of
      A.   baby talk.   B.   telegraphic speech.
      C.   babbling.   D.   motherese.

13.   A child's fundamental sense of maleness or femaleness that exists regardless of what one
      wears or does is called
      A.   gender schema.   B.   gender socialization.
      C.   gender identity.   D.   sex-typing.

14.   According to gender schema theory
      A.   gender-typed behavior increases once a gender schema is developed.
      B.   gender schemas do not develop until a child is about four years old.
      C.   gender schemas are formed early and basically do not change throughout life
      D.   gender schemas change dramatically during adolescence.

15.   Which of the following is evidence of the influence of the social context on gender
      development?
      A.   Specific situations evoke sex-typed behaviors.
      B.   Boys and girls do not consistently differ in the traits of passivity or activity; their
            behavior depends on the gender of the child with whom they are playing.
      C.   Among preschoolers, girls are seldom passive with each other.
      D.   all of the above

16. Kohlberg's theory describes
   A. moral emotions.
   B. moral behavior.
   C. moral reasoning.
   D. moral actions.

17. According to Kohlberg's theory, moral reasoning is based on trust, conformity and loyalty to others in the _____ stage.
   A. preconventional
   B. postconventional
   C. conventional
   D. egocentric

18. Critics of Kohlberg's theory of moral development argue that
   A. the hierarchy of stages actually reflects verbal, not moral, development.
   B. adults and children use the same moral reasoning in all ethical situations.
   C. Kohlberg's work implies that women are more moral than men.
   D. the stages are too similar to be meaningful.

19. When children understand that someone else is in distress, but they assume that the other person must feel as they do, they are experiencing
   A. empathy for another's life condition.
   B. "egocentric" empathy.
   C. empathy for another's feelings.
   D. global empathy.

20. The emotion that one feels when one has not lived up to one's own internal standard is
   A. guilt.
   B. shame.
   C. internal empathy.
   D. remorse.

21. Parents who rely on power assertion for discipline produce children who
   A. lack moral feelings and behavior.
   B. accept responsibility for their misbehavior.
   C. have a sense of internal control.
   D. feel guilty if they hurt others and, thus, are considerate of other children.

22. Which of the following is true about altruistic children?
   A. They are assigned many responsibilities.
   B. Parents depend on the children's contributions.
   C. They know that their work makes a genuine contribution.
   D. all of the above

23. The major sign of puberty for females is
   A. the development of pubic hair.
   B. the growth spurt.
   C. menarche.
   D. acne.

24. Which of the following is true about the idea adolescence is inevitably a time of great turmoil?
    A.   Research has supported that adolescence is a time of anguish and rebellion.
    B.   The vast majority of adolescents experience turmoil, but a minority do not.
    C.   More than half of the adolescents in a large-scale study experienced few emotional upsets.
    D.   The emotional turbulence of adolescence has to do with hormonal changes.

25. The effect of childhood experiences on adulthood is
    A.   not inevitable; early traumas do not necessarily have life-long consequences.
    B.   irreversible.
    C.   a straight and inflexible line to the future.
    D.   unknown.

1.   Embryos that are genetically male will begin to secrete _____ during the _____ stage of prenatal development.
    A.   adrenalin; embryonic   B.   testosterone; embryonic
    C.   hormones; fetal   D.   estrogen; germinal

2.   Jane has smoked heavily during her pregnancy. What are the risks?
    A.   increased chance of miscarriage   B.   premature birth
    C.   her child may be hyperactive   D.   all of the above

3.   Which of the following should Jane avoid during her pregnancy?
    A.   coffee   B.   over the counter drugs
    C.   teratogens   D.   all of the above

4.   Doris and Morris just had their first child. What behaviors can they expect?
    A.   The newborn will be passive and inert.
    B.   The newborn can see, hear, touch, smell and taste.
    C.   The newborn will not be able to identify the primary caregiver.
    D.   The newborn can only see light and dark but no other features of the environment.

5.   Doris worries that when she breast feeds her baby, she will not be able to sense what the baby needs, when she is full or how to sit comfortably with her. What is likely to occur?
    A.   They will develop a synchrony of simultaneous movement.
    B.   They will begin to move at the same pace and rhythm.
    C.   They will develop a synchrony of coordination and smoothness.
    D.   all of the above

6.   While on a walk with his father, Butch points to a cardinal and his father says, "Birdie." A little bit later, Butch sees a blue jay and says, "Birdie." This is an example of
    A.   assimilation.   B.   conservation.
    C.   accommodation.   D.   an operation.

7.   The next day while walking with his dad, Butch points to a butterfly and says, "Birdie." His dad says, "That's a butterfly." Butch says, "Butterfly." This is an example of
    A.   assimilation.   B.   a schema.
    C.   accommodation.   D.   an operation.

8.   Butch's ability to say "birdie" and "butterfly" are indicators that he
    A.   can use representational thought.   B.   can use formal operations.
    C.   is still egocentric.   D.   can use concrete operations.

9. Which of the following is an example of a challenge to Piaget's theory?
   A. Babies look longer at a ball if it seems to roll through a solid barrier.
   B. When four-year-olds play with two-year-olds, they modify and simplify their speech so the younger child will understand.
   C. By the time children are four or five years old, they have developed a theory of mind.
   D. all of the above

10. Based on the stages of language development, which of the following would a four- to six-month-old baby be able to do?
    A. say "mommy" and "daddy"
    B. use telegraphic speech
    C. recognize "mommy" and "daddy"
    D. all of the above

11. In the first months of life, a baby is most likely to respond to
    A. his or name.
    B. the words "mommy" and "daddy."
    C. the basic sounds of his or her native language.
    D. speech in which the pitch is higher and more varied and spoken with exaggerated intonation.

12. Both Fran and Dan know that girls play with dolls and become nurses and boys play with trucks and become doctors. This demonstrates
    A. gender socialization.   B. biological gender differences.
    C. gender identity.   D. all of the above.

13. When Jill grows up she says she is going to be a boy and marry Jane. This demonstrates that Jill
    A. has a psychological problem.
    B. is going to be a homosexual.
    C. has not established her gender identity.
    D. has not yet experienced gender socialization.

14. The belief by children that bears, fire, anger, dogs, and the color black are "masculine" and butterflies, hearts, the color pink, and flowers are feminine indicates that
    A. children have accurate gender identity.
    B. children have been reinforced for these types of distinctions.
    C. children are learning the metaphors of gender that relate to gender schemas.
    D. there is a biological basis for these distinctions.

15. Kathryn is playing in a group with only girls. Which of the following is likely to occur?
    A.   She will play independently and actively.
    B.   She will stay very close to the teacher.
    C.   She will stand on the sidelines.
    D.   none of the above

16. In Kohlberg's theory of moral development, your moral stage is determined by
    A.   your answers to questions such as "Do you think it is morally acceptable to steal?"
    B.   your answers to hypothetical moral dilemmas.
    C.   your ability to explain right and wrong in terms of results rather than intentions.
    D.   your performance on tests of moral feelings and behavior.

17. A man's wife is dying and she needs a special drug. The man can't afford the drug and the druggist won't lower his price. Jose was asked if he thought the man should steal the drug. Jose replied that he shouldn't because it is against the law. Jose would be in the _____ stage of moral development according to Kohlberg's theory.
    A.   preconventional   B.   conventional
    C.   postconventional   D.   principled

18. Deborah decides not to cheat on a test because she is afraid of the consequences if she is caught. However, she decides to sneak into the hospital after visiting hours to see her friend because her friend's needs are more important than the hospital rules. This is an example of which criticism of Kohlberg's theory?
    A.   Stages 1, 5 and 6 are extremely rare.
    B.   People's responses reflect verbal abilities more than moral reasoning.
    C.   Children and college-educated people are favored in this approach.
    D.   People's reasoning depends on the situation they are reasoning about.

19. Jon felt _____ because he let himself down, but he felt _____ when a friend caught him in a lie.
    A.   guilt; shame   B.   anger; embarrassment
    C.   shame; guilt   D.   remorse; guilt

20. _____ parents have children who have lower self-esteem and do more poorly in school, whereas _____ parents have children with high self-esteem and self-efficacy.
    A.   Authoritarian; permissive   B.   Authoritarian; authoritative
    C.   Authoritative; authoritarian   D.   Permissive; authoritative

21. Larry and Mary want their children to be the kind of people who offer help, support and unselfish suggestions. Which of the following should they do?
   A. They should encourage them to participate in outside activities such as athletics and music lessons.
   B. They should make them responsible for themselves at an early age.
   C. They should have them assume tasks for the family and be sure they know their work makes a genuine contribution to the family.
   D. all of the above

22. Early-maturing boys
   A. generally have a negative body image compared to late-developing boys.
   B. are more likely to smoke, drink, use drugs and break the law than later-maturing boys.
   C. feel worse about themselves than do late-developing boys at first, but they end up the healthiest group.
   D. have more self-control and emotional stability than late-developing boys.

23. Which of the following is true for Gary, who just reached puberty?
   A. He has roughly the same amount of androgens and estrogens as a female.
   B. He has higher levels of androgens and estrogens than females.
   C. He has higher levels of androgens and lower levels of estrogens than females.
   D. He is likely to experience a growth spurt, which will begin, on average, at age 10, will peak at age 12 or 13, and will stop at about age 16.

24. Which of the following is also true for Gary as he proceeds through adolescence?
   A. He is likely to experience emotional turmoil, since that is normative for adolescents.
   B. He is likely to experience emotional turmoil only if he is American, since this aspect of adolescence rarely appears in other cultures.
   C. Most likely he will not experience emotional turmoil, since great turmoil appears to be the exception for adolescents, not the rule.
   D. There is an equal change that he will experience emotional turmoil or proceed calmly through adolescence.

25. Wanda is an adult who was abused in childhood by a parent. What is most likely true for her?
   A. Most likely she will not be an abusive parent herself, because 70 percent of adults who were abused in childhood do not repeat the abuse.
   B. There is a very good chance she will become abusive with her own children.
   C. If she receives counseling she may be able to avoid becoming an abusive parent.
   D. Whether she becomes an abusive parents depends on how resilient she is.

PRACTICE TEST 3

1. Prenatal development is associated with several dangers. Identify the dangers associated with:
   A. X-rays
   B. cigarettes
   C. alcohol
   D. drugs

2. A. You are part of a pediatric medical team and you are conducting an evaluation of a newborn infant. Discuss all the behaviors and sensory abilities that a normal newborn should have.
   B. Many people think newborn attachment is instinctive. Discuss behaviors that contribute to attachment between the newborn and the caregiver.

3. A. A four-year-old girl insists small people must live in the TV because they are right there behind the glass. Identify her stage of cognitive development and the phenomenon being displayed by this child.
   B. A child adept at roller skating goes ice skating for the first time. She keeps trying to stand and move just as she would on roller skates but she falls again and again. According to Piaget, what is necessary for mastery of this new skill?
   C. A child threatened to tell his parents when his older brother gave him only one of the three candy bars they were supposed to share. The older child then broke his brother's bar in half and gave him two pieces. This satisfied both children because they each had two pieces. Identify the cognitive stages of these children and the disadvantage that allows the younger child to be cheated.
   D. Previously, whenever Johnny banged with a spoon, his mother would put it in a drawer and Johnny would quickly move on to something else. Now that he's eight months old, this isn't working. The child continues to demand the spoon even though he can't see it. Identify the cognitive stage of this child and the change that has taken place.

4. Harold has been babysitting for Jennie since she was an infant. She is now 23 months old. Harold has always tried to get Jennie to speak. He is now trying to get her to say, "The apple is on the table." Describe what Jennie's response might have been at 4 months old, 10 months old, 14 months old and at 23 months old.

5. Based on the description of the child, indicate what child-rearing styles each child's parents most likely used.

    A. Rosie feels good about herself and she sets high standards for her own performance. She is well-liked, helpful, independent and cooperative.

    B. Walter is quite timid and appears to have low self-esteem. He does not seem to know how to interact with other children.

    C. Henrietta is impulsive, immature, irresponsible and not particularly motivated.

6. Five people have been asked to explain why stealing is wrong. From the explanations provided, identify the most likely level of moral reasoning.

    A. Jim believes stealing is wrong because it hurts the feelings of others.

    B. Jane believes stealing is wrong because it is against the law.

    C. Joshua believes stealing is wrong because it violates the principle that everyone should work hard to acquire his or her own things.

    D. Jennifer believes most stealing is wrong, but in some cases, like saving someone's life, it can be justified.

    E. Joe believes stealing is wrong because you could be caught and punished.

7. Ron and Rita are going through adolescence.

    A. Describe the biological changes each is experiencing.

    B. Describe the psychological and social changes each is experiencing.

CHAPTER 14

Health, Stress, and Coping

LEARNING OBJECTIVES

1.   Describe Selye's stages of stress response and compare his theory to current theories.

2.   Describe the functioning of the immune system.

3.   Summarize the aims of psychoneuroimmunology and health psychology.

4.   List and discuss the major sources of stress.

5.   Describe four hypothesized relationships between emotion and disease.

6.   List and discuss the personality factors that affect health and the ability to cope with stress.

7.   Define locus of control and explain its relationship with health and well-being.

8.   Distinguish between primary and secondary control and explain how they differ across cultures.

9.   List and explain the major methods of coping with stress.

10.   Discuss the relationship between social networks and health and well-being.

11.   List and explain the psychological factors that are important to good health.

CHAPTER CONCEPT MAP

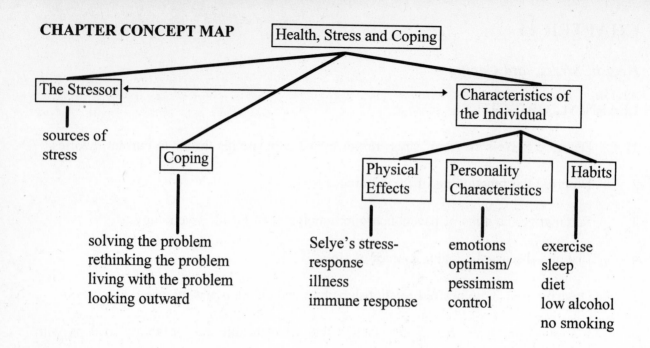

BRIEF CHAPTER SUMMARY

Chapter 14 examines the effects of stress on our lives. Selye's stress response cycle includes the alarm phase, the resistance phase and the exhaustion phase. Several fields, including health psychology and behavior medicine, study the relationship between psychological factors and health. Stress is no longer considered a purely biological condition that leads directly to illness, but rather an interaction between aspects of the individual and aspects of the environment. Current research is in the area of psychoneuroimmunology, which is an interdisciplinary field that looks at the relationship among psychological processes, the nervous and endocrine systems and the immune system. Personality characteristics of the individual, health habits and coping skills influence a person's physical and emotional response to stress. Several coping methods are reviewed, including solving the problem, thinking about the problem differently and living with the problem.

PREVIEW OUTLINE AND REVIEW QUESTIONS

Before you read the chapter, review the preview outline and Learning Objectives for each section of the text. Develop additional questions of your own based on key concepts and terms and write them in the designated spaces. Answer all questions as you read the text.

SECTION 1 - THE NATURE OF STRESS (PP. 518-526)

I.   **THE NATURE OF STRESS**
  A.   **Disciplines that study stress**
    1.   Health psychology
      a.   Looks at how psychological factors influence health
      b.   Takes a salutogenic approach
      c.   Studies and promotes factors that generate health
    2.   _____ medicine
      a.   An interdisciplinary approach to health and illness
      b.   Draws on findings from medicine, nutrition, physiology, psychology and other fields
    3.   Psychology and medicine have historically taken a pathogenic approach that focuses on why people get sick
  B.   **Alarm and adaptation**
    1.   Stressors
      a.   Environmental factors that throw the body out of balance
      b.   They force the body to respond by mobilizing its resources to fight or flee
      c.   Stress is not always negative - _____ is positive or good stress
    2.   Hans _____ focused on biological responses to stressors and identified three phases of the bodies response to stress
      a.   Alarm phase - the organism mobilizes
      b.   _____ phase - resists or copes with a threat which makes the body more susceptible to other stressors
      c.   Exhaustion phase - occurs if the stressor persists; body's resources are overwhelmed
    3.   Later studies have found that stress is not just a biological condition leading directly to illness
      a.   Qualities of the individual have an influence on the effects of stress
      b.   How the individual copes with stress has an effect
    4.   Definition of psychological stress - the result of an exchange between the person and the environment, in which the person believes that the situation strains or overwhelms his or her resources and is endangering well-being

C. **Illness and immunology**
  1. Different approaches
     a. Early approach came from _____ medicine within psychiatry and was based on the belief that many disorders caused by neuroses
     b. Today seen as a physical disorder affected by psychological factors
     c. Psychoneuroimmunology - examines why some people get sick and others don't
  2. Two functions of the immune system
     a. Recognize foreign substances (_____)
     b. Destroy or deactivate foreign substances
  3. Two types of white blood cells recognize and destroy foreign substances
     a. Lymphocytes - recognize and destroy foreign cells
        (1) Natural _____ cells - detect and reject tumors
            (a) B cells - produce antibodies
            (b) T cells - make direct contact with the antigen
                i) Killer T cells - destroy antigens
                ii) Helper T cells - enhance immune response
     b. _____ - ingest and eliminate those cells
  4. Stress can suppress these cells that fight disease and infection
D. **Sources of stress**
  1. Bereavement and tragedy
     a. Those who are bereaved taker poorer care of themselves
     b. Separation also has direct effect on the body
  2. Daily _____ - more hazardous to people who overreact
  3. Continuing problems - worse when interminable and uncontrollable

Answer these Learning Objectives while you read Section 1.

1. Describe Selye's stages of stress response and compare his theory to current theories.

2. Describe the functioning of the immune system.

3. Summarize the aims of psychoneuroimmunology and health psychology.

4. List and discuss the major sources of stress.

Write the questions that you have formulated below and answer them while you read.

A._____

B._____

II.   THE INDIVIDUAL SIDE OF HEALTH AND WELL-BEING

    A.   Personality and emotions

        1.   Possible links between emotion and disease

            a.   Disease may cause the emotion rather than the opposite

            b.   Unhealthy habits may cause the disease

            c.   Something else entirely may cause both the emotion and the disease

            d.   Mind and _____ interact

        2.   Two views about the relationship between negative emotion and disease

            a.   The way people manage emotion predicts well who will get sick

            b.   The way people manage emotion is unrelated to who gets sick

        3.   Personality type and illness

            a.   Type A behavior pattern - ideas about this have changed

                (1)   _____ is the characteristic in this pattern that is dangerous

                (2)   Neurotic hostility unrelated to heart disease

                (3)   Antagonistic hostility related to heart disease in men

            b.   _____ personality styles may be at highest risk for illness

        4.   Connection between negative emotions and disease is elusive - may be that both extremes of expression of negative emotions may be more at risk

    B.   Optimism and pessimism

        1.   Explanatory styles associated with characteristic responses to bad events

            a.   Optimistic

                (1)   Explains events as external, _____ and limited in impact

                (2)   May produce good health and greater longevity

            b.   Pessimistic

                (1)   Explains events as internal, stable and global

                (2)   Associated with less self-esteem and achievement and more illness and slower recovery from trauma

        2.   May have to do with how individuals cope with stress

    C.   Healthy habits

        1.   Include sleep, exercise, diet, moderate alcohol intake, not smoking

        2.   Obstacles to healthy habits

            a.   Many habits become entrenched in _____

            b.   Consequences of bad habits not immediate - reduces incentive

            c.   Healthy habits largely _____ of one another

            d.   Healthy habits unstable over time

        3.   Factors that influence ability to overcome obstacles

            a.   Social system

            b.   Cultural environment

            c.   Access to _____ services

D. **The question of control: Fight or flow?**
1. Self-_____ - a predictor of good health practices
2. Locus of control - expectation that the results of one's actions are under one's control
   a. Internal locus of control - believe they have control
   b. External locus of control - believe they don't have control
3. The benefits of control
   a. Difficult events more tolerable if more predictable
   b. Feeling in control reduces chronic pain, improves adjustment to surgery and illness, speeds up recovery from diseases
   c. Sense of control affects _____ and immune systems
4. Some problems with control
   a. Trying to control the uncontrollable can be a problem
   b. Doesn't help people to believe they could have controlled a past event that they felt unable to cope with
   c. A middle-class, _____ view - some groups are less optimistic
   d. One study showed the only type of control related to health was self-efficacy
   e. Influenced by _____
      (1) Westerners emphasize _____ control - modify the situation
      (2) Easterners emphasize _____ control - modify perceptions, goals or desires
      (3) Combining both types of control works best

Answer these Learning Objectives while you read Section 2.

5. Describe four hypothesized relationships between emotion and disease.

6. List and discuss personality factors that affect health and the ability to cope with stress.

7. Define locus of control and explain its relationship with health and well-being.

8. Distinguish between primary and secondary control and explain how they differ across cultures.

Write the questions that you have formulated below and answer them while you read.

A._____

B._____

328

III.   **COPING WITH STRESS**
    A.   **Coping**
        1.   Constantly changing _____ and behavioral efforts to manage demands in the environment or in oneself that one feels or believes to be stressful
        2.   Not a single strategy; people cope differently with different stressors over time
    B.   **Four general strategies**
        1.   Solving the problem
            a.   _____-focused coping
            b.   Problem-focused coping
                (1)   Begins with _____ the problem correctly
                (2)   Benefits - increases person's self-esteem, control and effectiveness
            c.   Good to use combination of emotion and problem-focused coping
        2.   Rethinking the problem - thinking about problems in new ways
            a.   _____: "It's not so bad"
            b.   Social comparisons: "I'm better off than some people, and I can learn from those who are doing better than I am"
            c.   _____ vs. avoidance: "Tell me everything" vs. "It's not important; let's go to the movies" - advantages and disadvantages to both
            d.   Humor: "People are funny" - humor is helpful
        3.   Living with the problem
            a.   _____ - benefits on the immune system; can use meditation
            b.   Exercise - good for physical and mental health
        4.   Looking outward - compassion; "healing through helping"

Answer this Learning Objective while you read Section 3.

9.   List and explain the major methods of coping with stress.

Write the questions that you have formulated below and answer them while you read.

A._____

B._____

IV.   THE SOCIAL SIDE OF HEALTH AND WELL-BEING
   A.   When friends help you cope
          1.   Studies show positive effects of social network
          2.   May effect _____ functioning
          3.   Most helpful for those with _____ levels of stress; neutral for those with
                 average levels of stress; harmful for those with low levels of stress
          4.   Parents are important source of support
          5.   What is defined as support is influenced by _____ expectations
   B.   Coping with friends
          1.   Several factors affect whether support helps or not
                 a.   _____ of support
                 b.   Timing of support
                 c.   Type of support
                 d.   Density of support
                        (1)   Dense networks are those in which friends all know one
                               another
                        (2)   Generally works well for women
          2.   Close relationships can provide support if good, stress if bad
V.   THE MIND-BODY CONNECTION
   A.   The degree of influence of psychological factors is unclear
   B.   General conclusions
          1.   Social support is a fundamental human need
          2.   People should practice habits associated with health
          3.   The effects of stress are worsened when a person feels _____
          4.   Once in a stressful situation, some ways of coping are better than others

Answer these Learning Objectives while you read Sections 4 and 5.

10.   Discuss the relationship between social networks and health and well-being.

11.   List and explain the psychological factors that are important to good health.

Write the questions that you have formulated below and answer them while you read.

A._____

B._____

FLASH CARDS

Cut the following chart along the borders and test yourself with the resulting flash cards.

14.1 HEALTH PSYCHOLOGY	**14.6 RESISTANCE PHASE OF STRESS**	**14.11 PSYCHO-NEUROIMMUNOLOGY**
14.2 BEHAVIORAL MEDICINE	**14.7 EXHAUSTION PHASE OF STRESS**	**14.12 HASSLES**
14.3 PATHOGENIC	**14.8 EUSTRESS**	**14.13 TYPE A BEHAVIOR PATTERN**
14.4 SALUTOGENIC	**14.9 PSYCHOLOGICAL STRESS**	**14.14 NEUROTIC HOSTILITY**
14.5 ALARM PHASE OF STRESS	**14.10 PSYCHOSOMATIC**	**14.15 ANTAGONISTIC HOSTILITY**

14.11 The study of the relationships among psychology, the nervous system and the immune system.	**14.6** The second phase of the stress response cycle identified by Selye in which the organism attempts to resist or cope with a threat that cannot be avoided.	**14.1** A field within psychology that addresses psychological factors that influence how people stay healthy and why they become ill.
14.12 Everyday irritations that some psychologists argue are a greater source of stress than the bigger problems.	**14.7** The third phase of the stress response cycle identified by Selye in which the body's resources become overwhelmed.	**14.2** A field that takes an interdisciplinary approach to health and illness, drawing on findings in medicine, nutrition, physiology and psychology.
14.13 A set of qualities proposed as a predictor of heart disease. It describes people who are irritable, ambitious and impatient.	**14.8** Positive or beneficial stress.	**14.3** An approach to the topic of health that focuses on why people get sick, emphasizing those who are at high risk of becoming ill.
14.14 The type of hostility felt by people who are complaining and irritable. It is not related to heart disease.	**14.9** The result of a relationship between a person and the environment in which the person believes the situation is overwhelming.	**14.4** An approach to the topic of health that focuses on wellness and on people who theoretically should become sick but don't.
14.15 The type of hostility felt by people who are aggressive, confrontational, rude, cynical and uncooperative. It is linked to heart disease for men.	**14.10** A term that describes the interaction between a physical condition and psychological states; literally means mind (psyche) and body (soma).	**14.5** The first phase in the stress response cycle identified by Selye in which the organism mobilizes to meet a threat with basic biological responses.

14.16 "DISEASE-PRONE PERSONALITY"	14.21 PRIMARY CONTROL	14.26 REAPPRAISAL
14.17 PESSIMISTIC EXPLANATORY STYLE	14.22 SECONDARY CONTROL	14.27 SOCIAL COMPARISONS
14.18 OPTIMISTIC EXPLANATORY STYLE	14.23 COPING	14.28 AVOIDANCE AND VIGILANCE
14.19 INTERNAL LOCUS OF CONTROL	14.24 EMOTION-FOCUSED COPING	14.29 SOCIAL INTEREST
14.20 EXTERNAL LOCUS OF CONTROL	14.25 PROBLEM-FOCUSED COPING	14.30 DENSE NETWORK

14.26 Reassessing the meaning of a problem. This is one way to think about a problem in a new way.	**14.21** An effort to modify reality by changing other people, the situation, or events; a "fighting back philosophy."	**14.16** People who are chronically depressed, angry and hostile, worried and anxious.
14.27 A way to rethink the problem is to compare oneself to others who are less fortunate.	**14.22** An effort to accept reality by changing one's own attitudes, goals or emotions; a "learn to live with it" philosophy.	**14.17** One type of characteristic response to bad events associated with less self-esteem, less achievement, more illness, slow recovery.
14.28 Vigilance involves scanning all information for evidence of threat. Avoidance involves avoiding threatening information using distraction.	**14.23** Cognitive and behavioral efforts to manage demands in the environment or oneself that one feels to be stressful.	**14.18** One type of characteristic response to bad events associated with external, unstable and specific explanations of bad events.
14.29 The ability to understand other people's needs, feel empathy and attachment, and cooperate with others for the common welfare.	**14.24** A coping style that concentrates on the emotions the problem caused, whether anger, anxiety or grief.	**14.19** A general expectation that one's actions are under one's own control.
14.30 A network of friends in which friends all know one another.	**14.25** A coping style that generally includes defining the problem, learning about it and considering possible actions.	**14.20** A general expectation that one's actions are beyond one's control.

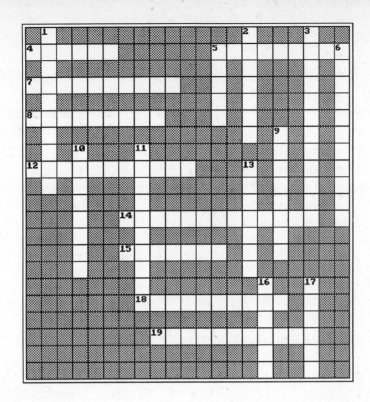

ACROSS

4. type of psychology that looks at how people stay healthy
5. coping style that involves distracting oneself from threatening information
7. approach to health that focuses on why people get sick
8. coping style that involves scanning all information for evidence of threat
12. approach to health that focuses on wellness
14. interaction between a physical illness and psychological states
15. everyday irritations
18. third phase of Selye's stress response model
19. reassessing the meaning of a problem

DOWN

1. type of medicine that takes an interdisciplinary approach to health and illness
2. primary and secondary _____
3. type of hostility linked to heart disease for men
5. first stage in Selye's stress response syndrome
6. optimistic or pessimistic _____ style
9. type of hostility not related to heart disease
10. positive or beneficial stress
11. second stage in Selye's stress response model
13. type of control involving a "fighting back" philosophy
16. efforts to manage stressful demands
17. optimistic and pessimistic

PRACTICE TEST 1

1. According to Selye, the body mobilizes to meet a threat during which stage?
   A. alarm
   B. resistance
   C. activation
   D. exhaustion

2. Current theories of stress response emphasize
   A. central nervous system sensitivity.
   B. psychological factors that mediate between the stressor and the stress.
   C. psychoneuroimmunology.
   D. how aversive the stressor actually is.

3. The immune system
   A. keeps us stress free.
   B. prepares our bodies for the fight or flight response.
   C. recognizes and defends the body against foreign substances.
   D. is designed to do all of the above.

4. Recognizing and destroying foreign cells are the primary job of
   A. red blood cells.
   B. lymphocytes.
   C. phagocytes.
   D. all of the above.

5. Which of the following are lymphocytes?
   A. natural killer cells
   B. B cells
   C. T cells
   D. all of the above

6. Which field takes an approach to health and illness that includes findings from medicine, nutrition, physiology and other fields?
   A. health psychology
   B. psychosomatic medicine
   C. behavioral medicine
   D. all of the above

7. Scientists interested in exploring the links between the psychological and physical processes involved in illness created an interdisciplinary field called
   A. health psychology.
   B. psychosomatic medicine.
   C. psychoneuroimmunology.
   D. behavioral medicine.

8. Most researchers believe that the most serious threat to health is posed by
    A. bereavement and separation.   B. emotional coping styles.
    C. continuing problems.   D. an external locus of control.

9. The stressfulness of noise depends on _____, whereas reactions to crowding as a stressor depend in part on _____.
    A. whether it can be controlled; whether you like the people
    B. whether it is unpleasant; whether it is desired
    C. whether it can be controlled; culture
    D. how loud it is; the amount of room there is

10. Which of the following is true about the relationship between emotion and disease?
    A. Emotions seem unrelated to physical health.
    B. Large scale studies have found that depressed women are far more likely to get breast cancer.
    C. The disease may cause the emotion.
    D. The way people manage negative emotions predicts with great accuracy whether they will become ill.

11. The part of the Type A personality pattern that seems to be hazardous to health is
    A. a fast work pace.   B. intensity.
    C. an achievement orientation.   D. hostility.

12. Which of the following is NOT one of the hypothesized relationships between emotion and disease?
    A. Unhealthy habits may cause the disease.
    B. Certain types of emotions seem to cause certain diseases.
    C. Something else entirely may cause both the emotion and the disease.
    D. The mind and body interact.

13. Which of the following is most associated with health risks?
    A. depression   B. Type A personality
    C. repressive personality styles   D. Type B personality

14. Explaining negative events as external, unstable and specific is characteristic of a(n)
    A. optimistic explanatory style.   B. repressive personality style.
    C. pessimistic personality style.   D. Type A personality.

15. Which of the following is related to an internal locus of control?
    A. astrology   B. playing the lottery
    C. wearing seat belts   D. emotion-focused coping

16. Scheduled exams are more stressful than pop quizzes because
    A. students can vent their emotions.
    B. students are more optimistic.
    C. students have more control.
    D. students can get more rest.

17. Compared to Western cultures, Eastern cultures, such as Japan's, emphasize
    A. primary control.
    B. internal control.
    C. secondary control.
    D. external control.

18. Which of the following demonstrates a problem with believing that an event is controllable?
    A. People could be unrealistically confident and try to control the uncontrollable.
    B. People could blame themselves for a problem they could not control.
    C. For some people, the realities of their lives are less controllable than for others.
    D. all of the above

19. Properly defining the problem is part of
    A. emotion-focused coping.
    B. rethinking the problem.
    C. problem-focused coping.
    D. vigilance.

20. When Susan has a medical procedure, she wants all the facts and information she can collect. She is exhibiting
    A. vigilance.
    B. avoidance.
    C. external locus of control.
    D. looking outward.

21. Which of the following is NOT one of the three ways of coping with stress?
    A. solving the problem
    B. resisting the problem
    C. reappraising the problem
    D. living with the problem

22. Which of the following quotes demonstrates strategies for reappraising the problem?
    A. "It's not so bad."
    B. "I'm better off than some people, and I can learn from those who are doing better than I am."
    C. "Tell me everything." or "It's not important."
    D. All of the above are strategies for reappraising the situation.

23. Friends may help you cope with stress by suggesting plans of action. This is an example of
    A. emotional support.
    B. reappraisal.
    C. cognitive guidance.
    D. tangible support.

24. Social support can actually be harmful if your stress level is
    A.   very high.   B.   average.
    C.   highly variable.   D.   very low.

25. Which of the following is a conclusion from findings related to health psychology?
    A.   Social support is a fundamental human need.
    B.   It is important to follow good health habits.
    C.   The effects of stress are worsened when a person feels helpless.
    D.   all of the above

1. Ellen is in finals week and she has been getting by on very little sleep. She is managing to prepare for her tests, but she is more irritable than usual and feels like she might be getting the flu. This would be compatible with the _____ of Selye's model.
    A. alarm stage   B. exhaustion stage
    C. resistance stage   D. activation stage

2. What would current models of stress predict about other students' reactions to finals week?
    A. An individual's reaction will depend on qualities such as personality traits, perceptions and his or her coping style.
    B. All students will find finals week stressful.
    C. A student's reaction will depend on how hard he or she has studied.
    D. The stress will result in physiological arousal (the alarm phase), which will be followed by the resistance phase.

3. You have the flu. The _____ recognize and destroy these foreign flu cells and the _____ ingest and eliminate these cells.
    A. lymphocytes; antigens   B. phagocytes; lymphocytes
    C. lymphocytes; phagocytes   D. phagocytes; natural killer cells

4. Which of the following is NOT one of the kinds of lymphocytes that aid in the recognition and destruction of foreign cells?
    A. B cells   B. Killer T cells
    C. Helper K cells   D. Natural killer cells

5. Dr. Weller is conducting research on the health behaviors of people who become ill and those who do not. What field of study does this represent?
    A. health psychology   B. psychoneuroimmunology
    C. behavior medicine   D. any of the above

6. The study mentioned in question 5 takes a _____ approach to health.
    A. salutogenic   B. pathogenic
    C. psychopathological   D. medical

7. Lucinda has just been diagnosed with breast cancer. She is convinced that if she has the right attitude, curing her illness is simply a question of "mind over matter." This is an example of
   A. one interpretation of the major conclusions in health psychology.
   B. one of the major conclusions from psychoneuroimmunology.
   C. a misconception that has mistakenly come out of health psychology.
   D. optimistic thinking.

8. In a study of police officers, the most stressful things reported included
   A. arresting people.   B. paper work.
   C. undercover work.   D. high-speed chases.

9. Crowding is most stressful
   A. in a small room.   B. on a hot day.
   C. in a crowd of strangers.   D. when you feel crowded.

10. Which of the following would most stress researchers believe to be the most serious threat to health?
    A. being chronically unemployed   B. crowding
    C. traffic jams   D. the demands of executives

11. After learning that Lucinda has cancer, Sally said, "She was so depressed, it's no wonder she got cancer." What are some other possible explanations for the relationship between depression and cancer?
    A. Perhaps the cancer caused the depression.
    B. Perhaps being depressed caused her to have poor health habits.
    C. Perhaps something else entirely caused both the cancer and the depression.
    D. All of the above are possible explanations.

12. Who among the following men has a higher risk for coronary heart disease?
    A. John is intense, ambitious, hard-driving and successful.
    B. Ron is complaining and irritable.
    C. Don is aggressive, confrontational, rude, cynical and uncooperative.
    D. Lon is easy-going and calm.

13. Which personality style may be at greater risk of serious illness and, once he or she has contracted a disease, which person may die sooner than the others?
    A. Phil has been diagnosed with clinical depression.
    B. Bill is a classic Type A personality.
    C. Lil is never angry, fearful, or anxious.
    D. Will is a true Type B personality.

14. Which of the following is likely to have been said by someone with a pessimistic explanatory style?
     A.   "This problem is all my fault and it's going to ruin my life."
     B.   "I couldn't do anything about this."
     C.   "I have had terrible luck today."
     D.   "Everything will be fine."

15. Maria has been diagnosed with cancer. She has gotten several opinions from different doctors, has read several articles and books on the subject, and has spoken with other cancer patients. She plans to have input into her treatment. She is exhibiting
     A.   internal locus of control.   B.   optimistic control.
     C.   self-efficacy.   D.   all of the above.

16. "To lose is to win" and "The true tolerance is to tolerate the intolerable" are statements that reflect
     A.   primary control.   B.   secondary control.
     C.   locus of control.   D.   self-control.

17. Which of the following statements reflects the only variety of control that, in one study, was related to health?
     A.   "I am basically in charge of my own life and well-being."
     B.   "Whatever goes wrong with my health is my fault."
     C.   "If I eat right, I can avoid all illness."
     D.   "If I become sick, it was meant to be."

18. Which of the following examples reflects the best strategy for solving a problem?
     A.   "I must make a plan of action."
     B.   "I must deal with my feelings about what happened."
     C.   "It is best not to think about this, since there is very little I can do."
     D.   "I must deal with my feelings and make a plan of action."

19. Shelley's mother recently died at age 68. Thinking about her friend Sara, whose mother died at age 49, makes her feel better and more accepting about her situation. This is an example of
     A.   social comparisons.   B.   vigilance.
     C.   humor.   D.   avoidance.

20. The strategy used by Shelley in the previous question is an example of which category of coping techniques?
     A.   solving the problem   B.   living with the problem
     C.   rethinking the problem   D.   vigilance

21. When is it best to use vigilance and when is it desirable to use avoidance strategies?
    A. Vigilance should be used at all times; it is never desirable to use avoidance.
    B. Vigilance is called for when action is possible and necessary, but once the decision is out of one's hands, avoidance and distraction are good coping tactics.
    C. Vigilance is called for when stressors are continuous or can be prepared for; avoidance should be used when the stressor is sudden.
    D. Vigilance should be used by people with Type A personalities, and avoidance is appropriate for those with repressive personality styles.

22. Amanda has experienced high levels of stress lately. She is coping with it by meditating regularly, exercising daily and doing some volunteer work. These are examples of which category of coping techniques?
    A. solving the problem
    B. reappraising of the problem
    C. living with the problem
    D. making social comparisons

23. Who among the following is most likely receive health benefits from social support?
    A. Anyone receiving social support is likely to receive health benefits.
    B. Cal, who has been experiencing very high levels of stress, will benefit.
    C. Hal, who has been experiencing average levels of stress, will benefit.
    D. Sal, who has been experiencing low levels of stress, will benefit.

24. Anne's mother died last week and her friend, Carl, is trying to cheer her up and help her to stop feeling so sad. This is an example of
    A. a situation in which a friend might contribute to stress.
    B. efforts to stem her grief prematurely, which is not helpful.
    C. bad timing; it is too soon after her loss for this type of help, however, it could be helpful later on.
    D. all of the above.

25. Which of the following is a psychological factor that is thought to be important to good health?
    A. social support
    B. health habits
    C. feelings of control
    D. all of the above

PRACTICE TEST 3

1. Indicate which member of each pair is likely to experience greater stress. Explain why.

    A. Air traffic controllers versus fishermen
    B. Type A personalities versus Type B personalities
    C. Subjects with an external locus of control versus subjects with an internal locus of control
    D. Subjects with a large social network versus single subjects
    E. Subjects with an optimistic versus pessimistic explanatory style

2. Apply Hans Selye's phases of stress response to people being held hostage. Describe what they would experience in the alarm, resistance and exhaustion phases.

3. Over a period of years, David has been under treatment for a variety of disorders, including depression and ulcers. Visits to the doctor and prescriptions have been fairly regular because symptoms recur or new ones break out whenever medication is stopped. The doctor is now beginning to suggest that the origin of the problems must be related to stress or his depression.

    A. How could stress make recurring symptoms possible?
    B. What are some possible relationships that might exist between David's depression and his illnesses?
    C. What must David examine about himself and his life?

4. Assume that a group of hostages has been held by terrorists for several years. For each description, indicate whether stress has been reduced through attempts to solve, reappraise or live with the problem, and identify the specific coping strategy being used.

    A. Margaret has decided her captors have no bad intentions and are just trying to make an important philosophical point.
    B. Frank believes escape would be difficult but not impossible. He keeps formulating escape plans and explaining them to others, hoping for one that is reasonable.
    C. Joe believes this disaster has a bright side. Had another terrorist group taken them, there might have been torture as well as captivity.
    D. Like Frank, Tony believes escape is possible, but only if the terrorists unexpectedly slip-up. His goal is to remain as calm as possible and look for an opportunity. He refuses to waste energy and lose hope by developing or considering unrealistic escape plans.
    E. Joan believes the group will remain in captivity virtually forever. Her goal is to eat as regularly as possible and combat inactivity through exercise.

CHAPTER 15

Psychological Disorders

LEARNING OBJECTIVES

1. Discuss the ways in which abnormal behavior has been defined.

2. Distinguish between projective and objective tests.

3. Summarize the positions supporting and criticizing the *Diagnostic and Statistical Manual of Mental Disorders* (DSM).

4. List and describe the principle characteristics of the anxiety disorders.

5. Distinguish among major depression, dysthymia and bipolar disorder.

6. Explain the various theories that attempt to account for depression.

7. List the general features of personality disorders and three specific personality disorders.

8. Describe the features of antisocial personality disorder and theories explaining the causes.

9. List and discuss the characteristics of the three types of dissociative disorders.

10. Describe the current controversy about the validity and nature of dissociative identity disorder (multiple personality disorder).

11. List the signs of substance abuse.

12. Distinguish between the disease model of addiction and the learning model of addiction.

13. List the components that interact to influence addiction and abuse.

14. Describe the symptoms of schizophrenia.

15. Explain the vulnerability-stress model of schizophrenia.

CHAPTER CONCEPT MAP

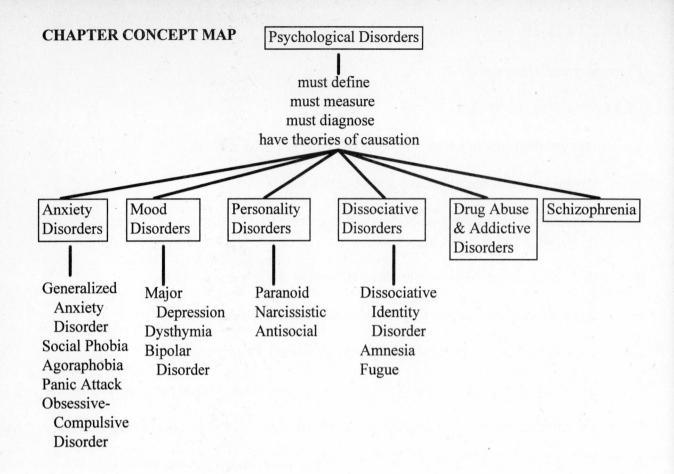

Psychological Disorders

must define
must measure
must diagnose
have theories of causation

| Anxiety Disorders | Mood Disorders | Personality Disorders | Dissociative Disorders | Drug Abuse & Addictive Disorders | Schizophrenia |

Generalized
Anxiety
Disorder
Social Phobia
Agoraphobia
Panic Attack
Obsessive-
Compulsive
Disorder

Major
Depression
Dysthymia
Bipolar
Disorder

Paranoid
Narcissistic
Antisocial

Dissociative
Identity
Disorder
Amnesia
Fugue

BRIEF CHAPTER SUMMARY

Chapter 15 defines mental disorder and examines the difficulties involved in reaching an acceptable definition for abnormality. The issues involved in measuring abnormal behavior and developing a reliable and valid diagnostic system are also discussed. Objective and projective psychological tests are described. The *Diagnostic and Statistical Manual*, which is the manual that contains descriptions of all diagnostic categories, is reviewed. Some of the problems with the diagnostic system are described. Six general categories of disorders are reviewed. The text describes symptoms, predisposing factors and theories of causation for specific mental disorders under each category of disorder.

PREVIEW OUTLINE AND REVIEW QUESTIONS

Before you read the chapter, review the preview outline and the Learning Objectives for each section of the text. Develop additional questions of your own based on key concepts and terms and write them in the designated spaces. Answer all questions as you read the text.

SECTION 1 - DEFINING DISORDER (PP. 553-555) AND
SECTION 2 - DILEMMAS OF DIAGNOSIS (PP. 555-561)

I. **DEFINING DISORDER**
- A. **Current definitions** - each is useful, none enough by itself
  1. Violation of cultural _____ - depends on the culture
  2. Maladaptive behavior
  3. Emotional _____
  4. Legal definition - impaired judgment and lack of self-control
- B. **Definition used by text** - any behavior or emotional state that causes an individual great _____ or worry; is self-defeating or self-destructive; or is maladaptive and disrupts the person's relationships or the larger community

II. **THE DILEMMAS OF DIAGNOSIS**
- A. **Measuring mental disorders**
  1. Psychological tests
     - a. Projective tests
       - (1) Rely on the projection of _____ conflicts
       - (2) Weak reliability and validity
     - b. Objective tests or inventories
       - (1) Standardized questionnaires
       - (2) Have better reliability and validity than projective tests
       - (3) Minnesota _____ Personality Inventory (MMPI)
         - (a) One of the most widely used
         - (b) Developed in the 1930's and revised in 1989
         - (c) Criticisms of the MMPI
           - i) May be _____ and culturally biased
           - ii) Some scales overlap
           - iii) Some scales based on inadequate and outdated norms
           - iv) Some items affected by the respondent's tendency to give the appropriate answer
           - v) Reliability and validity questioned for use with normal population
  2. Critics of tests believe that they cannot replace clinical judgment

B. **Diagnosis: Art or science?**

1. The *Diagnostic and* _____ *Manual of Mental Disorders* ("DSM") is the "bible" of psychological and psychiatric diagnosis
   a. Primary aim - _____; to provide criteria of diagnostic categories
   b. Makes no assumptions about the causes of the disorders
   c. Classifies each disorder according to five _____ or factors
      (1) Primary diagnosis
      (2) Ingrained aspects of the individual's _____
      (3) General medical conditions relevant to the disorder
      (4) "Psychosocial and environmental problems" that can make the disorder worse
      (5) Global assessment of the patient's overall functioning
2. Limitations of the DSM
   a. It may foster overdiagnosis and self-fulfilling prophecies
   b. It confounds serious "mental disorders" with _____ problems in living
   c. Diagnoses can be misused for social and political purposes
   d. It implies that the subjective art of diagnosis can be made _____ scientific
      (1) Weak reliability of diagnostic categories indicates subjectivity
      (2) Inclusion and exclusion of disorders not always based on empirical evidence but on pressures and cultural standards
3. Advocates say when used correctly, diagnoses are more accurate and bias is reduced

Answer these Learning Objectives while you read Sections 1 and 2.

1. Discuss the ways in which abnormal behavior has been defined.

2. Distinguish between projective and objective tests.

3. Summarize the positions supporting and criticizing the *Diagnostic and Statistical Manual of Mental Disorders* (DSM).

Write the questions that you have formulated below and answer them while you read.

A. _____

B. _____

III. ANXIETY DISORDERS
A. Anxiety and phobias
    1. Generalized anxiety disorder
        a. Symptoms
            (1) Continuous, _____ anxiety or worry
            (2) Feelings of foreboding and dread
        b. Causes - no single cause, but there are _____ factors
            (1) Hereditary predisposition
            (2) Inadequate coping skills
            (3) Traumatic events
            (4) Psychological dispositions
        c. There are precipitating factors
    2. Posttraumatic stress disorder (PTSD) or acute stress disorder
        a. When anxiety results from
            (1) Uncontrollable and unpredictable danger such as rape
            (2) Natural disasters such as _____ or hurricanes
        b. PTSD is diagnosed when reaction is delayed
        c. _____ stress disorder is diagnosed when reaction is immediate
        d. Symptoms of both disorders
            (1) Reliving the trauma
            (2) "Psychic numbing"
            (3) Increased physiological arousal
    3. Phobias
        a. Unrealistic fear of a specific situation, activity or thing
        b. Social phobia - persistent, irrational fear of situations in which they will be _____ by others
        c. Agoraphobia - fear of being alone in a public place from which _____ might be difficult or help unavailable
            (1) The most disabling phobia
            (2) May begin with _____ attacks - sudden onset of intense fear, then avoiding situations that might provoke another attack
            (3) Panic attacks not uncommon; whether it develops into a disorder depends on how the reactions are _____
            (4) Symptoms of panic attacks include heart palpitations, dizziness and faintness
            (5) Hypothesized causal factors of panic attacks
                (a) Biological abnormalities
                (b) Heritable component

B. Obsessions and compulsions

     1. _____
         a. Recurrent, persistent, unwished for thoughts
         b. May be frightening or repugnant

     2. Compulsions
         a. Repetitive, ritualized behaviors
         b. People feel a lack of control over the compulsion
         c. Common compulsions include repeated hand washing, counting, touching and checking things

     3. They are serious when they interfere with a person's life

Answer this Learning Objective while you read Section 3.

4. List and describe the principle characteristics of the anxiety disorders.

Write the questions that you have formulated below and answer them while you read.

A._____

B._____

SECTION 4 - MOOD DISORDERS (PP. 565-569)

IV. MOOD DISORDERS
  A. **Depression and mania**
    1. Major depression - disrupts ordinary functioning
      a. Symptoms - emotional, _____, cognitive and physical
      b. Incidence - higher rates in women
    2. _____ - depressed mood which is milder but more chronic
    3. Bipolar disorder - depression alternates with mania
      a. Mania - an abnormally high state of exhilaration
      b. Mania almost always occurs with depression as bipolar disorder
  B. **Causes of depression**
    1. Biological explanations - genetics and brain chemistry
      a. _____ and/or serotonin levels
        (1) Depression may be associated with deficiencies
        (2) Antidepressant drugs increase levels
      b. Possible genetic component to bipolar disorder, major depression
    2. Social explanations - conditions of people's lives; may explain gender differences in depression rates
      a. Marriage and _____ associated with lower rates of depression
      b. Being a mother associated with higher rates of depression
      c. Social-economic factors and history of _____ abuse are related
    3. Attachment explanations - disturbed _____ and separations
      a. Disruption of a primary relationship most often sets off a depressive episode
      b. Cause and effect is not clear
    4. Cognitive explanations and the _____ theory of depression
      a. Try to pinpoint cognitive styles associated with depression
      b. Problem of cause and effect

Answer these Learning Objectives while you read Section 4.

5. Distinguish among major depression, dysthymia and bipolar disorder.

6. Explain the various theories that attempt to account for depression.

Write the questions that you have formulated below and answer them while you read.

A._____

B._____

351

V. PERSONALITY DISORDERS

    A.   **Definition** - _____, maladaptive traits that cause great distress or inability to get along with others

    B.   **Problem personalities**

        1.   Paranoid personality disorder - pervasive, unfounded _____ and mistrust

        2.   Narcissistic personality disorder - exaggerated sense of self-importance

    C.   **Antisocial personality disorder**

        1.   Individuals who lack _____, morality, emotional attachments, empathy and shame

        2.   Must distinguish between antisocial _____ and antisocial personalities

            a.   Most antisocial behaviors peak in late adolescence and drop off by late-twenties and are a result of age, situation, and peer group

            b.   Antisocial personalities begin with problem behaviors in childhood

        3.   Other characteristics

            a.   More common in males

            b.   Lack of emotional arousal

            c.   About half of them "burn out" after age 40

        4.   Theories of causation

            a.   Central nervous system abnormalities have been suggested

            b.   One theory centers around behavioral _____ - an inherited characteristic shared by those who are antisocial, hyperactive, addicted or impulsive

            c.   May have suffered neuropsychological impairments from physical abuse or birth complications

            d.   Brain damage can interact with social _____ or neglect

            e.   Can be encouraged/discouraged by the values of the culture

Answer these Learning Objectives while you read Section 5.

7.   List the general features of personality disorders and three specific personality disorders.

8.   Describe the features of antisocial personality disorder and theories explaining the causes.

Write the questions that you have formulated below and answer them while you read.

A._____

B._____

VI. DISSOCIATIVE DISORDERS

   A. **Definition** - disorders in which consciousness, behavior and identity are split
      1. Dissociative states are intense and seem out of one's control
      2. Often are in response to _____ events
   B. **Amnesia and fugue**
      1. Amnesia - sudden inability to remember important personal information
         a. When organic condition not responsible, called psychogenic
         b. Only _____ (threatening) information is forgotten
      2. _____ states - person forgets identity and habits and wanders far away
         a. Often takes on new identity and life
         b. Can last for days or many years
   C. **Dissociative identity disorder ("Multiple personality")**
      1. The appearance of two or more identities within one person
      2. Two opposing views among mental health professionals
         a. A real disorder, common but often underdiagnosed or misdiagnosed
            (1) Believed to develop in childhood as a response to _____
            (2) Physiological differences between the personalities lend veracity to the disorder
         b. A creation of mental health clinicians who believe in it
            (1) Research used to support the diagnosis is seriously flawed
            (2) Clinicians are creating it through the power of _____
      3. Alternative _____ explanation
         a. Seen as an extreme form of a normal human process: the ability to present different aspects of our personalities to others
         b. May be a way for troubled people to understand their problems
         c. Other personalities are rewarded by clinicians with attention

Answer these Learning Objectives while you read Section 6.

9. List and discuss the characteristics of the three types of dissociative disorders.

10. Describe the current controversy about the validity and nature of dissociative identity disorder (multiple personality disorder).

Write the questions that you have formulated below and answer them while you read.

A._____

B._____

VII.   DRUG ABUSE AND ADDICTION

  A.   **From use to abuse** - definition of substance _____: maladaptive pattern of substance use leading to clinically significant impairment or distress

  B.   **Addiction: Disease or social problem?**

  1.   Explanations for why people become addicts

  a.   Personality explanations - _____ seekers

  b.   Environment explanations - family history and peer pressure

  2.   Results from longitudinal study on alcoholism

  a.   Some people went through times of problem drinking, then stopped

  b.   Factors thought to cause alcoholism were found to be a result of it

  3.   Models of addiction

  a.   Disease model of alcoholism promotes abstinence - widely accepted

  (1)   Supports the notions of tolerance and withdrawal

  (2)   Supports the idea that there is an _____ predisposition

  (3)   Research is contradictory and inconclusive

  (4)   Opposition to the disease model cites that

  (a)   Addiction patterns vary according to _____

  (b)   Not all drug users go through physiological _____

  (c)   Abstinence policies can _____ rates of alcoholism

  b.   Learning model - causes are physical, personal and social

  c.   Life-process model - addiction is a way of coping

  4.   Models disagree about whether former alcoholics can drink in _____

  5.   Factors that predict whether controlled drinking is possible include: previous severity of dependence, social stability, _____ about abstinence

  C.   **Physiology, psychology, personality and culture interact to cause addiction**

Answer these Learning Objectives while you read Section 7.

11.   List the signs of substance abuse.

12.   Distinguish between the disease model of addiction and the learning model of addiction.

13.   List the components that interact to influence addiction and abuse.

Write the questions that you have formulated below and answer them while you read.

A._____

B._____

VIII. **SCHIZOPHRENIA**
    A.   **Schizophrenia** - a psychosis or condition involving distorted perceptions of
                _____ and an inability to function in life
    B.   **The nature of the "schizophrenias"**
        1.   Active or _____ symptoms - distortions of normal processes and behavior
            a.   Bizarre _____ - beliefs
            b.   Hallucinations - usually auditory; seem intensely real
            c.   Disorganized, incoherent speech - illogical jumble of ideas
            d.   Grossly _____ and inappropriate behavior like catatonia
        2.   Negative symptoms - loss of former abilities
            a.   Loss of _____ - inability to pursue goals
            b.   Poverty of speech - empty replies reflecting diminished thought
            c.   Emotional flatness - general unresponsiveness
        3.   Severity and duration of symptoms vary; onset can be abrupt or gradual
        4.   Prognosis is unpredictable and falls into the "rule of thirds"
    C.   **Theories of the schizophrenias**
        1.   There is disagreement about whether it is one, or more than one disorder
        2.   Some symptoms appear cross-culturally
        3.   Biological factors that have been studied
            a.   Brain abnormalities - some found but none consistently
               (1)   Possibly a result of early brain damage
               (2)   Possibly a result of a genetic problem
            b.   _____ abnormalities possibly related to dopamine receptors; research is inconclusive
            c.   Infectious prenatal _____ theory - explains some characteristic patterns of the disease
        4.   Vulnerability-stress model - combines biological _____ and stress

Answer these Learning Objectives while you read Section 8.

14.   Describe the symptoms of schizophrenia.

15.   Explain the vulnerability-stress model of schizophrenia.

Write the questions that you have formulated below and answer them while you read.

A._____

B._____

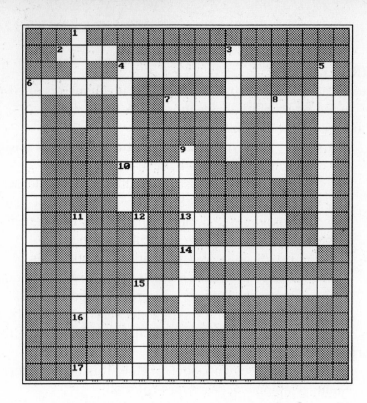

ACROSS

2. category of disorders that includes depression
4. mood disorder involving disturbances in emotion, behavior, cognition and body function
6. category of disorders that includes phobias and PTSD
7. category of disorders that includes amnesia and fugue
10. the opposite of depression
13. one model of addiction
14. general term that refers to disorders involving distorted perceptions of reality - includes schizophrenia
15. a psychotic disorder or disorders
16. one theory of depression involving early relationships between infant and caregiver
17. the learned _____ theory of depression

DOWN

1. type of phobia involving irrational fear of being observed by others
3. mood disorder in which mania and depression alternate
4. chronic depressed mood
5. objective tests
6. "fear of fear"
8. maladaptive pattern of substance use
9. a type of substance use characteristic of abuse
11. partial or complete loss of memory for threatening information
12. personality disorder characterized by lying, stealing and manipulating others

FLASH CARDS

Cut the following chart along the borders and test yourself with the resulting flashcards.

15.1 MENTAL DISORDER	**15.7 GENERALIZED ANXIETY DISORDER**	**15.13 PANIC ATTACK**
15.2 INSANITY	**15.8 POSTTRAUMATIC STRESS DISORDER**	**15.14 OBSESSIVE-COMPULSIVE DISORDER**
15.3 OBJECTIVE TESTS (INVENTORIES)	**15.9 ACUTE STRESS DISORDER**	**15.15 MAJOR DEPRESSION**
15.4 PROJECTIVE TESTS	**15.10 PHOBIA**	**15.16 DYSTHYMIA**
15.5 MINNESOTA MULTIPHASIC PERSONALITY INVENTORY (MMPI)	**15.11 SOCIAL PHOBIA**	**15.17 MANIA**
15.6 DSM	**15.12 AGORAPHOBIA**	**15.18 BIPOLAR DISORDER**

15.13 A feeling of intense fear and impending doom, accompanied by intense physiological symptoms such as rapid breathing and dizziness.	15.7 A continuous state of anxiety marked by feelings of worry and dread, apprehension, difficulties in concentration and signs of motor tension.	15.1 Any behavior or emotional state that causes great suffering; is self-destructive; is maladaptive and disrupts the community or relationships.
15.14 An anxiety disorder in which a person feels trapped in repetitive, persistent thoughts (obsessions) and repetitive behaviors (compulsions).	15.8 Delayed anxiety resulting from experiencing an uncontrollable or unpredictable danger or a natural disaster.	15.2 A legal term used to indicate that someone is incompetent to stand trial. The term is not used in relation to mental disorders.
15.15 A mood disorder involving disturbances in emotion, behavior, cognition and body function.	15.9 Immediate anxiety resulting from experiencing an uncontrollable or unpredictable danger or a natural disaster.	15.3 Standardized objective questionnaires requiring written responses; typically include scales on which people are asked to rate themselves.
15.16 A chronic depressed mood in which the symptoms are milder than in major depression; a person's customary way of functioning.	15.10 An unrealistic fear of a specific situation, activity or object.	15.4 Tests used to infer a person's unconscious motives, thoughts and conflicts based on interpretations of ambiguous stimuli.
15.17 The opposite of depression; an abnormally high state of exhilaration.	15.11 Persistent, irrational fear of situations in which people know they will be observed by others. They fear doing or saying something embarrassing.	15.5 A widely used objective personality test.
15.18 A mood disorder in which depression alternates with mania (excessive euphoria).	15.12 "Fear of fear;" a set of phobias, often set off by a panic attack, involving the basic fear of being away from a safe place or person.	15.6 The "bible" of psychological and psychiatric diagnosis; contains descriptions and diagnostic criteria of more than 300 mental disorders.

15.19 PERSONALITY DISORDERS	**15.25 AMNESIA (PSYCHOGENIC)**	**15.31 TOLERANCE**
15.20 PARANOID PERSONALITY DISORDER	**15.26 FUGUE STATE**	**15.32 LEARNING MODEL OF ADDICTION**
15.21 NARCISSISTIC PERSONALITY DISORDER	**15.27 DISSOCIATIVE IDENTITY DISORDER (MULTIPLE PERSONALITY DISORDER)**	**15.33 SCHIZOPHRENIA**
15.22 ANTISOCIAL PERSONALITY	**15.28 SUBSTANCE ABUSE DISORDER**	**15.34 PSYCHOSIS**
15.23 DISSOCIATIVE DISORDERS	**15.29 DISEASE MODEL OF ADDICTION**	**15.35 "WORD SALADS"**
15.24 SOCIOCOGNITIVE EXPLANATION (OF DISSOCIATIVE DISORDERS)	**15.30 WITHDRAWAL**	**15.36 VULNERABILITY-STRESS MODEL (OF SCHIZOPHRENIA)**

15.31 Greater and greater amounts of a drug are required to produce the same effect.	**15.25** When no organic causes are present, a dissociative disorder involving partial or complete loss of memory.	**15.19** Rigid, maladaptive personality patterns that cause personal distress or an inability to get along with others.
15.32 This position argues that alcoholism is a result of physical, personal and social factors. It is "a central activity of an individual's way of life."	**15.26** A person not only forgets his or her identity, but gives up customary habits and wanders far from home, possibly taking on a new life and identity.	**15.20** A disorder characterized by a pervasive, unfounded suspicion and mistrust of other people, irrational jealousy and secretiveness.
15.33 A psychotic disorder or disorders with some or all of these symptoms: hallucinations, delusions, disorganized speech, emotional abnormalities.	**15.27** A rare dissociative disorder marked by the appearance within one person of two or more distinct personalities.	**15.21** A disorder characterized by an exaggerated sense of self-importance and self-absorption.
15.34 An extreme mental disturbance involving distorted perceptions and irrational behavior. It may have psychological or organic causes.	**15.28** According to the DSM-IV, it is "a maladaptive pattern of substance use leading to clinically significant impairment or distress."	**15.22** A disorder characterized by antisocial behavior, such as lying, stealing, manipulating others, and sometimes violence and a lack of social emotions.
15.35 The illogical jumble of ideas and symbols, linked by meaningless rhyming words or remote associations, sometimes used by schizophrenics.	**15.29** The position that alcoholism is a disease over which an individual has no control and from which he or she never recovers.	**15.23** Conditions in which normally integrated consciousness or identity is split or altered, as in psychogenic amnesia.
15.36 A theory of schizophrenia that suggests biological vulnerability and stress are necessary to produce schizophrenia.	**15.30** When an individual discontinues the use of a substance, he or she experiences severe physiological reactions.	**15.24** This explanation suggests that multiple personality disorder is an extreme form of a normal human process.

PSYCHOLOGICAL DISORDERS

Complete the following chart indicating the major symptoms, predisposing factors and explanatory theories for each of the disorders described in the left-hand column

TYPE OF DISORDER	MAJOR SYMPTOMS	PREDISPOSING FACTORS	EXPLANATORY THEORIES
ANXIETY DISORDERS **Generalized Anxiety Disorder**			
Social Phobia			
Agoraphobia			
Panic Attack			
Obsessive-Compulsive Disorder			
MOOD DISORDERS **Major Depression**			
Dysthymia			
Bipolar Disorder			
PERSONALITY DISORDERS **Paranoid**			
Narcississtic			
Antisocial			
DISSOCIATIVE DISORDERS **Dissociative Identity Disorder**			
Amnesia			
Fugue			
SUBSTANCE ABUSE			
SCHIZOPHRENIA			

PRACTICE TEST 1

1. According to the _____ definition of mental disorder, a person who shows a total lack of sexual interest exhibits abnormal behavior.
    A. maladaptive behavior
    B. violation of cultural standards
    C. emotional distress
    D. impaired judgment

2. Which of the following is <u>NOT</u> one of the definitions of mental disorder?
    A. statistical deviation
    B. lack of self-control
    C. violation of cultural standards
    D. emotional distress

3. In general, _____ tests have better reliability and validity than _____ tests.
    A. objective; subjective
    B. objective; projective
    C. written; verbal
    D. projective; objective

4. The primary aim of the *Diagnostic and Statistical Manual of Mental Disorders* ("DSM") is
    A. to provide clear criteria of diagnostic categories.
    B. to describe the causes of particular disorders.
    C. to describe the best course of treatment for a particular disorder.
    D. all of the above.

5. Which of the following is <u>NOT</u> one of the criticisms of the DSM?
    A. It confounds serious "mental disorders" with normal problems in living.
    B. Its heavy emphasis on theory may alienate clinicians from different perspectives.
    C. It implies that the subjective art of diagnosis can be made objectively scientific.
    D. It fosters overdiagnosis and self-fulfilling prophecies.

6. Generalized anxiety disorder is marked by
    A. unrealistic fears of specific things or situations.
    B. continuous, uncontrollable anxiety or worry.
    C. the sudden onset of intense fear or terror.
    D. unwished-for thoughts and repetitive behaviors.

7. The most disabling fear disorder that accounts for more than half of the phobia cases for which people seek treatment is called
    A. panic disorder.
    B. social phobia.
    C. claustrophobia.
    D. agoraphobia.

8. Checking the furnace repeatedly before one can sleep and washing one's hands many times in a hour are examples of
   A. obsessions.
   B. phobias.
   C. compulsions.
   D. superstitions.

9. Dysthymia refers to _____ symptoms of depression.
   A. sudden, intense
   B. chronic, intense
   C. sudden, mild
   D. chronic, mild

10. Unlike normal sadness or grief, major depression involves
    A. panic attacks.
    B. low self-esteem.
    C. a lack of interest in outside activities.
    D. a negative mood.

11. Most manic episodes alternate with
    A. episodes of depression.
    B. panic attacks.
    C. obsessive-compulsive episodes.
    D. periods of elation.

12. Social theories of depression suggest that women are more likely to be depressed than men because they are more likely to lack
    A. endorphins and key neurotransmitters.
    B. positive self-images.
    C. fulfilling work and family relations.
    D. a stable network of friends.

13. Individuals with _____ personality disorder are unreasonably and excessively suspicious, jealous and mistrusting.
    A. narcissistic
    B. paranoid
    C. antisocial
    D. phobic

14. Individuals suffering from antisocial personality disorder are often charming and can be highly successful
    A. psychotherapists.
    B. con men.
    C. actors.
    D. business executives.

15. Hypothesized causes of antisocial personality disorder include
    A. problems in behavioral inhibition.
    B. neurological impairments.
    C. social deprivation.
    D. all of the above.

16. A sudden inability to remember certain important personal information describes
    A. psychogenic amnesia.
    B. a fugue state.
    C. dissociative identity disorder.
    D. post-traumatic stress disorder.

17. The controversy among mental health professionals about dissociative identity disorder has to do with
    A. whether it is a common and underdiagnosed disorder or whether it is concocted by mental health professionals and suggestible patients.
    B. whether it should be treated with traditional techniques or whether special treatments should be utilized.
    C. whether it is a biologically-based disorder or whether it results from psychosocial factors.
    D. whether the alternate personalities should be "seen" in treatment or whether they should be ignored by the therapist.

18. According to the DSM-IV, the key feature of substance abuse is
    A. the length of time a person has been using the drug.
    B. the inability to stop using the drug or to cut down on use.
    C. a maladaptive pattern of use leading to significant impairment or distress.
    D. all of the above.

19. The disease model of addiction
    A. requires abstinence.
    B. maintains that people have an inherited predisposition for alcoholism.
    C. holds that addiction is a biochemical process involving tolerance and withdrawal.
    D. incorporates all of the above.

20. At the heart of the debate between the disease and learning models of addiction is the question of whether
    A. moderate drinking is possible for former alcoholics.
    B. alcoholics should be blamed for their alcoholism.
    C. there is an alcoholic personality.
    D. alcoholics are "bad" or "sick".

21. Bizarre delusions, hallucinations, incoherent speech, disorganized and inappropriate behavior are _____ symptoms of schizophrenia.
    A. positive or active   B. negative
    C. catatonic   D. maladaptive

22. Negative symptoms of schizophrenia
    A. may begin before and continue after positive symptoms.
    B. include loss of motivation.
    C. include diminished thought and emotional flatness.
    D. include all of the above.

23. Support for the idea of an infectious virus during prenatal development as a cause of schizophrenia comes from the fact that
    A. there are seasonal patterns in the births of schizophrenic children.
    B. most schizophrenics have very low immune functioning.
    C. most schizophrenics show abnormalities on chromosome 5.
    D. most schizophrenics have extra dopamine receptors.

24. Which of the following has been advanced as one of the biological explanations of schizophrenia?
    A. brain abnormalities   B. extra dopamine receptors
    C. genes   D. all of the above

25. The idea that genetic or brain abnormalities combine with family or other pressures to trigger schizophrenia reflects the
    A. interactionist model   B. learning theory model
    C. vulnerability-stress model D. biology-pressure model

PRACTICE TEST 2

1. Jody is very fearful of being far from a hospital or in a situation in which she could not get help quickly. She won't go out in traffic or crowds and refuses to travel. This behavior is beginning to effect her job. It meets which definition of mental disorder?
    A.   maladaptive behavior   B.   impaired judgment
    C.   violation of cultural standards   D.   lack of self-control

2. You are taking a psychological test in which you respond in writing to a questionnaire with multiple choice items. What type of test is this?
    A.   projective   B.   objective
    C.   Thematic Apperception   D.   none of the above

3. Projective is to objective as
    A.   reliable is to valid.   B.   conscious is to unconscious.
    C.   unconscious is to conscious.   D.   abnormal is to normal.

4. The diagnoses of Disorder of Written Expression and Caffeine-Induced Sleep Disorder represent which criticism of the DSM?
    A.   the idea that diagnosis can be made objectively scientific
    B.   misusing diagnoses for social and political purposes
    C.   confounding serious "mental disorders" with normal problems in living
    D.   the fostering of overdiagnosis and self-fulfilling prophecies

5. Advocates of the DSM argue that
    A.   when the manual is used correctly, diagnoses are more accurate and bias is reduced.
    B.   correct labeling of a disorder leads people to the proper treatment.
    C.   while some diagnoses reflect society's biases, some mental disorders occur in all societies.
    D.   all of the above are valid.

6. Whenever Linda has to speak in public, she feels intensely anxious and uncomfortable. She fears she will humiliate herself. The only reason she agrees to do so is to keep her job. Linda has
    A.   an antisocial personality disorder.   B.   a generalized anxiety disorder.
    C.   a social phobia.   D.   agoraphobia.

7. Teresa has experienced panic attacks. She is now afraid to go to the place where she experienced the panic in case it happens again. Teresa is at risk of developing
    A. social phobia.   B. agoraphobia.
    C. obsessive-compulsive disorder.   D. acute stress disorder.

8. Josephine is trying to stop herself from checking the oven for the 21st time before she leaves the house. Not checking the oven results in
    A. feelings of depression.   B. a phobia.
    C. mounting anxiety.   D. none of the above.

9. John has been overeating, having difficulty sleeping through the night and trouble concentrating. These physical changes can be signs of
    A. a phobia.   B. mania.
    C. depression.   D. dysthymia.

10. Ricardo is full of energy and has grand plans for himself. He thinks he can do just about anything. As he is telling you his plans, you notice he is speaking very dramatically, and rapidly. Which diagnosis best fits Ricardo's symptoms?
    A. mania   B. bipolar disorder
    C. mood disorder   D. all of the above

11. Duane is taking anti-depressants. How do they alleviate symptoms of depression?
    A. They decrease levels of dopamine.
    B. They increase levels of serotonin and norepinephrine.
    C. They decrease levels of serotonin and norepinephrine.
    D. They increase levels of dopamine.

12. More women receive a diagnosis of depression than men. Which of the following is a possible explanation for this gender difference in depression?
    A. Women are more likely to have a history of sexual abuse.
    B. Men express depression differently and may be overlooked.
    C. Mothers are vulnerable to depression.
    D. all of the above

13. I believe that "nothing good will ever happen for me and there is nothing I can do about this." This statement is an example of the _____ explanation of depression.
    A. cognitive   B. social
    C. attachment   D. biological

14. Bob and Babs have been diagnosed with personality disorders. The central feature of Bob's personality disorder is that he doesn't trust anyone. The main characteristic of Babs' problem is that she is totally self-absorbed. Which personality disorder best fits Bob and which best fits Babs?

    A.   paranoid; antisocial   B.   antisocial; narcissistic
    C.   paranoid; narcissistic   D.   narcissistic; narcissistic

15. Fred has a diagnosis of antisocial personality disorder. He has just been found with a stolen car. What reaction will Fred be most likely to display?

    A.   He will be quite nervous and will be unlikely to repeat the offense.
    B.   He will act very sorry but, in fact, he will feel little regret.
    C.   He will act very angry and get himself into more trouble.
    D.   He will be extremely upset about being caught.

16. What do people who are antisocial, hyperactive, addicted and impulsive share?

    A.   a personality disorder   B.   the same behaviors
    C.   an explanatory style   D.   behavioral inhibition

17. Having a genetic disposition toward impulsivity, addiction, hyperactivity; being neglected or rejected by parents; having a history of physical abuse or birth complications are all

    A.   contributors to mood disorders.
    B.   risk factors for antisocial personality disorder.
    C.   foundations for any mental disorder.
    D.   paths to dissociative disorders.

18. People with psychogenic amnesia forget _____, whereas those experiencing a psychogenic fugue state forget _____.

    A.   certain (threatening) information; their identities and habits
    B.   a trauma; entire periods of time before and sometimes after the trauma
    C.   their names; specific incidents
    D.   an hour or less; more than an hour

19. Which of the following has been used both to support and refute the veracity of dissociative identity disorder?

    A.   certain physiological changes   B.   court transcripts
    C.   records of hypnosis sessions   D.   research method errors

20. As a result of his drinking, Michael cannot make it to his classes or complete his assignments. He drinks even when he is the designated driver, and Susan has told him that unless he stops drinking, she will not continue to date him. Michael shows signs of
    A. substance abuse.
    B. problem drinking.
    C. tolerance.
    D. a disease.

21. Joel believes alcoholism is a disease. Which of the following supports this model?
    A. There is strong evidence for a genetic contribution to alcoholism.
    B. There are rapid rises and falls in addiction rates.
    C. Not all drug users go through physiological withdrawal.
    D. There is not a lot of research that supports this model.

22. Elizabeth thinks she is Madonna. When she speaks she often does not make any sense at all and at times she appears to be talking to herself. She is experiencing
    A. positive symptoms of schizophrenia.
    B. negative symptoms of schizophrenia.
    C. catatonic symptoms of schizophrenia.
    D. emotional flatness.

23. Which of the following is NOT considered to be a factor that increases the likelihood of a schizophrenic breakdown?
    A. parents who give children mixed messages
    B. the existence of schizophrenia in the family
    C. physical trauma during childbirth that might damage the brain
    D. unstable, stressful environments in adulthood

24. According to the vulnerability-stress model of schizophrenia, who among the following would be most likely to develop schizophrenia?
    A. Harry has schizophrenia in his family, but he lives in a very stable, loving environment.
    B. Jerry has no biological risks for schizophrenia, but he lives in a stressful environment with emotionally disturbed parents.
    C. Gary was exposed prenatally to the flu and, as an adult, he lives in a very stressful environment.
    D. It is impossible to say.

25. Brain abnormalities that have been found to be associated with schizophrenia include
    A. decreased brain weight.
    B. reduced numbers of neurons in specific layers of the prefrontal cortex.
    C. abnormalities in the thalamus.
    D. all of the above.

PRACTICE TEST 3

1.   Jason spends all day at the shopping mall. Every day he stops people who look in his direction and literally begs for their forgiveness. What makes Jason so noticeable are his boldly colored sweatshirts. These are worn every day, over his coat when it's cold, and each one has exactly the same inscription: "Jason is not a thief." Discuss the aspect of Jason's behavior that conforms with each of the definitions of mental disorder.

   A.   Violation of cultural standards
   B.   Maladaptive behavior
   C.   Emotional distress
   D.   Impaired judgment and self-control

2.   In the formulation of Jason's diagnosis according to the DSM-IV, indicate whether the types of information identified below would be included or excluded. Explain your answers.

   A.   A diagnostic label for Jason's condition
   B.   The suspected cause(s) for Jason's symptoms
   C.   An estimate of potential treatment effects
   D.   How well Jason is functioning
   E.   Any medical condition that Jason might have

3.   For each description below, indicate whether the anxiety that is present is normal or abnormal. When it is abnormal, suggest the most likely diagnostic category.

   A.   Carl loves the racetrack but he will not go there again. The last time he was there he suddenly felt his heart racing, he was gasping for breath, his hands began to tremble and he broke out into a cold sweat.
   B.   Sandy is very clean! She feels contaminated unless she bathes and changes her clothes at least four times a day, and she is meticulous about the house as well. Every room is scrubbed at least twice a week and the bathroom is cleaned daily.
   C.   A college student becomes anxious whenever assigned a project that requires speaking in front of class. The anxiety motivates meticulous preparation and the student rehearses material again and again.
   D.   Marsha was stranded in a building for over two hours. The stairway was blocked by men moving large cartons, and the only path downward was the elevators. Elevators cause Marsha to sweat, tremble and suffer from images of being crushed. She decided to wait instead.
   E.   Harry has had problems since returning from Vietnam. He is listless and quarrelsome, and has fitful sleeps, reliving his past in nightmarish dreams.

370

4.   Decide whether each of the statements below is correct or incorrect. When it is incorrect, rewrite it in a more factual form.

A.   Mood disorders consist primarily of emotional symptoms and have little impact on behavioral, cognitive or physical functioning.
B.   In bipolar disorder, periods of sluggishness alternate with active attempts to commit suicide.
C.   Antidepressant drugs work by altering the activity level of the limbic system.
D.   Lack of fulfilling work and family relationships are a good predictor of depression.
E.   Negatively distorted thinking is the result, not the cause, of depression.
F.   Repeated failure is an unlikely source of major depressive episodes.

5.   Josephine is highly mistrustful of airline personnel. She believes that airplanes dirty the streets and sidewalks by dripping oil and that pilots have a power called "telectic penetration." On hearing a plane, Josephine becomes introspective and claims she is being used as a radar. She feels the pilots are tuning in to her latitude and longitude and asking her questions about her location. She is unable to speak until they are through.

A.   Does Josephine have delusions? If so, what?
B.   Is Josephine hallucinating? If so, describe her hallucinations.
C.   Is Josephine having any disorganized or incoherent speech? If so, describe.
D.   Is Josephine demonstrating any disorganized or inappropriate behavior? If so, what?
E.   Is Josephine demonstrating emotional flatness? If so, describe.

CHAPTER 16

Approaches to Treatment and Therapy

LEARNING OBJECTIVES

1. Describe the historical relationship between medical and psychological approaches to psychological problems.

2. Discuss the uses of antipsychotic drugs, antidepressants, minor tranquilizers and lithium in treating emotional disorders.

3. Summarize the problems inherent in treating psychological disorders with drugs.

4. Describe the procedures used in attempts to alter brain function directly.

5. Describe the two types of errors that can occur in diagnosis and treatment that are related to the mind-body debate.

6. List and explain the goals and principles of the four major schools of psychotherapy, and explain what is meant by eclectic therapy.

7. Discuss the goals and methods of various alternatives to psychotherapy, including community programs and self-help groups.

8. Describe the results of efforts to evaluate the effectiveness of psychotherapy.

9. Discuss the factors most likely to lead to successful therapy and discuss the role of the therapeutic alliance.

10. Discuss which therapies and which therapeutic structures work best for specific problems.

11. Discuss the circumstances in which therapy can be harmful.

12. Explain the limitations of psychotherapy.

CHAPTER CONCEPT MAP

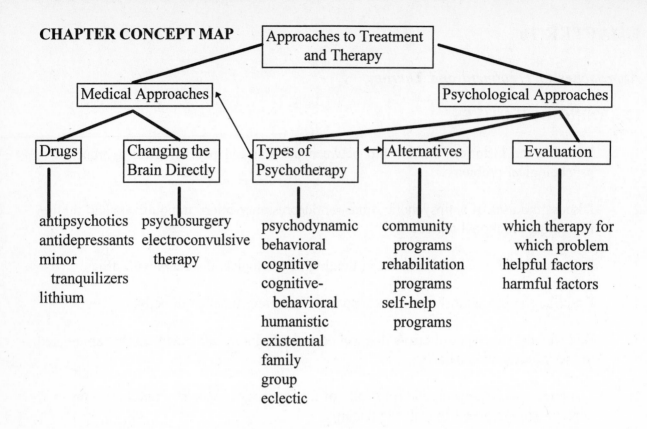

BRIEF CHAPTER SUMMARY

Chapter 16 describes various approaches to the treatment of mental disorders. Three general types of approaches are reviewed. Medical approaches include drug treatments, psychosurgery and electroconvulsive therapy. Drug treatments include medications that treat psychoses (antipsychotic medications), depression (antidepressants), anxiety (minor tranquilizers) and bipolar disorder (lithium carbonate). While drugs have contributed to significant advances in the treatment of mental disorders, they require great caution in their use. Psychosurgery, which was used more commonly in the 1950s, is rarely used any longer because of its serious and irreversible side effects. Electroconvulsive therapy is still used for serious cases of depression that do not respond to other treatments. Types of psychotherapy exist based on each of the major perspectives. The general principles and techniques of each of these approaches are reviewed along with research on their effectiveness. While there are certain commonalities among all the different types of psychotherapy, research indicates that some approaches are more effective for particular problems. Alternative treatment approaches include community and self-help programs. These approaches can be helpful in certain circumstances.

PREVIEW OUTLINE AND REVIEW QUESTIONS

Before you read the chapter, review the preview outline and the Learning Objectives for each section of the text. Develop additional questions of your own based on key concepts and terms and write them in the designated spaces. Answer all questions as you read the text.

SECTION 1 - MEDICAL TREATMENTS (PP. 593-600)

I.   **MEDICAL TREATMENTS**

    A.   **Historical approaches**

        1.   Organic model claims mental problems have _____ causes

        2.   Psychological model claims mental problems have psychological causes

    B.   **The question of drugs**

        1.   Two lines of support for the role of biology in some disorders

            a.   There is evidence for a genetic, biochemical or neurological component to some disorders

            b.   Medications affect people with disorders but have no effect on others who lack the disorders

        2.   Main classes of drugs used for treatment of mental and emotional disorders

            a.   Antipsychotic drugs, or major _____; have transformed the treatment of psychoses and schizophrenia

                (1)   Can have dangerous side effects, including tardive _____ and neuroleptic malignant syndrome

                (2)   Affect positive symptoms more than negative symptoms

                (3)   Overall success is modest

            b.   Antidepressant drugs - alter levels of _____

                (1)   Monoamine oxidase (MAO) inhibitors - elevate levels of norepinephrine and _____

                (2)   Tricyclic antidepressants - also elevates levels of norepinephrine and serotonin, but in a different way

                (3)   Fluoxetin (Prozac) - elevates _____

                (4)   Prescribed for anxiety, agoraphobia and obsessive-compulsive disorder as well as depression

                (5)   Also have side effects

            c.   "Minor" tranquilizers - prescribed for anxiety and unhappiness

            d.   _____ carbonate - prescribed for bipolar disorder; must be administered in the correct dose or can be dangerous

        3.   Cautions about drugs

            a.   Numerous research problems including include placebo effects, getting true double-blind studies and lack of long term testing

            b.   The _____ window - the amount that is enough but not too much

      c.   Relapse and drop-out rates - high drop-out rates from side effects
      d.   Race, gender and age all influence dosage
      e..   Many _____ work as well or better and teach people how to cope
      f.   Because a disorder may have biological origins does not mean the only appropriate treatment is medical
      g.   Concern about the prescription of medications without therapy

C.   **Probing the brain: Surgery and electroshock**
    1.   Psychosurgery - surgery to destroy selected areas of the brain thought to be responsible for emotional disorders
      a.   First attempt was a prefrontal _____
        (1)   Was never assessed scientifically
        (2)   Left patients with personality changes
      b.   Rarely used today
    2.   Electroconvulsive therapy (ECT) or "_____ treatments"
      a.   Treatment procedure modified so trauma is minimized
      b.   Affects every aspect of brain activity
      c.   Most effective with the suicidally depressed, who cannot wait for antidepressants to take effect; not effective with other disorders
      d.   Main drawback is _____ loss and other cognitive impairments

D.   **The hoofbeats of a zebra** - there is potential to misdiagnose mind/body problems

Answer these Learning Objectives while you read Section 1.

1.   Describe the historical relationship between medical and psychological approaches to psychological problems.

2.   Discuss the uses of antipsychotic drugs, antidepressants, minor tranquilizers and lithium in treating emotional disorders.

3.   Summarize the problems inherent in treating psychological disorders with drugs.

4.   Describe the procedures used in attempts to alter brain function directly.

5.   Describe the two types of errors that can occur in diagnosis and treatment that are related to the mind-body debate.

Write the questions that you have formulated below and answer them while you read.

A._____

B._____

II.   **KINDS OF PSYCHOTHERAPY**
    A.   **Commonalities among psychotherapies** - help clients think about their lives in new ways
    B.   **Psychodynamic therapy**
        1.   Probes the past and the mind to produce _____ and emotional release to eliminate symptoms
        2.   Psychoanalysis evolved into psychodynamic therapies
        3.   Considered "depth" therapies because they explore the unconscious by using techniques such as _____ association and transference
        4.   Do not aim to solve an individual's immediate problem
        5.   Many psychodynamic therapists use Freudian principles but not methods
        6.   Brief psychodynamic therapy does not go into whole history, but focuses on main issue or dynamic focus as well as self-defeating habits
    C.   **Behavioral and cognitive therapy**
        1.   Behavioral therapy - techniques derived from behavioral principles
            a.   Behavioral records and contracts identify current behaviors and behavioral _____
            b.   Systematic _____ - a step by step process of "desensitizing" a client to a feared object or experience
            c.   Aversive conditioning - substitutes _____ for a reinforcement that has perpetuated a bad habit
            d.   Flooding or exposure treatment - therapist accompanies client into the feared situation (called "in vivo" exposure)
            e.   Skills training - practice in specific acts
        2.   Cognitive therapy
            a.   Aim is to identify thoughts, beliefs and expectations that might be prolonging a person's problems
            b.   Albert Ellis and _____ Emotive Behavior Therapy - therapist challenges illogical beliefs directly with rational arguments
            c.   Other cognitive approaches are less direct
        3.   Cognitive-behavior therapy - combines the above two approaches; most common treatment
    D.   **Humanistic and existential therapy**
        1.   Humanistic therapies - assume that people seek self-_____ and self-fulfillment
        2.   Do not delve into the past, help people to feel better about themselves "here and now"
        3.   Client-centered or nondirective therapy by Carl _____
            a.   Therapist offers unconditional positive regard to build self-esteem

      b.   No specific techniques, but therapists must be warm, genuine and empathic; client adopts these views and becomes self-_____ _

    4.   Existential therapies - help client explore meaning of existence and utilize the power to choose a destiny and accept self-responsibility

E.   **Beyond the person: Family and group therapy**

    1.   Family therapy - the problem is not in the person but in the social _____, therefore often the whole family is treated

      a.   The family kaleidoscope - the family as a changing pattern in which all parts affect each other

         (1)   Observing the family together reveals family tensions and imbalances in power and communication

         (2)   Some use a multigenerational approach that identifies repetitive patterns across generations

         (3)   Some use _____ - family tree of psychologically significant events

      b.   Family systems approach - if one member in the family changes, the others must change too

      c.   Solution-focused or "strategic" family therapy - helps clients specify their goals and find ways to achieve them

    2.   Group therapy

      a.   Group therapy may be run by psychodynamic therapists, cognitive-behaviorists, family therapists and humanists

      b.   Basic format of self-revelation in a group is the same

      c.   Different from encounter groups

F.   **Psychotherapy in practice** - eclecticism

    1.   Most psychotherapists are _____ - using techniques from different approaches

    2.   A common process in all therapies is to replace self-defeating narratives or life stories with one that is more hopeful and attainable

Answer this Learning Objective while you read Section 2.

6.   List and explain the goals and principles of the four major schools of psychotherapy, and explain what is meant by eclectic therapy.

Write the questions that you have formulated below and answer them while you read.

A._____

B._____

SECTION 3 - ALTERNATIVES TO PSYCHOTHERAPY (PP. 608-612)

III. **ALTERNATIVES TO PSYCHOTHERAPY**
   A. **The community and rehabilitation movements**
      1. Majority of people with mental illness live in the community
      2. _____ psychologists
         a. Deal with assessment and treatment of people who are physically or mentally disabled
         b. Approach is eclectic
            (1) Behavior therapy
            (2) Group counseling
            (3) Job training
            (4) Community intervention
      3. Community programs have been very successful in helping the mentally ill who have disabilities
      4. Types of community support
         a. _____-way houses, clubhouse models
         b. Establishment of support systems including family therapy, foster care, family home alternatives and family support groups
   B. **The self-help movement**
      1. Organized around a common concern
      2. Support groups offer three ingredients: understanding, empathy, advice
      3. Different from psychotherapy
         a. Do not focus on specific problems
         b. Not for those with serious psychological difficulties

Answer this Learning Objective while you read Section 3.

7. Discuss the goals and methods of various alternatives to psychotherapy, including community programs and self-help groups.

Write the questions that you have formulated below and answer them while you read.

A._____

B._____

SECTION 4 - EVALUATING PSYCHOTHERAPY AND ITS ALTERNATIVES (PP. 612-621) AND
SECTION 5 - THE VALUE AND VALUES OF PSYCHOTHERAPY (PP. 622-624)

IV.   **EVALUATING PSYCHOTHERAPY AND ITS ALTERNATIVES**
- A.   **The scientist-practitioner gap**
  1. Conflict between scientists and practitioners about the relevance of research findings to clinical practice
     - a. Scientists want the effectiveness of psychotherapy scientifically demonstrated
     - b. Practitioners believe it is very difficult to empirically study psychotherapy
  2. Overall conclusions from research on the effectiveness of therapy
     - a. Psychotherapy is better than doing nothing at all
     - b. Those who do best in psychotherapy have treatable problems and are _____ to improve
     - c. For many common, mild disorders and everyday problems, paraprofessional therapists may be as effective as professional therapists
     - d. In a significant minority of cases, psychotherapy is harmful because of the therapist's incompetence, bias against the client, or unethical behavior
- B.   **When therapy helps**
  1. When there is a good fit between client and therapist
  2. When clients have a strong sense of self and sufficient distress to motivate them to change
  3. When clients exhibit a commitment to therapy, willingness to work, expectation to succeed
  4. When clients are cooperative and have _____ feelings during therapy
  5. When therapists are _____, warm, genuine and imaginative
  6. When a therapeutic _____, or bond between client and therapist forms
  7. In general, support, learning and action factors are associated with positive psychotherapy results
- C.   **Which therapy for which problem?**
  1. Depth therapies not highly successful with major depression, anxiety, fears, panic, agoraphobia, sex problems, personality disorders, drug abuse or on sex offenders
  2. Behavior therapies helpful for agoraphobia
  3. Cognitive therapy is successful in treatment of _____ disorders, panic attacks, anxiety and moderate depression; it is often more effective than antidepressant drugs for relapse prevention

4. Cognitive-behavior therapies don't succeed well with _____ disorders and psychoses, severe depression, recovery from trauma
5. "Pure" versus combined approaches
   a. For certain problems, combinations of treatments work best
   b. _____ treatment model - psychiatrists and psychologists working together

D. **When therapy harms**
   1. Coercion by the therapist to accept the therapist's advice, sexual intimacies, or other unethical behavior
   2. Bias on the part of a therapist who doesn't understand some aspect of the client
   3. Therapist-_____ disorders - unconsciously inducing the client to produce the symptoms they are looking for

V. **THE VALUE AND VALUES OF PSYCHOTHERAPY**
   A. **The limitations of psychotherapy**: it cannot transform you into someone you're not, cure you overnight, provide a life without problems
   B. **What psychotherapy can do**: it can help you make decisions, provide support, improve morale and energy

Answer these Learning Objectives while you read Sections 4 and 5.

7. Discuss the goals and methods of various alternatives to psychotherapy, including community programs and self-help groups.

8. Describe the results of efforts to evaluate the effectiveness of psychotherapy.

9. Discuss the factors most likely to lead to successful therapy and discuss the role of the therapeutic alliance.

10. Discuss which therapies and which therapeutic structures work best for specific problems.

11. Discuss the circumstances in which therapy can be harmful.

12. Explain the limitations of psychotherapy.

Write the questions that you have formulated below and answer them while you read.

A._____

B._____

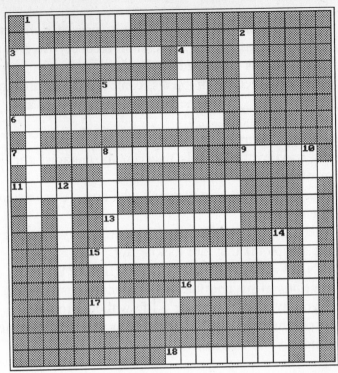

ACROSS

1. fake treatment used as a control in an experiment
4. late-appearing neurological effects of drugs taken over many years
5. a salt used to treat bipolar disorder
6. Freud's original method of psychotherapy
7. patient transfers emotional feelings for his or her parents to the therapist
9. type of therapy with several people at once
11. behavioral technique; step-by-step process intended to reduce fear
13. kind of drug that prevents reabsorption of norepinephrine and serotonin
15. regard offered by Rogerian therapy
16. life story
17. type of therapy in which problem is not seen as in the individual but in the social context
18. behavioral technique in which punishment is substituted for reinforcement

DOWN

1. operation designed to destroy selected areas of the brain
2. the therapist takes the client right into the feared situation
4. antipsychotic or antidepressant
8. type of psychotherapy that helps the client explore the meaning of life
10. general term for treatment that helps people through talking
12. type of therapy that borrows methods from different approaches
14. the bond that develops between the therapist and the client

382

FLASH CARDS

Cut the following chart along the borders and test yourself with the resulting flash cards.

16.1 ANTIPSYCHOTIC DRUGS (MAJOR TRANQUILIZERS)	16.7 COGNITIVE THERAPIES	16.13 PSYCHOSURGERY
16.2 ANTIDEPRESSANT DRUGS	16.8 RATIONAL EMOTIVE THERAPY	16.14 LOBOTOMY
16.3 MINOR TRANQUILIZERS	16.9 HUMANISTIC THERAPIES	16.15 ELECTROCONVULSIVE THERAPY (ECT)
16.4 LITHIUM CARBONATE	16.10 CLIENT-CENTERED THERAPY	16.16 PSYCHOANALYSIS
16.5 AVERSIVE CONDITIONING	16.11 ACTIVE PLACEBO	16.17 PSYCHODYNAMIC ("DEPTH") THERAPIES
16.6 FLOODING	16.12 THERAPEUTIC WINDOW	16.18 FREE ASSOCIATION

16.13 Any surgical procedure that destroys selected areas of the brain believed to be involved in emotional disorders or violent, impulsive behavior.	16.7 A type of therapy in which the aim is to help clients identify the thoughts, beliefs and expectations that might be prolonging their problems.	16.1 Major tranquilizers primarily used in the treatment of schizophrenia and other psychotic disorders.
16.14 Psychosurgery done in the mid-1900s that was supposed to reduce the patient's emotional symptoms without impairing intellectual ability.	16.8 A type of cognitive therapy in which the therapist challenges the client's illogical beliefs directly with rational arguments.	16.2 Stimulants that influence neurotransmitters in the brain; they are used in the treatment of mood disorders, usually depression and anxiety.
16.15 A procedure occasionally used for cases of prolonged major depression, in which a brief brain seizure is induced to alter brain chemistry.	16.9 A type of therapy that is based on the assumption that people seek self-actualization and self-fulfillment.	16.3 Medication often prescribed for patients who complain or unhappiness of worry.
16.16 Freud's original method in which unconscious dynamics of personality are explored.	16.10 A type of humanistic therapy developed by Carl Rogers. The therapist's role is to listen and offer unconditional positive regard.	16.4 A salt used to treat bipolar disorder.
16.17 Different forms of therapy that evolved from Freudian psychoanalysis, which share the goal of exploring unconscious dynamics.	16.11 Fake treatments that mimic the physical effects of real drugs so that neither subjects nor researchers know which the subject has received.	16.5 A behavioral technique that substitutes punishment for the positive reinforcement that has perpetuated a bad habit.
16.18 In psychoanalysis, a method of recovering unconscious conflicts by saying freely whatever comes to mind.	16.12 The amount of drug that is enough but not too much.	16.6 A behavioral technique in which the therapist takes the client right into a feared situation and remains with the client until the panic declines.

16.19 TRANSFERENCE	16.25 FAMILY THERAPY	16.31 REHABILITATION PSYCHOLOGY
16.20 BRIEF PSYCHODYNAMIC THERAPY	16.26 GENOGRAM	16.32 SUPPORT/SELF-HELP GROUPS
16.21 BEHAVIORAL THERAPIES	16.27 SOLUTION-FOCUSED (STRATEGIC) FAMILY THERAPY	16.33 SCIENTIST-PRACTITIONER GAP
16.22 SYSTEMATIC DESENSITIZATION	16.28 GROUP THERAPY	16.34 THERAPEUTIC ALLIANCE
16.23 UNCONDITIONAL POSITIVE REGARD	16.29 ECLECTIC APPROACHES	16.35 SPLIT TREATMENT
16.24 EXISTENTIAL THERAPY	16.30 NARRATIVE METHOD	16.36 PSEUDOMEMORIES

16.31 Type of psychologist who is concerned with the assessment and treatment of people who are physically or mentally disabled.	16.25 A type of therapy that conceptualizes individual problems in terms of the social context or family.	16.19 In psychodynamic therapies, a critical step in which the patient transfers emotional feelings for his or her parents to the therapist.
16.32 Groups organized around a common concern.	16.26 A technique used by family therapists that involves drawing a family tree of psychologically significant events across generations.	16.20 A form of psychodynamic therapy that is time-limited. It usually consists of 15 to 25 sessions.
16.33 The gap created by the disagreement between scientists and therapists about the relevance of research findings on clinical practice.	16.27 An approach to family therapy that focuses on helping clients specify their goals and finding ways to achieve them.	16.21 A type of therapy based on techniques derived from behavioral principles.
16.34 The bond of confidence and mutual understanding established between therapist and client that allows them to work together.	16.28 A form of therapy based on self-revelation in a group that can be based on family, psychodynamic, behavioral, cognitive, humanistic principles.	16.22 A behavioral technique involving a step-by-step process of "desensitizing" a client to a feared object or experience.
16.35 A model in which a psychiatrist prescribes medication while a psychologist focuses on the psychological aspects of treatment.	16.29 The practice of psychotherapy that borrows methods and ideas from different schools or approaches.	16.23 A humanistic technique in which the client is helped to feel that he or she is loved and respected no matter what; approach developed by Rogers.
16.36 Constructed fantasies shaped by the suggestions and expectations of the therapist.	16.30 A therapeutic tool to help clients form new stories about their lives.	16.24 A type of therapy that helps clients explore the meaning of existence and deal with the great questions of life.

APPROACHES TO PSYCHOTHERAPY

Complete the following chart by listing specific techniques and general goals of therapy for each of the approaches in the left-hand column.

THERAPY APPROACH	SPECIFIC TECHNIQUES	GENERAL GOALS OF THERAPY
PSYCHODYNAMIC APPROACHES		
BEHAVIORAL APPROACH		
COGNITIVE APPROACHES		
HUMANISTIC APPROACHES		
GROUP THERAPY		
FAMILY THERAPY		

PRACTICE TEST 1

1. The medical model of psychological disorders regards mental problems as having
   A. biological causes.
   B. psychological causes.
   C. environmental causes.
   D. any of the above.

2. Antipsychotic drugs do <u>NOT</u>
   A. restore normal thought patterns.
   B. lessen hallucinations.
   C. reduce dramatic symptoms.
   D. have side effects.

3. Lithium carbonate is often effective in treating people who
   A. have schizophrenia.
   B. have tardive dyskinesia.
   C. complain of unhappiness or anxiety.
   D. have bipolar disorder.

4. The drugs that are most effective in treating mood disorders are
   A. antipsychotic drugs.
   B. minor tranquilizers.
   C. antidepressant drugs.
   D. major tranquilizers.

5. A problem with using drugs in treating psychological disorders is that
   A. there are high drop-out rates.
   B. tests of drug effects in long-term usage are often missing.
   C. there is a strong placebo effect in evaluating their effectiveness.
   D. all of the above are potential problems.

6. The original intention of prefrontal lobotomy was to
   A. reduce the patient's anxiety without impairing intellectual capacity.
   B. "ventilate" evil impulses or mental pressures.
   C. remove an abnormal organic condition, such as a tumor.
   D. replace drugs and electroconvulsive therapy, which were considered dangerous.

7. The main drawback of electroconvulsive therapy (ECT) is that it
   A. only helps people with minor psychological problems.
   B. produces memory loss and other cognitive impairments.
   C. requires high voltages that could be fatal.
   D. causes epileptic seizures.

8. A problem that can result from having a "mind" or a "body" orientation to psychological problems is
   A. misdiagnosing a physical illness for a psychological problem.
   B. reducing complex psychological problems to matters of biochemistry.
   C. making errors in diagnosis and treatment.
   D. all of the above.

9. In psychodynamic therapies, the patient's displacement of emotional elements in his or her inner life onto the therapist is called
   A. free association.
   B. transference.
   C. insight.
   D. dynamic focus.

10. The factor considered to be most helpful in psychodynamic therapies is
    A. insight.
    B. behavior change.
    C. changing conscious beliefs.
    D. the reduction of symptoms.

11. A type of therapy that takes the individual right into the most feared situation is called
    A. systematic desensitization.
    B. aversive conditioning.
    C. flooding or exposure treatment.
    D. brief psychodynamic therapy.

12. Systematic desensitization, aversive conditioning, flooding and skills training are all
    A. techniques used in cognitive therapies.
    B. psychodynamic techniques.
    C. methods employed by humanists.
    D. behavioral techniques.

13. Which two therapies often borrow each other's methods, so that a combination of the two is more common than either method alone?
    A. psychoanalysis; behavior therapy
    B. family therapy; group therapy
    C. cognitive therapy; behavior therapy
    D. support groups; group therapy

14. In which approach does the therapist challenge the client's illogical beliefs?
    A. cognitive therapy
    B. humanistic therapy
    C. psychodynamic therapy
    D. existential therapy

15. What type of therapist would try to provide unconditional positive regard and act as an "ideal parent?"
    A. cognitive
    B. humanistic
    C. psychodynamic
    D. existential

16. Which type of therapist might make use of insight, exposure, challenging irrational thoughts and unconditional positive regard?
    A. a humanistic therapist
    B. a behaviorist therapist
    C. an eclectic therapist
    D. a cognitive therapist

17. Professionals who help those who are physically or mentally disabled to work and live independently are called
    A. behavioral psychologists.
    B. family therapists.
    C. rehabilitation psychologists.
    D. group therapists.

18. Based on controlled clinical trials, which of the following is true about the effectiveness of therapy?
    A. Psychotherapy is better than doing nothing at all.
    B. People who do best in psychotherapy are those who can form very strong attachments to the therapist.
    C. In general, paraprofessionals get poorer results as therapists than professionals.
    D. all of the above

19. Good therapeutic candidates are those who
    A. are introspective and want to talk about their childhoods.
    B. want a chance to talk about their feelings without any limits.
    C. recognize the expertise of the therapist.
    D. are committed to therapy, willing to work on their problems, and expect to succeed.

20. A therapeutic alliance is
    A. an organization of therapists who advocate for the benefits of therapy.
    B. a group of consumers who were harmed because of a therapist's incompetence or unethical methods.
    C. a bond between the client and therapist that depends on their ability to understand each other.
    D. a support group in which people share common problems.

21. Depth therapies work best for
    A. anxiety disorders.
    B. people who are introspective and want to explore their pasts and examine their current lives.
    C. people with sex problems.
    D. people who are drug abusers.

22. Research suggests that cognitive and behavioral approaches are very successful with many types of problems, however, they are NOT thought to work well for
    A. personality disorders and psychoses.
    B. phobias and panic disorder.
    C. moderate depression.
    D. agoraphobia and anxiety disorders.

23. Which factors can cause psychotherapy to be harmful?
    A. coercion   B. bias
    C. therapist-induced disorders   D. all of the above

24. One explanation for the growing number of patients diagnosed with Multiple Personality Disorder is that the diagnosis is a result of
    A. bias.   B. therapist inducement.
    C. incompetence.   D. coercion.

25. A realistic expectation for the outcome of psychotherapy is
    A. to learn that any change is possible.
    B. to help make decisions and get through difficult times.
    C. to be happy all, or almost all, of the time.
    D. to help eliminate the problems from one's life.

1. Dr. Grace views Herbert's depression as biochemical, whereas Dr. Fine believes that it is due to early attachment problems. Dr. Grace represents the _____ model and Dr. Fine represents the _____ model.
   A. organic; medical
   B. psychological; organic
   C. organic; psychological
   D. physical; organic

2. Randolf is taking antipsychotic medication. Which of the following should concern him?
   A. the possibility of tardive dyskinesia
   B. the fact that while the more dramatic symptoms may be helped, normal thinking may not
   C. though he may be well enough to be released from a hospital, he may not be able to care for himself
   D. All of the above are concerns.

3. Jay is taking a medication that elevates the levels of norepinephrine and serotonin in his brain. What is his most probable diagnosis?
   A. depression
   B. an anxiety disorder
   C. bipolar disorder
   D. a psychosis

4. Felicia has been prescribed an antidepressant. Which of the following might she be taking?
   A. a major tranquilizer
   B. a tricyclic
   C. lithium
   D. a minor tranquilizer

5. Based on the cautions about drug treatment, Felicia should probably have concerns about
   A. whether the drug is more effective than a placebo.
   B. whether the drug has been tested for long-term use.
   C. whether the right dosage has been identified.
   D. all of the above.

6. Among the following patients, who would be a likely candidate for electroconvulsive therapy (ECT)?
   A. Fran is suicidally depressed.
   B. Dan is anxious.
   C. Stan is moderately depressed.
   D. ECT should not be used on any of them, since it is outdated and barbaric.

7. Which of the following would avoid diagnosis and treatment errors that result from being on one side of the mind-body debate?
   A. Require all patients who come to a psychologist to have a physical exam.
   B. Require all patients who come to a physician to have a psychological exam.
   C. Consider symptoms from both a medical and psychological point of view.
   D. Get a second opinion in all cases.

8. During her first visit to Dr. Bhoutos, Patrece is told to say whatever comes to mind. Dr. Bhoutos is using _____ as part of _____ psychotherapy.
   A. transference; behavioral   B. flooding; behavioral
   C. free association; psychodynamic   D. transference; psychodynamic

9. After several months of therapy, during one session Patrece had a momentous awareness about how her relationship with her father had been affecting her for years. This realization
   A. is called insight.
   B. along with emotional release, should cause her symptoms to disappear, according to psychodynamic principles.
   C. is the key to therapeutic gains in psychodynamic approaches.
   D. incorporates all of the above.

10. To help Bob with his fear of flying, Dr. Rose teaches Bob to relax while they proceed through a series of steps that go from reading a story about an airplane, to visiting an airport, to boarding a plane, to taking a short flight. This _____ technique is called

    _____.
    A. cognitive; rational emotive therapy   B. humanistic; flooding
    C. behavioral; systematic desensitization   D. behavioral; flooding

11. Cognitive therapies focus on changing _____, whereas humanistic therapies focus on _____.
    A. beliefs; self-acceptance   B. behaviors; changing families
    C. behaviors; insight into the past   D. thoughts; skills

12. A cognitive therapist would treat a procrastination problem by
    A. helping the client gain insight through free association and transference.
    B. having the client keep a diary of how time is actually spent and then establishing specific goals.
    C. asking the client to write down negative thoughts about work, to read the thoughts as if someone else had said them, and then to write a rational response to each one.
    D. building self-esteem and putting the client in touch with his or her real feelings.

13. Dr. Smith is treating procrastination by having Stuart keep a diary of how much time he spends working, establishing goals, identifying his negative thoughts about his abilities, gaining insight into his fears of succeeding and the origins of the negative thoughts, changing these thought patterns, and helping him to feel better about himself. Dr. Smith is what type of therapist?

    A. behavioral
    B. cognitive
    C. eclectic
    D. humanistic

14. Of the following people diagnosed with schizophrenia, the one who has the best chance of functioning successfully is

    A. someone who has lived for a long time in an institution.
    B. someone who lives alone and is fairly isolated.
    C. someone who has community support and close contact with family and friends.
    D. someone who is an ongoing participant in deep psychotherapy.

15. Frank participates in a self-help group because he gets many things out of it, including

    A. help that focuses on specific problems.
    B. help that focuses on his underlying issues and problems.
    C. the fact that others have been there and know what he is going through.
    D. none of the above.

16. _____ maintain that effectiveness of therapy must be demonstrated, whereas _____ wish that academic psychologists would pay more attention to clinical evidence.

    A. Scientists; paraprofessionals
    B. Scientists; practitioners
    C. Practitioners; clinicians
    D. Researchers; scientists

17. Sandra is trying to decide whether to seek psychotherapy. She has done some reading on its effectiveness and has found that

    A. people in almost any professional treatment improve more than people who do not get help.
    B. people who do best in psychotherapy are those who have the most serious problems to begin with.
    C. unfortunately, psychotherapy is harmful in about 30 percent of all cases.
    D. psychotherapy helps in all types of psychological problems.

18. Sandra decides she is going to start psychotherapy. She should look for a psychotherapist

    A. of the same race and gender.
    B. whom she respects and whom she feels respects and understands her.
    C. who is detached and objective.
    D. who gives her a lot of information.

19. Sandra will be most successful in therapy if she
    A.   challenges the therapist whenever she disagrees.
    B.   is aware of any mistakes the therapist makes and is willing to point them out.
    C.   goes along with whatever the therapist says or suggests.
    D.   is cooperative and committed to therapy and expects it to work.

20. Based on research on the effectiveness of psychotherapy, which of the following clients should benefit most from therapy?
    A.   Hank has a narcissistic personality disorder.
    B.   Frank is schizophrenic.
    C.   Mary is having trouble dealing with her divorce.
    D.   Larry has never held a job nor moved out of his parents home, though he is 40 years old.

21. Helen is suffering from agoraphobia. Which type of therapy would be most helpful?
    A.   exposure therapy   B.   flooding
    C.   behavioral approaches   D.   all of the above

22. Cassandra wants to understand herself better; she wants to know why she does some of the things she does and to know what she is feeling. She believes that her past has a big impact on her present. Which type of therapy would best meet these goals?
    A.   cognitive therapy   B.   behavioral therapy
    C.   depth therapy   D.   solution-oriented therapy

23. In which of the following cases is Melina most likely to find the therapeutic experience harmful?
    A.   Her therapist firmly believes that Melina was sexually abused in childhood, though she has no memories of this and does not believe it is so.
    B.   Her therapist disagrees with her about several issues.
    C.   Her therapist does not always give her an immediate appointment when she calls.
    D.   All of the above may be harmful.

24. It is considered acceptable for a therapist to engage in sexual relations or other intimate behaviors with a client
    A.   when it is necessary to learn about close and loving relationships.
    B.   to help him or her overcome sexual difficulties.
    C.   when the client invites it or asks for it.
    D.   under no circumstances.

25. Ophelia says that all of her friends are in therapy and she wants to be in therapy also. Which of the following is a reasonable expectation for her to have of therapy?
    A. It may help her to make decisions.
    B. It may help her get through bad times.
    C. It may help improve her morale and restore energy to cope.
    D. all of the above

PRACTICE TEST 3

1. Identify the three major categories of approaches to psychological problems and briefly describe the help they offer. Indicate under what circumstances each would be desirable.

2. Identify the drugs typically employed for each of the disorders listed below and then briefly explain why drugs alone may not be sufficient treatment.

    A.   Anxiety disorders
    B.   Mood disorders
    C.   Psychotic disorders

3. Summarize the major features of each of the five major approaches to psychotherapy. Specify the goals and common techniques of each.

4. Identify the features of the client, the therapist, and their relationship that are associated with therapeutic success.

5. Identify and briefly describe the factors that contribute to therapeutic harm.

CHAPTER 17

Principles of Social Life

LEARNING OBJECTIVES

1. Discuss the focus of the field of social psychology, including the influences of norms, roles and groups on behavior and cognition.

2. Describe three controversial studies and discuss how they illustrate the influence of roles on behavior.

3. List and explain reasons that people obey authority.

4. Summarize the principles and components of attribution theory.

5. Define attitudes and identify important influences on attitudes.

6. List and explain persuasive and manipulative techniques of attitude change.

7. Discuss some reasons for conforming to social pressure in a group.

8. Explain the ways decision making and individual behavior can be influenced by group processes, including diffusion of responsibility, deindividuation, groupthink and group polarization.

9. Summarize the effects of competition, cooperation and interdependence.

10. Discuss the factors that lead to dissent and nonconformity.

11. Discuss the factors that lead to altruistic behavior.

12. Relate the principles of social psychology to the banality of evil.

CHAPTER CONCEPT MAP

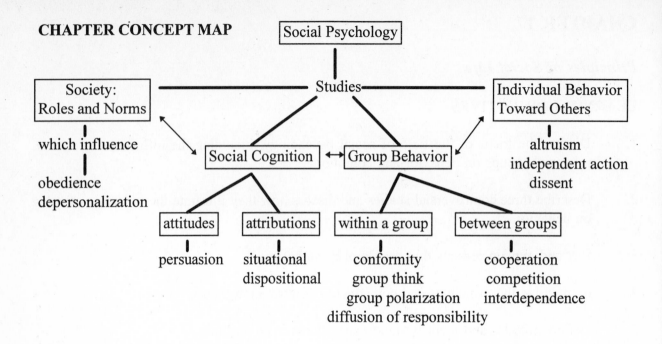

BRIEF CHAPTER SUMMARY •

Chapter 17 examines some of the main topic areas in the field of social psychology, which studies the individual in the social and cultural context. The influence of the social context begins with norms or rules that people are expected to follow. Each of us fills many social roles that are governed by norms about how a person in that position should behave. The roles we fill and the rules that govern those roles heavily influence our behavior, as demonstrated by three classic studies. These studies show how roles can override our own beliefs and values. The social context also influences our thought processes. Efforts to change our attitudes are ever present. To resist unwanted persuasion, one must think critically about information from all sources. Attributions--the way we explain events--influence our responses to the world. Certain types of attributional errors and tendencies can occur that may cause misinterpretations of events. Group behaviors are also examined. Certain group processes can occur as a result of the presence and influence of other group members. Finally, the chapter examines the factors that influence independent action, particularly altruism and dissent. Studying individuals in a social context helps to identify the normal social influences that contribute to behaviors we often think result from individual or personality factors.

PREVIEW OUTLINE AND REVIEW QUESTIONS

Before you read the chapter, review the preview outline and the Learning Objectives for each section of the text. Develop additional questions of your own based on key concepts and key terms and write them in the designated spaces. Answer all questions as you read.

SECTION 1 - ROLES AND RULES (PP. 627-636)

I. **ROLES AND RULES**
    A. **Definitions**
        1. Norms - the _____ people are expected to follow
        2. Roles - positions in society that are regulated by norms about how people in those positions should behave
    B. **The prison study by Zimbardo**
        1. Method
            a. College students randomly assigned to be prisoners or guards
            b. Given no further instructions on how to behave
        2. Results
            a. "Prisoners" quickly became _____, helpless and panicky and begged to be let out of the study
            b. Guards acted like guards; one-third became tyrannical
            c. Researchers terminated the study early
        3. Conclusions
            a. Critics said students knew those roles from the media
            b. Researchers say that is their point - people's behavior depends in part on their roles
    C. **The hospital study by Rosenhan**
        1. Method
            a. Eight normal adults presented themselves at 12 hospitals saying they heard certain words
            b. Otherwise they gave all correct information about themselves
        2. Results
            a. All admitted, all but one received a diagnosis of _____
            b. Once admitted, they acted like themselves and were kept for from 7 to 52 days
            c. Once in the role of patient, all their behavior seen through that lens
        3. Conclusions
            a. Role of mental patient encourages _____ - the loss of one's individuality
            b. To the staff, patients are not full human beings

D. **The obedience study by Milgram**
1. Method
    a. Subjects thought they were in an experiment about learning and were instructed to shock another subject when an error was made
    b. No one received shocks, but the subjects did not know this
2. Results
    a. Two-thirds obeyed the experimenter and gave all the shocks, though they thought the victim was in pain
    b. Subsequent studies examined conditions for disobedience
        (1) When the victim protested it made no difference
        (2) When the experimenter left the room
        (3) When shocks had to be administered _____
        (4) When two experimenters issued conflicting demands
        (5) When ordinary man, not an authority figure, issued commands
        (6) When _____ refused
3. Conclusions
    a. Obedience is a function of the _____, not of personalities
    b. The nature of the relationship to authority influences obedience

E. **The power of roles** - when do people obey when they would rather not
1. _____ of authority, which allows people to feel absolved of responsibility for their actions
2. Routinization - behavior becomes normalized
3. The rules of good manners - people can lack a language of protest
4. Entrapment - obedience escalates through a commitment to a course of action

Answer these Learning Objectives while you read Section 1

1. Discuss the focus of the field of social psychology.

2. Describe three controversial studies and discuss how they illustrate the influence of roles on behavior.

3. List and explain reasons that people obey authority.

Write the questions that you have formulated and answer them while you read.

A._____

B._____

II.　SOCIAL COGNITION: ATTRIBUTIONS AND ATTITUDES
　　A.　Explanations and excuses
　　　　1.　Attribution theory - the motive to make sense of one's own behavior and that of others in order to _____ and control events
　　　　2.　Type of attributions have consequences on emotions and actions
　　　　　　a.　Two types of attributions
　　　　　　　　(1)　_____ attributions - identify the cause of an action as something in the environment
　　　　　　　　(2)　Dispositional attributions - identify the cause of an action as something in the _____, such as a trait or motive
　　　　　　b.　Fundamental attribution error
　　　　　　　　(1)　Tendency to overestimate _____ factors and underestimate the influence of the situation when explaining someone else's behavior
　　　　　　　　(2)　More prevalent in Western nations
　　　　　　c.　Self-serving bias
　　　　　　　　(1)　When explaining one's own behavior, people take credit for _____ actions and attribute the bad ones to the situation
　　　　　　　　(2)　Also affected by culture
　　　　　　d.　Just-world hypothesis
　　　　　　　　(1)　The need to believe the world is fair and that good people are _____ and bad people are punished
　　　　　　　　(2)　This can lead to blaming the victim
　　B.　The social origins of attitudes
　　　　1.　Attitudes
　　　　　　a.　Relatively stable opinions containing a _____ element and an emotional element
　　　　　　b.　Can be changeable opinions or major convictions
　　　　2.　Affected by many social and environmental influences
　　　　　　a.　Some arise from the _____ effect - attitudes of an age group
　　　　　　b.　Events that occur when a person is between the ages of 16 to 24 are often very influential
　　　　3.　Relationship between attitudes and behavior
　　　　　　a.　Often attitudes and behaviors can be independent of one another
　　　　　　b.　Each can affect the other
　　　　4.　Cognitive _____
　　　　　　a.　When two attitudes or an attitude and a behavior conflict
　　　　　　b.　People are motivated to resolve the conflict by changing an attitude or a behavior

5.   Persuasion - some influences on attitudes result from others trying to change them
     a.   Friendly persuasion
         (1)   Repetition of information increases the likelihood it will be believed
         (2)   Called the validity effect
     b.   Exposure to an argument from someone admired
     c.   Fear - often causes people to _____ arguments
     d.   Coercive persuasion or brainwashing techniques
         (1)   The person is put under physical or emotional _____
         (2)   The person's problems are defined in simplistic terms and simple answers are offered repeatedly
         (3)   The leader offers unconditional love, acceptance, attention, and answers to personal problems
         (4)   A new _____ based on the group is created
         (5)   The person is subjected to entrapment
         (6)   Once a person accepts the new philosophy, access to information is severely controlled

Answer these Learning Objectives while you read Section 2.

4.   Summarize the principles and components of attribution theory.

5.   Define attitudes and identify important influences on attitudes.

6.   List and explain persuasive and manipulative techniques of attitude change.

Write the questions that you have formulated below and answer them while you read.

A._____

B._____

III. **INDIVIDUALS AND GROUPS**
   A. **Conformity**
       1. Asch's conformity study
       2. Reasons people conform
           a. Those most likely to conform have a strong need for social approval, are highly rigid or have low _____
           b. Depends on the group situation and the reasons people adapt
   B. **The anonymous crowd**
       1. Diffusion of responsibility
           a. Individuals fail to take action because they believe someone else will do so
           b. May explain why crowds of people fail to respond to an emergency
       2. Social _____
           a. Diffusion of responsibility in work groups
           b. Individuals slow down and let others work harder
           c. Does not happen in all groups
               (1) Increases
                    (a) When members not accountable for their work
                    (b) When working harder duplicates efforts
                    (c) Work is uninteresting
               (2) Declines
                    (a) With challenging work
                    (b) When each member has a different job
                    (c) When evaluations are individual or compared to another group
       3. _____
           a. Losing all awareness of individuality and sense of self
           b. Individuals don't take responsibility for their actions
           c. Increases under anonymous conditions
           d. The situation influences what deindividuated people do
           e. Gender roles influenced by deindividuation
           f. Deindividuation can be voluntary or involuntary
   C. **Groupthink and group thinking**
       1. Groupthink - the tendency for all members of the group to think alike and suppress _____
           a. Occurs under the following conditions
               (1) Need for agreement overwhelms the need for the wisest decision
               (2) Needs to be liked overwhelm members ability to disagree

405

                 b.   Features of groupthink
                       (1)   Group avoids challenging leader's preference
                       (2)   Doesn't want to disagree
                       (3)   Avoids outside information
                       (4)   Group suppresses dissent
                 c.   Criticisms of groupthink
                       (1)   Easy to see retrospectively, harder to see prospectively
                       (2)   Many things contribute to its occurrence
          2.   Group polarization - average decision of a group is more _____ than
                members' individual decisions
                 a.   Groups thought to make riskier decisions - "the risky shift"
                 b.   The direction of the group's decision depends on the topic
                 c.   Certain topics are immune to group polarization
          3.   Jury decisions
                 a.   Lean toward the majority
                 b.   If split then the _____ bias occurs - the more the group talks, the
                       more lenient the verdict
          4.   Individuals influence groups through repetition, by expressing minority
                views consistently, firmly, and articulately and by finding allies
   D.   Competition and cooperation
          1.   Competition often _____ work motivation and has many negative effects
          2.   Most businesses depend on cooperation
          3.   Interdependence is successful at reducing competitiveness and hostility
          4.   Cooperative groups work better than working competitively or alone

Answer these Learning Objectives while you read Section 3.

7.   Discuss some reasons for conforming to social pressure in a group.

8.   Explain the ways decision making and individual behavior can be influenced by group
      processes.

9.   Summarize the effects of competition, cooperation and interdependence.

10.   Discuss the factors that lead to dissent and nonconformity.

Write the questions that you have formulated below and answer them while you read.

A._____

B._____

SECTION 4 - ALTRUISM AND DISSENT: THE CONDITIONS OF INDEPENDENT ACTION (PP. 654-658) AND
SECTION 5 - THE QUESTION OF HUMAN NATURE (PP. 658-660)

IV. **ALTRUISM AND DISSENT: THE CONDITIONS OF INDEPENDENT ACTIONS**
    A. **Altruism**
        1.   The willingness to take _____ or dangerous action on behalf of others
        2.   Reasons for altruistic action
            a.   Moral values
            b.   Personal feelings for the victim
            c.   Social and situational influences
    B. **Factors that predict independent action and altruism**
        1.   The individual perceives the need for intervention or help, but this is influenced by population _____ and cultural rules
        2.   The individual decides to take responsibility or feels personal responsibility
        3.   The individual has an _____; the presence of another dissenter increases the likelihood of protest
        4.   The individual decides that the costs of doing nothing outweigh the costs of getting involved
        5.   The individual feels competent
        6.   The individual becomes _____; once initial steps have been taken, most people will increase their commitment
V. **THE QUESTION OF HUMAN NATURE**
    A.   **"The banality of evil"** - refers to the fact that evil acts are not just committed by evil people, but by otherwise good people
    B.   **Normal _____ processes explain "evil" acts according to social psychology**
        1.   Adherence to roles, obedience to authority, vulnerability to self-serving biases, conformity, entrapment, deindividuation and competition
        2.   These phenomena result from social organization not human nature

Answer these Learning Objectives while you read Sections 4 and 5.

11.   Discuss the factors that lead to altruistic behavior.

12.   Relate the principles of social psychology to the banality of evil.

Write the questions that you have formulated below and answer them while you read.

A._____

B._____

ACROSS

2. a given social position governed by norms
4. hypothesis that the world is fair
5. the willingness to take selfless action on behalf of another
7. treating another without regard for his or her individuality
13. social conventions that regulate human life
17. gradual process by which individuals escalate their commitment to a course of action
18. the opposite of cooperation

DOWN

1. forceful type of persuasion
2. the tendency for all group members to think alike
6. loss of awareness of one's own individuality
7. type of attribution that sees something within the person as the cause of an action
8. type of attribution that sees something external as the cause of an action
9. an explanation for behavior
10. a relatively stable opinion
11. social conventions
12. cognitive _____
14. when each member of a team slows down, letting others work harder
15. classic study in which college students were placed in one of two roles
16. conducted the obedience study

408

FLASH CARDS

Cut the following chart along the borders and test yourself with the resulting flash cards.

17.1 SOCIAL PSYCHOLOGY	17.6 ENTRAPMENT	17.11 FUNDAMENTAL ATTRIBUTION ERROR
17.2 NORMS	17.7 SOCIAL COGNITION	17.12 SELF-SERVING BIAS
17.3 ROLE	17.8 ATTRIBUTION THEORY	17.13 JUST-WORLD HYPOTHESIS
17.4 DEPERSONALIZATION	17.9 SITUATIONAL ATTRIBUTIONS	17.14 BLAMING THE VICTIM
17.5 LANGUAGE OF PROTEST	17.10 DISPOSITIONAL ATTRIBUTIONS	17.15 ATTITUDE

17.11 The tendency to overestimate personality factors and underestimate the influence of the situation when explaining other peoples' behavior.	**17.6** A gradual process in which individuals escalate their commitment to a course of action to justify their investment of time, money or effort.	**17.1** An area of psychology that examines the individual in the social context.
17.12 The tendency to take credit for one's good actions and rationalize one's mistakes when explaining one's own behavior.	**17.7** An area in social psychology that studies social influences on thought, memory, perception and other cognitive processes.	**17.2** Social conventions that regulate human life, including explicit laws and implicit cultural standards.
17.13 The notion that many people need to believe that the world is fair and that justice is served; bad people are punished and good people rewarded.	**17.8** The theory that people are motivated to explain their own behavior and that of others by attributing causes to a situation or disposition.	**17.3** A given social position that is governed by a set of norms for proper behavior.
17.14 The argument that the victim of an event deserved, provoked or wanted the situation to occur.	**17.9** Identifying the cause of an action as something in the environment.	**17.4** Treating another person without regard for his or her individuality as a human being.
17.15 A relatively stable opinion containing a cognitive element and an emotional element.	**17.10** Identifying the cause of an action as something in the person, such as a trait or motive.	**17.5** Lacking the words to refuse to obey; not knowing what to say.

17.16 COHORT	17.21 BRAINWASHING	17.26 GROUPTHINK
17.17 GENERATIONAL IDENTITY	17.22 CONFORMITY	17.27 LENIENCY BIAS
17.18 COGNITIVE DISSONANCE	17.23 DIFFUSION OF RESPONSIBILITY	17.28 GROUP POLARIZATION
17.19 THE VALIDITY EFFECT	17.24 SOCIAL LOAFING	17.29 ALTRUISM
17.20 COERCIVE PERSUASION	17.25 DEINDIVIDUATION	17.30 THE BANALITY OF EVIL

17.26 The tendency for all members in close-knit groups to think alike for the sake of harmony and to suppress disagreement.	17.21 Called undesired social influence or coercive persuasion; it suggests that a person has a change of mind and is unaware of what is happening.	17.16 An age group, such as school class or a whole generation, that shares common experiences or demographic traits.
17.27 When a jury is equally split, the more the group talks, the more lenient its verdict.	17.22 Taking action or adopting attitudes as a result of real or imagined group pressure.	17.17 An identity of a particular cohort or age group. Often events that occur between the ages of 16 and 24 are critical in its formation.
17.28 The tendency for a group's decision to be more extreme than its members' individual decisions.	17.23 The tendency of members in organized or anonymous groups to avoid taking responsibility for actions, assuming others will do so.	17.18 Tension that occurs when a person holds two cognitions that are psychologically inconsistent, or when a belief is incongruent with behavior.
17.29 The willingness to take selfless or dangerous action on behalf of others.	17.24 Diffusion of responsibility in work groups. Each member of a team slows down, letting others work harder.	17.19 The tendency of people to believe that a statement is true or valid simply because it has been repeated many times.
17.30 Under certain conditions, good people can be induced to do bad things.	17.25 The loss of awareness of one's own individuality in groups or crowds and the abdication of mindful action.	17.20 Severe tactics used to force someone to change his or her attitudes.

PRACTICE TEST 1

1. Rules that regulate "correct" behaviors for a manager or an employee are called
   A. norms.
   B. occupational roles.
   C. social rules.
   D. depersonalization.

2. Roles, attitudes, the behavior of groups, attitudes, conformity and persuasion are
   A. all examples of norms.
   B. major areas in cultural psychology.
   C. major areas in attribution theory.
   D. major areas in social psychology.

3. The major point of the prison study was
   A. to demonstrate that certain personality types should not be in positions of authority.
   B. that peoples' behavior depends to a large extent on the roles they are asked to play.
   C. that students are very suggestible and are not good research subjects.
   D. how quickly people are corrupted by power.

4. The process of _____ allowed the staff to treat the patients without regard for their individuality in the hospital study.
   A. depersonalization
   B. role violations
   C. institutionalization
   D. deindividuation

5. In the obedience experiments, Milgram found that people were more likely to disobey the experimenter and refuse to administer shock when
   A. the experimenter stayed in the room.
   B. the subject administered shocks directly to the victim in the same room.
   C. authority figures, rather than "ordinary" people, ordered subjects to continue.
   D. the subject worked with a peer who also administered shocks.

6. In the obedience experiments, what percentage of the subjects administered the maximum amount of shock to the victim?
   A. only 1 to 2 percent
   B. approximately two-thirds
   C. 30 percent
   D. all of the subjects

7. Which of the following causes people to obey when they really would rather not?
   A. entrapment
   B. good manners
   C. routinization
   D. all of the above

8. In attributing causes to other peoples' behaviors, the tendency to overestimate the effects of personality factors and underestimate the effects of situational factors is called
    A. a dispositional attribution.
    B. the just-world hypothesis.
    C. the fundamental attribution error.
    D. the self-serving bias.

9. "Sally rides her bike to school because she is athletic" is an example of
    A. a dispositional attribution.
    B. the self-serving bias.
    C. the fundamental attribution error.
    D. situational attribution.

10. "Jennifer rides her bike to school because she can't get a ride" is an example of
    A. a dispositional attribution.
    B. the self-serving bias.
    C. the fundamental attribution error.
    D. situational attribution.

11. "People get what they deserve" is an example of
    A. the just-world hypothesis.
    B. situational attribution.
    C. the fundamental attribution error.
    D. the self-serving bias.

12. Attitudes are affected by
    A. thinking.
    B. conformity.
    C. habit.
    D. all of the above.

13. The fact that mere repetition increases the perception that familiar statements are true demonstrates
    A. cognitive dissonance.
    B. generational identity.
    C. the validity effect.
    D. coercive persuasion.

14. One of the techniques that facilitates coercive persuasion is
    A. repeating a piece of information over and over.
    B. exposing people to arguments from someone they admire.
    C. defining a person's problems in simplistic terms, and offering simple answers.
    D. offering people food while listening to an argument.

15. People are most likely to conform if
    A. they must in order to keep their jobs, win promotions or win votes.
    B. they wish to be liked.
    C. they are highly rigid.
    D. they are characterized by all of the above.

16. A woman was stabbed and none of the numerous onlookers called for help. What accounts for this?
    A. social loafing
    B. conformity
    C. diffusion of responsibility
    D. deindividuation

17. In friendly, close-knit groups, there is a tendency for all members to think alike and suppress dissent. This phenomenon is called
    A. group polarization.
    B. risky shift.
    C. diffusion of responsibility.
    D. groupthink.

18. To increase the influence of a minority opinion, a group member should
    A. use coercion.
    B. introduce a reasonable doubt.
    C. repeat the opinion.
    D. capitalize on group think.

19. Group polarization predicts that a group's average decision will be
    A. very similar to its members' individual decisions.
    B. more moderate than its members' individual decisions.
    C. more cautious than its members' individual decisions.
    D. more extreme than its members' individual decisions.

20. According to research, what are some of the effects of competition?
    A. Though it fosters jealousy, it increases achievement.
    B. It makes people feel insecure and anxious, jealous and hostile.
    C. It energizes people and improves self-confidence.
    D. It is favorable for the winners and destructive for the losers.

21. Working together or interdependently to reach mutual goals
    A. results in a decrease in performance.
    B. reduces competition and hostility.
    C. is less effective than working in competitive teams.
    D. increases hostility because it forces people to work together.

22. Which of the following is NOT one of the factors that predicts independent action, such as whistleblowing and altruism?
    A. The individual has an altruistic personality.
    B. The individual becomes entrapped.
    C. The individual feels competent.
    D. The individual has an ally.

23. Before a bystander will behave altruistically, he or she must first
    A. have a "helpful" personality.
    B. have had a similar experience in the past.
    C. perceive the need for help.
    D. experience all of the above.

24. The willingness to take selfless or dangerous action on behalf of others is called
    A. interdependence.   B. individuation.
    C. altruism.   D. all of the above.

25. Which characteristic is most likely to lead to evil actions?
    A. adherence to roles, obedience to authority, conformity, entrapment
    B. lack of developed conscience
    C. mental illness
    D. an evil nature

PRACTICE TEST 2

1. A social psychologist would conduct research on
   A. the causes of antisocial personality disorder.
   B. whether personality types are related to social behaviors.
   C. what circumstances promote helpful behavior.
   D. what type of therapeutic approach best treats social phobia.

2. In the prison study, subjects
   A. exhibited both the behaviors and emotions of the roles of guard and prisoner.
   B. who played prisoners developed emotions associated with their roles, but the guards did not.
   C. who were guards became very distressed that the prisoners played their part so well.
   D. guards played their role but did not enjoy it.

3. In the hospital study, the hospital staff avoided eye contact and conversation with the patients as much as possible. Often, the psychiatrists moved on without replying or even looking at the person. These behaviors demonstrate
   A. deindividuation.   B. prejudice.
   C. norms.   D. depersonalization.

4. In the obedience study, the person most likely to disobey would be a subject who
   A. felt very upset about administering shocks to another person.
   B. worked with peers who refused to go further.
   C. had strong moral and religious principles.
   D. had a very passive personality.

5. The conclusion of the obedience study was that
   A. obedience was more a function of the situation than of the particular personalities of the participants.
   B. obedience was more a function of the particular personality types of the participants.
   C. participants with a past history of problems with authority were more likely to obey.
   D. obedience was a function of how much the victim complained.

6. Which conclusion is shared by the prison study, the hospital study and the obedience study?
   A.   The roles people played influenced their behavior more than their personalities.
   B.   What people did depended on the role they were assigned.
   C.   Social roles and obligations have a powerful influence on behavior.
   D.   all of the above

7. You take Mike out for a drink to console him about his dissolving marriage. Next, you occasionally babysit his two-year-old. Then, you find yourself taking care of the child every weekend. This sequence is an example of
   A.   good manners.   B.   routinization.
   C.   lacking a language of protest.   D.   entrapment.

8. When Ashley's husband forgot to run an errand, she attributed his forgetting to his selfishness. When Andy's wife forgot to run an errand, he attributed her forgetting to her being preoccupied with problems at work. Ashley made a(n) _____ attribution, while Andy made a(n) _____ attribution.
   A.   dispositional; situational   B.   situational; dispositional
   C.   self-serving; external   D.   internal; dispositional

9. I believe that I got an A in geometry because I'm a hard worker, but I got a "D" in biology because the teacher doesn't like me. This demonstrates
   A.   the just-world hypothesis.   B.   the self-serving bias.
   C.   the fundamental attribution error.   D.   dissonance.

10. I'm trying to understand why Jamie snubbed me today. Based on the fundamental attribution error, which explanation am I most likely to choose?
    A.   Jamie is a moody person.   B.   Jamie had a bad day.
    C.   It had to do with the fight we had.   D.   I've done something wrong.

11. When Hortense was diagnosed with cancer, she believed that she must have done something wrong to have deserved such an illness. Her belief is an example of
    A.   a situational attribution.   B.   guilt.
    C.   the just-world hypothesis.   D.   a dispositional attribution.

12. "It's no wonder Jane was attacked. It's her own fault; she never should have been out alone." This is an example of
    A.   the fundamental attribution error.   B.   blaming the victim.
    C.   self-serving bias.   D.   none of the above.

13. The Vietnam war shaped the values and attitudes of many people who were college students during that era. This is an example of a(n)
A. social attitude.
B. dispositional attribution.
C. generational identity.
D. individual identity.

14. Students were asked to publicly advocate the importance of safe sex, and then list the reasons for their own past failure to use condoms. Afterwards, they experienced
A. friendly persuasion.
B. cognitive dissonance.
C. coercive persuasion.
D. insight.

15. Following their confrontation with the discrepancy between their attitudes and their behaviors, what would the students in question 14 be most likely to do?
A. increase their use of condoms
B. make no change in their behavior
C. decrease their use of condoms
D. none of the above

16. Dr. Wyatt wants to persuade his colleagues about a particular point. He should
A. utilize the validity effect.
B. use the emotion of fear.
C. appeal to their generational identity.
D. use all of the above techniques.

17. Several years ago, Maxine became part of a cult. Looking back, she describes what happened. Which of the following probably happened to Maxine?
A. She was not allowed to eat, sleep or exercise.
B. She was offered unconditional love, acceptance and attention by the leader.
C. She was given a new last name that was shared by all other members.
D. all of the above

18. Dr. Patel is assigning a group project in her psychology class. She has structured the assignment so that to successfully complete the project each student must rely on the work of all the other students in the group. Patel has designed this project in these ways in order to promote
A. deindividuation.
B. social loafing.
C. cooperation.
D. generational identity.

419

19. According to the diffusion of responsibility theory, you would be more likely to receive assistance with a car problem
    A.   on a small road with almost no other traffic.
    B.   on a crowded highway with many other automobiles.
    C.   on a city street with numerous other cars.
    D.   anywhere that a lot of people could see that you needed help.

20. Geraldo's boss always likes to be right and to be the "expert" on any topic. He becomes irritated with whomever disagrees with him. Although he requests "honest feedback and input" from employees, he is likely to get
    A.   groupthink.   B.   group polarization.
    C.   social loafing.   D.   deindividuation.

21. Healthy competition
    A.   occurs in situations in which the rules are clear.
    B.   occurs in situations in which both sides are equally capable.
    C.   is a contradiction in terms because, in general, competition results in many negative outcomes and does not appear to be too healthy.
    D.   encourages achievement.

22. Which of the following promotes interdependence?
    A.   competition for prizes
    B.   having prizes for all competitors
    C.   having a task that requires cooperative effort to be successful
    D.   dividing a project and having each part developed by different individuals

23. Rachel and her daughter spend every Christmas working at the shelter.
    A.   They are volunteering because they have deeply held moral values.
    B.   They work at the shelter because they have personal feelings for the victims.
    C.   They help at the shelter because have become entrapped.
    D.   Any of the above reasons could explain their altruistic behavior.

24. Evil deeds are a result of
    A.   extreme and unusual circumstances.   B.   normal psychological processes.
    C.   people who have been traumatized.   D.   mental illness.

25. Who among the following is most likely to commit an evil act according to the idea of the banality of evil?
    A.   a person with a disturbed personality   B.   an immoral person
    C.   an ordinary person   D.   an evil person

PRACTICE TEST 3

1. Identify the influences and effects of roles and norms in the prison study, the hospital study and the obedience study.

2. A group of students were asked to explain the source of a person's grades. They provided the explanations below. Examine each explanation and identify the explanatory device it relies upon.

   A. Grades result from a person's intelligence and self-discipline. When these are high, grades are good and vice versa.

   B. Grades depend on doing the right things. A person should earn good grades for reading instructions, meeting deadlines, turning in assignments. If a person does not do these things, he or she should receive bad grades.

   C. Grades depend on quality teaching and educational materials. If the teacher is good, students should be motivated and do well.

   D. Grades depend on luck. Sometimes it doesn't matter whether a person has studied or not if the test is tricky.

3. You need to get a "B" in all of your classes to get the scholarship you need. You are right on the border between a "B" and a "C" in your Spanish class. Using information on persuasion, discuss how you might approach your Spanish teacher to attempt to persuade him to give you the benefit of the doubt.

4. Dr. Wong requires a group project in her sociology class. She wants each group to design a federally funded project to reduce the number of homeless and provide appropriate services for those who remain homeless. She is aware of all the principles of group behavior and she wants to reduce the likelihood of social loafing, diffusion of responsibility, groupthink, deindividuation, group polarization and competition. She wants to increase cooperation and independent action. Develop a set of instructions she should use to meet all of her goals for this assignment.

5. Dr. Sullivan is starting his own private high school. He wants this school to be different than other schools. He wants this school to develop cooperation among students rather than competition. He wants students to have a feeling of commitment to their fellow students, their classmates and the school as much as to their own individual ambitions. Describe the rules, norms, grading system, extracurricular system and approach to teaching that would achieve the goals Dr. Sullivan seeks to attain.

CHAPTER 18

The Cultural Context

LEARNING OBJECTIVES

1. Define culture.

2. List and explain some of the problems in the study of culture.

3. Discuss cultural similarities and differences in body language, and distinguish between high-context and low-context cultures.

4. Distinguish between monochronic and polychronic cultures, and describe the influences on how time is organized in a particular culture.

5. Compare and contrast individual-centered cultures and collectivist, or group-centered, cultures.

6. List and explain various sources of social identity.

7. Describe problems and potential solutions related to balancing one's ethnic identity in culturally diverse societies.

8. Describe the social constructionist view of gender differences and the status of women.

9. Define ethnocentrism and explain its consequences.

10. Describe ways in which stereotypes are useful and three ways they distort reality.

11. Define prejudice and describe the psychological, social and financial functions that cause it to persist.

12. Describe the debates that surround the definitions of racism, sexism and other prejudices.

13. Discuss the approaches that have been taken to try to reduce prejudice and conflict between groups, and describe their outcomes.

14. Discuss the benefits and dangers of cultural research.

CHAPTER CONCEPT MAP

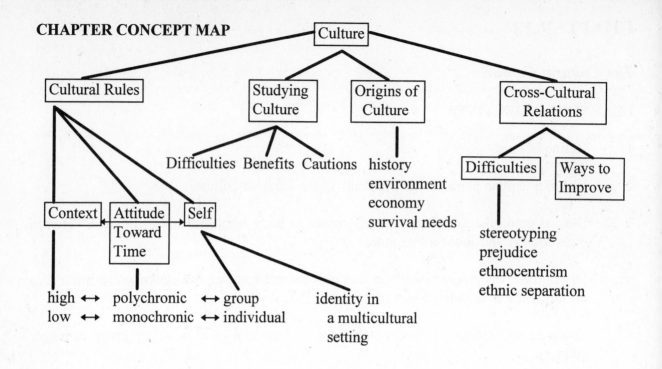

BRIEF CHAPTER SUMMARY

Chapter 18 examines some of the rules that govern culture. Some cultures are very homogeneous; they are considered high-context cultures. People in these cultures operate according to shared experiences; therefore, they rely on nonverbal language rather than the exact meaning of their words. People in these cultures tend to have a polychronic way of organizing time and are more likely to define themselves according to their group. Cultures that are hetereogeneous are considered low-context cultures, and they rely more on verbal than nonverbal communication. These cultures organize time in a monochronic fashion, and people tend to define themselves individualistically. Studying culture has certain difficulties that must be addressed, including the problematic tendency to believe that some cultures are superior to others. Among those who study culture, many believe that cultural rules are socially constructed based on economics, ecology and reproductive issues. Understanding culture is important; stereotyping and prejudice can interfere with relationships between people from different cultures. Many attempts to improve cross-cultural relationships have not been successful. Better cross-cultural relationships require common goals, equal status and economic standing, support from authorities and opportunities to work and socialize together.

PREVIEW OUTLINE AND REVIEW QUESTIONS

Before you read the chapter, review the preview outline and the Learning Objectives for each section of the text. Develop additional questions of your own based on key concepts and terms and write them in the designated spaces. Answer all questions as you read the text.

SECTION 1 - STUDYING CULTURE (PP. 663-669)

I. **STUDYING CULTURE**
    A.   **Definitions**
        1.   Culture - shared _____ that govern the behavior of members of a society and a set of values, beliefs and attitudes shared by most members
        2.   Cultural psychologists - study how people are affected by their culture
        3.   Cross-cultural psychologists - compare members of different societies
    B.   **Issues that make research on culture different from other areas in psychology**
        1.   The problem of methods and _____
        2.   The problem of _____ results - linguistic or functional equivalence
        3.   The problem of stereotyping - individual differences must be recognized
        4.   The reification of culture - regarding culture as an explanation in itself
        5.   Cross-cultural findings can be politically and _____ sensitive
    C.   **One study used matched samples and found cultural differences on four key dimensions**
        1.   The extent to which people accept and expect unequal distribution of _____ in organizations and families
        2.   The extent to which they are integrated into groups or are expected to be "individualistic"
        3.   The extent to which they endorse "masculine" assertiveness or "feminine" _____
        4.   The extent to which they can tolerate uncertainty

Answer these Learning Objectives while you read Section 1.

1. Define culture.

2. List and explain some of the problems in the study of culture.

Write the questions that you have formulated below and answer them while you read.

A._____

B._____

II. **THE RULES OF CULTURE**
   A. **Context and communication**
      1. High-context cultures - homogeneous; nonverbal signs very important
      2. Low-context cultures - people pay more attention to words than _____
   B. **The organization of time**
      1. _____ cultures - time is experienced as linear; in low-context cultures
      2. Polychronic cultures - time organized along parallel lines, people do many things at once; demands of people take precedence; in high-context cultures
   C. **The self and self-identity**
      1. Individual-centered versus _____, or group-centered, cultures influences how the self is defined, which affects individual psychology, the perception of relationships and the strength of bonds
      2. Social identities are based on _____, ethnicity, religion and roles, which must be balanced; there are four types of ethnic identities
         a. Bicultural - ties to ethnicity and larger culture
         b. _____ - weak ethnic feelings, strong acculturation
         c. Ethnic separatists - strong ethnic identity, weak acculturation
         d. Marginal - connected to neither ethnicity nor main culture

Answer these Learning Objectives while you read Section 2.

3.   Discuss cultural similarities and differences in body language, and distinguish between high-context and low-context cultures.

4.   Distinguish between monochronic and polychronic cultures, and describe the influences on how time is organized in a particular culture.

5.   Compare and contrast individual-centered and collectivist, or group-centered, cultures.

6.   List and explain various sources of social identity.

7.   Describe problems and potential solutions related to balancing one's ethnic identity in culturally diverse societies.

Write the questions that you have formulated below and answer them while you read.

A._____

B._____

SECTION 3 - THE ORIGINS OF CULTURE (PP. 678-686)

III.   **THE ORIGINS OF CULTURE**
    A.   **A culture's attitudes and practices are embedded in its _____, environment, economy and survival needs**
    B.   **Cultural origins of gender roles serve as an example**
        1.   Two views about the origins of gender roles
            a.   Social _____ suggest they are a result of culture
            b.   Sociobiologists and _____ psychologists believe that biology heavily influences gender roles
        2.   Aspects of gender roles that seem to be universal
            a.   Men have had, and continue to have, more _____ and power
            b.   Men, on average, are more _____ and violent than women
            c.   Men generally hunt, travel and make weapons; women generally cook, clean and take care of children
            d.   Masculinity must be achieved through effort; femininity is seen as developing without intervention
        3.   Aspects of gender that vary across cultures
            a.   The status of women is not uniformly low; many variations exist
            b.   The content of "men's work" and "women's work" varies culturally
            c.   Cultures differ in the daily _____ permitted between the sexes
            d.   Attitudes vary about female chastity
            e.   In some cultures, men and women regard one another as opposites; in other cultures, they do not regard one another as very different
        4.   Factors affecting the variation in gender roles
            a.   Production - economic matters
                 (1)   Rigid concepts of manhood exist where there is great _____ for resources
                 (2)   Gender roles are related to a culture's development - the more industrialized, the more modern the gender role
            b.   Reproduction - child bearing and raising

Answer this Learning Objective while you read Section 3.

8.   Describe the social constructionist view of gender differences and the status of women.

Write the questions that you have formulated below and answer them while you read.

A._____

B._____

**SECTION 4 - CROSS-CULTURAL RELATIONS (PP. 686-697) AND
SECTION 5 - CAN CULTURES GET ALONG? (PP. 698-700)**

IV.   **CROSS-CULTURAL RELATIONS**
    A.   **Ethnocentrism and stereotypes**
        1.   Ethnocentrism
            a.   The belief that one's own culture is _____
            b.   Generates "us-them" thinking
        2.   Stereotypes
            a.   Summary impression of a group in which a person believes that all members of that group share a common trait
            b.   They are cognitive _____ that help us organize experience
            c.   Illusory _____ contribute to stereotyping - two variables that occur together on one occasion become permanently linked
            d.   Stereotypes lead to three distortions of reality
                (1)   Accentuate differences between groups
                (2)   Produce selective perception
                (3)   Underestimate differences within other groups
            e.   They often contain a "grain of truth," but not the whole truth
            f.   People have positive stereotypes about groups they like and negative stereotypes about groups they dislike

    B.   **Prejudice**
        1.   An unreasonable negative feeling toward a category of people or a cultural practice
        2.   The sources of prejudice
            a.   Psychodynamic approach attributes prejudice to scapegoating
            b.   It is related to low feelings of self-worth
            c.   Socialization - taught by parents
            d.   Social benefits
            e.   Economic _____ and justification of discrimination
        3.   The varieties of prejudice
            a.   Those who are trying not to be prejudiced
            b.   Those who do not feel guilty about having prejudicial feelings
            c.   Symbolic _____ - racism is less common against individuals but now is expressed toward racial symbols like "welfare abuse"
            d.   People may control their prejudice until they are angry, stressed or receive a blow to their self-esteem
            e.   Researchers have identified two types of sexism
                (1)   _____ sexism - strong negative feelings about women
                (2)   Benevolent sexism - positive and paternalistic feelings

4. Reducing prejudice
    a. Different approaches that have been not been fully successful
       (1) Focus on individual change through education, improvement of self-esteem or religion
       (2) The _____ hypothesis
       (3) Legal changes should be used to eradicate prejudice
       (4) The groups in conflict should work together
    b. Conditions necessary to reduce prejudice - to work all must exist
       (1) Both sides must cooperate toward a common goal
       (2) Both sides must have equal _____ and economic standing
       (3) Both sides must believe they have the moral, legal, and economic support of the authorities
       (4) Both sides must have opportunities to work and socialize together, formally and informally

V. CAN CULTURES GET ALONG?
A. General concerns and questions
    1. Old biases may be replaced with new ones
    2. All cultures are subject to psychological processes like ethnocentrism
    3. Cultural research can inflame intolerance
B. Realistic goal - accept that conflict occurs and find nonviolent ways to resolve it

Answer these Learning Objectives while you read Sections 4 and 5.

9. Define ethnocentrism and explain its consequences.

10. Describe ways in which stereotypes are useful and three ways they distort reality.

11. Define prejudice and the psychological, social and financial functions that perpetuate it.

12. Describe the debates that surround the definitions of racism, sexism and other prejudices.

13. Discuss the approaches that have been taken to try to reduce prejudice and conflict between groups, and describe their outcomes.

14. Discuss the benefits and dangers of cultural research.

Write the questions that you have formulated below and answer them while you read.

A._____

B._____

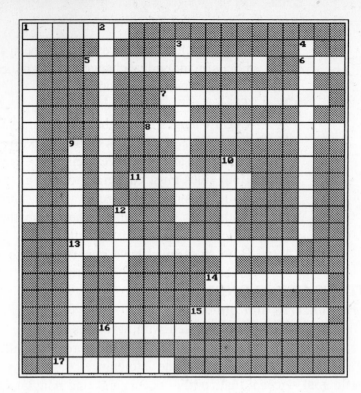

ACROSS

1. shared rules that govern the behavior of members of a community
5. cultures in which people pay close attention to nonverbal forms of communication
6. anatomical category
7. cultures in which people tend to do several things at once
8. the belief that one's own group is superior
13. social _____
14. a type of racism in which the focus of dislike is no longer on individuals
15. an unreasonable negative feeling toward a category of people
16. the duties, rights, and behaviors a culture considers appropriate for males and females
17. type of correlation in which two variables become linked on one occasion so people expect them always to be linked

DOWN

1. cultures in which the group is given greater emphasis than the individual
2. to regard an intangible process as if it were a literal object
3. cultures in which time is organized sequentially
4. having a weak feeling of ethnicity but a strong sense of acculturation
9. a type of psychology that compares members of different societies
10. a cognitive schema in which a person believes that all members of the group share a common trait
12. how close people normally stand to one another when they are speaking

FLASH CARDS

Cut the following chart along the borders and test yourself with the resulting flash cards.

18.1 CULTURE	18.7 HIGH-CONTEXT CULTURES	18.13 SOCIAL IDENTITY
18.2 CULTURAL PSYCHOLOGISTS	18.8 LOW-CONTEXT CULTURES	18.14 ETHNIC IDENTITY
18.3 CROSS-CULTURAL PSYCHOLOGISTS	18.9 MONOCHRONIC CULTURES	18.15 ASSIMILATION
18.4 REIFICATION	18.10 POLYCHRONIC CULTURES	18.16 ETHNIC SEPARATISM
18.5 BODY LANGUAGE	18.11 INDIVIDUAL-CENTERED CULTURES	18.17 MARGINAL IDENTITY
18.6 CONVERSATIONAL DISTANCE	18.12 COLLECTIVIST CULTURES	18.18 SEX

18.13 Part of a person's self-concept that is based on his or her identification with a nation, culture or ethnic group or with gender or other roles in society.	18.7 Cultures in which people pay close attention to nonverbal forms of communication and assume a shared context for their interactions.	18.1 Shared rules that govern the behavior of members of a community, and a set of values, beliefs and attitudes shared by the community members.
18.14 Having a close identification with one's own race, religion or ethnic group.	18.8 Cultures in which people do not take a shared context for granted, and instead emphasize direct verbal communication.	18.2 Psychologists who study the many ways in which people are affected by the rules of the culture in which they live.
18.15 People who have a weak feeling of ethnicity but a strong sense of acculturation.	18.9 Cultures in which time is organized sequentially; schedules and deadlines are valued over people.	18.3 Psychologists who compare members of different societies, searching both for their commonalities and their specific cultural differences.
18.16 People who have a strong sense of ethnic identity but a weak feeling of acculturation.	18.10 Cultures in which time is organized horizontally; people tend to do several things at once and value relationships over schedules.	18.4 To regard an intangible process, such as a feeling, as if it were a literal object.
18.17 People who do not feel connected to either their ethnicity or to the dominant culture.	18.11 Cultures in which the individual, rather than the group, is given greater emphasis.	18.5 The nonverbal signals of body movement, posture, gesture and gaze that people constantly express.
18.18 Classification based on universal, unchangeable anatomical reproductive functions.	18.12 Cultures in which the group, rather than the individual, is given greater emphasis.	18.6 How close people normally stand to one another when they are speaking.

18.19 SOCIAL CONSTRUCTIONISM	**18.25 ILLUSORY CORRELATION**	**18.31 BICULTURAL IDENTITY**
18.20 PRODUCTION	**18.26 PREJUDICE**	**18.32 SEXISM**
18.21 REPRODUCTION	**18.27 SYMBOLIC RACISM**	**18.33 CONTACT HYPOTHESIS**
18.22 ETHNOCENTRISM	**18.28 HOSTILE SEXISM**	**18.34 DE FACTO SEGREGATION**
18.23 "US-THEM" THINKING	**18.29 BENEVOLENT SEXISM**	**18.35 GENDER**
18.24 STEREOTYPE	**18.30 ACCULTURATION**	**18.36 SELECTIVE PERCEPTION**

18.31 An identity in which people have ties both to their ethnicity and to the larger culture.	**18.25** When two variables that are unusual or distinct in some way become linked on one occasion, people tend to expect them always to be linked.	**18.19** The view that there are no universal truths about human nature, because people construct reality based on their culture, history, and power.
18.32 Prejudice based on sex.	**18.26** An unreasonable negative feeling toward a category of people or a cultural practice.	**18.20** Matters pertaining to the economy. Offered as one factor that accounts for the variation in gender roles around the world.
18.33 An approach to reducing prejudice that advocates bringing members of both sides together to let them get acquainted.	**18.27** The focus of dislike is not on individuals but on racial symbols and issues such as "forced busing."	**18.21** Matters pertaining to the bearing, raising and nurturing of children. One factor that accounts for the variation in gender roles around the world.
18.34 Segregation that exists even when legal reforms have been instituted.	**18.28** A type of sexism that involves strongly negative feelings about women, such as anger, hatred and contempt.	**18.22** The belief that one's own ethnic group, nation or religion is superior to all others.
18.35 All the duties, rights and behaviors a culture considers appropriate for males and females.	**18.29** A type of sexism that involves positive feelings about women along with paternalistic and stereotyped attitudes toward them.	**18.23** A type of thinking that occurs when any two groups perceive themselves to be in competition.
18.36 The tendency to see only what fits a stereotype and to reject any perceptions that do not fit.	**18.30** The process by which members of minority groups in a given society come to identify with and feel part of the mainstream culture.	**18.24** A cognitive schema or an impression of a group, in which a person believes that all members of the group share a common trait or traits.

PRACTICE TEST 1

1. Culture is
   A. a program of shared rules that govern the behavior of community members.
   B. a set of values, beliefs and attitudes shared by most community members.
   C. a system of rules that is passed from one generation to another.
   D. defined by all of the above.

2. Study samples of individuals who are similar in all aspects of their lives except their nationality, including age, economic status, and education are called
   A. matched samples.   B. reification samples.
   C. stereotyped samples.   D. cross-cultural samples.

3. One of the problems in studying culture is
   A. it is very difficult to define.
   B. it is difficult to get subjects.
   C. the problem of interpreting results.
   D. the differences in body language.

4. The difference between cross-cultural psychology and stereotyping is that
   A. stereotyping identifies negative features of a group, whereas cross-cultural psychology identifies positive, negative and neutral features of a group.
   B. stereotypes are untrue, whereas cross-cultural findings are generally accurate.
   C. unlike stereotypes, the study of culture does not assume that all members of a culture behave the same way.
   D. unlike stereotypes, cross-cultural findings do not have political consequences.

5. Some aspects of body language seem to be universal, however, most aspects are specific to particular cultures. An aspect of body language that is particular to a given culture is
   A. facial expressions.   B. conversational distance.
   C. body movements that reveal status.   D. all of the above.

6. High-context cultures are those in which
   A. people pay close attention to nonverbal signs.
   B. people pay far more attention to words than nonverbal language.
   C. people assume little shared knowledge and history.
   D. people generally refuse requests very directly.

7. High-context cultures are usually _____, while low-context cultures are _____.
   A. monochronic; polychronic   B. heterogeneous; homogeneous
   C. polychronic; monochronic   D. verbal; nonverbal

8. People from _____ cultures are likely to do many things at once, are highly distractible and change plans often and easily.
   A. monochronic
   B. polychronic
   C. low-context
   D. all of the above

9. A culture's way of organizing time
   A. develops arbitrarily.
   B. is based on the climate of the country.
   C. is a direct result of the natural terrain of the country.
   D. stems from the culture's economic system, social organization, political history and ecology.

10. People from individualistic cultures identify themselves
    A. by personality traits or occupation.
    B. in ways that reflect their integration into the community.
    C. by their descendants.
    D. by their social roles, such as uncle, cousin or daughter.

11. One's social identity is based on
    A. nationality.
    B. ethnicity.
    C. religion.
    D. all of the above.

12. A person with a(n) _____ identity is likely to say, "I am proud of my own ethnic heritage, but I identify just as much with my country."
    A. assimilated
    B. ethnic separatist
    C. bicultural
    D. marginal

13. Cultural researchers' explanation for gender differences involves
    A. the idea that there are biological constraints on our gender roles.
    B. two fundamental factors: production and reproduction.
    C. the fact that men have had more status and power than women.
    D. the fact that men, on average, are more aggressive and violent than women.

14. The belief that one's own culture or ethnic group is superior to all others is called
    A. ethnic separatism.
    B. ethnocentrism.
    C. social constructionism.
    D. prejudice.

15. "Us-them" thinking is a natural outcome of
    A. ethnic separatism.
    B. ethnocentrism.
    C. social constructionism.
    D. prejudice.

16. A stereotype
    A. may be positive, negative or neutral.
    B. is the belief that all members of a group share a common trait or traits.
    C. is a cognitive schema by which we map the world.
    D. incorporates all of the above.

17. Stereotypes can be helpful because they
    A. provide illusory correlations.
    B. help us form opinions about particular individuals.
    C. help us to organize experience and process new information.
    D. improve our ability to perceive differences and similarities among people.

18. Stereotypes distort reality by
    A. accentuating differences between groups.
    B. producing selective perceptions.
    C. underestimating differences within other groups.
    D. propagating all of the above.

19. An unreasonable negative feeling toward a category of people or a cultural practice is called
    A. ethnocentrism.   B. a stereotype.
    C. a prejudice.   D. an illusory correlation.

20. Prejudice continues to exist because
    A. of the just-world hypothesis.
    B. there are economic benefits to justifying discrimination.
    C. people have had no contact with those against whom they are prejudiced.
    D. of symbolic racism.

21. According to some social scientists, "forced busing," "welfare abuse," "reverse discrimination" and "hard-core criminals" are examples of
    A. old prejudices in disguise.
    B. symbolic racism.
    C. code words for continuing animosity that most whites have for blacks.
    D. all of the above.

22. Someone who holds positive feelings about women, along with paternalistic and stereotyped attitudes toward them, is engaging in
    A. benevolent sexism.   B. hostile sexism.
    C. traditional sexism.   D. mainstream attitudes.

23. The idea that people will reduce their prejudices if they get together with and get to know members of the other group is called
   A.   de facto segregation.   B.   the contact hypothesis.
   C.   the legal approach.   D.   the jigsaw approach.

24. To reduce prejudice and conflict, it is necessary
   A.   to have the cooperation of both sides.
   B.   that both sides have equal status and economic standing.
   C.   that both sides have opportunities to work and socialize together.
   D.   to meet all of the above conditions.

25. Cultural research can
   A.   make people aware of the dangers of ethnocentrism.
   B.   inflame intolerance rather than reduce it.
   C.   promote ethnic, societal and gender-based separatism.
   D.   cause all of the above to happen.

PRACTICE TEST 2

1. Being on time, not jay-walking and shaking hands when meeting a new person are all examples of
   A. stereotypes.
   B. shared rules that govern the behavior of members of a community.
   C. the reification of culture.
   D. body language.

2. According to the definition, culture consists of
   A. shared rules, behaviors, values, beliefs and attitudes.
   B. expectations, motivations and cognitions.
   C. roles, norms, attributions and attitudes.
   D. a set of behaviors shared by members of the community.

3. When Janine travelled in Europe, she found that many people sunbathed in the nude. She concluded that Europeans engage in looser sexual behavior than people in the United States. Of the problems involved with studying culture, Janine is having a problem with
   A. not using matched samples.
   B. determining which behavior is superior.
   C. interpreting differences.
   D. all of the above.

4. "Americans are so violent because of their culture." This statement is an example of
   A. the shared rules of a culture.
   B. the reification of culture.
   C. passing value judgments about a culture.
   D. how culture gets passed along genetically.

5. Though Catherine is trying to tell Stephanie politely that she is upset, Stephanie does not seem to believe her. Stephanie is paying more attention to the fact that Catherine is speaking quietly and smiling during the discussion. Stephanie is probably from
   A. a low-context culture.   B. a monochronic culture.
   C. a high-context culture.   D. an ethnic culture.

6. The reason people from cultures like Stephanie's pay more attention to nonverbal language is because
   A. these cultures are generally homogeneous and close-knit, and people assume a shared knowledge and history.
   B. people assume little shared knowledge and history.
   C. verbal behavior can be manipulated, whereas nonverbal language is more honest.
   D. they are more emotional cultures and information is generally communicated through gestures.

7. People from some cultures tend to stand closer to one another during conversation than those from other cultures because
   A. those who stand closer are from friendlier cultures.
   B. those who stand closer are from cultures in which sexual values differ.
   C. of differences in rules governing conversational distance.
   D. of differences in the way each type of culture organizes time.

8. Jake likes his "own space" and doesn't particularly like it when plans change suddenly. Jake is most likely from
   A. a monochronic culture.   B. an individual-centered culture.
   C. a low context-culture.   D. all of the above.

9. Darleen knows that whenever she goes back to the country where her parents were born and raised she will find everyone in the same home and neighborhood. People have known each other for many years and are life-long friends. The culture of this country is most likely
   A. collectivist.   B. monochronic.
   C. individual-centered.   D. low-context.

10. Vivian emigrated from China at age 18 and she has been a U.S. citizen for three years. When she is asked, she says that she is an American and she seems to have no interest in her Chinese heritage. This is an example of
    A. biculturalism.   B. ethnic separatism.
    C. marginalism.   D. acculturation.

11. Maria was born in Brazil but came to the U.S. when she was one month old. She has always lived in the U.S., but when she is asked, she says she is Brazilian. She has strong loyalty and interest in Brazil and very little affiliation with mainstream U.S. culture. This is an example of
    A. biculturalism.   B. ethnic separatism.
    C. marginalism.   D. acculturation.

12. During the first meeting of psychology class, the professor asks students to introduce themselves to the class by sharing something important about themselves. Liza introduces herself by saying that she is Russian and she is a mother. These are
    A. examples of biculturalism.   B. stereotypes.
    C. social identities.   D. ethnic identities.

13. A culture's attitudes and practices develop from
    A. its history.   B. its economy.
    C. its environment and survival needs.   D. all of the above.

14. In Sambian society, all adolescent boys are required to engage in oral sex with older males as part of their initiation into manhood, yet they are required to marry someone of the other sex. In the United States, this behavior would be viewed differently. Diverse sexual practices support
    A. the social learning view of gender.
    B. the view that gender is socially constructed.
    C. the idea that there are no universal truths about human nature.
    D. all of the above views.

15. According to cultural researchers, the two fundamental factors that account for the wide variation in gender roles around the world are
    A. size and stature.   B. religion and biology.
    C. production and reproduction.   D. culture and religion.

16. When Sam visited Italy, he observed that many men walk together arm in arm. He concluded that their moral standards are clearly inferior to those of his own country. This is an example of
    A. a stereotype.   B. ethnic identity.
    C. cultural bias.   D. ethnocentrism.

17. Sara had a friend from England who told many lies about her background. Sara has concluded that the English are dishonest and superficial. She is basing this on
    A. an illusory correlation.   B. scapegoating.
    C. socialization.   D. all of the above.

18. Students are shown a slide of a white male committing a crime against a black male. Later, when they are asked what they saw, most reported seeing a black male committing a crime against a white male. This error is a result of the fact that stereotypes
    A. produce selective perception.
    B. accentuate differences between groups.
    C. underestimate differences within other groups.
    D. cause none of the above to happen.

19. Stereotypes
    A. confirm illusory correlations.
    B. help us process new information and retrieve old memories.
    C. are not useful and invariably result in negative consequences.
    D. contain no aspect of truth.

20. Unemployment is high and the economy is in a recession. It is likely that
    A. prejudice will decline as people feel more empathy for one another.
    B. the poor economy will cause an increase in symbolic racism.
    C. prejudice will increase as a result of economic insecurity.
    D. economic conditions will have very little effect on stereotyping and prejudice.

21. Jane very loudly disagrees with comments that reflect prejudice. She says that if everyone would do this, the _____ that reinforce(s) prejudice would be eliminated.
    A. economic benefits   B. socialization
    C. scapegoating   D. social benefits

22. Sean does not consider himself prejudiced. He has friends of different races and ethnic backgrounds. He tries hard not to be influenced by old prejudices that may come up, yet he still sometimes feels uncomfortable with members of some other groups. Sean is
    A. prejudiced.
    B. not prejudiced.
    C. engaging in symbolic racism.
    D. considered prejudiced by some and not by others; there is considerable debate about what constitutes prejudice.

23. Jeff always is putting women down in very obvious ways and it is clear that he considers them inferior. Peter is very polite to women, but in subtle ways he talks down to them and never gives them important, responsible tasks to do. Which describes both men best?
    A. Jeff is sexist, Peter is not.
    B. Jeff is showing hostile sexism and Peter is showing benevolent sexism.
    C. Both men are displaying hostile sexism.
    D. Both men are displaying sexism but not prejudice.

24. Dr. Rollins is trying to reduce prejudice at her institution. She should
   A.   implement the contact hypothesis.
   B.   help educate individual community members.
   C.   change laws.
   D.   provide both sides with the moral, legal and economic support of the authorities.

25. Some critics have suggested that the focus on culture
   A.   can be used to inflame intolerance.
   B.   diminishes the real importance of biological differences.
   C.   helps us see that all humans are subject to psychological processes.
   D.   promotes all of the above behavior.

PRACTICE TEST 3

1. Dr. Katz is developing a research project to study gender differences in five different countries. Discuss some difficulties she should avoid and some considerations in constructing her research study.

2. Michael is from a high-context culture and he is spending his junior year abroad in a low-context culture. Michael will be attending the local university there. Develop a description about Michael and discuss what kinds of problems or difficulties he might experience in the low-context culture. Include information about his daily life, classes, social relationships and his efforts to make plans with people, schedule appointments, run errands, go to stores and banks. Discuss observations he might make about his fellow students and how they live.

3. Simone is at a party in which another guest is discussing her beliefs about gender differences. The other guest believes that gender differences are, for the most part, biologically based and universal. Present the arguments that support and refute this position.

4. Jan and her sister are having a debate about the Agyflops, people from a country located in the Pacific Ocean. Jan's sister does not like the Agyflops and is explaining why to Jan. Most of her reasons are based on stereotypes. For each statement Jan's sister makes, indicate which cognitive distortion it exemplifies.

   A. "When I visited Agyflopia, everyone was so unfriendly. No one smiled."

   B. "They are so different from us. Americans are so direct, but you never know what the Agyflops are thinking."

   C. "I guess that there are many Agyflops in school with us, but they never seem to speak correctly and they always seem so stupid."

   D. "Once I saw two Agyflops being stopped by the police. I think they are basically dishonest people."

5. Why is prejudice so hard to eliminate? You are the principal of a school with students from many different backgrounds. Design a program that attempts to improve cross-cultural relationships.

APPENDIX A

Statistical Methods

LEARNING OBJECTIVES

1.   Describe a frequency distribution and explain how one is constructed.

2.   Describe the different types of graphs and explain how graphs can mask or exaggerate differences.

3.   Describe the three measures of central tendency and how each is calculated.

4.   Define standard deviation and describe how it is calculated.

5.   Compare and contrast percentile scores and z-scores.

6.   Describe a normal distribution and the two types of skewed distributions.

7.   Describe the characteristics of a normal curve.

8.   Distinguish between the null and the alternative hypothesis.

9.   Explain what is meant by statistical significance, and discuss the relationship between statistical significance and psychological importance.

10. Define sampling distribution.

SECTION BY SECTION PREVIEW OUTLINE AND REVIEW QUESTIONS

Before you read the Appendix, review the preview outline and the questions for each section of the text. Develop additional questions of your own based on key concepts and key terms and write them in the designated spaces. Answer all the questions as you read.

SECTION 1 - ORGANIZING DATA (PP. 710-712)

I. **ORGANIZING DATA**
    A.   **Constructing a frequency distribution** - often the first step in organizing data
         1.   Shows how often each possible score actually occurred
         2.   To construct one, order all possible scores from _____ to lowest
         3.   Then tally how often each score is obtained
         4.   Grouped frequency distributions
             a.   Groups adjacent scores into equal-sized classes or intervals
             b.   Grouped frequencies are used when there are _____ scores
             c.   Frequencies within each interval are tallied
    B.   **Graphing the data**
         1.   A graph is a picture that depicts numerical relationships
         2.   Types of graphs
             a.   _____ or bar graph - draw rectangles or bars above each score indicating the number of times it occurred from the bar's height
             b.   Frequency polygon, or line graph - each score is indicated by a dot placed directly over the score on the horizontal axis, at the appropriate height on the vertical axis
         3.   Caution about graphs - they can mask or _____ differences

Answer these Learning Objectives while you read Section 1.

1. Describe a frequency distribution and explain how one is constructed.

2. Describe the different types of graphs and explain how graphs can mask or exaggerate differences.

Write the questions that you have formulated and answer them while you read.

A._____

B._____

II. DESCRIBING DATA

    A.   Measuring Central Tendency - characterizes an entire set of data in terms of a single representative number

        1.   The mean

            a.   To calculate the mean, add up a set of scores and _____ the total by the number of scores in the set

            b.   Means can be misleading because very high or very low scores can dramatically raise or lower the mean

        2.   The median

            a.   The median is the _____ in a set of scores ordered from highest to lowest

            b.   The same number of scores falls above the median as below it

            c.   A more representative measure when extreme scores occur

        3.   The mode

            a.   The score that occurs _____ often

            b.   Used less often than other measures of central tendency

    B.   Measuring variability

        1.   Tells whether the scores are clustered closely around the mean or widely scattered

        2.   The _____

            a.   The simplest measure of variability

            b.   Found by subtracting the lowest score from the highest one

        3.   The standard deviation

            a.   Tells how much, on the average, scores in a distribution differ from the _____

            b.   To compute the standard deviation

                (1)   Subtract the mean from each score yielding deviation scores

                (2)   Square deviation scores

                (3)   Average the squared deviation scores

                (4)   Take the square root of the result

            c.   Large standard deviations signify that scores are _____ scattered and the mean is probably not very representative; small standard deviations signify that scores cluster near the mean and that the mean is representative

    C.   Transforming scores - used when researchers don't want to work directly with raw scores

        1.   Percentile scores

            a.   Percentage of people scoring at or below a given raw score

        b.   A drawback to percentiles is that they do not tell how far apart people are in terms of raw scores

    2.   Z-scores or _____ scores

        a.   Tell how far a given raw score is above or below the mean, using the standard deviation as the unit of measurement

        b.   To calculate, subtract the mean of the distribution from the raw score and divide by the standard deviation

        c.   They preserve the relative spacing of the original raw scores

        d.   Z-scores comparisons must be done with caution

D.   **Curves,** or the _____ of the distribution

    1.   A normal distribution has a symmetrical, bell-shaped form when plotted in a frequency polygon - called a normal curve

    2.   Characteristics of a normal curve

        a.   Right side is the mirror image of the left side

        b.   Mean, median and mode have the _____ value and are at the center of the curve

        c.   The percentage of scores falling between the mean and any given point on the horizontal axis is always the same when standard deviations are used on that axis

    3.   Not all types of observations are distributed normally, some are lopsided or skewed

        a.   When the tail goes to the left, it is a negative skew

        b.   When the tail goes to the right, it is a _____ skew

Answer these Learning Objectives while you read Section 2.

3.   Describe the three measures of central tendency and how each is calculated.

4.   Define standard deviation and describe how it is calculated.

5.   Compare and contrast percentile scores and z-scores.

6.   Describe a normal distribution and the two types of skewed distributions.

7.   Describe the characteristics of a normal curve.

Write the questions that you have formulated and answer them while you read.

A._____

B._____

III. **DRAWING INFERENCES** with inferential statistics
    A.   **The null versus the _____ hypothesis**
        1.   The null hypothesis states the possibility that the experimental manipulations will have no effect on the subjects' behavior
        2.   The alternative hypothesis states that the average experimental group score will differ from the average control group score
        3.   The goal is to _____ the null hypothesis
    B.   **Testing hypotheses**
        1.   Goal - to be reasonably certain the difference did not occur by _____
        2.   Sampling distribution is used - the theoretical distribution of differences between means
        3.   When the null hypothesis is true, there is no difference between groups
        4.   If there is a difference, how likely is it to occur by chance?
        5.   If it is highly improbable that a result occurs by chance, it is said to be _____ significant
        6.   If more than chance was operating, it is safe to assume the independent variable had some influence
        7.   Characteristics of statistical significance
            a.   Psychologists accept a finding as statistically significant if the likelihood of its occurring by chance is five percent or less
            b.   Statistically significant results are not always psychologically interesting or important
            c.   Statistical significance is related to sample _____ - results from a large sample are likely to be found statistically significant

Answer these Learning Objectives while you read Section 3.

8.   Distinguish between the null and the alternative hypothesis.

9.   Explain what is meant by statistical significance, and discuss the relationship between statistical significance and psychological importance.

10.   Define sampling distribution.

Write the questions that you have formulated and answer them while you read.

A._____

B._____

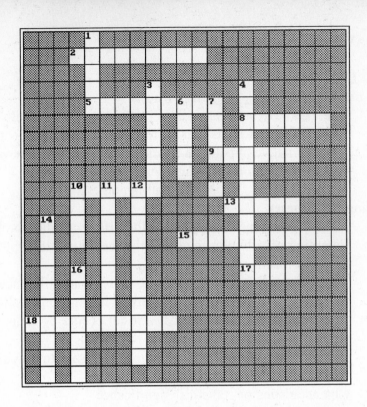

ACROSS

2. _____ distribution
5. bar graph
8. a lopsided curve
9. a symmetrical, bell-shaped curve
10. the midpoint of a distribution
    of scores
13. the pattern of distribution of
    scores
15. when a result is extremely unlikely
    to have occurred by chance, it is
    considered statistically _____
17. type of hypothesis that asserts that
    the independent variable in a study
    will have no effect on the dependent
    variable
18. type of score that indicates the
    percentage of people who scored at
    or below a given raw score

DOWN

1. a drawing that depicts numerical
    relationships
3. a line graph
4. frequency _____
6. calculated by subtracting the lowest
    score in a distribution from the
    highest score
7. the most common measure of central
    tendency
10. the most frequently occurring score
    in a distribution
11. standard _____
12. type of hypothesis, sometimes
    called the research hypothesis
14. the null or alternative _____
16. standard score

450

FLASH CARDS

Cut the following chart along the borders and test yourself with the resulting flash cards.

APP.1 FREQUENCY DISTRIBUTION	APP.8 MODE	APP.15 NORMAL CURVE
APP.2 GRAPH	APP.9 RANGE	APP.16 RIGHT-SKEWED DISTRIBUTION
APP.3 HISTOGRAM/BAR GRAPH	APP.10 STANDARD DEVIATION	APP.17 LEFT-SKEWED DISTRIBUTION
APP.4 FREQUENCY POLYGON/LINE GRAPH	APP.11 DEVIATION SCORE	APP.18 NULL HYPOTHESIS
APP.5 MEASURE OF CENTRAL TENDENCY	APP.12 PERCENTILE SCORE	APP.19 ALTERNATIVE HYPOTHESIS
APP.6 MEAN	APP.13 Z-SCORE (STANDARD SCORE)	APP.20 SAMPLING DISTRIBUTION
APP.7 MEDIAN	APP.14 NORMAL DISTRIBUTION	APP.21 STATISTICALLY SIGNIFICANT

451

APP.15 A symmetrical, bell-shaped frequency polygon representing a normal distribution.	APP.8 A measure of central tendency; the most frequently occurring score in a distribution.	APP.1 A summary of how frequently each score in a set occurred.
APP.16 A non-normal distribution of observations in which the "tail" of the curve is longer on the right; it is said to be positively skewed.	APP.9 A simple measure of variability, calculated by subtracting the lowest score in a distribution from the highest score.	APP.2 A drawing that depicts numerical relationships.
APP.17 A non-normal distribution of observations in which the "tail" of the curve is longer on the left; it is said to be negatively skewed.	APP.10 A commonly used measure of variability that indicates the average difference between scores in a distribution from their mean.	APP.3 A graph in which the heights (or lengths) of bars are proportional to the frequencies of individual scores or classes of scores in a distribution.
APP.18 An assertion that the independent variable in a study will have no effect on the dependent variable.	APP.11 The difference between each individual score in a distribution and the mean of that distribution.	APP.4 A graph showing a set of points obtained by plotting score values against score frequencies. Adjacent points are joined by straight lines.
APP.19 An assertion that the independent variable in a study will have a certain predictable effect on the dependent variable.	APP.12 A number that indicates the percentage of people who scored at or below a given raw score.	APP.5 A number intended to characterize an entire set of data.
APP.20 The theoretical distribution of an entire population that would occur if only chance were operating.	APP.13 A number that indicates how far a given raw score is above or below the mean, using the standard deviation of the distribution.	APP.6 A measure of central tendency; an average calculated by adding up all the scores in a set and dividing the sum by the number of quantities in the set.
APP.21 The term used to refer to a result that is extremely unlikely to have occurred by chance.	APP.14 A theoretical frequency distribution having certain special characteristics.	APP.7 A measure of central tendency; the value at the midpoint of a distribution of scores when the scores are ordered from highest to lowest.

PRACTICE TEST 1

1. The first step in organizing raw data is to
   - A. get a measure of the central tendency.
   - B. establish the range.
   - C. construct a frequency distribution.
   - D. identify the standard deviation.

2. A "histogram" is the technical term that describes a
   - A. bar graph.
   - B. polygon.
   - C. mean.
   - D. line graph.

3. The most frequently occurring score in a distribution is called the
   - A. mean.
   - B. median.
   - C. standard deviation.
   - D. mode.

4. The mean, median and mode are
   - A. measures of central tendency.
   - B. measures of variability.
   - C. characteristics of a normal distribution, but not a skewed distribution.
   - D. characteristics of a skewed distribution, but not a normal distribution.

5. A measure of variability that indicates the average difference between scores in a distribution and their mean is called the
   - A. range.
   - B. standard deviation.
   - C. mode.
   - D. z-score.

6. A score that indicates how far a given score is from the mean is called a
   - A. range.
   - B. mode.
   - C. standard deviation.
   - D. z-score.

7. A lopsided distribution in which scores cluster at the high or low end of the distribution is referred to as
   - A. normal.
   - B. bimodal.
   - C. skewed.
   - D. standard.

8. What asserts that experimental manipulations have no effect?
   - A. null hypothesis
   - B. sampling distribution
   - C. alternative hypothesis
   - D. statistical signific nce

9. Results that are not attributable to chance are referred to as
   - A. non-chance fluctuations.
   - B. skewed.
   - C. statistically significant.
   - D. all of the above.

10. The theoretical distribution of the results of the entire population is called the
    A. null hypothesis.
    B. sampling distribution.
    C. statistical significance.
    D. random error.

PRACTICE TEST 2

1. Dr. Starr gives 10-question quizzes in her psychology class. When she returns quizzes, she puts on the board how many people scored a 10, 9, 8, 7, 6, 5, 4, 3, 2 and 1. This is called a
   A. normal curve.
   B. frequency distribution.
   C. frequency polygon.
   D. histogram.

2. A histogram is to a polygon as
   A. a line is to a bar.
   B. null is to alternative.
   C. a bar is to a line.
   D. normal is to skewed.

3. Students in Dr. Friedlander's class got the following scores on their first test: 75, 77, 87, 63, 93, 77, 72, 80, 57, 68, 76. What is the mode?
   A. 77
   B. 75
   C. 36
   D. 76

4. What is the median in the distribution of scores in question 3?
   A. 77
   B. 75
   C. 36
   D. 76

5. What is the range in the distribution of scores in question 3?
   A. 77
   B. 36
   C. 30
   D. 76

6. Because the sum of the deviation scores is always zero, the standard deviation is based on
   A. the squared deviation scores.
   B. the mean of the deviation scores.
   C. the square root of the deviation scores.
   D. none of the above.

7. If the mean is 10, and the standard deviation is 2, a person with a score of 8 has a z-score of
   A. 8.
   B. -1.
   C. 1.
   D. 2.

8. A distribution in which there are many low scores and a small number of very high scores is referred to as
   A. normal.
   B. positively skewed.
   C. bimodal.
   D. negatively skewed.

9.   If the null hypothesis is true, differences between experimental and control groups are due to
        A.   standard deviations.   B.   skew.
        C.   chance fluctuations.   D.   true differences.

10.   Statistical significance
        A.   suggests that a result would be highly improbably by chance alone.
        B.   does not necessarily have anything to do with psychological importance.
        C.   is a likely outcome with a large sample.
        D.   incorporates all of the above

PRACTICE TEST 3

1. Researchers organize and describe data in a variety of ways. Below, different statistical devices have been grouped together. Examine each grouping and describe the common purpose of the statistics within each.

    A.   Mean, median, mode
    B.   Range and standard deviation
    C.   Frequency distributions, bar graphs (histograms) and line graphs (frequency polygons)
    D.   Percentile scores and z-scores

2. Assume that the height of the male population is normally distributed with a mean of 70 inches and a standard deviation of 3 inches. Given such information, examine each of the statements below and decide whether it is justified or unjustified. Explain the basis for your answer.

    A.   The most frequently occurring male height is 70 inches.
    B.   The percentage of men above 70 inches is much higher than the percentage below this height.
    C.   If the height requirement for entering the police academy were set at 73 inches, less than half the male population would qualify.
    D.   A curve depicting the height of players in professional basketball would also be normally distributed.

3. Below are two inaccurate statements about hypothesis testing and statistical significance. Revise each statement so that it is accurate.

    A.   The null hypothesis is accepted whenever results are statistically significant.
    B.   Statistical significance is a measure of the relative strengths of experimental and control treatments.

Sociocultural psychologists would look to the attitude in the culture toward alcohol use. They would understand the role alcohol plays for people and how it is expected to be used. For example, attitudes and expectations for alcohol use are different in other countries where alcohol is used as a beverage at meals and is consumed at meal times by adolescents and sometimes children.

According to humanists, Harold's drug abuse represents a choice. He is freely choosing to use drugs and is equally free to choose not to do so. Humanists may inquire whether he believes it assists him in dealing with questions about reaching his full potential.

Feminist psychologists would be interested in gender differences in drug abuse. They would see Harold's drug use as a way of dealing with emotions that are compatible with the male gender role in this society. Since the expression of certain emotions is not considered masculine, they might speculate that drug use would be a way of dealing with "unmasculine" emotions.

3.   A sociologist would be most likely to conduct this study because sociologists study groups and institutions in a given society.

An anthropologist would be most likely to conduct this study because anthropologists compare different cultures.

A psychologist would be most likely to conduct this study because psychologists study the mental processes and behavior of an organism or individual. This study examines mental illness and its treatment in this society.

4.   A psychologist would use psychotherapy based on psychological theories to treat Juanita's depression. The psychologist would have formal training and would hold either a Ph.D., an Ed.D., or a Psy.D. A psychiatrist would be likely to prescribe medication for Juanita's depression. A psychiatrist is a medical doctor (M.D.) with a residency in psychiatry. A psychoanalyst would use psychoanalysis, which is a type of psychotherapy based on the work of Sigmund Freud. To practice psychoanalysis, specialized training at a recognized psychoanalytic institute is required. A psychotherapist would use psychotherapy. A psychotherapist may or may not have formal education in psychology or a related field.

CROSSWORD PUZZLE ANSWER KEY

ACROSS		DOWN	
1.	biological	2.	learning
4.	functionalism	3.	basic
6.	cognitive	5.	nonclinical
8.	school	7.	experimental
11.	psychology	9.	disciplines
14.	Freud	10.	forerunners
16.	feminist	12.	Wundt
17.	practice	13.	humanist
18.	industrial	15.	applied

ANSWER KEYS FOR CHAPTER 2

ANSWER KEY - PRACTICE TEST 1

1. B (p. 43)	2. A (pp. 44-46)	3. C (p. 44)	4. D (p. 44)
5. A (p. 44)	6. B (p. 47)	7. D (p. 47)	8. D (p. 48)
9. C (p. 49)	10. A (p. 52)	11. B (p. 52)	12. D (pp. 54-55)
13. B (p. 57)	14. B (p. 57)	15. C (p. 58)	16. B (p. 59)
17. A (p. 60)	18. D (p. 60)	19. B (p. 61)	20. C (p. 62)
21. A (pp. 64-65)	22. D (p. 66)	23. A (p. 68)	24. B (p. 69)
25. D (p. 72)			

ANSWER KEY - PRACTICE TEST 2

1. A	2. C	3. C	4. A
5. C	6. C	7. B	8. C
9. A	10. C	11. C	12. A
13. C	14. B	15. A	16. D
17. C	18. B	19. A	20. C
21. C	22. C	23. C	24. D
25. A			

ANSWER KEY - PRACTICE TEST 3

1

A. Survey. Adolescents constitute a large population and the information sought should be accessible through questionnaires or interviews. Care is needed to construct a sample that is representative of the population under consideration.

B. Psychological tests. The goal is to measure psychological qualities within an individual. Other methods (e.g., case history, naturalistic observation) might be employed, but they are more time-consuming and do not offer the degree of standardization, reliability and validity found in a well-constructed test.

C. Experiment. Cause-and-effect information is being sought. In science this information is obtained through experiments in which the proposed causal variable is manipulated under controlled conditions.

D. Correlation. This technique is used to determine if and how strongly two variables are related. Establishing that a correlation exists, however, does not address the problem of why two things are related.

E. Naturalistic observation. A description of behavior as it occurs in a real-life situation is being sought. Making the observations without arousing suspicion in subjects could be problematic.

F. Case study. Making this determination requires in-depth information about the way a variety of psychological factors - expectation, values, motives, past experiences, and so forth - blend together within the person. This kind of information is unique to the person under consideration and could not be assessed through standardized tests.

G. Laboratory observation. The goal is to identify what the parents are doing that may be contributing to the child's problems and help them to parent differently. To ascertain what is currently going on in the family, observing them interact in the laboratory would be the best way to actually see what is occurring. Information could be collected with an interview or questionnaire, but parents may not be aware of what they are doing.

2   A. Hypothesis: Caffeine improves studying
Independent variable and its operational definition: caffeine; ounces
Dependent variable and its operational definition: studying; test score
Experimental condition: group receiving caffeine
Control group: group receiving decaffeinated beverage

B. Hypothesis: Heavy metal music increases aggression
Independent variable and its operational definition: music; jazz, classical, heavy metal
Dependent variable and its operational definition: aggression; amount of time spent punching bag
Experimental condition: groups exposed to jazz, classical and heavy metal music
Control group: group exposed to white noise machine

C. Hypothesis: Exercise increases relaxation
Independent variable and its operational definition: exercise; aerobics, number of sit-ups and push-ups
Dependent variable and its operational definition: relaxation; heart rate, muscle tension, respiration, blood pressure
Experimental condition: groups engaging in aerobics, sit-ups and push-ups
Control group: group having supervised study session

3	A.	Positive	B.	Negative
	C.	Negative	D.	Positive
	E.	Zero	F.	Negative
	G.	Negative	H.	Positive
	I.	Negative	J.	Zero

4   A.   Unethical. Requiring research participation for a course, without providing an alternate way of satisfying the course requirement, violates the principle of voluntary consent.

        B.   Unethical. Not only should subjects be free to withdraw at any time, but they should also be informed of this right before they begin to participate.

        C.   Ethical. Although it is controversial, outright deception has not been ruled out by the American Psychological Association's guidelines.

        D.   Ethical. Under the American Psychological Association's guidelines, the use of animals is acceptable in research that reduces human suffering and promotes human welfare.

        E.   Ethical. The investigator is obligated to protect subjects from physical and mental discomfort by using both voluntary and informed consent.

CROSSWORD PUZZLE ANSWER KEY

ACROSS		DOWN	
1.	theory	2.	reliability
4.	independent	3.	mean
7.	survey	5.	naturalistic
8.	methodology	6.	deception
9.	validity	11.	experiment
10.	negative	12.	placebo
12.	postmodern	13.	norms
14.	control	16.	range
15.	variance		
17.	correlation		
18.	skepticism		

ANSWER KEYS FOR CHAPTER 3

ANSWER KEY - PRACTICE TEST 1

1. C (p. 79)	2. B (p. 79)	3. C (p. 79)	4. D (p. 80)
5. A (p. 80)	6. C (p. 80)	7. C (p. 80)	8. A (p. 80)
9. B (p. 81)	10. D (p. 81)	11. B (p. 80)	12. A (p. 84)
13. B (p. 84)	14. C (p. 88)	15. D (p. 89)	16. D (pp. 89-90)
17. B (p. 92)	18. C (p. 92)	19. D (pp. 93-94)	20. A (p. 96)
21. A (p. 97)	22. A (p. 100)	23. C (p. 104)	24. D (p. 107)
25. B (p. 115)			

ANSWER KEY - PRACTICE TEST 2

1. B	2. C	3. A	4. C
5. B	6. D	7. A	8. B
9. A	10. D	11. C	12. C
13. A	14. B	15. B	16. A
17. B	18. A	19. C	20. D
21. B	22. B	23. C	24. D
25. C			

ANSWER KEY - PRACTICE TEST 3

1   A.   The basic elements of DNA within the genes influence protein synthesis in the body by specifying the sequence of amino acids, which are the building blocks of the proteins. The sequence of amino acids are affected by the arrangement of the basic elements, which comprises a chemical code. Proteins then go on to affect virtually all structural and biochemical characteristics of the organism. Genes for alcoholism might influence the basic elements of DNA or their arrangement, which then go on to influence the amino acids, the proteins and the structures or biochemistry of the body.

     B.   This statement misinterprets heritability estimates. Heritability estimates do <u>NOT</u> apply to individuals, only to variations within a group. No one can determine the impact of heredity on any particular individual's trait. For one person, genes may make a tremendous difference; for another, the environment may be more important. This statement ignores the fact that even highly heritable traits can be modified by the environment. This statement ignores environmental influences.

C. One might use a linkage study, which would examine large families in which alcoholism is common.

2 A. The feeling of disgust may have been useful in warding off contamination from disease and contagion.

B. Intuition may have allowed people to anticipate others' behaviors based on their beliefs and desires and thereby prepare for problems.

C. Self-concept may have been useful in knowing one's value to others.

D. Feelings of kinship may have promoted protection and help to one's kin, thereby insuring their survival.

E. Male promiscuity has the effect of increasing the offspring of any individual male, thereby continuing his genes.

F. Female selectivity increases the chances of conceiving with the best genes.

3. Until the middle of this century, views about language acquisition suggested that language is learned (not inborn) bit by bit and that children learn to speak by imitating adults and paying attention when adults correct their mistakes. Chomsky stated that language was too complex to learn in this way. He said that children learn not only which sounds form words, but can apply the rules of syntax and discern underlying meaning. He said that the capacity for language is inborn and that the brain has a language acquisition device, or a "mental module" that allows children to develop language if they are exposed to an adequate sampling of speech. According to Chomsky, human beings are designed to use language. The following support his position:

1. Children everywhere seem to go through similar stages of linguistic development.
2. Children combine words in ways that adults never would, and so could not simply be imitating.
3. Adults do not consistently correct their children's syntax.
4. Even children who are profoundly retarded acquire language.

4 A. The study would use pairs of identical twins reared apart. IQ tests would be given to both members of the pairs and the following comparisons would be made:

1. Scores of both members of the pairs of identical twins
2. Scores of identical twins reared together
3. Scores of siblings reared apart
4. Scores of siblings reared together
5. Scores of unrelated people

The conclusions would depend on the results of these comparisons. Similarity of IQ scores based on genetic similarity, regardless of shared environment, would be supportive evidence for heritability estimates. Cautionary statements would include:

1. Heritable does not mean the same thing as genetic.
2. Heritability applies only to a particular group living in a particular environment, and estimates may differ for different groups.
3. Heritability estimates do not apply to individuals, only to variations within a group.
4. Even highly heritable traits can be modified by the environment.

B. The following recommendations would be made:
1. Develop a prenatal care program for mothers-to-be that involves education about drug use, nutrition, health, environmental pollutants
2. Nutrition program for young children
3. Assistance related to exposure to toxins
4. Information on the importance of mental stimulation
5. Family therapy and support to reduce stressful family circumstances
6. Training in parent-child interactions

CROSSWORD PUZZLE KEY

ACROSS		DOWN	
1.	psycholinguistics	2.	syntax
5.	empiricist	3.	nativist
7.	Chomsky	4.	linkage
10.	genome	6.	toxins
12.	nutrition	8.	heritability
14.	Darwin	9.	deep
17.	language	11.	mutate
19.	evolution	13.	chromosomes
20.	monozygotic	15.	dizygotic
21.	intelligence	16.	genes
		18.	mating

ANSWER KEYS FOR CHAPTER 4

ANSWER KEY - PRACTICE TEST 1

1. D (p. 118)	2. B (p. 119)	3. D (pp. 120-121)	4. A (p. 120)
5. C (p. 121)	6. C (p. 120)	7. C (p. 120)	8. D (p. 122)
9. A (p. 123)	10. B (p. 123)	11. A (p. 123)	12. C (p. 125)
13. B (p. 125)	14. B (p. 126)	15. D (p. 128)	16. C (p. 129)
17. A (p. 129)	18. B (p. 131)	19. D (p. 133)	20. A (p. 137)
21. B (p. 137)	22. A (p. 143)	23. C (p. 146)	24. D (pp. 148-150)
25. C (p. 125)			

ANSWER KEY - PRACTICE TEST 2

1. A	2. C	3. B	4. D
5. B	6. A	7. B	8. A
9. B	10. C	11. D	12. B
13. D	14. B	15. D	16. A
17. C	18. D	19. B	20. D
21. D	22. B	23. A	24. B
25. B			

ANSWER KEY - PRACTICE TEST 3

1   A.   The dendrites of neurons in the ear are stimulated and the message is sent to the cell body, which causes an inflow of sodium ions and an outflow of potassium ions that result in a wave of electrical voltage travelling down the axon. At the end of the axon, synaptic vesicles held in the synaptic end bulb release neurotransmitters, which cross the synaptic cleft and lock into receptor sites on the next neuron.

        B.   The sound causes neurons in the ear to fire, going via sensory neurons to the thalamus, which directs the message to the auditory cortex in the temporal lobes, to the prefrontal lobes to figure out what to do and make a plan, to the motor cortex in the frontal lobe, out of the brain via motor neurons to the skeletal muscles to get up and move.

C.   Information from the ears goes to the brain via the somatic nervous system of the peripheral nervous system. Once at the thalamus, it is in the central nervous system. As information exits the brain from the motor cortex, the somatic nervous system gets involved again as messages go to the muscles that allow you to cross the room. Your feeling nervous involves the autonomic nervous system, which carries messages from the central nervous system about your preparedness for the test to the glands and organs.

2   A.   Hypothalamus; forebrain
        B.   Thalamus; forebrain
        C.   Prefrontal lobe; forebrain
        D.   Broca's area; forebrain
        E.   Hippocampus; forebrain
        F.   Cerebellum; hindbrain

3.   It is difficult to say exactly, but the forebrain, which is responsible for higher functioning, has been damaged. Parts of the hindbrain, specifically the medulla, which is responsible for heart rate and respiration, are still in tact, but because Helen is not conscious, it is possible that the pons, which is responsible for sleeping and waking, may be damaged.

4   A.   Frontal lobes; personality, planning, initiative
        B.   Parietal lobes; body senses and location
        C.   Occipital lobes; vision

5   A.   Right
        B.   Left
        C.   Right
        D.   Left
        E.   There are problems with functions controlled by the left hemisphere, but not with the right hemisphere.

CROSSWORD PUZZLE KEY

ACROSS

2.   amygdala
5.   dendrite
7.   hypothalamus
9.   parietal
10. holistic
11. synapse
13. cerebrum
14. cortex
16. forebrain
17. axon
18. insulin
19. pons
21. neurotransmitter

DOWN

1.   Broca
3.   glial
4.   frontal
6.   neuropsychology
7.   hormone
8.   limbic
12. neuron
15. endorphins
20. sensory

ANSWER KEYS FOR CHAPTER 5

ANSWER KEY - PRACTICE TEST 1

1. C (p. 157)	2. B (p. 158)	3. B (p. 158)	4. A (p. 159)
5. C (p. 158)	6. D (p. 161)	7. B (p. 163)	8. A (p. 164)
9. D (pp. 167-168)	10. A (p. 169)	11. B (p. 170)	12. C (p. 170)
13. B (p. 170)	14. C (pp. 174-175)	15. B (p. 172)	16. C (p. 172)
17. D (p. 177)	18. C (p. 177)	19. B (p. 179)	20. C (p. 181)
21. D (p. 182)	22. C (p. 191)	23. C (p. 189)	24. A (p. 187)
25. C (p. 186)			

ANSWER KEY - PRACTICE TEST 2

1. B	2. A	3. C	4. A
5. A	6. D	7. D	8. D
9. A	10. A	11. C	12. D
13. B	14. D	15. A	16. C
17. D	18. D	19. A	20. C
21. D	22. A	23. C	24. D
25. C			

ANSWER KEY - PRACTICE TEST 3

1. A. Ultradian, because the cycle repeats several times a day
    B. Infradian, because the cycle repeats less than once a day
    C. Ultradian, because the cycle repeats several times a day
    D. Could be Circadian if cycle repeats daily; could be ultradian if cycle repeats more than once a day; could be infradian if cycle repeats less than once a day
    E. Ultradian, because the cycle repeats several times a day
    F. Infradian, because the cycle repeats less than once a day

2. A. The definition of PMS is important because physical and emotional symptoms often appear on the same questionnaire. Because many women may experience physical symptoms, they are likely to have a higher score than if these two categories of symptoms were presented separately.

B. Negative moods are likely to be attributed to PMS when they occur just prior to the onset of menstruation, whereas negative moods that occur at different stages of the menstrual cycle are likely to be attributed to other factors. Another problem related to the self reporting of PMS symptoms is the tendency to notice negative moods that occur before menstruation, and to ignore the absence of negative moods before menstruation.

C. Expectations can influence perceptions. The very title of a widely used questionnaire, the Menstrual Distress Questionnaire, can bias responders to look for and find certain symptoms, while ignoring other, more positive, symptoms.

D. Research findings include:
1. Women and men do not differ in the emotional symptoms or number of mood swings they experience over the course of a month.
2. For most women, the relationship between cycle stage and symptoms is weak or nonexistent.
3. There is no reliable relationship between cycle stage and behaviors that matter in real live.
4. Women do not consistently report negative psychological changes from one cycle to the next.

3. A. Sleep consists of REM and four distinct non-REM periods.
B. The extra alertness results from the fact that the body is synchronized to wake itself up as the morning approaches. Loss of sleep is not invigorating.
C. Although theorists do not agree on the exact functions of sleep, rest is one of its presumed functions. We can "catch up" on several nights of sleep deprivation in just one night.
D. Though people can function pretty well after losing a single night's sleep, mental flexibility, originality and other aspects of creative thinking may suffer.
E. We display four to five REM periods each night, and laboratory research indicates that we dream every night.

4. A. Activation-synthesis theory or dreams as interpreted brain activity
B. Dreams as information processing
C. Dreams as unconscious wishes or psychoanalytic theory
D. Dreams as problem-solving

5. A1. Depressant
A2. Disinhibition, anxiety reduction, slower reaction times, memory loss, poor coordination
A3. Death, psychosis, organic damage, blackouts

473

B1. Depressant
B2. Sedation, anxiety and guilt reduction, release of tension
B3. Tolerance and addiction, sensory and motor impairment, coma, death   C1.
    Opiate

C2. Pain reduction, euphoria
C3. Addiction, convulsions, nausea, death

D1. Stimulant
D2. Elevated metabolism and mood, increased wakefulness
D3. Nervousness, delusions, psychosis, death

E1. Stimulant
E2. Appetite suppression, excitability, euphoria
E3. Sleeplessness, sweating, paranoia, depression

F1. Psychedelic
F2. Hallucinations and visions, feelings of insight, exhilaration
F3. Psychosis, panic, paranoia

G1. Classification unclear, some say mild psychedelic
G2. Relaxation, increased appetite, culturally determined effects
G3. Controversial abusive effects

CROSSWORD PUZZLE KEY

ACROSS

2.	consciousness
6.	REM
8.	marijuana
9.	lucid
11.	alpha
15.	latent
16.	withdrawal
17.	activation
18.	tolerance
19.	opiates

DOWN

1.	menstruation
2.	circadian
3.	infradian
4.	ultradian
5.	psychoactive
7.	delta
10.	depressants
12.	hypnosis
13.	steroids
14.	stimulants

ANSWER KEYS FOR CHAPTER 6

ANSWER KEY - PRACTICE TEST 1

1. C (p. 197)   2. C (p. 197)   3. A (p. 198)   4. C (p. 199)
5. B (p. 199)   6. A (p. 203)   7. C (p. 202)   8. D (p. 204)
9. A (PP. 203-204)   10. B (p. 205)   11. A (p. 206)   12. B (p. 208)
13. D (p. 207)   14. D (p. 208)   15. B (pp. 210-211)   16. D (p. 213)
17. D (pp. 213-214)   18. A (p. 214)   19. B (p. 219)   20. C (p. 221)
21. A (p. 223)   22. C (p.226)   23. A (p. 227)   24. B (p. 228)
25. D (pp. 229-230)

ANSWER KEY - PRACTICE TEST 2

1. B   2. D   3. A   4. B
5. C   6. D   7. A   8. D
9. C   10. C   11. B   12. C
13. A   14. C   15. C   16. C
17. A   18. B   19. D   20. B
21. A   22. C   23. A   24. C
25. B

ANSWER KEY - PRACTICE TEST 3

1.   A.   When a person compares two stimuli (the scarf and the car), the size of the change necessary to produce a just noticeable difference is a constant proportion of the original stimulus. In this case, $2.00 is a much larger proportion of $10 than it is of $10,000. Therefore, $2.00 on the price of a car would not produce a just noticeable difference. Two dollars represents 1/5 of the price of the scarf. One-fifth of the price of the car would be $2,000 and would produce a j.n.d.

    B.   Signal detection theory indicates that active decision making is involved in determining an absolute threshold. The fatigue, as well as attention, of subjects may be interfering with decision making.

    C.   A reduction in sensitivity results from unchanging, repetitious stimulation or sensory adaptation. John may be having trouble feeling the glasses on his head because they have been there for a while.

D. When people find themselves in a state of sensory overload, they often cope by blocking out unimportant sights and sounds and focusing only on those they find useful. Unimportant sounds are not fully processed by the brain. This capacity for selective attention protects us from being overwhelmed by all the sensory signals impinging on our receptors.

2. Light, the stimulus for vision, travels in the form of waves. Waves have certain physical properties: length, which corresponds to hue or color; amplitude, which corresponds to brightness; complexity, which corresponds to saturation or colorfulness. The light enters the cornea and is bent by the lens to focus. The amount of light getting into the eye is controlled by muscles in the iris, which surrounds the pupil. The pupil widens or dilates to influence the amount of light let in. The light goes to the retina located in the back of the eye. The retina contains rods and cones, which are the visual receptors. The cones are responsible for color vision and the rods for black-and-white vision and seeing things in dim light. The fovea, where vision is sharpest, is in the center of the retina and contains only cones. Rods and cones are connected to bipolar neurons that communicate with ganglion cells. The axons of the ganglion cells converge to form the optic nerve, which carries information out through the back of the eye and on to the brain.

3. A. Three colors will be needed - blue, red and green - corresponding to three types of cones. Combining such colors produces the human color spectrum.
   B. Four colors will be needed - blue, yellow, red and green. They must be paired in a way that allows them to function as opposites.

4. A. Loudness is increasing as indicated by changes in the amplitude of the waves.
   B. Pitch changes are related to changes in wave frequency.
   C. The quality of sound, called timbre, is being altered by mixing various waves.

5. A. Proximity is the tendency to perceive objects that are close together as a group.
   B. Closure is the tendency to fill in gaps to perceive complete forms.
   C. Similarity is the tendency to see things that are alike as belonging together.
   D. Continuity is the tendency for lines and patterns to be perceived as continuous.

6. A. Your expectation could influence your interpretation of what you saw and what happened.
   B. Your belief about your neighbor's character could influence your perception that he was sneaking around.
   C. Your emotions could influence your perception that someone was at the door.

CROSSWORD PUZZLE ANSWERS

ACROSS

2. pain
3. kinesthesis
7. sensation
9. cochlea
10. psychophysics
12. audition
13. fovea
14. retina
17. constancies
18. basilar
19. receptors
20. pheromones

DOWN

1. ganglion
2. pitch
4. perception
5. wave
6. gustation
8. olfaction
9. cones
11. hue
14. rods
15. timbre
16. codes

ANSWER KEYS FOR CHAPTER 7

ANSWER KEY - PRACTICE TEST 1

1. C (p. 245)	2. B (p. 247)	3. A (p. 247)	4. D (p. 252)
5. B (p. 250)	6. A (p. 249)	7. C (p. 248)	8. D (p. 251)
9. B (p. 252)	10. D (p. 255)	11. C (p. 255)	12. B (p. 257)
13. C (p. 257)	14. A (p. 259)	15. B (p. 261)	16. C (p. 264)
17. A (p. 263)	18. B (p. 263)	19. C (p. 266)	20. C (p. 268)
21. D (pp. 270-271)	22. C (p. 269)	23. A (p. 275)	24. D (p. 275)
25. B (p. 275)			

ANSWER KEY - PRACTICE TEST 2

1. C	2. A	3. C	4. B
5. C	6. A	7. A	8. C
9. C	10. C	11. B	12. A
13. C	14. B	15. C	16. D
17. D	18. C	19. A	20. C
21. C	22. B	23. D	24. A
25. B			

ANSWER KEY - PRACTICE TEST 3

1.
    A. CS = first and middle name; US = father's anger; UR = anxiety; CR = anxiety
    B. CS = closet and leash; US = walk; UR = excitement; CR = excitement
    C. CS = perfume; US = true love; UR = happy; CR = happy
    D. CS = Park Place and Main Street; US = accident; UR = fear; CR = anxiety

2.
    A. Dogs are often disciplined by being swatted (US) with rolled-up newspapers (CS). Fear is a natural response (UR) to being hit and a learned response to such objects (CR). Furthermore, stimulus generalization is demonstrated in that the dog gives the CR to other types of rolled-up papers.
    B. When attacked (US) by a Doberman (CS) in the past, Joan experienced fear (US). Since that time, she has been nervous about all Dobermans (stimulus generalization), though not around other dogs (stimulus discrimination). Her reduction of fear toward Dobermans represents extinction.
    C. The sudden noise of screeching tires (CS) often causes people to tense up and flinch (CR). The lack of response during a car race is stimulus discrimination.

D. Getting sick (UR) from spoiled chicken (US) caused Bill to experience stimulus generalization to turkey (CS), which is similar to the chicken on which he originally became ill, and to experience a CR to the turkey.

3. A. The tendency to buckle-up is strengthened through negative reinforcement (the desire to eliminate the sound of the buzzer).
   B. Punishment is weakening the tendency to smoke around the roommate. This becomes more complicated because of the addictive process, which negatively reinforces smoking by removing uncomfortable withdrawal symptoms.
   C. Reinforcement is strengthening Warren's dishwashing behavior.
   D. Punishment is weakening Fred's tendency to go down the most difficult slopes.

4. A. Sara is on a partial reinforcement schedule. While this may be enough to maintain a behavior once it is well established, when a response is weak it should be reinforced each time it occurs (continuous reinforcement).
   B. By picking him up sometimes in response to his cries, Ari's parents have put him on a partial reinforcement schedule, which causes behaviors to be very persistent and difficult to extinguish. To change this pattern, they must consistently respond by not picking him up when he cries and eventually the behavior will extinguish. It will take longer to do so now that he is on this intermittent schedule.
   C. It appears that all the things the teacher is trying to use as punishment are reinforcing Sue's behavior. They all involve extra attention, so by finding a consequence that is unpleasant and does not involve attention, this behavior might be decreased by using punishment. She might also try teaching her and then reinforcing her for other types of attention.

5. The initial punishment occurs long after the marks are made and therefore may not be associated with the behavior that is being punished. The parent is also scolding the child when he or she is feeling angry and therefore he or she may be harsher than usual. The child may also be aroused because of the punishment. Ideally, the behavior should be directed to an appropriate medium, such as paper or coloring books, and then that behavior should be reinforced.

6. A. Variable-interval
   B. Fixed-ratio
   C. Fixed-interval
   D. Fixed-ratio

7.   Similarities:
    1.   Agree about the importance of laws of operant and classical conditioning
    2.   Recognize the importance of reinforcers and the environment

    Differences:
    1.   In addition to behaviors, study attitudes, beliefs, and expectations
    2.   Emphasize interaction between individuals and their environment

CROSSWORD PUZZLE ANSWER KEY

ACROSS

2.   Skinner
3.   Pavlov
5.   conditioned
8.   behaviorism
11.   fixed
12.   schedule
13.   cognitive
16.   intermittent
17.   shaping
18.   observational

DOWN

1.   unconditioned
4.   variable
5.   classical
6.   extinction
7.   reinforcement
9.   response
10.   stimulus
14.   insight
15.   latent

ANSWER KEYS FOR CHAPTER 8

ANSWER KEY - PRACTICE TEST 1

1. D (p. 288)	2. A (p. 288)	3. B (p. 289)	4. D (p. 289)
5. A (p. 290)	6. C (p. 290)	7. A (p. 292)	8. D (p. 293)
9. A (p. 294)	10. D (pp. 294-296)	11. B (p. 297)	12. B (pp. 300-301)
13. C (p. 300)	14. B (p. 300)	15. A (p. 306)	16. B (p. 306)
17. C (p. 312)	18. D (p. 309)	19. C (p. 312)	20. B (p. 312)
21. A (p. 313)	22. B (p. 313)	23. D (p. 316)	24. D (p. 317)
25. B (p. 320)			

ANSWER KEY - PRACTICE TEST 2

1. D	2. C	3. B	4. C
5. B	6. D	7. D	8. C
9. B	10. A	11. B	12. B
13. B	14. D	15. A	16. B
17. D	18. B	19. D	20. C
21. B	22. C	23. C	24. D
25. C			

ANSWER KEY - PRACTICE TEST 3

1. A. Coat   B.   Horse
    C. Dog   D.   Uncle

2. A. The ship's position must be deduced. The position of the North Star and the formula are two premises that, once known, will allow the conclusion to be determined with certainty.
    B. Scientists of all types rely on inductive reasoning. Enough cases must be collected before a conclusion can be drawn.
    C. The overall process is dialectical reasoning, which is likely to incorporate inductive and deductive reasoning. It will be necessary to assess potential outcomes, risks, losses and appropriate considerations.
    D. Again, the overall process is dialectical reasoning, which will probably incorporate inductive and deductive reasoning.

3. A. Exaggerating the improbable
    B. Cognitive dissonance and justification of effort
    C. Confirmation bias

4. A. Sternberg's componential intelligence; Gardner's logical-mathematical intelligence
   B. Sternberg's contextual intelligence; Gardner's interpersonal intelligence
   C. Sternberg's experiential intelligence; Gardner's interpersonal intelligence and intrapersonal intelligence

5. A. Evidence supporting cognitive abilities in nonhumans:
   1. Evidence on herons, sea otters and assassin bugs related to their food gathering habits reflects behaviors that appear intelligent.
   2. Some chimpanzees use objects as rudimentary tools, and there is evidence for some summing abilities and the use of numerals to label quantities.
   3. Some primates demonstrate the ability to use some aspects of language like: learning signs from sign language, understanding words and some sentences, using signs to converse with each other, ability to manipulate keyboard symbols to request food without formal training, use of some simple grammatical rules.
   4. Other evidence exists from dolphins and parrots.

   B. Evidence against cognitive abilities in nonhumans:
   1. The meaning of these abilities is questioned; human meaning may be attributed to these actions.
   2. Early studies were overinterpreted and biased.
   3. It's unclear whether the use of signs and symbols were strung together without any particular order or syntax.
   4. While an animal may be "conscious," in the sense of being aware of its environment, it does not know that it knows and is unable to think about its own thoughts in the way that human beings do.

CROSSWORD PUZZLE KEY

ACROSS

1. confirmation
2. set
4. thinking
5. propositions
13. dissonance
14. reasoning
16. deductive
17. componential

DOWN

1. concept
2. experiential
5. heuristics
6. intelligence
8. prototypical
9. schemas
10. inductive
11. nonconscious
12. metacognition
14. triarchic

ANSWER KEYS FOR CHAPTER 9

ANSWER KEY - PRACTICE TEST 1

1. A (p. 328)	2. D (pp. 332-333)	3. C (p. 337)	4. B (p. 337)
5. C (p. 338)	6. C (p. 338)	7. D (p. 343)	8. D (p. 340)
9. C (p. 341)	10. B (p. 341)	11. A (p. 343)	12. B (p. 343)
13. C (p. 344)	14. A (p. 345)	15. C (p. 346)	16. C (pp. 346-347)
17. C (p. 348)	18. C (p. 348)	19. B (p. 349)	20. A (p. 251)
21. D (p. 354)	22. B (p. 360)	23. D (pp. 361-362)	24. D (p. 367)
25. C (p. 368)			

ANSWER KEY - PRACTICE TEST 2

1. D	2. A	3. D	4. B
5. C	6. D	7. A	8. C
9. C	10. D	11. C	12. D
13. D	14. D	15. A	16. C
17. B	18. B	19. A	20. D
21. C	22. C	23. D	24. A
25. B			

ANSWER KEY - PRACTICE TEST 3

1. To be remembered, material first must be encoded into the form in which it is to be retained. Storage takes place in various areas of the brain, which appears to correspond to structural changes in the brain. Retrieval is the process by which stored material is located for current use.

2. Information entering through the senses is briefly held in sensory memory, where preliminary sorting and encoding take place. It is then transferred to short-term storage, where it is rehearsed. Finally, as a result of deep processing or elaborative rehearsal, it is forwarded to long-term storage, where it is indexed and organized to become part of the network of more permanent material.

3. A. Procedural memory
   B. Episodic memory
   C. Semantic memory

4. Memory processes are subject to distortion in recall. Selection pressures bias information within sensory memory. Short-term memory simplifies, condenses and even adds meaning as information is being processed. In long-term storage, information is organized and indexed within the pre-existing framework, allowing memories to become intermixed. As information is retrieved, distortion can result from interferences and reasoning involved in reconstructing the event.

5. A. According to decay theory, virtually all the details should be forgotten because of the long time interval involved. The only memories remaining should be those used from time to time as the person grew older.

   B. The absence of retrieval cues is often a source of forgetting. The example suggests that the mental image created by the description of the homeroom was a cue that released a set of associated memories.

   C. Some emotionally unpleasant situations may be forgotten more rapidly and may be harder to recall than other situations. For the sake of emotional comfort, Henry may be motivated to forget situations associated with personal distress.

6. Interference arises as memory incorporates similar material in succession. Assuming there is greatest similarity between Italian and Spanish, these should be kept as separate as possible, as well as overlearned and frequently reviewed. Breaks would also help as you go from one topic of study to another. A sequence like Italian, math, English, history and Spanish would be better than Spanish, Italian, English, math and history.

CROSSWORD PUZZLE KEY

ACROSS

1. memory
3. semantic
5. recognition
6. cues
8. storage
9. recall
11. narratives
14. short-term
16. amnesia
17. episodic
18. primacy
19. proactive

DOWN

1. mnemonics
2. reconstruction
3. sensory
4. consolidation
5. retrieval
7. deep
10. long-term
12. retroactive
13. procedural
15. decay

ANSWER KEYS FOR CHAPTER 10

ANSWER KEY - PRACTICE TEST 1

1. D (p. 376)	2. A (p. 382)	3. B (pp. 376-377)	4. C (p. 377)
5. A (p. 377)	6. C (p. 379)	7. D (p. 379)	8. D (pp. 379-380)
9. C (p. 380)	10. B (pp. 380-381)	11. A (p. 380)	12. B (p. 381)
13. D (p. 381)	14. A (p. 381)	15. A (p. 382)	16. D (p. 382)
17. B (pp. 385-386)	18. B (p. 383)	19. C (p. 387)	20. D (p. 390)
21. C (p. 392)	22. D (pp. 392-393)	23. A (p. 392)	24. B (p. 396)
25. D (pp. 396-397)			

ANSWER KEY - PRACTICE TEST 2

1. A	2. B	3. D	4. C
5. D	6. D	7. D	8. C
9. D	10. B	11. C	12. B
13. B	14. A	15. D	16. D
17. D	18. C	19. B	20. D
21. D	22. D	23. C	24. C
25. C			

ANSWER KEY - PRACTICE TEST 3

1. A. The facial-feedback hypothesis assumes that emotion and facial expression are intimately interconnected. Distinct facial expressions not only identify emotions but contribute to them as well. By posing the face, performers may actually engender emotions in themselves.

    B. They indicate that outward expressions can be masked or even faked. More importantly, they indicate that learning is important in the expression of emotion.

    C. Emotion work might be defined as the ability to intentionally alter facial expression and body language to simulate a chosen emotion.

    D. For Darwin, facial expression was biologically wired because of its adaptive communication value. Because the face rather than the body is the focal point of social interaction, body expressions need not be similarly wired.

2. A. An increase in epinephrine and norepinephrine is brought about by the adrenal glands and under the control of the autonomic nervous system. Involvement of the amygdala, limbic system and cortex contribute to this arousal response.

B. The patient is functioning according to the display rules for men, which dictate that men should not feel fear or anxiety. The nurse is doing the emotion work associated with the role of a nurse. Nurses are supposed to be comforting and pleasant to patients.

C. Cerebral cortex

3. These results are consistent with the idea that it is our interpretation of events that is instrumental in the experiencing of emotion rather than the event. The students' reactions are based on their explanations and interpretations of why they got those grades. Larry studied hard and expected a better grade. His depressive reaction may have to do with the fact that since he studied and did not do better, he may see himself as stupid, which is an internal and stable interpretation. Curly studied a little bit for the test so he felt relieved that he got a "C". The grade has no bearing on his view of himself. He did not expect to fail, but did not really expect a better grade. Moe did not study at all so he interpreted the grade as very lucky. The grade did not influence his view of himself, but rather he interpreted it as due to external luck.

4. A. Display rules govern the recipients of gifts.
B. Emotion work involves acting out emotions not truly felt.
C. The facial expression of anger is universally recognizable. Moreover, the husband's familiarity with Mary should make any idiosyncratic expressive features easily identifiable.
D. The emotion work is implied by gender roles.
E. She has a combination of lower status, high familiarity, sexual similarity and gender.
F. All of the reactions do.

CROSSWORD PUZZLE KEY

ACROSS

1. facial-feedback
3. James-Lange
4. secondary
7. emotion
11. primary
12. control
13. internality
14. arousal
15. cognitions

DOWN

2. display
5. epinephrine
6. amygdala
8. norepinephrine
9. two-factor
10. prototypes

ANSWER KEYS FOR CHAPTER 11

ANSWER KEY - PRACTICE TEST 1

1. C (p. 405)	2. C (p. 406)	3. C (p. 406)	4. D (p. 406)
5. A (p. 406)	6. C (p. 407)	7. A (p. 406)	8. C (p. 410)
9. B (p. 410-411)	10. C (p. 411)	11. D (p. 416)	12. D (p. 416)
13. D (p. 416-417)	14. C (p. 418)	15. B (p. 418)	16. C (pp. 418-419)
17. B (p. 420)	18. D (p. 422)	19. D (p. 422)	20. D (p. 424)
21. B (p. 425)	22. B (pp. 425-426)	23. A (p. 427)	24. A (p. 431)
25. B (p. 432)			

ANSWER KEY - PRACTICE TEST 2

1. C	2. B	3. A	4. B
5. D	6. B	7. C	8. B
9. D	10. C	11. C	12. B
13. B	14. B	15. C	16. C
17. C	18. B	19. D	20. A
21. A	22. B	23. B	24. A
25. D			

ANSWER KEY - PRACTICE TEST 3

1. We cannot be certain what motivates any given behavior. Each behavior described may be activated by a variety of different motives. Below are some possible explanations.
    a. Calling her friend shows need for affiliation.
    b. Visiting her boyfriend demonstrates the motivation for love.
    c. Doing extra credit assignments and an extra work project could reflect need for achievement, performance goals or learning goals.

2. Ludus: "Want to play hide and seek? Come find me for fun and excitement."
    Eros: "For passion, romance and intensity; I'm looking for the love of my life."
    Storge: "Looking for a soul-mate, friend, lover, companion to walk through life with."
    Mania: "Looking for someone made for me; intense, emotional, inseparable."
    Pragma: "Looking for a non-smoker, who likes to travel and listen to jazz. NO children."
    Agape: "Let me spoil you. I want to be there for you and be your main support."

487

3.   Information that supports homosexuality as a choice and refutes the biological argument:
  a.   The fluidity of women's experiences
  b.   There are flaws in the biological evidence
            *Methodological problems in the findings on brain differences
            *The majority of homosexuals do not have a close gay relative
  c.   Psychological theories have not been well-supported

Information that supports the biological information and refutes the choice position:
  a.   Research findings that women with a history of prenatal exposure to estrogen are more likely to become bisexual or lesbian
  b.   Research findings on differences in brain structures of homosexual and heterosexual men
  c.   Studies that show a moderate heritability

Political implications include: If homosexuality is biological, then it is a fact of nature and not a choice, and therefore, people should not be prejudiced. Those who are prejudiced against homosexuals suggest that the biological evidence says that it is a "defect" and should be eradicated or "cured." Those who say it is a choice, say it can be "unchosen."

4.   A.   People high in achievement enjoy challenges. Opportunities for succeeding and overcoming failure increase their motivation. Issues of self-efficacy are involved. If John does not think he can do it, this can become a self-fulfilling prophecy.
  B.   Specific patterns of moderate difficulty are associated with sustained motivation. Joe's goals are vague and extremely difficult to accept on a long-term basis. They decrease motivation.
  C.   Sustained motivation is facilitated by feedback, goal-setting, incentives and job enrichment. In unstructured courses, students not only must cope with content, they must find ways to evaluate on-going understanding, pat themselves on the back and enrich day-to-day drudgery.

5.   A.   Multiple approach-avoidance conflict
  B.   Avoidance-avoidance conflict
  C.   Approach-approach conflict
  D.   Approach-avoidance conflict

CROSSWORD PUZZLE ANSWER KEY

ACROSS

3. motivation
6. teamwork
11. attachment
12. avoidant
14. value
15. glass
18. companionate
19. achievement
20. self-efficacy

DOWN

1. social
2. power
4. implicit
5. affiliation
7. incentive
8. secure
9. stranger
10. separation
13. anxious
16. approach
17. scripts

ANSWER KEY - PRACTICE TEST 1

1. C (p. 437)	2. A (p. 438)	3. C (p. 438)	4. B (p. 438)
5. C (p. 438)	6. D (p. 441)	7. A (p. 442)	8. D (pp. 443-444)
9. B (p. 445)	10. A (p. 447)	11. C (p. 448)	12. D (p. 450)
13. A (p. 452)	14. A (p. 453)	15. C (p. 453)	16. A (p. 454)
17. C (pp. 455-456)	18. C (pp. 455-456)	19. D (p. 457)	20. B (p. 458)
21. C (p. 461)	22. C (pp. 464-465)	23. A (p. 468)	24. A (p. 466)
25. B (p. 470)			

ANSWER KEY - PRACTICE TEST 2

1. B	2. C	3. B	4. C
5. D	6. C	7. C	8. D
9. C	10. C	11. C	12. C
13. D	14. B	15. A	16. B
17. B	18. D	19. D	20. D
21. C	22. A	23. C	24. D
25. C			

ANSWER KEY - PRACTICE TEST 3

1.
   A. Cognitive social learning approach
   B. Trait approach
   C. Psychodynamic approach
   D. Humanistic approach

2.
   A. According to the reality principle, the ego would seek to prepare for the test.
   B. The id seeks pleasure and immediate gratification, according to the pleasure principle.
   C. The id seeks pleasure and is not concerned with the consequences of reality.
   D. The ego is appraising reality.
   E. The internalized parental values of the superego are discouraging him from cheating.
   F. The ego is defending against threats from the superego.
   G. Violations of the superego produce guilt.

3. A. Reaction formation
    B. Projection
    C. Repression
    D. Denial
    E. Regression
    F. Displacement

4. A. Phallic stage
    B. Oral stage
    C. Phallic stage
    D. Anal stage

5. A. Adler
    B. Jung
    C. Horney
    D. Object-relations school

6. The behavioral school:
    Classical and operant conditioning are the central processes of the behavioral school. Parents are therefore viewed in terms of the way they associate stimuli and reinforce responses for the child. Parental impact is related to the consistency of their procedures and is limited by the conditioning that takes place outside their sphere of influence.

    The cognitive social learning school:
    Observational learning, self-regulation and interpretation and perception of events are central processes. Parents are therefore seen as role models and sources of information about values, expectations and perceptions. They can influence a child's perceptions about his or her locus of control and self-efficacy.

7. Abraham Maslow:
    Self-actualization was a basic need for Maslow. However, its achievement depended on gratifying even more fundamental needs, such as physiological drives and social needs.

    Rollo May:
    May believes that alienation, loneliness and helplessness are basic components of human existence. The person strives to overcome these through effective choices.

Carl Rogers:
According to Rogers, self-actualization and full functioning are related to the presence of unconditional positive regard. However, most children and adults live in situations in which they receive conditional positive regard.

8. A. Low levels of neuroticism, high levels of extroversion and agreeableness
    B. High levels of conscientiousness, and probably agreeableness, and a low level of openness to experience
    C. High levels of neuroticism and openness to experience, but a low level of extroversion

CROSSWORD PUZZLE KEY

ACROSS

1.   personality
7.   Cattell
9.   ego
10. projective
11. Freud
14. superego
15. internal
17. Oedipus
19. identification
20. denial
20. denial

DOWN

1.   psychoanalysis
2.   repression
3.   archetypes
4.   trait
5.   humanistic
6.   collective
8.   temperaments
12. complex
13. intrapsychic
16. Horney
18. Adler

ANSWER KEYS FOR CHAPTER 13

ANSWER KEY - PRACTICE TEST 1

1. C (p. 478)	2. A (p. 478)	3. D (pp. 478-479)	4. B (pp. 480-481)
5. A (p. 482)	6. A (p. 482)	7. D (pp. 486-487)	8. A (p. 486)
9. C (p. 487)	10. D (p. 488)	11. C (p. 490)	12. B (p. 491)
13. C (p. 493)	14. A (p. 495)	15. D (p. 497)	16. C (p. 498)
17. C (p. 498)	18. A (p. 499)	19. C (pp. 500-501)	20. A (p. 501)
21. A (p. 502)	22. D (p. 506)	23. C (p. 508)	24. C (p. 510)
25. A (p. 512)			

ANSWER KEY - PRACTICE TEST 2

1. B	2. D	3. D	4. B
5. D	6. A	7. C	8. A
9. D	10. C	11. D	12. A
13. C	14. C	15. A	16. B
17. B	18. D	19. A	20. B
21. C	22. B	23. C	24. C
25. A			

ANSWER KEY - PRACTICE TEST 3

1.
    A. Fetal abnormalities and deformities
    B. There is an increased likelihood of miscarriage, premature birth, abnormal fetal heartbeat and underweight babies; and after the child's birth, there are increased rates of sickness and Sudden Infant Death Syndrome; in later childhood, hyperactivity and difficulties in school.
    C. Fetal alcohol syndrome
    D. Effects vary with specific drugs; extreme caution must be exercised, even with prescribed and over-the-counter drugs.

2.
    A. Newborns should have the following reflexes: rooting, sucking, swallowing, Moro, Babinski, grasp, stepping. They should follow a moving light with their eyes and turn toward a familiar sound. They should be able to distinguish contrasts, shadows and edges, and be able to discriminate their primary caregiver.
    B. Newborns are sociable from birth and show a preference for the human face. They can distinguish their primary caregiver by smell, sight or sound almost immediately. They establish synchrony with the primary caregiver very early.

3.   A.   The child is in the preoperational stage and is demonstrating egocentric thinking.
     B.   The child is inappropriately trying to use assimilation; she needs to use accommodation.
     C.   The younger child is in the preoperational stage and lacks the ability to conserve; the older child is in the concrete operations stage.
     D.   Johnny is in the sensory-motor stage and has developed object permanence.

4.   At 4 months old: Jennie would cry and coo and respond to high-pitched and more varied verbalizations in which the intonation is exaggerated. She can recognize her own name.
     At 10 months old: She would be increasingly familiar with the sound structure of her native language. She might be making babbling sounds such as "ba-ba" or "goo-goo".
     At 14 months old: She could begin using gestures.
     At 23 months old: She would use telegraphic speech because she is not yet able to use article and auxiliary words. She would probably say, "Apple table."

5.   A.   Authoritative parenting
     B.   Authoritarian parenting
     C.   Permissive parenting

6.   A.   Conventional morality
     B.   Conventional morality
     C.   Postconventional morality
     D.   Postconventional morality
     E.   Preconventional morality

7.   A.   The biological changes for Ron include: Development of primary and secondary sex characteristics - hormone production in the testes produce sperm, males now have higher androgen levels than girls, nocturnal emissions, the growth of the testes, scrotum and penis, deepened voice, facial, chest and pubic hair. Later he will experience a growth spurt.

     The biological changes for Rita include: Development of primary and secondary sex characteristics - hormones stimulate the ovaries, which release eggs and mark the beginning of menstruation or menarche. She now has higher levels of estrogens than males. She develops breasts and pubic hair and has a growth spurt that occurs earlier than in males.

     B.   Both will be dealing with issues related to identity, but they will not necessarily experience emotional turmoil. They will begin to learn the rules of adult sexuality, morality, work and family. They will try to develop their own standards and values. They will begin to individuate from their parents.

KEY FOR CROSSWORD PUZZLE

ACROSS

1. development
6. teratogens
9. germinal
13. shame
14. accommodation
16. Piaget
17. representational
18. conservation
19. authoritarian

DOWN

2. egocentric
3. empathy
4. maturation
5. fetal
7. synchrony
8. puberty
10. induction
11. assimilation
12. menarche
15. operations

ANSWER KEY - PRACTICE TEST 1

1. A (p. 520)	2. B (p. 521)	3. C (p. 522)	4. B (p. 522)
5. D (p. 522)	6. C (p. 519)	7. C (p. 522)	8. C (p. 525)
9. C (p. 524)	10. C (p. 526)	11. D (p. 527)	12. B (p. 527)
13. C (p. 528)	14. A (p. 529)	15. C (p. 532)	16. C (p. 532)
17. C (p. 533)	18. D (p. 533)	19. C (p. 536)	20. A (p. 538)
21. B (p. 536)	22. D (pp. 537-538)	23. C (p. 543)	24. D (p. 543)
25. D (p. 548)			

ANSWER KEY - PRACTICE TEST 2

1. C	2. A	3. C	4. C
5. D	6. A	7. C	8. B
9. D	10. A	11. D	12. C
13. C	14. A	15. D	16. B
17. A	18. D	19. A	20. C
21. B	22. C	23. B	24. D
25. D			

ANSWER KEY - PRACTICE TEST 3

1.
   A. Air traffic controllers are likely to face a higher degree of daily irritation and uncontrollable events than fisherman.
   B. Type A people, particularly if they have antagonistic hostility and experience greater stress.
   C. Those with an external locus of control are less likely to feel they can predict and control their environments, and prediction and control reduce stress.
   D. Generally, those with social networks experience buffers to stress.
   E. Pessimistic explanatory styles result in the perception that the stressor is unchangeable, therefore these people will feel less control over the stress.

2.
   A. The alarm phase will be the most prominent as the person is being captured. Bodily resources will be mobilized as the person attempts to fight or flee.
   B. Resistance will coincide with early captivity. Its duration is related to the victim's capacity to manage potentially overwhelming events. Signs of arousal will be prominent and bodily preparedness is the rule. Biologically, use of energy resources will be above normal. Psychologically, the victim is actively fighting the situation.

C.   The timing of exhaustion depends on individual characteristics, such as coping styles. Biologically, it is signaled by bodily fatigue and susceptibility to illness. Psychologically, the person shows signs of giving up and wearing down.

3.   A.   Prolonged stress is capable of suppressing the disease and infection fighting cells of the immune system. As this happens, bodily defenses are impaired and susceptibility to symptoms increases.

    B.   Though the evidence is mixed, it is possible that the depression is contributing to his illness by affecting the immune system. It is also possible, however, that his continuous illness is contributing to the depression. It may be that poor health habits are causing both or that an entirely different thing is causing both. Finally, the depression and the illnesses could be mutually influencing each other.

    C.   David must examine his personality for antagonistic hostility; his personal style of evaluating and managing changes, daily hassles, and problems; the quality and quantity of his social relationships and interest; and everyday habits relating to rest exercise, and diet.

4.   A.   Margaret is rethinking the problem and using some denial.

    B.   The situation is being directly attacked with a problem-focused strategy.

    C.   Frank is reappraising the problem using social comparisons.

    D.   Tony is using an emotion-focused strategy.

    E.   Joan is trying to live with the problem.

CROSSWORD PUZZLE ANSWER KEY

ACROSS

4.	health
5.	avoidance
7.	pathogenic
8.	vigilance
12.	salutogenic
14.	psychosomatic
15.	hassles
18.	exhaustion
19.	reappraisal

DOWN

1.	behavioral
2.	control
3.	antagonistic
5.	alarm
6.	explanatory
9.	neurotic
10.	eustress
11.	resistance
13.	primary
16.	coping
17.	styles

ANSWER KEY - PRACTICE TEST 1

1. B (p. 554)   2. A (pp. 554-555)   3. B (pp. 555-556)   4. A (p. 557)
5. B (pp. 558-560) 6. B (p. 561)   7. D (p. 562)   8. C (p. 564)
9. D (p. 565)   10. B (p. 565)   11. A (p. 565)   12. C (p. 567)
13. B (p. 569)   14. B (p. 570)   15. D (p. 571)   16. A (p. 573)
17. A (p. 573)   18. C (p. 576)   19. D (p. 578)   20. A (p. 581)
21. A (pp. 583-584) 22. D (p. 584)   23. A (p. 587)   24. D (p. 586)
25. C (p. 587)

ANSWER KEY - PRACTICE TEST 2

1. A   2. B   3. C   4. C
5. D   6. C   7. B   8. C
9. C   10. D   11. B   12. D
13. A   14. C   15. B   16. D
17. B   18. A   19. A   20. A
21. D   22. A   23. A   24. C
25. D

ANSWER KEY - PRACTICE TEST 3

1.   A.   This definition considers the violation of norms and standards to be abnormal. Jason violates norms governing social interaction, appearance and good taste.
      B.   Maladaptive behavior is behavior that results in disharmony and distress. Jason is behaving disruptively toward others.
      C.   This definition relies on signs of distress. Jason is apparently seeking forgiveness based on some internal experience of guilt or distress.
      D.   Jason does not seem to be able to distinguish between acceptable and unacceptable behavior, or, if he makes this distinction, he is unable to control himself.

2.   A.   Included
      B.   Excluded
      C.   Excluded
      D.   Included
      E.   Included
      Explanation: The DSM-IV classifies disorders on five axes: primary diagnosis, ingrained aspects of personality, relevant medical conditions, current stressors and overall level of functioning. The included items reflect those axes and the others do not.

498

3. A. Abnormal: panic attack
    B. Abnormal: obsessive-compulsive disorder
    C. Normal
    D. Abnormal: phobia
    E. Abnormal: post-traumatic stress disorder

4. A. Mood disorders involve emotional, behavioral, cognitive and physical symptoms.
    B. In bipolar disorder, mania alternates with depression.
    C. Antidepressant drugs raise the levels of the neurotransmitters, serotonin and norepinephrine.
    D. There is no change.
    E. Negative thinking seems to be both a result and a cause of depression.
    F. Repeated failure can be a source of learned helplessness, a characteristic related to depression.

5. A. Josephine has delusions. The fact that she believes that airplanes dirty the streets and sidewalks by dripping oil, that pilots have a power called "telectic penetration" and that she is being used as a radar are all examples of delusions.
    B. Josephine is experiencing hallucinations. She hears the pilots talking to her about her location.
    C. Josephine is demonstrating incoherent associations, including "telectic penetration," her latitude and longitude, and airplanes.
    D. Josephine's behavior is inappropriate in that she withdraws and is unable to speak.
    E. From the description, it is unclear if Josephine is exhibiting emotional flatness.

CROSSWORD PUZZLE ANSWER KEY

ACROSS

2. mood
4. depression
6. anxiety
7. dissociative
10. mania
13. disease
14. psychosis
15. schizophrenia
16. attachment
17. hopelessness

DOWN

1. social
3. bipolar
4. dysthymia
5. inventories
6. agoraphobia
8. abuse
9. maladaptive
11. amnesia
12. antisocial

ANSWER KEYS FOR CHAPTER 16

ANSWER KEY - PRACTICE TEST 1

1. A (pp. 593-394)   2. A (p. 594)   3. D (p. 595)   4. C (p. 594)
5. D (pp. 596-597)   6. A (p. 598)   7. B (p. 599)   8. D (p. 600)
9. B (p. 601)   10. A (p. 600)   11. C (p. 602)   12. D (pp. 601-602)
13. C (p. 603)   14. A (p. 602)   15. B (p. 603)   16. C (p. 607)
17. C (p. 609)   18. A (p. 614)   19. D (p. 615)   20. C (p. 615)
21. B (p. 618)   22. A (p. 619)   23. D (p. 620)   24. B (p. 621)
25. B (p. 622)

ANSWER KEY - PRACTICE TEST 2

1. C   2. D   3. A   4. B
5. D   6. A   7. C   8. C
9. D   10. C   11. A   12. C
13. C   14. C   15. C   16. B
17. A   18. C   19. B   20. D
21. D   22. C   23. A   24. D
25. D

ANSWER KEY - PRACTICE TEST 3

1.   Medical treatments feature drugs and other forms of organic intervention. Drugs are very useful for psychotic disorders, and, in combination with psychotherapy, they are useful for other disorders, including: major depression, bipolar disorder, some anxiety disorders.

Psychotherapies attempt to change thinking, emotional and behavioral processes. They're designed to help clients think about their lives in new ways in order to find solutions to the problems that plague them. They have been shown to be very useful with mood disorders, anxiety disorders, eating disorders, chronic fatigue syndrome.

Community services tend to be problem-oriented and offer counseling, support groups, and skills training. They can be useful for those with mental or physical disabilities, including schizophrenia.

2.   A.   Anxiety disorders: minor tranquilizers
     B.   Mood disorders: antidepressants
     C.   Psychotic disorders: antipsychotics

Drug treatments are limited by the complications of side effects and finding the right dosage. They may not be effective for everyone or may work effectively only in the short-term. Often there is little research on the effects of long-term usage. Moreover, drugs relieve symptoms and do nothing to help people learn new coping skills.

3. Psychodynamic therapies strive for insight into the unconscious processes that produce a problem. With insight and emotional release, symptoms should disappear. The goal of treatment is not to solve an individual's immediate problem, since it is only the tip of the iceberg. Techniques include free association and transference. Psychoanalysis was the original model proposed by Freud in which a patient was seen multiple times in a week for many years.

    Cognitive therapy aims to correct distorted, unrealistic thoughts, beliefs and expectations. Techniques vary but revolve around examining negative thoughts, formulating reasonable responses and using realistic perspectives.

    Behavior therapy attempts to eliminate maladaptive responses and behavior patterns. Techniques are based on learning principles and include systematic desensitization, aversive conditioning, flooding and operant strategies.

    Humanistic therapy is designed to increase self-esteem, positive feelings and self-actualization. Approaches include client-centered therapy and existential therapy. Client-centered therapy utilizes unconditional positive regard, empathy and genuineness.

    Family therapy aims to correct the forces in the family that are contributing to the expression of a problem. The family may be analyzed from a multigenerational standpoint, using a genogram, or as a social system.

    The shared features include: support factors, which allow the client to feel secure and safe; learning factors, which allow the client to see and experience his or her problems in a new light and think about how to solve them; and action factors, which allow the client to reduce fears, take risks and make necessary changes.

4. Client features: commitment to therapy, willingness to work on their problems, and expectations of success; cooperativeness with suggested interventions and positive feelings during the therapy session.

    Therapist features: empathy, warmth, genuineness and imagination; make clients feel respected, accepted, and understood; expressive and actively invested in the interaction with the client.

Therapeutic alliance: a relationship in which both parties respect and understand one another, feel reaffirmed and work toward a common goal.

5.   Coercion by the therapist to accept the therapist's advice, sexual intimacies, or other unethical behavior. Bias on the part of a therapist who doesn't understand the client because of the client's gender, race, religion, sexual orientation, or ethnic group. Therapist-induced disorders can be harmful. When a therapist so zealously believes in the prevalence of certain problems that they induce the client to produce the symptoms they are looking for.

CROSSWORD PUZZLE KEY

ACROSS

1.   placebo
3.   dyskinesia
5.   lithium
6.   psychoanalysis
7.   transference
9.   group
11. desensitization
13. tricyclic
15. unconditional
16. narrative
17. family
18. aversive

DOWN

1.   psychosurgery
2.   flooding
4.   drugs
8.   existential
10. psychotherapy
12. eclectic
14. alliance

ANSWER KEY - PRACTICE TEST 1

1. B (p. 628)   2. D (p. 628)   3. B (p. 630)   4. A (p. 631)
5. B (p. 633)   6. B (p. 632)   7. D (pp. 634-635) 8. C (p. 637)
9. A (p. 637)   10. D (p. 637)   11. A (p. 638)   12. D (pp. 639-640)
13. C (p. 641)   14. C (p. 643)   15. D (p. 645)   16. C (p. 646)
17. D (p. 649)   18. B (p. 651)   19. D (p. 650)   20. B (p. 652)
21. B (p. 653)   22. A (pp. 656-657) 23. C (p. 654) 24. C (p. 654)
25. A (pp. 658-659)

ANSWER KEY - PRACTICE TEST 2

1. C   2. A   3. D   4. B
5. A   6. D   7. D   8. A
9. B   10. A   11. C   12. B
13. C   14. B   15. A   16. A
17. D   18. C   19. A   20. A
21. C   22. C   23. D   24. B
25. C

ANSWER KEY - PRACTICE TEST 3

1. The prison study: The students were either playing the roles of prison guards or prisoners. These roles were governed by norms of how prisoners and guards should behave. The students knew the roles and the norms that governed them and played the parts.

    The hospital study: In this case, the staff - including the psychiatrists - and the patients knew the norms of their own roles as well as the norms for the other role. All participants played their real-life roles. The roles allowed the staff to depersonalize the patients.

    The obedience study: The role of the research subject and authority figure was known to the study participants, who then played that role. Knowing the norms for both sets of roles made it difficult for subjects to violate their roles and the roles of the authority.

2. A.   Dispositional attribution
    B.   Just-world hypothesis
    C.   Situational attribution - self-serving bias
    D.   Situational attribution

3.	You might want to use some techniques of friendly persuasion. You could use the validity effect by repeating that you have worked very hard in this class. Repeatedly referring to your effort may make it seem more believable to the faculty member. You also might want to make a reference to a class you have taken by a well-respected colleague in which you did very well. This is attempting to influence your teacher's attitude by using the respected colleague's opinion. You might try to link your message with a good feeling by telling your professor how much you enjoyed the class.

4.	To reduce social loafing, Dr. Wong should make sure each student is responsible for a different part of the project that is essential to the whole project. She might make part of the grade an individual grade and part of the grade a group grade. To reduce groupthink she might want to make grades dependent on the presentation of multiple points of view and different positions and approaches. She will want to structure the project so that success depends on the cooperation and interdependence of all students. Finally, to promote altruism and independent action, she might want students to volunteer at a homeless shelter to get to know some homeless people personally.

5.	The norms of the school would be based on interdependence, cooperation and group support. Competition and individual self-promotion would not be rewarded and might even be penalized. Rules would reflect these norms. For example, in athletic events, students might be applauded for any success, and for working together rather than for winning. Winning would not be a goal for any event, whether athletic, artistic or academic. Participation, effort and cooperation would be rewarded. Traditional grades would not be used. Rather, students would be rewarded with grades that reflect effort and cooperation. Teaching activities would be structured in a way to foster interdependence, and competition among students would be discouraged. The norms of cooperation would determine the rules, policies, activities and teaching techniques.

CROSSWORD PUZZLE KEY

ACROSS

3.	roles
4.	just-world
5.	altruism
7.	depersonalization
13.	rules
17.	entrapment
18.	competition

DOWN

1.	coercive
6.	deindividuation
8.	situational
10.	attitude
12.	dissonance
15.	prison

2.	groupthink
7.	dispositional
9.	attribution
11.	norms
14.	loafing
16.	Milgram

ANSWER KEYS FOR CHAPTER 18

ANSWER KEY - PRACTICE TEST 1

1. D (p. 664)	2. A (p. 666)	3. C (p. 666)	4. C (p. 667)
5. B (p. 670)	6. A (p. 671)	7. C (p. 673)	8. B (p. 672)
9. D (p. 673)	10. A (p. 675)	11. D (p. 675)	12. C (p. 676)
13. B (p. 682)	14. B (p. 686)	15. B (p. 686)	16. D (p. 687)
17. C (p. 687)	18. D (p. 689)	19. C (p. 690)	20. B (p. 691)
21. B (pp. 694-695)	22. A (p. 695)	23. B (p. 696)	24. D (pp. 696-697)
25. D (p. 698)			

ANSWER KEY - PRACTICE TEST 2

1. B	2. A	3. C	4. B
5. C	6. A	7. C	8. D
9. A	10. D	11. B	12. C
13. D	14. D	15. C	16. D
17. A	18. A	19. B	20. C
21. D	22. D	23. B	24. D
25. A			

ANSWER KEY - PRACTICE TEST 3

1. Dr. Katz needs to use matched samples. Matched samples include individuals who are similar in all aspects of their lives except their nationality, including age, economic status, and education. Dr. Katz needs to be aware that linguistic and functional equivalence do not always exist. This means that the same words or behaviors may have different meanings in different cultures. Some terms cannot be adequately translated at all, or they may have different meanings in subtle or obvious ways. Finally, Dr. Katz should be aware of stereotyping. It is difficult to study general rules about a culture without sounding like stereotypes. However, it is important to recognize that though general rules may be identified, not all members of the culture engage in certain behaviors or have certain characteristics.

2.   Michael is from a culture that is generally homogeneous and close-knit. People pay more attention to nonverbal language than to words. Generally, people from Michael's culture do not feel the need to explain their exact meaning, since it is assumed they share certain basic understandings. They have a polychronic organization of time, which means that many things may be done at once, appointments do not take priority over people and that plans can be changed often and easily. People from Michael's culture do not over-value privacy and feel comfortable sharing work and living space. Promptness is not a high value nor is private property. People in his culture tend to build life-long friendships. Michael is likely to find the low-context culture cold and disengaged by comparison to his culture. In his daily life, he may get into some trouble if he does not arrive on time to classes, turn in assignments on time or keep appointments on time. He will probably be surprised by how much this upsets others. He is likely to find it sad or unusual how distant many of the students are from their families. They all may seem rather lonely to him. Finally, he may become confused by how friendships are formed. People seem friendly, but then they do not really want to become close, life-long friends. Michael may find that he is seen by others as irresponsible.

3.   While it is true that cross-culturally there are many commonalities among the behavior of men and women, there are also many differences. The many cultural differences suggest that notions of gender are socially constructed and are influenced by economic, ecological and other practical considerations.

        Commonalities include:

a.   Men have had, and continue to have, more status and power than women.

b.   Men typically fought wars and, on the average, are more aggressive and violent than women.

c.   Typically, men engage in hunting large game, traveling a long way from home or making weapons.

d.   Typically, women have primary responsibility for cooking, cleaning and child-care.

e.   Males must pass physical tests, endure pain, confront danger and separate themselves psychologically and even physically from their mothers and the world of women.

f.   Femininity tends to be associated with responsibility, obedience and childcare, and it is seen as something that develops without any special intervention.

Differences include:

a. The status of women is not uniformly low.

b. The content of what is considered "men's work" and "women's work" varies from culture to culture.

c. Cultures differ in the degree of daily contact that is permitted between the sexes.

d. Attitudes about female chastity vary considerably.

e. In some cultures, men and women are seen as opposite in nature, ability and personality; in other cultures, they do not regard each other as opposites.

4. A. Underestimating differences within other groups
    B. Accentuating differences between groups
    C. Producing selective perceptions
    D. Illusory correlations

5. Factors that contribute to the persistence of prejudice include:

    1. Socialization - children learn prejudices from their parents.

    2. Social benefits - prejudices bring support from others who share them and the threat of losing support when one abandons the prejudice.

    3. Economic benefits and justification of discrimination - when economic or social times are difficult, prejudice increases.

    Reducing prejudice: efforts that have not been particularly successful include: the contact hypothesis, efforts aimed at individuals, such as education, and the legal approach.

    A program to reduce prejudice must include: multiple efforts, the cooperation of both sides, equal status and economic standing of both sides, comprehensive support from authorities and the opportunity to work and socialize together, formally and informally.

ANSWER KEY FOR CROSSWORD PUZZLE

ACROSS

1. culture
5. high-context
6. sex
7. polychronic
8. ethnocentrism
11. identity
13. constructionism
14. symbolic
15. prejudice
16. gender
17. illusory

DOWN

1. collectivist
2. reification
3. monochronic
4. assimilation
9. cross-cultural
10. stereotype
12. distance

ANSWER KEYS FOR APPENDIX A

ANSWER KEY - PRACTICE TEST 1

1. C (p. 711)	2. A (p. 711)	3. D (p. 713)	4. A (pp. 712-713)
5. B (p. 713)	6. D (p. 714)	7. C (p. 715)	8. A (p. 716)
9. C (p. 717)	10. B (p. 718)		

ANSWER KEY - PRACTICE TEST 2

1. B	2. C	3. A	4. D
5. B	6. A	7. B	8. B
9. C	10. D		

ANSWER KEY - PRACTICE TEST 3

1.   A.   These descriptive statistics are measures of central tendency and describe data by a single, representative number.

         B.   These descriptive statistics measure variability and reflect the spread of obtained scores.

         C.   These statistical pictures are used to organize data in terms of an overall visual summary.

         D.   These transformations are used when scores are put in a standardized format for easier comparisons.

2.   A.   This statement is justified because the mean and mode are equal in a normal distribution.

         B.   This statement is unjustified because the normal distribution is symmetrical, with either side of the mean mirror-imaging the other.

         C.   This statement is justified because less than 16 percent of the population get a score about one standard deviation from the mean.

         D.   This statement is unjustified because this curve is likely to be skewed to the right given that basketball players are chosen for their height.

3.   A.   The null hypothesis is rejected whenever results are statistically significant.

         B.   Statistical significance occurs when differences between the experimental and control groups are very unlikely to be caused by chance or random errors.

ANSWER KEY FOR CROSSWORD PUZZLE

ACROSS

2. frequency
5. histogram
8. skewed
9. normal
10. median
13. curve
15. significant
17. null
18. percentile

DOWN

1. graph
3. polygon
4. distribution
6. range
7. mean
10. mode
11. deviation
12. alternative
14. hypothesis
16. z-score